FOOTBALL, TAUGHT BY

MATT BUSBY

FOOTBALL, TAUGHT BY
MATT BUSBY

WAYNE BARTON

Reach Sport

In memory of Patrick Barclay
My hero
My mentor

Reach Sport

www.reachsport.com

1

Published in Great Britain and Ireland in 2025 by Reach Sport.

www.reachsport.com
@Reach_Sport

Reach Sport is a part of Reach PLC.

Hardback ISBN: 9781916811249
eBook ISBN: 9781916811256

Photographic acknowledgements:
Wayne Barton collection, Mirrorpix, Alamy, Getty.

Every effort has been made to trace the copyright.
Any oversight will be rectified in future editions.

Editor: Simon Monk.
Production: Christine Costello.
Cover Design: Chris Collins

Printed and bound in Great Britain by
Clays Ltd, Elcograf S.p.A.

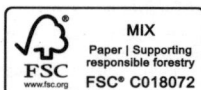

MIX
Paper | Supporting
responsible forestry
FSC® C018072
FSC
www.fsc.org

This book is dedicated to Tony Park
For the encouragement to believe

CONTENTS

"Manchester, Manchester United. A bunch of bouncing Busby Babes, they deserve to be knighted. If ever they're playing in your town, you must get to that football ground. Take a look and you will see, football taught by Matt Busby"

– Manchester United Calypso,
Written by Eric Watterson & Ken Jones

FOREWORD

By Tony Whelan

I PAID A VISIT TO OLD TRAFFORD RECENTLY TO ATTEND a meeting and, as usual arrived early because I did not want to miss the opportunity to go on the 'Grand Tour' of the four famous statues which are placed, considerately, at various points of the ground. They attract visitors from all over the world every single day. Quite simply, I never tire of wanting to see Sir Matt Busby, Jimmy Murphy, Sir Alex Ferguson, and the incomparable 'Trinity' standing gloriously on their dais. They represent the very best of Manchester United Football Club – it really is a marvellous sight. Along the way, I can pay tribute to the players and staff who died at Munich as I walk slowly and reflectively down the tunnel which reverently preserves the memory of those heroes.

Therefore, when I saw the title of Wayne Barton's wonderful book, it filled me with an unbelievable surge of happiness, joy, excitement, and nostalgia because it reminded me of when I joined the club as an apprentice professional in July 1968 after leaving school when I was 15. Believe me, I was like Alice in Wonderland!

FOOTBALL, TAUGHT BY MATT BUSBY

The team had fulfilled Matt Busby's dream of winning the European Cup just a few months earlier. And yet, here I was, at The Cliff, training in the morning and, in the afternoon, cleaning the boots of those legends and collecting their kit to take to the laundry. Ironically, I (we) did not see it as chore, but rather a labour of love. As for The Boss (Matt Busby), he was magisterial, everyone was in awe of him.

During my time at the club (1968-1973), I was taught by the staff to love the game for its own sake, enjoy playing, work hard and express myself as a player to the best of my ability. Furthermore, a high standard of behaviour, discipline and manners was expected. It was instilled in you that if you did all these things, it enhanced your chance of realising your potential as a footballer and human being. As you can imagine, I had the time of my life coupled with the honour and privilege of serving under the great man, albeit briefly. This was certainly Football, Taught by Matt Busby as I understood it, and I tried to follow these guidelines throughout my playing and coaching career.

I first became acquainted with Wayne when I read his superb biography of George Best published in 2021. He has written books on various aspects of the club's history, tradition and culture, but this is, undoubtedly, his magnum opus.

He writes with such energy, passion, eloquence, knowledge, and authority that the reader can't wait to turn the page to see what he's going to reveal next. He has been meticulous in his research and has no peers when it comes to articulating the nature and essence of our magnificent football club. In short, he is a master craftsman, this book being ample proof of that. He takes you on a dazzling roller-coaster ride, discussing myriad aspects of club history to present a coherent synopsis of what has come to be known as Football, Taught by Matt Busby in all its manifestations.

It is challenging and thought-provoking, but the reward for persevering is well worth the effort. You are invited to examine the club's identity in a wholly different way by traversing some hitherto untrodden territory.

For example, I am a veritable child of the 60s and the lens through which I view the football world differs from someone who was born in the 1980s and so forth. We must also consider that tactics have changed over the decades, and the modern game has input from sport science experts in the form of fitness training, psychology, performance analysis, statistics and so on. The laws of the game have also been modified which has a major influence on tactical innovation. All these factors must be pondered when studying the phenomenon of Matt Busby's philosophy of football.

The author probes the complex scope of experience regarding what it takes to be a member of staff or supporter of the club, and what it feels like to be a member of the family. He achieves this in a remarkable way, by connecting the different eras through a common theme – its identity – from Newton Heath to Carrington. Thus, if you want to become an avid student of the club, this is precisely the text for you.

The book's importance lies in the fact that it delves deeply into a tradition and heritage which has a profound impact on the identity and tactical vision of one of the foremost sports institutions on the planet. Indeed, we are treated to a host of eminent celebrities from the history of football: managers, coaches, scouts, players, officials; as well as the way tactics have evolved from the classic WM formation of Herbert Chapman to the sophistication of the present day.

We now return to the striking statues that adorn the perimeter of Old Trafford, but one has special importance in the context of our subject. It is Sir Matt, peering across the forecourt, surveying the empire he did so much to create. He glances to where the three players who are, arguably, most closely associated with him face him directly – it's an extremely poignant sight for any supporter to witness. That is because those players encapsulate everything that Matt Busby stood for by the way they played the beautiful game.

Their talent was unique. Denis Law was a dynamo in the penalty area: lightning quick and brave as a lion. George Best was, well, irrepressible – a dribbler par excellence. As for Bobby Charlton, has there ever been a more graceful, elegant mover with the ball in full flow who, at the same time, packed such a ferocious shot in both feet? You must view the footage of the innumerable goals they scored between them to fully comprehend the veracity of these words. It is a measure of Busby's genius that he was able to assimilate their sensational gifts into the team so seamlessly.

Finally, it is you that will choose how best to describe 'Football, Taught by Matt Busby' whether it be celestial, magical, youthful, entertaining, fearless, never-say-die, artistic, pioneering among other things. Football at Old Trafford has captured the heart, mind, and spirit of millions of people for a generation or more. It remains a primary reason why the stadium is packed to the rafters for every game, no matter who the opposition are.

In the light of this, we should be immensely grateful to Mr Barton not least for offering a new perspective on the extraordinary legacy the venerable Sir Matt has left, which continues to inspire and enchant football lovers wherever the game is played.

Dr Tony Whelan
The Cliff Training Ground,
Salford, 2025

INTRODUCTION

ROMANCE IS A CURIOUS THING. IN ITS MOST traditional form it is connected to love and relationships. It is found in a chance meeting, a locking of eyes. In the unexpected encounter. In the searching for something or somebody and finally finding it. In the long-term friend who suddenly looks a little different. It's found in a gesture, big or small.

Romance can be found in the elements. It's in the allure of fire. The calm of water. The mystery of the stars and the galaxy. The wonder of an aurora. You might be overwhelmed by the feeling of romance on the streets of Paris or New York.

Of course, romance can be found in art. The wonderful thing about art is its ability to transfer its very meaning based on the perception of the individual appreciating it; and diving further, the life experiences of that individual. Art is a painting. A sculpture. A creation, an expression, an application, a rhythm. It's music. Literature. Movement. Dance. Your favourite television show or movie. Romance is not necessarily spontaneous; the creators coax and conjure it. It is contrived, sometimes beautifully so, appreciated even more when it is *so* contrived as to appear left to chance.

Is sport art? Can sport be romantic? The answer is yes, because the truth is that everything can be, relative to our own experiences. Let's cut to the chase and apply this thought train to the topic at hand, which is football, and specifically here, Manchester United Football Club. Romance and art in all the above forms can be translated to the sport of football. You might have been born into the following of your team. A rite of passage to go to the match from an early age. You might have fallen in love in a different way; mesmerised by the way the team played football. You might have been drawn to the history of the club. The colour of the shirt. You might have moved house and needed a new team. You might have been there from the start of a journey. You could have been on holiday and passed by the stadium of your new favourite side.

Entire lives are shaped around the choice of a football club. People fall in love through this mutual connection. Children are named after heroes. Lives revolve around it; you can be lucky enough to live a stone's throw from the stadium. You can travel to different continents to watch your team play. You can live in a different country and get up at 3am to watch a meaningless pre-season friendly. You can fall so deeply in love with the game itself that you can make a career from it.

It becomes, eventually, almost like a religion. The congregation is usually much larger in number than you'd see at a church but you're all praying for the same thing. Something better. You go to watch your team play. You hope to be entertained. You hope to see them win. You're happy to be surrounded by people you like or love. You're happy to be alone. You're happy to be there. Sometimes you're not happy to be there. Sometimes it feels like a test of endurance. An unhappy relationship where you feel powerless to affect change. You're happy when you win. When you see the team play well. When you see your team reach a moment that represents a journey fulfilled. You are sad when your team loses. If you see your team reach the conclusion of a journey only to taste defeat at the final moment. You see the supporters of the other side celebrating. You are unhappy with that, but on a subconscious level, you understand it's part of the journey. The openness with which you present yourself to the emotion of this profound disappointment is part of the communal sacrifice you make with your rival in order to enrich the feeling that winning brings. It's a ritual played out every week at football stadiums all over the world, and those feelings of ecstasy and despair are heightened depending on the stakes and the journey. A long cup run? A battle for the league title or for safety? The geographical proximity of the opposition? Some historical connection?

Twenty-two men or women kick a ball around, 11 trying to kick it into one goal and 11 trying to kick it into the other. The thrill of the neutral spectator is found in the pursuit of witnessing something unexpected; the thrill of a coach is found in the pursuit of manipulating events. Goals are scored or not scored. Games are won, lost and drawn. A trophy may be handed to the victors. It means something to the players, the staff, the spectators. It might mean something to the television viewers. To the majority of the world, it means nothing. There is no emotional significance to the moment, no matter how much you try and explain the value of a player scoring the winning goal in the last minute against your closest rivals. There is some wider resonance, some tangible change, when allegiances move – if those 11 players are representing their country as opposed to their club, then nations may pause. Shops may close early. The news will become dominated by it. It transcends the insular arena of sport and creeps into everyday life. Otherwise, sport only makes that leap when there is something notable. Something exceptional on a human level to make it of interest to the common man.

Otherwise, professional sports remain a somewhat insular environment, where the value of the moments are appreciated by the competitors and the audience. Those moments become contextualised in the acute sense, in the relevance of the particular game, and then in a wider sense, where they become attached to the supporter's personal history of following the team. You can feel the moments as they happen and you can sometimes sense them before they do. That's what football provides. The anticipation. The greater your personal connection, the higher the propensity for that feeling of anxiety, the hope for something special. The butterflies. The endorphins. Sometimes it's wanting the feeling to be over – victory can be relief. Usually it's the sweet release of a goal, that moment you know you'll remember for the rest of your life. The stronger that connection, the greater the feeling of romance. Yes, it's contrived; somewhere between art and a movie, where a storyline is presented and the actors perform their interpretation. You have some idea of what you're going to see, and you'll be entertained if it's successfully executed, but what is going to have you talking afterwards are the elements you were not expecting. The extraordinary contributions.

Unless your team loses.

In which case it can be a mournful walk from the stadium. Some supporters can shrug off defeat more easily than others. Some are consumed by it and it ruins their day, or even week. Some can even take value from a defeat. The feeling of being alive that the anticipation of the game provided. The feeling of being able to experience it because one day you might not. The feeling of being with people. The feeling of supporting. Belonging. The self-worth of knowing you supported, even when it didn't go right. There's an even smaller number who become fascinated by the why and how. What does it mean? Does it mean anything?

Manchester United's identity – their style of play, their cultural legacy – has been more closely scrutinised than any other club in the modern era. It has transcended the postcode of M16 ORA to become a subject of national media discussion. It's a major subject in the post-mortems and the analyses of perceived failure. Philosophy. DNA. Sir Alex Ferguson. Sir Matt Busby. It's a riddle, a conundrum; those old enough to experience either just Ferguson's era, but especially both his and Busby's, will recall the style of those managers never really being appreciated in comparison with their peers. Busby was seen as a gentleman of the sport but not as a tactical mastermind. Ferguson was omnipresent in an era where Arsene Wenger and Jose Mourinho were deemed to have transformed British football, and triumphed over both without ever receiving the same sort of intellectual credit from the so-called minds of the game – professors, as Mourinho might call them.

The post-Sir Alex Ferguson era has seemed familiar to those who were around when Busby retired. Managers have been and gone, their suitability discussed in relation to the club's identity. So, what is that identity? Clearly, it has much to do with winning trophies. But you can take trophies aside for a moment. You know what a Sir Alex Ferguson team looked like when it played. And, when he finally tasted his own success after a difficult start, he was widely judged to have built a team as entertaining as Busby's. Despite Ferguson's larger trophy haul, it was Busby who set the standard, and it could be argued that Ferguson was only *as* successful because his journey so closely resembled Busby's. With that in mind, any study of what Manchester United are, what their identity is, what they stand for and what they represent, has to start with Matt Busby and go from there.

It's winning. It's playing with young players developed by the club. It's a freedom of expression. It's the closest professional football feels to playground football; the chaos, the gambles, the glory. You know what it is to look at it. You can create a list of attributes that it possesses. Never before has anyone taken the exhaustive task of studying every nook and cranny in order to define, with certainty and clarity, what Manchester United's identity actually is. It's football taught by Matt Busby; but it's much more complex than just five words.

1

FOOTBALL BEFORE MATT BUSBY

TO UNDERSTAND MANCHESTER UNITED'S TACTICAL history, you must first understand the evolution of tactics within football itself. The early years of association football help us to do this because the generational changes were straightforward. As in life, sporting evolution is influenced by many factors. Time, experience, environment, technology and original human thought – these all impact the speed of change. Philosophies of sport and life, financial constraints, language, even the weather – all of these external elements have some bearing on the shaping of tactics and strategies within it.

When major changes occur, the significance of the shift is not always obvious. Such a change can yield an instant return. Other times, the change can be gradual. In some cases, it is possible to analyse the start of an influence and wonder how it is even comparable with the traditionally accepted incarnation of that philosophy.

The most famous example is Holland's 1974 World Cup campaign. Rinus Michels had been hired to oversee the tournament after his vision of football, 'Total Football', had been successful at Ajax and Barcelona. Total Football required every player to be adept at playing almost every position, so when one player made a run out of his natural area, another could fill the vacated space to ensure the structure of the team remained the same. The idea was that any outfield player could play in any role – and while perfection has never been achieved, the most successful versions of this system have indeed included a high number of defenders who could moonlight as midfielders, and midfielders who could do likewise as forwards. There are modern iterations which spring easily to mind and the key elements tend to be domination of the ball and relentless movement of players.

It was successful for Holland in 1974. Ajax had tasted European glory with this approach but the World Cup was seen as its first global impression. The Netherlands destroyed Argentina and comfortably defeated Brazil – the reigning World Cup holders. To look back on the tapes of that tournament, though, one is not treated to the sophistication they might expect. The Holland team hunted in packs to retrieve the ball with a sort of recklessness that should have seen calmer teams take advantage. Indeed, at times it seems contradictory to the vision. Even the most celebrated styles, which at the time made an impact due to being so revolutionary, were refined over time.

As British football fanatics enthused over the flair of these continental styles – football on these shores seen as a hard-working, long-ball game – few would have known that the concept of Total Football was given to Europe by men born in England. At the time it was largely felt that Michels was following the Hungarian coach, Gusztav Sebes. Sebes led the 'Magical Magyars', featuring the likes of Ferenc Puskas, in an era where they lost just once in six years – a spell which included famous wins against England. There was no doubt the Hungarians had, in their approach to the game, the future: Sebes was bucking the trend, exposing traditional formations to the extent that many people within the English game felt there was some unsportsmanlike skulduggery at play. Such stories we'll cover in due time; but it is worth referencing now to illustrate how the English game was resistant to major change and how influential figures were suspicious of anything unfamiliar. If only those influential figures had embraced the trio of Jimmy Hogan, Jack Reynolds and Vic Buckingham more tightly. Two of these names would prove to have some contribution in Manchester United's future.

The very first football formations looked something like 1-1-8; there would be a goalkeeper, a defender, a midfielder, and the other eight players would arrange themselves in a forward line. To counter this, some teams would play a 2-1-7; hardly a watertight response. In the 1890s, team shapes changed as coaches aimed to bring some organisation. Having players scattered around the pitch could facilitate greater control of the ball. Shapes of 2-2-6 became more common; then 2-3-5 was established as the most-used formation in English football.

There was also the changing offside rule to consider. Prior to the turn of the century, the rules dictated that a player could be offside even if in their own half. This was changed in 1907, but the most significant amendment followed in 1925, where it was decided a player would be offside if there were fewer than two opponents in front of him when the ball was played.

To briefly explain the 2-3-5 formation: the team would consist of a goalkeeper, two full-backs, a wing-half line of a right, centre and left-half, and five forwards. An outside-right, inside-right, centre-forward, inside-left, and outside-left. When the offside rule changed in 1925, the new manager of Arsenal, Herbert Chapman, brought the centre-half into the back line, making it a 3-2-5 or a 3-2-2-3. It would become known as the W-M formation, because of its resemblance to the letters when the team was laid out positionally. This was copied by most managers in the Football League and adopted by many international teams.

This is a record of Manchester United, and we'll get there, but to best understand where we're going, it's important to remember where we're coming from. Manchester United were first, of course, Newton Heath Lancashire and Yorkshire Railway Cricket and Athletic Club, who were formed on June 1st, 1878.

It was a recreational sports team founded by superintendent Frederick Attock – his relatives who also worked on the railways suffered from ill-health and he was keen to provide workers with some athletic relief on their breaks. A committee was formed, the team did quite well, and over the years Attock leaned on political and journalist friends to further the development of this fledgling club. As the club became more established, its name would change to drop the railway association; we'll refer to this pre-1902 incarnation as Newton Heath.

Two early reference points to how Newton Heath played football can be observed in their 2-2-6 shapes, first in a home match against Bentfield in January 1880. The hosts won 3-0, all the goals coming in the second half. The team:

FULTON

BLACK   RIGBY

EDMONSON   CHARLTON

LATHAM   THOMPSON   THOMAS   KENYON   JARRATT   JONES

Black and Rigby were listed as 'backs', Edmonson and Charlton as 'half-backs', Latham and Thompson were both listed as 'right wing', Jarratt and Jones as counterparts on the left, with Thomas, the captain, and Kenyon, described as 'centres'.

Just over a year later, in February 1881, Newton Heath defeated Bootle in an Association match which ended 10-2. The Coachbuilders' (one of Newton Heath's nicknames, alongside Newtonians and Heathens) side that day:

HOPWOOD

SHAW   MORRIS

HINCHLEY   HALL

RICHARDS MYERS CRAMPHORN SWARBRICK WEBBER DUNN

It should be noted that Richards and Myers were simply described as playing on the 'right' by *Athletic News*, with Webber and Dunn on the 'left'.

A move to the common team shape of the generation was noted in the Manchester Senior Cup final of 1885, in which Newton Heath lost to Hurst:

FULTON

BLACK (CAPTAIN)   MITCHELL

HOWLES   KAY   MORAN

DAVIES SIDDONS EARP GOTHERIDGE DAVIES

Then came the first steps of another thread of the club's identity, as a team from Canada (appropriately titled 'The Canadians') visited Manchester to play in a friendly in 1888, thereby becoming the club's first-ever opponents from overseas. The Canadian tourists returned on November 8th, 1890, for which a match card was created. The card depicts both teams playing in a 2-3-5 shape – it is important to say that when match cards became match programmes, teams would be lined up in this way and this would be the case even going in to the late 1950s, when it was commonly accepted that the middle player of the '3' was in fact playing in the back line of defence.

HAY (GOALKEEPER)
POWELL   AN OTHER
BOURKE   DAVIES   OWEN
AN OTHER   R DOUGHTY   J DOUGHTY   GOTHERIDGE   GALE

There was a game against Walsall Town Swifts on November 8th, 1890, where Newton Heath's side lined up thus:

SLATER
MITCHELLS   CLEMENTS
DOUGHTY   RAMSEY   STEWART
FARMER   CRAIG   EVANS   SHARP   MALARVIE

Incidentally, it was a trip to Walsall – in March 1892 – which saw the first recorded reference to Newton Heath wearing a change strip. Their home colours were usually red and white halves with dark navy shorts and stockings. "The homesters were compelled to wear white shirts in consequence of the visitors having the same colours as Newton Heath: red and white," reported the *Manchester Courier*. It is believed that white shirts were the go-to due to them being the cheapest and easiest to obtain. I hear you, reader. Didn't Newton Heath play in green and gold halved shirts? The earliest noted reference to these colours actually came in an article in *The Clarion* on September 30th, 1883, where the club were said to have 'discarded the L&Y Railway colours, red and white jerseys, for green and gold'. These shirts were striped, not halved.

The club played at North Road in Clayton before moving to Bank Street in 1893. Perhaps here we see the birth of their tactics, though not in a traditional sense. The stadium at Bank Street was situated next to a chemical works – and legend had it that if Newton Heath were losing at half-time, fumes would be released from the chimneys to aggravate the visiting team.

Newton Heath's first venture into the Football League was eventful. Their first-ever First Division game was a 4-3 defeat at Blackburn. A 1-1 home draw with Burnley was followed by heavy defeats, first 4-1 at Burnley and then 6-0 at Everton. After drawing 0-0 at West Brom, the players were assembled for a training session on their North Road pitch, under the watchful eye of their trainer, Mr Smith. One of the activities included hammer-throwing. Willie Stewart, a Scottish centre-half, was more aggressive than accurate with his throw, and the hammer struck Bob Donaldson, a North Lanarkshire-born forward, knocking him 'insensible'. Donaldson recovered to score against West Brom in a 4-2 home defeat two days later – but with a week's rest, the result was even better, as Newton Heath won in the league for the first time, defeating Wolverhampton Wanderers 10-1 – Donaldson and Stewart both scoring hat-tricks!

The Birmingham Daily Gazette complained about the state of the pitch. "Pools of water lay here and there, and all the players were drenched to the skin before they had been on the field five minutes. Why, the Wanderers could not stand, much more kick the ball, and Newton Heath simply made rings round the visitors." Complaints about the surface were well-founded, and what started as an advantage started to become a nuisance even for the hosts – a 14-0 win over Walsall Swifts in 1895 was voided due to the state of the pitch. Newton Heath won the rescheduled encounter 9-0 in the 100th competitive match in the club's history; but they would have to seek a long-term solution.

Eventually, after starting life as unpaid footballers, players were paid around £1 per week and had to take other jobs to support their families. This meant little time for training – team gatherings were held either at the local fish and chip shop or at the house of a local chimney sweep by the name of 'Father' Bird, who would put on a hot-pot for the players. There was a great togetherness, which was just as well, as the players would never know until after a game whether they were getting paid. A local tailor, wanting to drum up some interest in his business, promised an overcoat to anyone who scored. When the full-backs started to bomb up the pitch, it left the defence even more vulnerable, and Newton Heath directors asked the tailor to withdraw his offer – which he did.

From the club's formation until 1914, the team was selected by a committee, led by a secretary, who was to all intents and purposes the team manager. Newton Heath's first recognised secretary was Alfred Hubert Albut, who was in charge from 1892 to 1900.

In Aston Villa's match programme of the game against Manchester United on February 26th, 1910, they spoke of the character of Albut. "Like other great clubs in their infancy, they played jolly hard football for the pure love of the game, and the founder's little dreams of the giddy heights of which they were to climb. About the time Newton Heath began to emerge from obscurity, its managers enlisted the services of Mr Albert Albut... a prominent all-round sportsman in Birmingham and a football missionary of nerve and adventure. Some of his experiences in search of players would read like a fairytale if he only cared to tell them."

Their style? The team contained a healthy blend of English and Scottish players. For countries that shared a border, their philosophy couldn't have been more different – the English preferring a running-based game and the Scots preferring to pass the ball around. The first famous success in English football –

Preston North End's invincible team – was coached by William Sudell, who brought no fewer than six Scots into his side. The Scottish game was described in some quarters as 'scientific'; Newton Heath's interpretation of it was to play an ultra-attacking style. The August 4th, 1949 edition of the *Grimsby Daily Telegraph* carried a fascinating line. "My colleague recalls a match between Grimsby and Newton Heath when all the Heath players, with the exception of the goalkeeper, were actually in the Grimsby penalty box, storming the Grimsby goal," wrote a correspondent. Albut's philosophy? The committee? Was it merely reflective of the early stages of organised sport? Whatever, it still carried a distinctive thumbprint which could be matched against any great side the club fielded over the next century.

Albut was succeeded by James West, who was in post when the club was renamed Manchester United on April 28th, 1902 – a decision taken as they were on the brink of bankruptcy. Debts of £2,670 seemed certain to end the club's existence. At a creditors' meeting, James West reported the club required £2,000 in order to be solvent again. Harry Stafford, the team captain, declared he had the names of five gentlemen who would provide the funds. One of those men, John Henry Davies of Old Trafford, would be elected the president – in a bizarre sequence of events, Stafford's dog, a St. Bernard named Major, went missing after a local bazaar that was being held to raise funds to rescue Newton Heath.

The dog was given to Davies by a man named John Roberts Thomas; and when Stafford tracked Major down, he shared with Davies the financial peril of his club. Davies' daughter, Elsie, had fallen in love with Major, and so the father was determined to acquire the dog for his little girl.

This led to conversations between Davies and Stafford, with the player eventually accepting the offer to buy the dog in exchange for help for the club. Some months later Davies – along with those other local businessmen – stepped in to save the day.

So, when Newton Heath played their last-ever match under that name – the Manchester Senior Cup final, against Manchester City at Hyde Road on April 26th, 1902 – the mood among the supporters was one of optimism. Newton Heath went a goal down, but levelled and then won in the second half thanks to a penalty scored by Fred Erentz, the club's longest-serving player. "The cheering which greeted this was loud and prolonged," reported the *Athletic News*. It was additionally fitting as it was Erentz's last-ever match.

Team for the Manchester Senior Cup final:

SAUNDERS
STAFFORD   ERENTZ
MORGAN   GRIFFITHS   CARTWRIGHT
SCHOFIELD   COUPAR   PRESTON   HAYES   LAPPIN

To mark the name change to Manchester United, the club officially adopted new colours – a red jersey, white shorts and black stockings.

The first league game played by the club under its new name came at Gainsborough Trinity on September 6th, 1902. The game was petering out to a draw until the 86th minute when debutant Charlie Richards scored a dramatic winner. Richards was an outside-right – these early days of the sport did not include numbers on shirts, but he was effectively the number seven. Considering the legacy that would be associated with Manchester United, the number seven and late winners, the first goal of the rebirth had been every bit as romantic as the last goal as Newton Heath.

James West remained in post until September 1903, when he

was succeeded by Ernest Mangnall. It was Mangnall who would lead United to their first successful period, which commenced with the 1907/08 First Division championship

Mangnall, then 37, was an old friend of John Bentley, one of United's staff. He arrived renowned for his work as Burnley secretary; he was charismatic and loved talking to the press. His approach to football was of its day – many then believed a player would be hungry for the ball on a Saturday if they didn't train with it during the week. His attitude to fitness *was* revolutionary, however, and he put players through their paces via cross-country running and swimming. Mangnall took advantage of a situation at Manchester City, who were found guilty of awarding their players bonuses – which was against FA regulations. Many players were banned from representing the club again, leading to a mass exodus. Mangnall was able to acquire four – two of the very best, Sandy Turnbull and Billy Meredith, and two very good players in Herbert Burgess and Jimmy Bannister. This transformed United into a side contending for the biggest honours, winning the league in 1908 and the FA Cup a year later.

How did this first great Manchester United team play? There was an 18-page booklet published in April 1908, soon after their title triumph was confirmed.

Mangnall's side looked like this:

MOGER
HOLDEN   STACEY
DUCKWORTH   ROBERTS   BELL
MEREDITH   BANNISTER   J TURNBULL   S TURNBULL   WALL

"It is not a difficult question to solve – how Manchester United won the League Championship," wrote the untitled author. "I shall base my remarks upon two words, namely: Greatness and Unity.

FOOTBALL, TAUGHT BY MATT BUSBY

As the poet tells us: 'Some are born great, some achieve greatness, some have greatness thrust upon them.' Manchester United come under the second quotation of the poet's. They have achieved greatness, by their triumphant march to the goal they set out to reach.

"It has been attained by sheer merit and skill. The prize has been won by the doggedness and tenacity of a great 11… never in the history of football has a team shown its greatness and superiority more than the United team since the dawn of season 1907/08."

Even with the understanding that almost any seminal team might claim to have similar traits, greatness and unity would become two significant qualities in any strong Manchester United team. It was clear that the players who had arrived from City had galvanised the United support to believe their team could now achieve great things. On his debut on New Year's Day 1907, against Aston Villa at Bank Street, Billy Meredith took a perfect corner that was planted on to Sandy Turnbull's head for the game's only goal.

"When (Charlie) Roberts led the United team with its famous recruits onto the field," reported the *Manchester Guardian*, "there was a scene of wonderful enthusiasm. A greater roar of cheering has probably never sounded over a football ground, nor probably has a football crowd ever been seen in more remarkable animation."

Roberts and Meredith were not only leaders on the pitch, but off it, too, as it was this duo whose combined voice effectively created the PFA. That revolution was led following the death of Tommy Blackstock, a full-back who collapsed during a Combination match against St. Helens in April 1907 after heading the ball. Roberts and Meredith were appalled to discover there was no support available for Blackstock's family, and this was the tipping point for players to unionise.

FOOTBALL BEFORE MATT BUSBY

The *Manchester Evening News* predicted big things in August 1907. "United have never in their history opened a season with so strong a playing combination," read the report from the Wanderer. "No club on either side of the border will have so dangerous an outside pair as Meredith and Wall."

United were better on the road than in front of their own fans. "For some reason," the *Manchester Guardian* reported after United's narrow 1-0 home win over Birmingham, "the league leaders play a much better game away from home. Possibly the Clayton enclosure has a depressing effect on the team, when the factories around are belching forth smoke and steam carelessly, and an atmosphere of gloom enraps the place like a pall." A 3-1 win at Goodison Park all but secured the title.

So United had doggedness, tenacity and skill – what about those players as individuals?

Goalkeeper Harry Moger was referred to as 'reliable', while Richard Holden had 'few superiors at right-back'. Left-back Herbert Burgess was 'capable of holding his own with any forward'. Burgess shared his spot with George Stacey, who was 'yet to play a poor game' for the club. Right-half Dick Duckworth had a 'real turn of speed'. Captain Charlie Roberts, the centre-half, was the best in his position 'either in this country or across the border... whose enthusiasm inspires the other members of the team'. Another report said: "Roberts has been the man of the club. He has led the side with an enthusiasm that has put life and confidence into the team."

Alex Bell, left-half, was 'exceptionally clever'. It was this half-back line, effectively a deep-set midfield, which was the most influential area of this side, providing a platform for entertaining forwards. The headline act in this team was Billy Meredith, 'the greatest outside-right in the country and in the opinion of many the finest that ever lived. A great dribbler who gets the better of his opponents in a manner bewildering'. Meredith was considered the first 'superstar' of the sport, his distinctive dribbling ability and the manner in which he chewed upon a toothpick whilst strolling on the pitch setting him apart. The showmanship quality had been present at the club since before the turn of the century. One disapproving report in the *Manchester Guardian* explained what they saw in a 4-1 win over West Brom in October 1893: "Every time one of the Newton Heath men scored his colleagues shook him warmly by the hand, and for a brief period the hero strutted around with an air of superiority and pride which an actor would find it difficult to stimulate." The supporters appeared to love that extroverted confidence; and when it was present in the individual form of Meredith, he naturally became an instant favourite.

The inside-right was Jimmy Bannister, described as a player who 'sinks his own individuality for the benefit of his partner'. The inside-left, Sandy Turnbull, was 'a prince of goal-getters', great in the air and 'equally clever' with his feet. Outside-left was George Wall, described as being like 'a cat after a mouse' who had 'no equal' as a gatherer of goals. Finally there was Jimmy Turnbull, the centre-forward, a 'bundle of energy' who used his physicality to help his team.

Mangnall was given praise for ensuring his 'team has worked together like one man; like a perfect human machine knowing that success comes only to the truly great'. "The greater the demand on the players the grander their response" was one tribute to a manager who had delivered "to the Manchester public a team that could reach the highest pinnacle of football and startle the football world."

In his 1962 book *Manchester United*, Percy Young gave an interesting summary of this team. "It was partly a matter of a shrewd appraisal, but rather more the talent to blend abilities into a composite machine-link unity," Young wrote. "Apart from Meredith, Wall and Charlie Roberts, the individuals concerned were of average ability, blessed chiefly with a talent for bringing out the best in each other."

In May 1908, United travelled by water to Czechoslovakia, Austria and Hungary to play a series of games against domestic opponents; there are multiple reasons for why this has a romantic connection to the club's identity. Firstly, it marks the birth of United's relationship with continental competition. Secondly, led by Ernest Mangnall, there was a desire to discover more about other cultures and their interpretation of the game.

How did United fare against foreign opposition? "Everyone then came to see the game of the team that won the English league this year by a record number and to witness the fight between them and our Czech representatives," read the *Sport A Hry* report of United's 2-0 wins over Slavia Prague over consecutive days on May 11th and 12th. "It was a great struggle. The game of the professional remains a daunting pattern for us."

United played eight games on the tour. The last attracted a crowd of 12,000, the biggest ever for a football match in Hungary at that time; Roberts and co won 7-0. The home referee blew for numerous free-kicks, presenting the impression the visitors had been overly physical. It incited some of the crowd to race on to the pitch to confront the players.

One unnamed United star wrote to the *Daily Dispatch* to share the ordeal: "Although mounted police and others with swords did their best to protect us, a few of us were hit by people standing near the entrance to the dressing tent. The fun really commenced when leaving the ground. As soon as we got into the landaus waiting outside the gates a wild and apparently uncivilised mob did all they possibly could to maim us." The player spoke of stones and brickbats, but expressed relief nobody was seriously hurt.

The *Manchester Courier* carried some thoughts from Mangnall. "The idea of foreign players seemed to be, said Mr Mangnall, that all they have to do is kick, push and hack. They go for the man and not the ball, and that is the chief fault of the players. But it was not so much with the players that they have to make complaint as with the referees. It was a rare thing that they found an official who knew the rules."

There was a clear respect from the foreign sportswriters at least and an admission that the European game had much to learn. In generations to follow, much attention would be given to the way United would set up on these continental jaunts, but on this maiden voyage they were simply encouraged to play their natural way.

United weren't the only team in this period to make trips to the continent; another was Bolton Wanderers. On one trip to Holland they defeated FC Dordrecht by 10 goals. This inspired Wanderers inside-forward Jimmy Hogan to pledge he would one day return to the city 'to teach those fellows how to play properly'. Hogan would spend two years in Dordrecht from 1910-1912 coaching ball control and fitness; in effect implementing what was known as 'the Combination Game', a brand of football that placed an emphasis on teamwork. Hogan returned to Bolton to conclude his playing career before travelling to Austria to coach the national team. At the outbreak of the First World War, he was interned as a prisoner of war; but he was smuggled to the Hungarian border, and became a coach at MTK Budapest between 1914 and 1918. They became the dominant team in Hungarian football, winning 10 consecutive titles and setting the foundation for a philosophy of soccer the country would adopt.

Hogan's influence was more widespread than Jack Reynolds, who would introduce a similar philosophy to Hogan's at Ajax. Former Watford and Grimsby winger Reynolds spent 27 years at Ajax in three separate spells between 1915 and 1947, winning multiple trophies. He not only encouraged a team game, but promoted individual skill and the concept of players being introduced into the senior team at a younger age. In his final season at Ajax, he gave a teenage striker by the name of Rinus Michels his first matches.

The third of these English pioneers is Vic Buckingham. Buckingham's time as a manager would come later, but he was identified by *The Observer* as leading the only team in England whose style of play resembled that of the Hungarian side which triumphed at Wembley in 1953. After that famous 6-3 victory, the Hungarian president Sandor Barcs paid tribute to Jimmy Hogan, saying: "He taught us everything we know about football." Buckingham's West Brom won the FA Cup that same year, and came close to winning the league title. In 1959, Buckingham was hired by Ajax, knitting together the footballing ideals of Hogan and Reynolds in a way that would shape football. He won the league title, but remained only for a short spell there before returning as manager in 1964/65, where he gave the 17-year-old Johan Cruyff his debut.

Justice for those names did not arrive for some time. And there is no evidence to suggest Ernest Mangnall shared the footballing vision of Hogan, Reynolds or Buckingham but there are nonetheless some interesting conclusions to draw from Manchester United's first title-winning team. It could be deduced that Mangnall had a balance of three cavalier stars – Meredith, Bell and Wall – and eight players who worked hard for the team. The author Geoffrey Green described an outstanding side with 'five artists and six other good players who blended into a composite whole'.

United's success continued into the following season, as the club won the Charity Shield and then the FA Cup, defeating Bristol City in the final. Further descriptions of the players were provided in the match brochure for the final. George Stacey, now at right-back (with Vince Hayes replacing Dick Holden in the full-back position), was noted as a quiet but fierce competitor. Charlie Roberts was described as 'England's most scientific centre-half-back' who directed United's play 'by the very strength of his individuality'. Harold Halse was a new name at inside-forward, and he "has the individualism necessary to enable him to make a gallant dash for goal… a speedy forward who makes a science of his dodging."

As for how those players combined, well, the *Athletic News* gave us an insight to their style after the semi-final win over Newcastle: "Manchester United, with valiant half-backs and a forward line which is distinguished by cleverness and dash, never looked like losing." The final was decided by Sandy Turnbull, who was not fit and only playing after captain Charlie Roberts convinced his manager to take the chance. Roberts also made a fateful choice on the coin toss – deciding to play with the wind behind his team in the first half. The United players were used to dealing with inclement weather more often than teams from the south, and Roberts understood that getting a lead and then protecting it was the best gameplan. After Sandy Turnbull had duly scored in the 22nd minute, United gave a professional second-half performance – at one point, slowing the game down so much that referee Jim Mason cautioned them for wasting time. Turnbull's goal was the only goal of the final and was the start of a suitably understated trend – that of the 'worker' star getting the decisive goal to win a trophy in a team with a star like Meredith.

Later that year, when the FA withdrew its recognition of the PFA due to concerns about its authority being undermined, players were pressured into either resigning from the union or having their playing registration cancelled. Charlie Roberts refused and his United team-mates backed him up; the club, under pressure from the FA, suspended their playing staff. Roberts and his colleagues continued to train, and the United captain took the opportunity when he saw a photographer taking pictures, creating a sign that read 'The Outcasts FC' and lining his team-mates up for a team picture. On August 31st, the day before United's 1909/10 season was due to start, the FA backed down.

Mangnall presided over one more notable triumph – a second league title, and then a second Charity Shield, in 1911. By now, United had moved to a new stadium called Old Trafford in Stretford, a decision influenced by Mangnall's ambition and the financing of Davies – the stadium was built at a cost of £60,000 and was ready to host its first game in February 1910. One journalist described it as "the most handsomest, the most spacious and the most remarkable arena I have ever seen. It is unrivalled in the world."

Davies' financing had transformed the club into the glamour team of the country. Little is known of the detail of that ambition, however in July 2005, there was an interesting if brief note in the *Daily Post*. "J H Davies was my late husband's grandfather and he always envisaged it as a club for the working man," Elizabeth Partington told the outlet. "It was a family club."

This period of success ended when Mangnall left for Manchester City in the summer of 1912. T.J. Wallworth stepped into the breach for a few games before John Bentley became the fourth full-time secretary of the club from October 1912. There was a decline caused partly by the age of the team, while the club was also embroiled in scandal when players from United and Liverpool were found guilty of match-fixing in a game on Good Friday, 1915. Seven players, including Billy Meredith, were given life bans. The other United players to face permanent suspensions were Sandy Turnbull, Enoch West and Arthur Whalley. However, all saw their bans lifted in thanks their service to their country in the First World War (Turnbull was killed in the war, but was posthumously reinstated) – all except for West, who protested his innocence for the rest of his life.

The result of the game – 2-0 to United – stood, in spite of the controversy, and it kept the club in the First Division. As soon as football resumed after the war, United's struggles continued, and they were relegated in 1922.

Jack Robson had been named the club's first-ever manager in 1914 and remained in post until October 1921, although this period was interrupted by the war. Robson was described as parsimonious and able to 'tell a footballer in his cradle', and signed many young players for United.

Robson was succeeded by John Chapman, who took the club back into the top flight in 1925. That was partly thanks to the leadership of centre-half Frank Barson, who was signed from Aston Villa specifically with the goal of taking United up – it was included in his contract that he would be given a pub if he did. Barson was a hugely popular figure with United fans – and unpopular with rival fans, who would often be waiting for him after games due to what they perceived to be overly rough treatment of their players. Barson would often be given a police escort to ensure his safety.

After promotion in 1925, the club honoured their promise and bought Barson the George & Dragon in Ardwick. On the opening night, the pub was so busy and the demand for Barson's attention was so high, that he gave the keys to the barman and told him to keep it for himself. Extra jobs in the hospitality industry were often presented to players who proved themselves worthy in the eyes of J.H. Davies, the club owner. Davies remained influenced by Louis Rocca's love of United and carried a paternal attitude towards the players, creating something of a family feel. Chapman blended well into that atmosphere, described as 'kindness personified'. The manager organised frequent get-togethers with his players, with the consequence being a team who enjoyed playing for their leader.

The team that won promotion back to the First Division by winning 4-0 against Port Vale in April 1925:

STEWARD

MOORE BARSON JONES

BENNION GRIMWOOD

SPENCE SMITH PAPE LOCHHEAD MCPHERSON

In 1926, Chapman was suspended by the FA in a bombshell announcement in early October – amid a vague accusation he had 'behaved improperly'. The writer Alf Clarke claimed to know 'full well all the circumstances', and that had Chapman made the matter public he would have cleared himself – but as the situation involved a player, he took the consequences. In August, one of the club's own directors, Mr J. Yates, had sent a letter to the FA to report Chapman over a sum of £56 and 19.4d. There was no confirmation what the money was related to, only an indication from a board meeting later that month to discuss what was described as 'lavish expenditure'. Chapman gave his version of events and even reimbursed that figure to the club from his own pocket. The board accepted this, but the FA acted on Yates' letter and the club received a letter informing them of the suspension. The board of directors instead decided to remove Chapman permanently. Ironically, it appeared his close relationship with his players ultimately cost him his job.

"I am at an utter loss to know what 'improper conduct' means in this case," Chapman told reporters. "I have nothing whatsoever on my conscience and, apart from my salary, I have never benefitted a penny piece in any shape or form." Disillusioned, Chapman dropped out of the game altogether, becoming general manager of Liverpool Greyhound Racing Club.

Clarence 'Lal' Hilditch, the veteran wing-half described by Clarke as a student of the game, stepped in as player-manager for the rest of the season before former Middlesbrough manager Herbert Bamlett took over. He was in charge for four-and-a-half years, seeing out the 1920s, which had been a difficult decade to say the least. There were few players who stayed for the long term over that period, a turnover which suggests the financial instability was so severe that a regular churn of players was necessary.

In 1931, the club were relegated again, the style they'd displayed in the heyday of Mangnall and Meredith a distant memory. United lost their first 12 games of the campaign, and were doomed to relegation by the time they travelled to Highbury to face Herbert Chapman's title-chasing Arsenal in February. The match programme showed sympathy for their visitors, while confessing a "strong desire to inflict on them yet another defeat, while to detract attention from the lugubrious present by recalling the glories of the Old Trafford club of 20 years ago smacks rather of the facile patter of the dentist, who prattles beguilingly to his victim while searching for an opportunity to effect his painful task."

Arsenal won 4-1.

When United failed to start the following season well, and lost 5-2 at home to Leeds, Bamlett was dismissed.

2

CRICKMER
AND ROCCA

WIGAN-BORN WALTER CRICKMER HAD BEEN IN POST as secretary since 1926, and worked for Manchester United before that as a clerk since 1919. When Herbert Bamlett was sacked, Crickmer took the reins as manager. He was clearly a loyal servant with a love for the club; but even Crickmer did not have the devotion of Louis Rocca, whose association with the club stretched back to when, as a 10-year-old, he snuck into a game at Newton Heath's Bank Street ground without a ticket.

When caught, he was told he would escape punishment if he agreed to make tea and coffee for the players at half-time. "The ground was not much to look at," Rocca said, "but I would have camped out on the terraces if I'd been allowed." He was paid 6d. a week – and it cost him more than that in tramcar fares to get to and from the ground.

Louis Rocca was born in Ancoats in 1882, and grew up in a community with a large population of Irish, Italian and Polish immigrants. Ancoats was described as 'the chimney of the world' and shared the attitude of the city at large. In July 1901, the Bridge Inn, on the corner of Beswick Street and Mill Street, was taken over by new landlord Harry Stafford, the Newton Heath captain, whose reopening event featured appearances from team-mates. It attracted a new legion of young supporters; Rocca was one of them.

Rocca went from tea-boy to looking after the kits and boots of the players, making him the most envied boy in the neighbourhood. He also claimed – though this has been disputed – to have been the person who suggested 'Manchester United' when the new names for the club were being discussed. One thing that could not be disputed was that in Crickmer and Rocca, Manchester United were blessed with a pair of ultra-loyalists who worked unreasonable hours to keep the club surviving. Despite now being on the club staff, Rocca would still write into the local newspaper to give his views on the team, once writing that a player should be picked on the consistency of his performance and not on reputation.

At the age of just 24, Rocca was appointed chief scout. He created a network of eyes around the country, especially with Roman Catholic priests and school teachers, in addition to his relentless scouring of local newspapers where he kept an eye on the junior team results. Rocca and Crickmer began to dream of a Manchester United team filled with local youngsters – at the AGM which followed the conclusion of the 1930/31 season, the *Manchester Guardian* reported this compelling anecdote: "The United's first business is to build up an efficient side from youth." However, the pair were forced to once again address the prospect of financial ruin in late 1931.

John Henry Davies had passed away in 1927 and the club struggled again from that moment; incidentally, one of Davies' last acts was to finance a post-season tour to Switzerland. United won all their games comfortably, while there was growing intrigue about football on the continent. United's handsome wins appeared to offer no conclusions, but their fascination with finding out more about the game abroad was shared by many domestic clubs, especially as talk grew of their emphasis of a passing game. When news of the English team's wins reached home, there was an emboldened resolve in the home Football Associations that they were doing the right thing.

When Davies died, United's finances fell into disarray again. There could be no more tours in the short term. As Crickmer and Rocca approached Christmas 1931, they could not pay the players' wages. A local sportswriter, Stacey Lintott, was aware of United's peril, so he contacted Salford-born businessman, James W. Gibson. He met with Crickmer, who explained that United needed £2000 to survive. Gibson promised more than that – £30,000, in fact, with at least £20,000 earmarked for transfer fees, on the condition that he was named chairman and could elect a board of directors. Crickmer and Rocca had little choice but to agree, but were suitably encouraged that their vision was shared.

The club was saved, but the financial situation could not immediately be resolved, so Rocca and Crickmer had to request that the players play without pay. "I saw one of the finest things in my long career with the club," Rocca recalled. "It was a Friday afternoon. 30-four professionals stood in the ground waiting for their wages – and there wasn't a penny piece to pay 'em with. We explained that Mr Gibson had offered to find some money, but not that day exactly. The players voluntarily agreed to play the match the next day without their wages. That was real loyalty! Fortunately none of these very gallant sportsmen had to wait long before the money was forthcoming."

FOOTBALL, TAUGHT BY MATT BUSBY

In early January 1932 Gibson attempted to raise funds by issuing 'Patron's Tickets' – "a postal order for one shilling from a working man who said he was never able to get to the matches on Saturdays, but hopes that his mite would help to keep the old Club together" (these were, in essence, a season ticket for multiple years) – but the response was disappointing. The new chairman was reassured by one letter he received from a supporter pledging funds even though he would be unable to attend. The resourceful Gibson had a back-up plan, and in a series of events similar to those instigated by Harry Stafford, the new owner found four local men who were prepared to offer financial assistance.

United were stabilised and attendances had, on average, trebled over the season – the galvanised team put in a strong run of form, winning seven from eight in a late winter run which helped to achieve a 12th-place finish in the second tier. An indication of the team's style of play could be found in Gibson's comments as chairman at that summer's AGM, where the *Manchester Guardian* reported he said "that a new type of spectator had taken the place of the old fair-weather sort, and he did not fear the competition of the motor cycle or the 'dog chasing dummies', provided the club supplied the right type of football."

The man identified as the permanent manager was Scott Duncan, a Scottish former outside-right who had played for Newcastle United and Glasgow Rangers. It was a significant move as it was the first time the club had appointed a former professional player. Rocca described the appointment as one of the 'most satisfying moments', saying Duncan was 'certainly the best manager I've ever known'.

Duncan was given a significant amount of money to create a promotion-worthy side, and invested it mainly in players from the Scottish and Irish leagues – an indication of the football the new

36

manager wanted to play. He had a track record of giving local players a chance at Cowdenbeath, and he also had some ideas which were considered bold. They were interesting enough to catch the attention of the *Topical Times*, who published a series of columns written by Duncan. His prescience could be noted by his observations on 'tactical' moves. He recalled an Old Firm game, back when he was a Rangers player, where the opponents had left their dressing-room door open to allow the Rangers players to hear the gameplan for the second half – to man-mark one of their rivals' star men. He also recalled a story of a cup tie at Falkirk where one player said, 'Don't give me the ball' because two players were marking him and they could outnumber the opponents by allowing that to continue. Duncan also imparted some wisdom on bringing players aged 17 or 18 into the first team. "At his age he isn't strong enough," he said. "He is 'burned out' before he reaches athletic manhood."

It was clear that Duncan had caught the imagination of those he was working with. "I decided to strip the team completely, coach the halfbacks to give added support to the forwards instead of the defence, get rid of half the playing staff and concentrate on youth," he said.

Improvement in the form of a sixth-placed finish was not enough to prevent press criticism about the wastage of money, and two of Gibson's appointed board members resigned. One of them was replaced by Harold Hardman, who had played a handful of times for United in the 1908/09 season. The pressure took its toll, and a hugely underwhelming second season for Duncan concluded with United in their lowest position since they had joined the Football League in 1892. On the final day of the season United travelled to Millwall, a straight relegation shoot-out, with Duncan's side needing to win to climb above their London rivals and escape relegation.

Team v Millwall on Saturday May 5th, 1934:

HACKING

GRIFFITHS JONES

ROBERTSON VOSE MCKAY

CAPE MCLENAGHAN BALL HINE MANLEY

United had used 38 players that season, an indication of the unstable events of it, and in the course of the game suffered an injury to one of their key players. In these days before substitutes, Ernie Hine, their inside-right, had to move to the outside position in order to not interfere with play. "Each man played as if prepared to die," Geoffrey Green wrote in his book *There's Only One United*. Tom Manley scored the game's crucial first goal, before a second goal after the break secured safety. It made it one of *the* crucial games in the club's history.

"That unbreakable spirit, which has been a facet of United's successes over the years, came to the surface," Duncan said. "Many regard that game as the turning point in United's history." It was certainly one of them – and, considering Manley's significance as one of the very first youth products to be blooded in the first team, it was the start of another significant thread.

"I was one of a boisterous party which reached Manchester on that Saturday night," recalled Alf Clarke, "to find cheering crowds plus a band gathered outside Central Station. You would have imagined that United had won the FA Cup judged by the deafening applause they received on getting from their saloon."

Over the next four years, United were promoted, relegated, and promoted again, though in that latter campaign, it was Walter Crickmer who was in the hot seat to guide United back into the top flight, after Duncan resigned in October to take up the manager's job at Ipswich. He had lowered the average age of the squad from

33 to 25, and he also oversaw the appointment of Tom Curry as trainer and Bill Inglis as assistant trainer in the summer of 1934. Jack Turley was also promoted 'from First Aid to massage'.

"Many people have said that I was the architect for these successes," Duncan later reflected of his contribution in 1958. "While I might claim a slice of credit, I am the first to say that the club could not have achieved so much without that careful, canny Scot, Matt Busby. I only laid the foundations. I started 'signing 'em young' because I could see the tempo of the game speeding up even before the war… at the last board meeting I attended, I told the directors, 'Don't worry about the future of Manchester United. You have players capable of taking the club to the pinnacle of success. I know they will do it."

Crickmer retained the United managerial job in the following season, consolidating their place in the top flight with a 14th-placed finish. Though still carrying a heavy debt of approximately £70,000, the club were beginning to turn a profit – in 1937, they'd made a profit of £10,486 – and Gibson was good on his word for development at the club as he sunk £35,000 into the development of Old Trafford.

This occurred at the same time as the realisation of another of Rocca and Crickmer's dreams: the formal creation of Manchester United Junior Athletic Club (MUJAC), with the ambition of "cultivating young players after they leave school." James Gibson went on record to stress: "United have no intention of buying any more mediocrities. Our aim is a United composed of Manchester players." In fact, similar statements were made at his first board meeting, just weeks after agreeing to salvage the club, where the suggestion of a 'colts' or 'nursery' team was proposed 'so that a common idea and technique shall unite the junior with the senior staff'.

A similar sentiment had been printed in the *Manchester Guardian* as far back as 1909, with a reference to the board's suggestion that the club could field a side of Manchester-born players. United had a reserve side, which won the Central League in only its second year of existence in 1913.

A couple of very young players made senior appearances – Sidney Tyler in the 1920s and Tom Manley in the 1930s – though this was not in itself evidence of a true pathway for younger players. The first steps towards that were taken in 1932, when United established an 'A' team. "By running a team in the Manchester League," Scott Duncan told the *Evening Chronicle*, "we shall be able to give all likely juniors a chance of showing their paces, and United hope to discover from their number more than average finds." He spoke of the purpose of those young players "held in reserve to develop their talents… so that in time they could step in and do themselves justice."

Duncan urged there would be patience shown. "To hurry along a youngster is a big mistake, but the junior must be assured that his time will come. I know of several instances of young, promising players who have gone out of the game because they have been put into senior football a year or two before they should have done."

Duncan was gone by 1939, when, after its first year of operation, MUJAC were entered into – and won – the Chorlton league. By then, chairman James Gibson had secured tenancy of training facilities in Lower Broughton. This property, known as The Cliff, was previously used by the Broughton Rangers rugby side. It was run by United for the 1938/39 season, and the club held trials at the facility at the start of the campaign.

The trials were so successful that the MUJACs were able to field two teams on their first match-day of September 3rd, 1938. "History was created in Manchester United football circles today,"

Alf Clarke wrote in the *Evening Chronicle*. "This afternoon there are no fewer than five United teams on duty… no club in the country is better served with junior players than Manchester United, and it is very pleasing to record that many teachers in the Manchester, Salford and Stretford areas, who are sponsoring the scheme, give many hours of their leisure time looking after the welfare of the junior players." Two of those men were James McClelland, a former United forward, and Arthur Powell, a trainer.

One of the players to turn up on day one was a left-sided local player by the name of John Aston. Rocca's scouting network proved invaluable as the club identified a north-east defender by the name of Allenby Chilton and another wide player, Charlie Mitten, from a Scottish junior team. It was clear in this approach that United were looking for the most talented boys from across the country, but it is equally compelling to hear the testimony of another young hopeful, Jack White, who lived next to Old Trafford and grew up as a United fan when they were struggling on and off the pitch. "I was thrilled to bits about playing for Manchester United," he told Tony Park and Steve Hobin in their book *Sons of United*, "I thought I was the bee's knees and looked forward to every game."

This would have been a source of pride for Rocca and Crickmer in particular; their dedicated personalities could hopefully be seen on the pitch. That mixture of talent and enthusiasm was remarkably successful in the first year – the MUJACs won their first 26 games, scoring 180 goals in the process. The reserves won the Central League and Manchester Senior Cup, while the A team won their league, too, meaning it was a year of cheer for United following their senior side's consolidation campaign.

It is interesting to note that the tactics used throughout the teams at the various different levels remained the same. A reserve team at Bury featured the United team in this fashion:

BEALE
WORRALL   ROUGHTON
SAVAGE   WINTERBOTTOM   WHALLEY
BRYANT   WASSALL   HANLON   CRAVEN   PART

If a few of those names look familiar, then your eyes are not deceiving you; Whalley is indeed Bert Whalley, and Winterbottom is indeed Walter Winterbottom. And front and centre is 21-year-old Jimmy Hanlon, who graduated into the first team, scoring 12 goals in 27 games – two of them coming on the final day of the 1938/39 season against Liverpool. He was not the only player to have made that step up, as the line-up proves.

BREEDON
REDWOOD   ROUGHTON
WARNER   VOSE   MCKAY
BRYANT   WASSALL   HANLON   CAREY   ROWLEY

It seems that these first-team selections were the very first signs of Manchester United's youth policy in successful practice.

The framework of what a Manchester United team should be was now clear: 'the right kind of football' as dictated by the chairman, young and talented (and, preferably local) players, as wished for by the club's most dedicated servants, and a sprinkling of that Rocca-esque commitment too. Indeed, Rocca had articulated his pride at the way United's players had responded to the news they wouldn't be paid in 1931; the idea had always been that United had been forced to fight harder than most in order to even exist, so to see that manifest itself in the player's dedication was something that was certain to leave an impression on young fans like, for example, Jack White.

So there were some basic principles in place, and while it is straightforward to credit Gibson, Crickmer and Rocca, it is also prudent to pay a tribute to the likes of Mangnall and Stafford, whose dedication had left a lasting impression on Rocca. What is most definitely fair to say is that all of these principles were essentially holistic; they were not attached to the shape of the team, nor was United's formation or style of play particularly distinctive outside of their glory period of 1907-1912. That said, there was a telling observation of United's 5-1 win against Chelsea in September 1938. The *Sunday Chronicle* reported: "Here, at Old Trafford, they are actually keeping the ball on the turf in attack, instead of thumping it all over the premises, and are running into position to receive passes." Three players who received particular praise were Carey, Pearson and Rowley.

However, just as it seemed a bright new future seemed to await Manchester United, war broke out in Europe in September 1939. The club suffered significant physical damage. The investment Gibson had poured into the development of Old Trafford was ruined by two air raids – the first on December 22nd, 1940, and the second on the night of March 11th, 1941. The main stand was destroyed; the terraces transformed into a landscape which resembled wasteland. Even the pitch was branded with 'a deep scar' in the middle. The club received some compensation from the War Damage Commission but could not commence rebuilding until fighting ceased. Until such time that rebuilding was complete, Manchester City offered to share their Maine Road ground at a cost of £5,000 per season. The long-held vision to develop Old Trafford into an arena with a capacity of 120,000 would have to wait.

Many of United's senior players were enlisted to fight; and while recognised professional competition went on hiatus, clubs still continued to fulfil fixtures, completing their team with players of other clubs who would 'guest', participating in the Wartime League. The war lasted six years, waging a naturally destructive impact on the lives and short careers of players. It is in this process that Crickmer and Rocca's vision resulted in its second great success (if we accept its first was to come into being at all).

In Rocca's contact book were three brothers – Abraham, Clifford and Frederick Gosling, greengrocers in Newton Heath who also ran a football team. The Goslings were big United fans – and Rocca worked with them to continue to give more young United players a chance playing in the Manchester Amateur League.

United were luckier than most when it came to their player's fates in the war. Perhaps the most impacted was their bright new thing Jimmy Hanlon, who suffered malnutrition as a prisoner of war, and whose career was never quite the same. Stadium aside, when the war was over, Manchester United were in a fairly strong position thanks to the foundation work done by James Gibson, Walter Crickmer and Louis Rocca – a trio who the club remain eternally indebted to.

3
___

ENTER MATT BUSBY...

MATT BUSBY WAS BORN IN BELLSHILL, SCOTLAND. HE was a right wing-half of international class, capped once for his country after impressing for Manchester City. Whilst at Maine Road, Busby had spent some time in the reserve team – and Louis Rocca, friendly with the player due to their connections in the local Catholic community, had attempted to bring him across the city to Old Trafford. Rocca was told he could sign Busby – but it would cost £150. Rocca replied the club did not even have 150 shillings, which was probably accurate.

It was rumoured that Scott Duncan had wanted to sign Busby as part of his Scottish influx, at which point he was quoted a price of £250, but the United boss declined. Busby instead moved to Liverpool in 1936 for £8,000 and did in fact play in that last game of the 1938/39 campaign at Old Trafford, where United had won by two goals to nil as the wheels of their new youth production line began to turn. Busby's performance drew particular acclaim from the *Guardian*, as well as that of United's Bill McKay: "The play of those two sage and seasoned wing half-backs McKay and Busby was worth everything else put together." Elsewhere, the *Guardian* also described Busby as 'the gentlest-mannered and most philosophic of footballers'.

Busby was just 30 years old when the war began. He was enlisted in the King's Liverpool regiment and became a sergeant major. He had as traumatic a relationship with war as one could have – his father and all of his uncles had been killed in the first war 25 years earlier. Busby confessed he 'wasn't a born soldier' and was grateful to FA secretary Stanley Rous for nominating him to be stationed in Aldershot, where he would learn to become a physical training instructor.

In 1942, James Gibson travelled to Dorset to spend time with Bill Williams, an old friend who was in charge of sport for the Southern Command. Gibson explained to his friend of the plans they were putting into place in Manchester. He expressed two concerns. The first was that Rocca was 60 years old and despite being as passionate as ever, he would not live forever. The second was that Crickmer, despite being 18 years younger than Rocca, was needed to fulfil the club's clerical duties in his usual role as secretary, and if push came to shove over whether he should be secretary or manager, he was a better fit for the former role. Williams told Gibson he had heard promising things about Busby, who had been made player-manager of an all-star team of enlisted men who were playing exhibition matches at home and abroad. Back in Manchester, Gibson had a meeting with Crickmer and Rocca and explained that he felt a new manager was needed. He said the two names that he had heard most about were Matt Busby and Joe Mercer. Rocca insisted that Busby was the right man and said he'd use his connections to make an approach.

ENTER MATT BUSBY...

Busby had begun to see himself as a manager. Most aspiring managers in the UK were driven by the prospect of creating a dynasty in the same manner as Herbert Chapman with Arsenal in the early part of the decade. But Busby also admired the intent of his Liverpool manager George Kay to populate his team with young players and, as the war went on, he grew in confidence due to the fact that the army team he was managing consisted of many top-class stars.

Kay had been sufficiently impressed to offer Busby a role as his assistant when he was demobbed, with a proposal that he could continue to play for as long as he wanted to. Busby had resisted because he was beginning to feel ready for management, even though he was self-conscious about his own confidence.

As it transpired, Louis Rocca, as he always did, managed to hear about this, and sent a letter to Busby care of his unit, 10 days before Christmas 1944.

"I could not trust a letter going to Liverpool," Rocca wrote, "as what I have to say is so important. I don't know if you have considered what you are going to do when war is over, but I have a great job for you if you are willing to take it on…"

In February of 1945, Busby agreed to meet James Gibson at one of his businesses, Cornbrook Cold Storage on 14 Hadfield Street, from where the club were forced to operate following the bombings a mile or so away at Old Trafford.

"Call it confidence, conceit, arrogance, or ignorance, but I was unequivocal about it," Busby later wrote. "At the advanced age of 35 I would accept the managership of Manchester United only if they would let me have all my own way. As the manager I would want to manage. I would be the boss… I had my theories about the psychology needed, the essential qualities I felt had been missing in the game. The gulfs must go." Busby wondered if the loss of his father at a young age had induced a "paternal, protecting feeling for other unfortunate or sensitive young people" and had felt attracted to the plan already drawn up at United to introduce young players through a system into the first team. "I did not set out to build a team," Busby said in his book *My Story*, "the task ahead was much bigger than that. What I really embarked upon was the building of a system which would produce not one team, but four or five teams, each occupying a rung on a ladder, the summit of which was my first XI… I wanted to build teams of world-class footballers, and to do the job efficiently, had to get hold of them young. As soon as they were available, in fact."

His demand for complete control was accepted; as was his insistence that he be given a five-year contract – like Chapman had received when he became manager of Arsenal – and not the three-year deal Gibson had offered. In the February 17th edition of the *Sunday Mail*, the news was revealed, forcing United to make a formal announcement the following day. Busby's contract was due to start when he was demobbed later that year; before that he rejoined his army colleagues in London ahead of a flight to Naples, from where the 'all-stars' would tour Italy and Greece. The travelling party were in tremendous spirits due to the German surrender in Italy.

It was in Italy – Bari to be precise – where Busby crossed paths with another former half-back with whom he'd battled on the pitch. His name was Jimmy Murphy, formerly of West Brom, and aside from their confrontations at club level, the pair had been on opposing sides for Busby's sole international cap – Wales emerging victorious. Where Busby was known as a player of class and poise, Murphy's nickname was 'Tapper' in reference to his aggressive tackling style. What really impressed Busby in Bari was the intensity with which his old pal was building up the importance of these practice matches. Murphy was in charge of a team and delivered a pre-match message as though the players were getting ready to play in the FA Cup final. That will to win was intoxicating.

"It was his attitude, his command, his enthusiasm and his whole driving, determined action and word-power that caused me to say to myself: 'He's the man for me,'" Busby recalled. "He was the man who would help me create a pattern that would run right through the several teams of players from 15 years of age upwards to the first team."

Murphy was sold on Busby's patter. It sounded perfect. "Our ideas were similar," said Busby, "and from this understanding, my conception of a crèche, a nursery, then a school with a curriculum of playing and character standards and my overall search for a pattern that would facilitate the interchanging of players from one team to another – from all these were born what eventually were known as the Busby Babes. It could be that what either Jimmy Murphy or I lacked the other had. He would always give a straightforward opinion. He was no yes-man. But once having made a point he would accept that mine was the decision. If he judged a player I found that his judgements almost always confirmed mine. He was invaluable in handling boys but his value did not rest there. He could tackle the established player with the same conviction and enthusiasm."

A week prior to this meeting, Busby's team had played in Florence against a side whose forward line comprised of players from the Brazilian Expeditionary Force; including José Perácio, the legendary forward who had scored three goals in the 1938 World Cup. Busby watched, impressed, as the forwards played with a freedom and liberation befitting the actual freedom and liberation of the time.

Murphy had his own coaching ideas. He'd been in France at

the same time that an Austrian team had a training camp there in the late 1930s. They were led by none other than Jimmy Hogan. Murphy was transfixed with Hogan's techniques – just as Busby had been with him. Hogan was conducting training sessions with the ball in play, which was revolutionary for the time; Hogan explained to Murphy how he liked his centre-half to be able to play with the ball rather than just hoofing it clear, and also expressed his belief that continental soccer was about to enter a new age where European nations would quickly accelerate past the English.

"Mastery of the ball and of the simple way of doing things were the basis of football," Murphy recalled. "I used a lot of Jimmy Hogan's ideas when I joined Matt Busby at Manchester United. He was a very influential coach."

Busby formally began work at Manchester United on Monday October 22nd, 1945 (Jimmy Murphy followed when he was demobbed the following spring). Busby told reporters that he was going to spend some time assessing the club's current players and looking over the scout's reports of young players. "It will not be easy to start building up," he said, "but I hope I may form some concrete plans for team strengthening later in the season. United have a first-class side if I could only get them together in one place!"

Crickmer and trainer Tom Curry had continued to select the side for the Wartime League games. Crickmer's day-to-day duties were consumed by the administration work, so training was most often taken by Jimmy McLelland and Jimmy Brown. Now Busby was in situ, he oversaw training and selected his first team for the following weekend's game against Bolton Wanderers at Maine Road on October 27th, 1945 in the North Regional section of the Wartime League. Some 30,000 turned up to see United go behind, and then equalise through Johnny Carey, before winning thanks to a goal by Fred Worrall. Busby was unbeaten in his first eight games in this league, winning four – and it was clear how important Carey was at inside-forward. When United won 6-1 against Preston on November 3rd, Carey was involved in almost every goal.

The new manager's first official, competitive game in charge was an FA Cup tie with Accrington Stanley at Peel Park. The team sheet read:

CROMPTON
WHALLEY CHILTON ROACH
WARNER COCKBURN
HANLON CAREY SMITH ROWLEY WRIGGLESWORTH

Of these, Crompton, Whalley, Cockburn and Hanlon could be said to be genuine youth products while there is also a fair claim for Chilton, too, given that he never played a senior game for Liverpool before Louis Rocca lured him to Manchester. Four or five homegrown players in a senior team would be a success in any era and is a testament to the fantastic work done by Crickmer and Rocca.

But Matt Busby wasted no time in making his plans known. United drew that game 2-2 – winning 5-1 in the second leg, but losing in the next round to Preston. It left Busby with seven more months to prepare for competitive action when the First Division resumed in August 1946, by which time there were even more graduates into the first team – John Aston, Billy McGlen, Johnny Morris, Stan Pearson and Charlie Mitten joining Crompton and Chilton. The line-up for the manager's first league game, a 2-2 draw at Middlesbrough's Ayresome Park, was as follows:

FOOTBALL, TAUGHT BY MATT BUSBY

CROMPTON
CAREY CHILTON ASTON
WARNER MCGLEN
MORRIS PEARSON
DELANEY ROWLEY MITTEN

Busby deployed the traditional 3-2-5 (by now, the centre-half had retreated into the defensive line) with inside-forwards that would drop a little deeper, making runs past Rowley or into the pockets of space between Rowley and the wide players.

Enough about the shape, for now. Let us finally dig into the Busby philosophy.

"What is this pattern of playing I keep going on about?" he asked in his book *Soccer At The Top*. "Only the naive would imagine that it is a drill to be followed by every Manchester United player. It is a pattern formed by the players and the staff, formed by individuals who are all different, and therefore the pattern over the years will gradually change. But only gradually… we didn't sign all the best (young players), but we managed more than our share, so that in our midst, ever maturing, ever growing into the Old Trafford pattern of play and behaviour, we had an extraordinary number of youths."

In an interview with Arthur Hopcraft in 1968, Busby explained further: "I always wanted creative football. I wanted method. I wanted to manage the team as I felt players wanted to be managed."

If talk of a pattern still seems vague then let's elaborate through the observation of the author Ralph L. Finn in his book *Champions Again*, who deduced there were two distinct approaches in English football. The first was the native: "The long-ball to fast raiding wingers," he wrote. "The centre from the wing. The big strong finisher in the middle. An occasional ball-playing inside-forward, but seldom more than one in a side. Strong, terrier-like wing-halves. Big robust backs."

The other, as referenced earlier, was 'Scottish in origin, not English', and explained by Finn thus: "The traditional Scots style is infinitely more subtle. It believes firmly in ball players in every forward and half-back position. It carves out openings by clever play, relying on skill to create those openings. It prefers the short pass on the ground to the wide flung pass in the air. The England style is exciting, exhilarating, good to watch. The Scots style appeals more strongly to those with a more cultured understanding of the game."

There was, as well, another line once uttered by Busby which provided an insight into his vision. "I would rather lose," he said, "than play defensively and play safe."

The manager discussed the value of youthfulness. "I thought that young players who could start their careers at Old Trafford would give you all they'd got at all times," he said, "and they'd give you loyalty which I think is so important."

Busby had a clear and defined vision in terms of desired qualities of players in each area of the team. So too did Jimmy Murphy.

"What are the basic needs?" Busby asked, when discussing goalkeepers. "From the back the need is for a goalkeeper who is in charge of the penalty area, who has an understanding with his colleagues by thought reading as well as shouting, as well as having an appreciation of angles and using the ball at the right time."

Jimmy Murphy's answer was a little more elaborate. "First impressions of a goalkeeper are all important," he said. "The best exude confidence even at the kick-in. I like them to be 6ft or over. This doesn't entirely rule out the smaller fellows, but the first essential of a 'keeper' is that he must have the size to dominate his area. If he is tall he can come out fearlessly and collect the dangerous high balls. And if he is powerful he is not likely to be knocked over. He must also have 'good hands'. If there is the slightest sign he drops the ball then he must be checked to discover whether this is a temporary lapse or a fatal fault.

"Then he needs anticipation, quick reflexes; and he must know how to angle himself when the ball is on the wings. Goalkeeping is the one position that has not changed much over the last 30 years, apart from the way they now use the ball in their own penalty area to initiate attacks. In the old days they just used to punt it upfield. Presence is the almost indefinable 'something' which stamps the great keeper. It is true one often sees small agile keepers diving and leaping to make seemingly impossible saves. But week in week out, year on year, give me the tall, powerful boys who are not afraid to come off the line."

Busby had inherited Jack Crompton in this role – and while he admired his goalkeeper, he was almost immediately tempted to look for a successor, coveting Frank Swift at Manchester City. The United manager had tremendous foresight in this particular area of the pitch as signings in future times would show.

As we'll discover, there was no era that experienced a shift in tactical approaches as profoundly as the era Busby was at the helm of Manchester United. His 26 years in charge at Old Trafford bore witness to the complete evolution from the old to the new – the three-man defence to the four-man defence and other variations which remain the basis of almost every modern system. The centre-half was assisted by the half-backs, who became the team's pacemakers – they were required to defend, attack, carry the ball and move it at the right time, at the same time as tracking the runs of the opposing inside-forwards. Ostensibly, by comparison the centre-half had only the centre-forward to look after; towards the end of Busby's tenure, one centre-half became two, and that second centre-half would usually be one of the half-backs dropping deeper. When five-man forward lines became three and four-man midfields, this was a consequence of those forwards dropping a little deeper, too.

In 1946, Busby was not in a hurry to deviate from the 3-2-5, but his following comments about the composition of a defence were made at a time when most of football had made the switch to backlines of four.

"Full-backs require strength, pace, and need to be quick on the turn – needs that are perhaps even more vital now than they were twenty years ago," Busby explained. "All the back men need to have command in the air, have to be able to read situations before they arise."

Murphy discussed the full-backs. "Of all positions the full-back has changed the most dramatically over the past ten years," he said in 1968. "When I played managers looked for big burly backs who could strike fear into wingers by their crunching tackles. Today one looks for a fast and perfectly balanced player who can keep pace with the fastest wing man. Indeed this is the most vital aspect of his game, for modern defences are so tight that an overlapping full-back is a key factor in a quick counter-attack.

"They play at times like an additional winger. Therefore speed is essential. Tackling is still important, but there are not so many sliding tackles as there were. These days a back must be able to read a move so instead of going for the first tackle he can force the opposing wing man down the touchline. I look for the boy who has speed, can turn quickly, can read the game and is a good striker of the ball – preferably with either foot. For this accuracy of passing is a 'must' to start attacking moves for his own side."

When it came to the centre of the defence, it was clear that Busby wanted someone who was capable on the ball. "What is now termed a sweeper is to be a smeller of danger, and this was never better done than by Nobby Stiles, who was taking up positions to counter situations when the ball was at the other end of the park," he said. "All these defenders, too, must use the ball accurately. The one thing to be avoided is giving the ball away – the team that does it least is the one that wins the prizes."

Murphy concurred, though seemed to prefer brawn over brains in this department. "Ideally one, if not both (centre-halves), should be tall, able to climb high and be mobile," he said. "Therefore, I ask myself: Has he plenty of spring like a gymnast? Is he safe when heading the ball from all angles? This is the number one on the list of skills. The centre-half must be dominant particularly in the air. He cannot afford to miss anything."

It is perhaps no surprise that Busby and Murphy, both former wing-halves, were in agreement that the midfield was the most crucial area of the pitch.

"The middle men, the creators, are the ones who really shape the game, the ones from whom most blessings flow," Busby observed. "Deep-lying inside-forwards and wing-halves used to do the job, so there is nothing actually new about middle men, the only difference now being whether the method is to use two mainly or three. Four is a policy of fear. Whatever the method, these are the men predominantly who start things. They have to have vision, imagination to hold the ball or pass it, and ability to beat a man, used if a pass that will do the same work for him more swiftly and economically is not on. But the middle man has also to be able to win the ball, so he has to be able to tackle, read, or smell when an interception is going to present itself."

High standards; and yet every great Manchester United side from this point on possessed one of these players. Busby's Manchester United had more than their fair share and it was not a coincidence that they were all moulded by the hands of Jimmy Murphy. "Even ten years ago a manager tried to build his side on the classic traditions of a powerful defensive type wing-half and a ball playing, attacking wing-half," Murphy said. "As a general rule the attacking winger had better ball control and greater mobility and he would move up behind the forward line to keep an attack going. True, the defensive wing-half would often go on an attacking sortie, in which case the normal attacking wing-half would cover for him. This was the broad principle, but today tactics are vastly different. The more defensive wing-half is used almost exclusively on defensive work as a 'sweeper' up or secondary centre-half. This player's chief asset must be his reading of the game.

"So much for the back four, which is the modern defensive set-up; now we must have two men working in midfield to link defence with attack. The old style attacking wing-half will be one of these men, only now he is used in a much more roving role. The first essential here is accuracy in passing. He may be absolutely brilliant on the ball, with a whole repertoire of tricks which will thrill the crowd, but he is no use to his team if the final pass is a bad one. The ratio must be five or six to one. That is to say, if he passes 30 times in a match I can excuse five bad balls....but no more!

"This class of player should never be in a hurry. No matter how much the crowd scream for him to 'get rid' he must hold the ball until his own men are in position to set up an attack. This is the man who sets the machine in motion, therefore he cannot afford to have his eyes glued on the ball. He should have an instinctive touch so he can stride forward confidently, getting a picture of the field of play so he knows which of his colleagues is in the best possible position to receive the ball. He must have an ice cold football brain and when I see a man of this calibre I don't necessarily blame him if a pass goes astray.

"So many football fans, keyed up with excitement, hoot with

derision at what appears to them a bad pass. Never forget it is not the man with the ball that makes a pass possible, it is the man off the ball who should get into an unmarked position. You can always tell immediately when a team is playing well, because there are a number of players in open spaces ready to receive the ball. That shows they want the ball and are full of confidence. Bad teams with bad players 'hide' themselves."

Murphy was no less straight-talking when it came to the qualities his perfect forwards would have. "This man must have pace and shot allied to his ball control," he insisted. "Alfredo Di Stefano did this job magnificently for Real Madrid and so too did Tom Finney. Such a player must have a natural attacking flair, smooth movement on the ball, good control, and the ability to put his foot on the accelerator to quicken up or slow down the tempo. This man is doubly dangerous if he is fast, has a body swerve and a powerful shot so he can come from behind to have a crack at goal.

"This is the major difference between the attacking wing-half and his partner, the deep-lying inside-forward or centre-forward. The man who starts the move is usually a one-pace player with a very keen football brain and wonderful ball control. His partner, who is generally a deep lying centre-forward or scheming inside-forward, is a faster player; makes a more direct attack on goal and has the forward's natural flair for snatching half chances."

Murphy described wingers as 'the match-winners' and insisted they must be team players. "The winger must be able to cross a ball at speed and above all he must be accurate," the Welshman said. "There is no point having a modern (Stanley) Matthews out there on the touchline practising his soccer sorcery if, when he crosses the ball, he miscues. There must be an end product: either a goal, or at least an attempt on goal. In modern football I think the wingers need courage more than ever before. If he loses possession he cannot stand still. He must double back and challenge. Therefore when I check on a wingman, I look for speed, courage, accuracy when centring, and the guts, speed and stamina to chase back and do a job in defence when his own team has lost possession."

Murphy closed on his thoughts about the forwards by explaining he felt world class goal-getters were the rarest commodities. "Point one is physique, for even if he is not a pretty ball player a team can use a tall man to play the ball off," he opined. "He must have perfect physical fitness and stamina so he can chase, even when he is given a bad pass."

Again, Busby's thoughts revealed he was on a similar wavelength. "Forwards must have great skill because they are facing the wrong way half the time when the ball comes to them," he said. "They have to be able to take a bump and bounce back. They, too, have to anticipate situations. They have to 'lose' opponents, which is one reason why really great players seem to have more time than lesser men, thus having escaped by anticipating the ultra-tight marking of today. A forward has constantly to give himself a view of the pitch before the ball reaches him, thus allowing him a preconceived notion of what he intends to do. Compared with 20 years ago, wingers are a rarity, but still most goals come from crosses, so all forwards have to have some of a winger's qualities and so do middle men and even full-backs. Then, of course, to provide the finish to the whole operation, the need is for two or three of those priceless characters who have the knack of putting the ball into the net, and of whom Manchester United have had more than their share..."

The thoughts are compelling; they reveal a philosophy and a vision behind a team, an ideal of football intelligence that was ahead of their time. It was just as well the pair were simpatico considering one was tasked with teaching players the basics of how the other would want them to perform once they were ready.

There was an area not yet discussed by either, and of course, having exhausted every area of the team, it did not apply to a specific position. Murphy was fire and Busby was ice; fire was necessary to create these young players and ice was needed for composure, better decision-making, independent and instinctive action. It was perhaps this perfect contrast that had Busby thinking a little further outside the box than Murphy in one specific area.

"A bonus is the genius in the ranks," Busby said. "United have had a few of those. These fellows are, by nature, nonconformists, inasmuch as they do things that the others cannot do. I have always believed that the brilliant individualist must be given scope for his nonconformism as long as it is not at the expense of the end product – the scoring of goals. Because the constant surprises inflicted on the opposition by these gifted players become confidence-sapping for them, making them disbelieve in themselves."

By the time of this statement, Busby had arguably accommodated five such players in his United teams over the years; Johnny Morris and Charlie Mitten from his first great team. Duncan Edwards, although he perhaps doesn't easily fit into the above categories on face value. Denis Law, by virtue of his individual goal-scoring excellence. And finally, of course, George Best, possibly the greatest example of those qualities.

If Busby could find a group of players with the perfect blend, then he could create the perfect team as per his vision. "The great Real Madrid had all these qualities plus the vital and often missing link, complete understanding, and it was this I was aiming for," Busby said. "It is the understanding that makes the pattern from the individuals in it. To create it, the first job is making a player aware of what his own position demands, whether it is destructive, creative, or both, what he is required to do in any situation. All players do things differently. But basic requirements are the same, and knowing the requirements laid down for offensive or defensive situations, they are given constant practice in them.

"Since the reserve and other young players also often take part in the practice, the pattern is constantly being formed throughout the club, varied, as I said, only slightly and gradually as the odd player moves on, whose individual style has affected the pattern. Thus also not only has a player learned the requirements and practised them, he has learned from sheer practice the requirements of his colleagues, and the idiosyncrasies of his colleagues until they become a team of thought-readers.

"I was sometimes accused of 'playing it off the cuff' when some other teams with lesser talents regiment themselves into becoming boring, defensive, mechanical morons. But if the care with which we of Manchester United created our pattern, which was adapted to change with changes of individuals, and which was torn to shreds at Munich, and then created again, if all this is playing it off the cuff, my critics know more about the game than I do."

Murphy's explanation on this point revealed the chain of command. "A great football team is the product of many people, directed by the manager," he said. "To find the right players to blend into a team pattern is a laborious process, extending over many years. The real professionals are rightly proud of their calling, for they never see a game in the same way as the average fan does."

In 1967, when he was awarded the Freedom of Manchester, Busby's speech included a wonderful reference to what thrilled him most about the sport. "I love its drama, its smooth playing skill and its great occasions," he said, "I feel a sense of romance, wonder, and mystery, a sense of poetry."

One point made by Busby from day one, in spite of making it clear he wanted that control, was that he was always never less than fully appreciative of the number of people working to make

Manchester United tick. He spoke of the work done by Walter Crickmer and his assistant, Les Olive. He described Crickmer as "a wise little man... his advice about procedures was invaluable."

Following his first season in charge, Busby appointed Bert Whalley as Murphy's assistant. Whalley, yet another half-back, had been forced to retire early due to an eye injury. Busby felt he was a "soft-spoken, studious type, a good judge and a particularly good influence on youngsters" which he reckoned would be a fine balance for Murphy's sometimes aggressive approach.

"We had Tom Curry and Bill Inglis as trainers," Busby continued, "priceless with their experience and their genius for keeping the dressing room happy. Tom Curry was so fond of Old Trafford that he used to bring his open razor to the ground so that he would not waste time shaving at home. If the team played badly he would leave his open razor on the dressing room table and say: 'Help yourself, lads.'" Curry was described by Alf Clarke as a 'grand personality' and 'one of the best trainers in the country'. He supervised training and sun-ray treatment via infra-red and radiant heat.

There would be no shying away from the fact that it was a team effort at Old Trafford but neither can it be disputed that the first great Busby team was almost all of his own making – or, at least it is fairer to say that it was Busby, Crickmer and Rocca's team, where the future might be Busby and Murphy's.

Even before the return of the First Division, Busby had seen enough in the Wartime League to begin to make changes. In February he had signed Jimmy Delaney, the veteran Celtic and Scotland outside-right. A fee of £4,000 seemed a lot of money for a 30-year-old who had been accused of being brittle-boned, but Busby was convinced it would be an astute signing, and argued to the board of directors that it would be money well spent if Delaney managed just one or two seasons (he eventually played six). Delaney made his debut against Liverpool, and a week later, was in the United side which won 5-0 at Anfield – Busby's first return there since leaving, which had been acrimonious to some extent as his former club felt he'd broken a gentleman's agreement to take the job at United.

By the time competitive league action resumed, Busby had a very strong idea of his best team, and he was also planning positional changes within the squad. The man himself had experienced a move from inside-forward to wing-half, which had a transformational impact on his own career. In the closing stages of the prior campaign, Busby had been forced to make a number of positional changes in a game against Manchester City – including moving Carey to full-back. He played a sensational game as United won 3-1, and remained there for the rest of the season with the club winning four from their last five. Jimmy Murphy was finally able to begin work at United and was at Maine Road to watch their last game of the 1945/46 season, a 2-1 win over Stoke.

So it was a new era that officially got underway for the 1946/47 campaign. United won their first three games comfortably and, in their fourth, welcomed Liverpool to Maine Road. It was still Maine Road, despite some rumblings that Old Trafford would be ready to welcome their team home – and United's financial difficulties were shown yet again when Busby welcomed his squad back for pre-season training admitting they'd have to have a 'whip round' to get enough training kit for them all.

On the pitch, though, things were looking great. The senior players who had lost many years to war were eager to make up for lost time, while they played with a discipline representative of what they had been through. Busby's influence was already tangible, though, as evidenced by the team that faced Liverpool:

FOOTBALL, TAUGHT BY MATT BUSBY

CROMPTON
CAREY   CHILTON   MCGLEN
WARNER   COCKBURN
PEARSON   ROWLEY
DELANEY   HANLON   MITTEN

Busby had made significant decisions to move Carey and Chilton; these alterations had been trialled before but were now permanent. The boldness should not be underestimated. Carey of course had played at inside-forward and Chilton's usual position to date had been wing-half. Later in the season, John Aston would become the regular left-back, and he was normally comfortable in forward positions; has there ever been another manager who was able to take two outright attackers and convert them into bedrocks of a defensive system?

"Most of the players had fought their right positions and the team was beginning to blend together and play the kind of swift, flowing football that the crowds loved to see," author Alec Shorrocks wrote. "Matt Busby was an effective manager and popular with the players… United were already beginning to build a reputation for the speed of their attack, their fast open play, and the rapidity with which their attacks changed positions. Opposing defenders, looking for a face or the number they were supposed to be marking, often saw their man 40 yards away and in trying to follow him were thereby drawn well out of position."

Busby's side again won 5-0 against his old employers; Don Davies of the *Manchester Guardian* describing the performance as 'masterly', adding it was 'one which even Manchester United will not easily repeat'. Their perfect start to the league season was interrupted by injuries and international call-ups (international matches would be held on the same day as club matches) – and United would eventually finish second behind Liverpool, who, despite being outclassed early in the season, won the definitive match which decided the destiny of the championship in early May.

A brief note, to return to the point of Aston's repositioning. Not all of these great changes in United history were made by design and this is one of the wonderful tales of chance (in spite of Carey describing the change of both his and Aston's positions as 'inspiration' on Matt's part). Over Christmas, United were suffering from an injury crisis, and both Carey and McGlen were out. The team travelled to Grimsby with Aston and Whalley taken as their replacements. On the morning of the game, the pair were walking in Grimsby town centre, and Whalley, as the elder, offered his team-mate the choice of whether he wanted to play on the left or right. Aston said he'd think about it. They stopped at a toy shop, as Aston wanted to get something for a doll's house he'd made his daughter for Christmas. The shopkeeper recognised their Mancunian accents and, thinking they were there as supporters, asked if they were going to the match. "I'd go," replied the shopkeeper, "but I saw them last week and I said if they pick that bloody outside-right again I'm not going!"

"Are you playing left-back then?" Whalley asked his pal outside the shop.

"I am that!" Aston laughed. And he played well in a 0-0 draw – a key decision, as the left-back position was more open due to Carey being a mainstay on the other side. Aston finished the season with 23 league appearances. While it is fair to say other influences were at play, it still took a tremendously bold decision from Busby to commit this into his team.

Another significant addition to the side was Johnny Morris, who was only able to start playing in late October after his national service. Morris was an instant hit as inside-forward, playing with a sense of ingenuity that thrilled the United fans.

At the conclusion of the season, Busby went to Jimmy Murphy's house to toast the Welshman's success with the reserve side, which won the Central League title – and was surprised to hear his number two admit that he felt nobody in the reserves would be able to make the step up to the first team. The pair resolved to go back to Rocca and concede that a higher quality of younger player would need to be found.

Busby's team continued to develop its personality in 1947/48. It had been a disappointing start – after winning two of their first three in the league, United won none of their next nine. A victory over Aston Villa stopped that run but it was going a goal down to Wolves the following week which provoked a turning point. The win at Molineux saw United's attack 'hit a new level of power and penetration', according to Alec Shorrocks. "United's players always believed that a goal against them brought out the best in their play," he wrote.

In the midst of the difficult run, Busby had gone to watch a game in Glasgow and bumped into an old friend. He asked what was going on at United – and Busby said he felt his side could win the FA Cup. His friend put a 'few pounds' on at 25-1. The resilience of his side was proven; not only did they win 6-2 at Wolves from being a goal down, no fewer than 11 positive results were rescued from losing positions over the rest of the season.

One of those results came at Villa Park in the third round of the FA Cup. The home side scored a goal registered at 13.5 seconds; but come half-time, the home fans were as stunned as the away team had been at that moment. Busby's men hit a devastating five-goal flurry with Delaney and Mitten in particular wreaking havoc on the wings. With nothing to lose, Villa staged an all-time classic comeback, getting back to 5-4 – before Stan Pearson broke their hearts with a decisive sixth, his second, to conclude the goalscoring for the day. "In my opinion," Pearson said afterwards, "that game was when we played the best football I've seen from anybody, anywhere, anytime. That's saying a lot, but we pinged that ball around so quickly first time – I've never seen anything like it before or since. We were shoving it around and darting here and there. It was magic."

Johnny Morris, one of the most exciting players, described it as one of the most exhilarating games he'd played in. Don Davies' match report was as exceptional as the football. "If Picasso and Matisse had been responsible for the design of this match they could not have given a more original twist to the proceedings," he wrote, and Geoffrey Green, an equally poetic writer, spoke of how "deep human qualities flowered before our eyes, and if the skies wept they proved to be tears of joy."

In the fourth round, United were drawn at home to Liverpool – but because City were also drawn at home, an alternative venue had to be found. Busby chose Everton's Goodison Park, even though it was of geographical favour to their opponents. "He told us it would suit our style of play," remembered John Aston. "It's a big, wide-open ground and we could really sling the ball around there." In seven first-half minutes – 30, 34, and 36 – Liverpool were blown away, Busby's side strolling into a 3-0 lead they wouldn't relinquish.

Opponents were quick to praise United's brand of football. Sam Bartram of Charlton, who were defeated in the fifth round, admitted he felt the game would go on forever "because we were so completely outplayed." Against Preston in the sixth round, Delaney and Rowley executed a perfect plan to frustrate the North End centre-half Paddy Waters. "Jack had him all over the place," Delaney recalled, "which meant that he couldn't cover the middle... every time I drifted into the centre and Jack went on to the wing you could hear Paddy shouting in his big Irish voice: 'Oh Jasus, watch dem, watch dem, dey're at it again.'"

Rowley scored the final goal in a 4-1 win – and United had a date at Wembley in the final when Derby County were defeated in the semi-final. Awaiting them would be Blackpool, who boasted in Stanley Matthews and Stan Mortensen two of the greatest players in the country. It was United's first FA Cup final since they won it in 1909 and the demand for tickets was so extreme that supporters made personal journeys to the club's office and even Matt Busby's house to make 'applications'.

In just his second full season with United, Busby had taken a team he'd largely inherited and crafted to Wembley, playing an exceptional brand of football. In the week before the final he had to make a call on the fitness of Jack Rowley, Jack Crompton and Jimmy Delaney, while Johnny Morris carried an ankle knock so significant he felt he was 'carried' at Wembley, but all made the game with varying degrees of comfort. The biggest selection call came at right-half. Jack Warner had usually been first choice but over Christmas, John Anderson had been called up in an emergency to play at Middlesbrough. Busby took 'a gamble' by picking Anderson, who had recently suffered the loss of his wife.

Team for the 1948 FA Cup final:

CROMPTON

CAREY ASTON

ANDERSON CHILTON COCKBURN

MORRIS PEARSON

DELANEY ROWLEY MITTEN

Included in the 99,842 crowd at Wembley were seven survivors of the 1909 FA Cup winning team, among them the most famous of them all, Billy Meredith, now 63. Families all over the country gathered around the radio to listen to the match. At half-time, Blackpool led 2-1.

"If we keep playing football we must win it," captain Johnny Carey told his team-mates, "if we start just kicking around we've no chance." Carey also explained the team's motto – "the ball should never stop."

United failed to muster much of an effort after the break until they won a free-kick following an injury stoppage. From there, Rowley drew his team level with a fine header. United were in the ascendancy and in the 80th minute, Stan Pearson went on a diagonal run across goal – cutting the ball back across the goalkeeper, and in via the post. A key moment had occurred just before. Crompton had denied Mortensen at the other end and launched a quick counter-attack. "Months before that," Alf Clarke wrote, "Crompton might have lacked the decisive split-second action to cover-up from such a situation. Matt Busby had emphasised to him the dangers and the way to combat them."

Within 100 seconds of scoring a third, Busby's side had a fourth – Blackpool had tried to attack from kick-off, but found themselves swarmed deep in their own defence. John Anderson unleashed a shot from 35 yards that caught all by surprise, flying into the roof of the net to seal a 4-2 victory – and the FA cup – for United.

The 13-minute goal blast, and United's recovery from a losing position, had captured the imagination of the nation. The variety of goals – a fine looping header, a mazy dribble and a good old long-range slobberknocker – showed this Busby brand of football as being both multi-dimensional and successful.

"I am always striving for perfection," Busby said, "and it was not until the 1947/48 season that I really saw such perfection from the players at Manchester United. United beat Blackpool in a match regarded by many as the best final ever played on the famous Wembley turf."

Jack Crompton felt that this team represented a pinnacle in his own career. "Why were we so good?" he asked rhetorically, "firstly, discipline… we'd all experienced discipline in the forces. We were easy to handle. Secondly, we had beautiful balance. We could all do our job well. We had a stable defence of destroyers, and a forward line of creators… they were a forward line without equal. They all had skill and pace. They were all so positive and they couldn't wait to get to the opposition goal. And physically we were all very strong. It was a side which would have won credit in any era."

John Aston had a similarly fond memory. "We blended well and played for each other, and the confidence in the team was amazing," he said. "Busby always used to preach to us to hold on during the first quarter of an hour. 'They'll come at you, and come at you,' he'd say. 'After the first 15 minutes or so,' he used to say, 'is when you can start playing your football.' His maxim was always 'Keep playing football'. Busby didn't have a ready-made team. Most of the players were there, but they needed organising, and that's what he did."

The forward line would get most of the praise – but one of them, Johnny Morris, was later keen to praise the half-back line and in particular Chilton (and his explanation further hints at the deployment of overlapping full-backs). "They were the ones who made it easy for the forward line," Morris said. "We had a great method of playing and I don't think there's anybody in this country who could tell you how we played. The kingpin was the centre-half and he made the full-backs play and he was good enough to cover the full-backs. Our understanding of each other was so natural. The way this team played, they made players."

Rowley's explanation of the Busby way was no less vague, saying it was 'fantastic', but "I don't think any of the players could explain it because you can't coach that type of football. The ball would come to me facing my own goal and I'd just flick it, then I'd turn around and it always went to one of our own players. I always remember we went to Wolves... Two of their defenders followed me so what did I do? I went lying deep so there was a big gap in the middle of the field and everything went through the middle."

Even Rowley had been a beneficiary of Busby's subtle approach to repositioning – he liked to drift wide, so his manager was happy to incorporate this into the fluidity of his front line. "He knew the brilliance of Pearson and Morris," Alf Clarke wrote, "two great inside-forwards whose styles, so vastly different, were the ideal blend for Jack Rowley. He hit upon the idea of the sudden switching of positions of Rowley and Delaney."

Stan Pearson would later concede that he felt the likes of Charlton, Law and Best were better individuals than any of the front line he played with, but insisted that the brand of football was no less thrilling. "Perhaps without realising it we had developed a sixth sense," he suggested. "Our understanding of each other's game was amazing. For example, if Charlie (Mitten) saw me getting the ball in a certain situation he'd already be on his way and I'd know he'd be on his way. It was a kind of instinct. Matt Busby was a man you wanted to play for. He made you want to play with him."

Young boys around the country raced onto their local fields to re-enact the final. They included boys by the names of Duncan Edwards and Bobby Charlton. The latter, an 11-year-old, selected United as 'his' team when they equalised in the first half – but was so eager to pretend he was at Wembley that he missed the entirety of the second half playing outside. "When, at last, someone came out and told us United had won 4-2," Charlton recalled, "I danced about in delight as if I had personally scored the winning goal."

The seeds of the future were planted, but United were still keen to pay tribute to their past. Before presenting the FA Cup to supporters back at Manchester Town Hall, the team made a detour to Hale to visit the ailing chairman James Gibson, who had missed the match through illness. The man who had saved the club was able to see the reward of his investment.

4

THE CHAMPIONS OF 1952

WHILE THE FABLED FA CUP WINNING TEAM OF 1948 wasn't ancient, it was clear it would need some regeneration. Even a man with a plan like Matt Busby would not have foreseen the areas in which that would be necessary within four years. Two players he would have probably felt he could count on for the longer term would have been Johnny Morris and Charlie Mitten; both were absent by the time United broke their championship duck under Busby.

Morris had struggled with the ankle injury he'd picked up before the cup final; and behind the scenes, Morris and Busby had clashed on the training pitch, with the former challenging the latter over a free-kick routine. The forward demanded a transfer, and within a year of winning the Cup with United, was on the move – to Derby County for a world record £24,000. Some £18,000 was immediately reinvested in Johnny Downie of Bradford Park Avenue, who was consistent but not quite as instinctive, or controversial, as Morris. In fact, reinvested is a misnomer – Downie's transfer was completed before that of Morris, showing that Busby was not in the mood to be messed around.

In the following months, Allenby Chilton also demanded a transfer, claiming his wife became more ill with the northern weather. Busby accepted the request and began to groom Sammy Lynn as his successor at centre-half – but when Chilton changed his mind and said he wanted to stay, the United manager was only too happy to keep him in his plans, first keeping Lynn in position and reintroducing Chilton at wing-half before he gradually moved back into his familiar position. This was a demonstration that Busby was happy to give players another chance rather than burning bridges.

That was not the case for Charlie Mitten, though. On a tour of North America in the summer of 1950, Mitten had been tempted by a lucrative offer to play in Colombia. The offer from Santa Fe was over six-and-a-half times what he was paid in England, and more than he'd earned in his career in total to date. It was too tempting – Mitten accepted the offer, knowing it was likely he would face sanctions from the English FA if he ever chose to return due to the domestic league in Colombia breaking away from FIFA control at the time.

Other players had been tempted by a move abroad. Henry Cockburn was so interested in different cultures he started to take a foreign language phrase book on his travels; however, he might have struggled, as England team-mate Tom Finney observed: "Henry once asked a head waiter what the time was and got a plate of spaghetti."

Mitten was replaced by a winger by the name of Harry

THE CHAMPIONS OF 1952

McShane, but even he would find himself a peripheral squad player by the time Busby's side won their league title in 1952. In fact, this is how that side looked, based on average appearances:

REG ALLEN

THOMAS MCNULTY JOHN ASTON

JOHNNY CAREY ALLENBY CHILTON HENRY COCKBURN

JOHN DOWNIE STAN PEARSON

JOHNNY BERRY JACK ROWLEY ROGER BYRNE

Until Byrne's emergence (he had been signed as a 19-year-old amateur in the same period as Mitten's departure), the left-side was competently filled by Ernie Bond. There had been an experiment in the previous season when Rowley was unfit; Aston was moved to centre-forward, with Byrne at left-back and Bond further forward. It had been a wise move. Aston, of course, was one of those who had begun his career as an inside-forward, and his return of 16 goals was exceptional. His return in the title-winning season was a modest four goals, but it served as evidence of Busby's intelligence in how to best use his squad's talents in an emergency – and also of his constant work on the training pitch.

"We linked together as a team… we were comrades," explained Henry Cockburn. "We were so enthusiastic and full of running. The way we played was never to stop the ball. Busby used to say, 'The ball is round to go round, so don't stop it, keep it rolling.' They call it one-touch nowadays. The game was so fluent. It was bloody great to watch from the back. In the days when we had wingers there was no finer sight than to see them running with the ball, taking players on, going past them."

Four of the 1948 team were gone completely and even Jack Crompton, though still at the club, had been replaced by Londoner Reg Allen, who had been signed for a world record fee for a goalkeeper of £11,000. Those negotiations had been handled in the summer of 1950 by Walter Crickmer and he sent news to Busby of the completed transfer. There was sadder news to send the manager that summer – Louis Rocca, Crickmer's long-time aid, and a man so devoted to Manchester United, sadly passed away. Indeed, neither Rocca nor James Gibson were alive to see United's league title triumph of 1952, with the chairman dying on September 11th, 1951. He was survived on the board of directors by his wife Lillian and son Alan. Gibson had been ill for some time, signing his last minutes as chairman on June 20th, 1950, after which Harold Hardman became acting chairman.

The reminder of the passing of time was evident all around Old Trafford; those who did remain in the side from the FA Cup victory were now all older than 30. There was not much career left if these players wanted to win the First Division title they so coveted; their finishes since the war had been second, second, second, fourth and second, so it was beginning to appear as though it might be a case of 'always the bridesmaids'. Busby's philosophy remained unmoved. "In the 1949/50 season," Percy Young wrote, "United won neither League Championship nor Cup, but they continued to play the same imaginative and scientific football."

It was evident that something seemed a little different even from the early stages of 1951/52. Jack Rowley started the season in a rich vein of form, scoring two hat-tricks in his first two games and another in the seventh as United started well. Johnny Berry, an outside-right from Birmingham, replaced Jimmy Delaney, and his direct youthfulness added a new dimension to Busby's front line. United had stumbled in the autumn but were arguably helped by an embarrassing early FA Cup exit to Hull City – this redefined the season's objective with only the First Division title left on the line. Busby's side concluded the season in fine fashion, defeating

Liverpool 4-0, Burnley 6-1, drawing at Blackpool and defeating Chelsea by three goals – a game in which club captain Carey starred, and the adventure of Busby's football was plain to see in action.

"For seven years Manchester United had been very close to winning the championship, but we never had reached that point," Carey recalled. "I was getting to an age when I was looking for a championship medal. I got the ball (against Chelsea) and I moved forward. The opposing team seemed to go and mark our fellows; they expected me to pass. And I kept going. And I'd gone from just outside our own penalty area, up towards the Stretford End, and I kept going, nobody was coming to challenge me. I got just outside the box. And I thought, well, I have to have a crack at it. I had to hit it with my left foot, and it went right up in the top corner and that made us two up, and virtually assured me of a First Division championship medal."

Marauding defenders scoring 25-yard blockbusters to win the title? Many years later, on the other side of town, Vincent Kompany would do something similar as his own Manchester City team were being credited with revolutionising the game, adopting the same principles that were on display at Old Trafford on that day in April 1952.

The win over Chelsea set up an extraordinary afternoon at Old Trafford where United welcomed Arsenal. The Gunners were the only side capable of stopping Busby's rampant reds from winning the title but to do so they'd have to win 7-0 and also win their game in hand. United, though, won 6-1, achieved through another Rowley hat-trick, and another of those familiar goal flurries, with strikes registered in the 74th, 82nd and 89th minutes. Rowley's hat-trick goal had been a penalty; he was renowned for being predominantly left-footed, but remembered having "the cheek to take it with my right foot." Some showmanship on the big day! The goal was Rowley's 30th of the campaign; it was the eighth time his team had scored four times or more in a game.

"Amid the noisy scenes of victory," author Alec Shorrocks opined, "Matt Busby's mind went back to 1945 when he had taken over a club without a ground and with very little money, but full of players rich in talent and enthusiasm. He would leave it to others to remind him of his place in the scheme of things: of how he had suggested positional changes and then blended them as a unit, and how his patient belief in the value of young players was beginning to show results. Maybe though, this team which in recent weeks had rediscovered something of the secret which had made it a matchless football machine in 1948, could be allowed to run for a little while longer."

United's had been a thrilling title victory, even if the names of the forward five did not quite roll off the tongue in the same fashion as the 1948 front line. Downie and Byrne were more low-key than Morris and Mitten; it might also be argued that this low-key consistency actually helped transform a successful cup team into a victorious league team.

"The title has never been better earned," read the *Manchester Guardian*. "Mr Busby has shown himself as great a coach as he was a player, with an uncannily brilliant eye for young local players' possibilities; a believer in the certainty of good football's eventual reward, and a kindly, yet when necessary, firm father of his family of players.

They have built up a club spirit which enables men to bear cheerfully disappointments and to ignore personal opportunities to shine for the good of the whole. Moreover, by eschewing the dangerous policy of going into the transfer market whenever a weakness develops and giving their chances instead to the many local citizens on the club's books, they have made it likely that this club spirit will persist."

United won the title by four points (in the days of two points for a win) and scored 95 goals – their goals conceded tally of 52 may seem high for a team that had won the league, but in these days where attack was heavily favoured over defence, it was still one of the meanest defences in the division.

5

YOUTHFUL PROMISE

GOING INTO THE 1952/53 CAMPAIGN, THE FIRST TEAM had McNulty, Aston, Cockburn, Pearson and Byrne as regulars who had come through the youth ranks. More compelling was the extra number of players – those brought in to play a smaller number of games. Crompton was still there to play nine, but it was in the number of those who were dipping their toes into the team that the future could be seen.

Billy Redman made 18 appearances, Don Gibson 17 and Frank Clempson eight, but in the names Jackie Blanchflower (one), Mark Jones (three), and Jeff Whitefoot (three), it was clear that the efforts made by Rocca before his death – and the man hired to effectually replace him, Joe Armstrong – were beginning to pay off in terms of getting youngsters of the requisite ability.

Armstrong had worked for Manchester City in a scouting capacity; Busby had once more made an astute choice. His enthusiasm was as strong as Rocca's, while he had a genial charm and a happy disposition. Armstrong's eye for a player was arguably better than Rocca's and the Central League team – once a resting home for veteran and convalescing players – was now a thriving environment in which some of these acquired kids were learning their trade. Ray Wood, Bill Foulkes, Eddie Lewis, Ronnie Cope, Geoff Bent – these were just some of the young lads cutting their teeth in the second string in addition to those who had been given a little taste of first-team football.

In this clear pathway, Armstrong had a convincing argument for parents deciding whether to send their boy to Manchester.

And those were just a few of the names. The real work was being done in the teams below the Central League team and the brand new FA Youth Cup almost seemed to have been created to showcase the work done by Jimmy Murphy and Bert Whalley with the junior players.

At the end of the 1951/52 season, Busby told shareholders who were concerned about the advanced age of the side that the club boasted approximately £200,000 of value in talent in the youth team and they would be soon writing a new, and more glorious, chapter in the history of Manchester United – the world record transfer fee at that time was £34,500, giving some perspective to the remarkable nature of his claim.

It still seemed a tad optimistic at the end of the following season even when United had triumphed in the inaugural FA Youth Cup, overcoming Wolves 9-3 on aggregate, having won the first leg 7-1. The team for both legs read:

CLAYTON

FULTON COPE KENNEDY

COLMAN EDWARDS

WHELAN PEGG

MCFARLANE LEWIS SCANLON

FOOTBALL, TAUGHT BY MATT BUSBY

The formation for these games was the 3-2-5, or 3-2-2-3, that was still widely used in football and through every level at Old Trafford. Of these players, only Bryce Fulton did not get a first-team opportunity, and seven would go on to give significant contributions to United's senior side. Overall, 'Murphy's Marvels' registered a staggering 50 goals in the competition that season, although 23 came in a single game against Nantwich; it was 10-0 at half-time, when a fired-up Jimmy Murphy barked at his players that under no circumstances were they to take it easy in the second period. This small anecdote was quintessential Murphy. His players were working to standards not set by footballing norms; they were working to standards set by Matt Busby and Jimmy Murphy, and those expectations were that they should shatter what was considered high achievement.

Wolves, under Stan Cullis, were following Busby's lead in this quest to develop their own talent. (Though Wolves had a long history in implementing a youth system – starting way back in 1927, under Major Frank Buckley.) United's great scouting network had stolen a march on the Midlands club by acquiring Dudley-born Duncan Edwards, widely seen as the greatest sporting prospect in the country.

Edwards of course was one of those smitten with the idea of Old Trafford after listening to the 1948 FA Cup final. His natural ability and prescient intelligence in reading a game made it obvious he would be an outstanding half-back who would dominate games for a generation; but his talent was so superior to his peers that he was deployed in other areas of the pitch to ascertain his best position.

It was by virtue of his advanced talent that Edwards became a special figure in the United philosophy and instigated perhaps the first slight concession Busby and Murphy had been forced to consider. In the rare times his youth team struggled, Murphy would push Edwards up front to score game-changing goals; without fail, he would deliver. In one fog-blanketed game at Manchester City, Edwards had told Murphy 'not to worry, chief' – he'd turn around a half-time deficit. He did. It led to Murphy trying to inspire the other boys to not have to rely so heavily on their pal.

Prior to one Youth Cup game at Chelsea, the Welshman expressed this in a positive way. He wanted a brilliant group of players – including Wilf McGuinness and Bobby Charlton, two of the premium talents in the country – to believe in themselves and carry the ball themselves. When Chelsea had a half-time lead, Murphy sent the boys back out with the message, "Give the fucking ball to Duncan."

They did – he scored twice – United won 2-1. Edwards had two great feet, a tremendous sense of sporting fairness, the finest range of passing in the country, and a frame which would not only made him impossible to knock off the ball, it gave injuries to those foolish enough to try. If he had a weakness, it was that he would be too impetuous in trying to win the game for his team.

In any analysis of Manchester United's tactical history, the case of Duncan Edwards warrants extra-special mention. That's not to say Busby would have to deviate from his plan of a team that was skilled in the arts of passing and moving, or sacrificing for the better of the team.

Edwards was a sponge of a player – he would happily take advice and learn from mistakes. Murphy could impress upon him his belief that a Manchester United team should never stop working if they were 1-0 down or 10 goals up; Busby could polish any rough edges with that paternal guidance. "How do you think you played today, son?" he would occasionally ask a player and that player would have to infer that the answer was that he could improve.

It spoke volumes that this type of conversation was never held with Edwards; it spoke louder that at 16, this beast of a boy was deemed ready for first-team football. He could be trusted to play maturely in the most crucial position on the pitch – and improve the team.

Most of the other 10 besides Edwards in the first FA Youth Cup-winning team – and many of those in future ones, like McGuinness and Charlton – subscribed to the Busby and Murphy philosophy keenly, if still not at the total abandon of their uniqueness. And it was the uniqueness that was encouraged by the United management, for it was these qualities which would determine team selections. These players still treated Busby as a god, and the devout Catholic Murphy saw nothing sacrilegious in that. He and Whalley encouraged it, in fact, in order to strengthen Busby's position of discipline.

The goal was to encourage these individual qualities in a responsible manner and introduce them into the team in a drip-drip effect. Busby had previously spoken of having five successful teams through the club's structure, so it stood to reason that the ultimate goal was to have a squad that was interchangeable for any particular fixture, while keeping that big roster on their toes with the threat of energetic young hopefuls. And how those young hopefuls were desperate to be a part of it; McGuinness had been the most highly-sought schoolboy in the country before he watched United's kids take apart Wolves and realised that Old Trafford was the place to be. He was not alone in having his head turned by the early successes of this conveyor belt.

These players would be complemented by the rare outside purchase; and the Old Trafford system would eventually be so plentiful that funds for transfers could be raised by the sale of a star who might find their own route to the side a little too competitive. To have all this and to have a successful team that played good football would be akin to footballing utopia – and yet over the next five years that is precisely what happened at Manchester United.

6

THE BIG WIDE WORLD

MATT BUSBY WAS THE MAN RESPONSIBLE FOR pioneering Manchester United's European adventures, and there is no question he was keen for his club to test itself against the very greatest sides anywhere in the world. But even Busby was a little sceptical about United's initial global footprint. The reputation of the style of football of his team, as well as consecutive second-placed finishes and the FA Cup win, had induced invitations from European clubs to play post-season friendlies. United declined these, deciding instead to play games across the Irish Sea, until one day in the 1949/50 season a letter arrived inviting the club on a post-season tour to play 12 games across North America.

The first two games of this tour were against a National League All-Stars team in Toronto and a New York All-Stars team in the Big Apple; United won 5-0 and 9-2 respectively. United made their way across the country and eventually faced Atlas Club Mexico in Los Angeles. A measure of how seriously these games were being treated could be found in captain Johnny Carey's *Evening Chronicle* columns, and he described the feeling around the game against Atlas as though United were 'playing for the championship of the world'. The team's arrival in Hollywood was marked by meeting celebrity figures like the former boxing heavyweight champion of the world, Primo Carnera, and the actor Clark Gable. "He looks as handsome off screen as on it," Carey wrote, "and I don't say that because he was courteous enough to come over to our table and bid us welcome."

The game against the Mexicans panned out more like a scarcely believable Hollywood blockbuster than your usual game of soccer and ended in a breathless 6-6 draw – with United dubiously awarded the trophy by virtue of their greater corner accumulation.

Throughout the tour, though, Busby's reservations had been proven time and time again by the advances made to his players by agents acting for South American clubs and the United manager was glad to get the headache over with once he was back in England.

Meanwhile, a more welcome South American influence was infiltrating the European consciousness. The Campeonato Sudamericano de Campeones (American Championship of Champions) commenced in 1948, and French journalist Jacques Ferran became obsessed with the idea of implementing a similar competition. "How could Europe not be able to accomplish a competition of the same kind as the South American one?" he said. "We needed to follow that example."

United's first post-war game on the continent had taken place all the way back in March 1946, when the FA invited them to Germany to face a British Army on the Rhine (BAOR) team. Busby's team lost 2-1 and further inconvenience was to follow when United struggled to make it back to England in time for their game at Bradford on the Saturday due to travel disruption. "League clubs have fixtures to fulfil at home," Busby complained, "and it is very unsatisfactory that we shall get back only a few hours before we are due at Bradford."

Football League secretary Fred Howarth was unimpressed. "The responsibility rests with Manchester United," he said. "If the match is postponed, then United will have to pay compensation to Bradford. Clubs will probably think twice about going to play matches on the Continent if they meet difficulties like this."

It was 1951 before United would play non-British or Irish clubs in Europe. As part of the Festival of Britain in 1951, Yugoslav champions Red Star Belgrade were invited to Old Trafford to play in a friendly – a match ending in a 1-1 draw.

Next came Busby's first European tour, as the club went to Denmark, with the club registering a couple of wins but also an embarrassing defeat to amateur side Aalborg. Hapoel Tel-Aviv accepted an invitation to travel to Manchester in late September – with Busby's side triumphing 6-0.

Following the championship win of 1952, United once again travelled to North America for another 12-game tour. By this time, Busby was a little more comfortable about his players' resistance to the finances on offer by South American clubs – Charlie Mitten, Neil Franklin and George Mountford had all made their way back to England, and all had been moved on by their original clubs after facing temporary suspensions.

The headline game of the tour was another Los Angeles-staged match against Atlas – in fact, so entertaining had the first game been, that two were scheduled this time around. United won 2-0 in the first, a game that was described as a 'free-for-all' and a 'fiasco' that incited 'near-riots' and fisticuffs on and off the pitch, with an Atlas player swinging a punch at the referee for awarding a penalty to Busby's side.

The United boss was keen to cancel the second game but his players, who had been blameless, insisted they were capable of handling it. They were – and won 4-3, in a game more entertaining for the football again. It did not pass without incident, however. No doubt feeling more fired up after the first game, United's stars were more aggressive from the off, and though Johnny Carey had been specifically instructed to keep order on the pitch, it was a thankless task. Byrne, at outside-left, was coming in for some particularly rough treatment. He reacted and was sent off – although Carey insisted the United winger walked off of his own accord.

"I was annoyed about this," Busby said. "I did not like Manchester United players being sent off… especially not abroad, where club and national reputations suffer more than an individual player's reputation. Nor did I like my instructions or my captain's instructions to be forgotten, even allowing for provocation, of which there was plenty." Busby ordered Byrne to apologise to Carey or he would be sent home. He did – and would probably have wished he had been sent home, for the tour concluded with two games against Tottenham in Toronto and New York, which were embarrassingly lost 5-0 and 7-1.

As explorations continued for more serious competition against European teams, United accepted an invitation to face Austria Vienna in Antwerp in November 1952. Some 50,000 supporters turned up to watch an exhibition between the two best sides from their respective countries. Moreover, Austria Vienna were seen as one of the best sides in the world, and had some evidence to back it up – namely their record in the Mitropa Cup, a competition held between the clubs of the successor states of the former Austria-Hungary. In the seven years prior to the war, Austria Vienna had won two of the titles.

Friendly v Austria Vienna, November 11th 1952. Line-up:

FOOTBALL, TAUGHT BY MATT BUSBY

CROMPTON

MCNULTY CAREY BYRNE

COCKBURN GIBSON

CLEMPSON DOWNIE ASTON PEARSON MCSHANE

(SUB: BERRY FOR CLEMPSON)

Even with Allenby Chilton back in Manchester, Busby made the bold decision to use Carey at centre-half. He instructed his team to start fast – and they obliged, registering a number of shots before finding the breakthrough in the 18th minute through Stan Pearson. Tensions rose towards the end of the game but United held firm to grind out a 1-0 victory.

"This was soccer at its best," wrote sportswriter Alf Clarke, while Busby admitted he was 'very proud indeed' and added he felt 'this success has put English soccer back on the map'. Their opponents were keen for a rematch, while invitations came in from Dutch teams, but United's next foray into European competition would be with their youth team in the Blue Stars tournament in Switzerland at the end of the following season (1953/54), by which time football as everyone knew it had changed.

The 1950 World Cup seemed a long time ago. Uruguay were the winners, but the plaudits went to Hungary, who won Olympic gold in 1952 and played a brand of football that almost seemed supernatural. Most of the players played for Budapest Honved, the state-sponsored Army team. Years had been spent perfecting the group's chemistry in a fashion that Busby and Murphy would have admired. Not only were their players technically excellent, they were also experimenting with formations and positioning.

Hungary were invited to play England at Wembley in November 1953 in a match billed by the British press as the 'Match of the Century' – the creators of the game against the best team of the time. Within a minute, it was clear that it would be a nightmare for the home fans and home Football Association alike. Nándor Hidegkuti scored – and if there should be no surprise, given he was wearing the number nine shirt, then tell that to the England defence, who were utterly bewildered by what was happening. Hidegkuti had dropped deeper than a centre-forward would, and Sándor Kocsis and Ferenc Puskás pushed higher than inside-forwards would. To compound matters, the trio would switch positions during the game, causing such mayhem that the visitors scored four times in the first 27 minutes. It was 6-2 after 53 minutes, at which point the Hungarians appeared to take a sporting pity on their opponents; a fate arguably more humiliating than the final score of 6-3, which sent shockwaves around all of Europe.

"The essential difference lay in attack," read the report from the *Guardian*, "where none of the English forwards except Matthews approached the speed, ball control and positional play of the Hungarians, which were as near perfect as one could hope to see."

The consequences were plentiful. First of all, there was a defiance from the FA; a rematch was arranged in Budapest the following May, with the murmur that revenge would be on the cards. Hungary won 7-1, underlining that theirs was a football from another planet – 'Mars', as Bobby Robson suggested. Others recognised it for what it was. The future. Don Revie was still a player for Manchester City and, alongside his manager, Les McDowall, identified the Hidegkuti role as one that could bring longevity to his career, the concept repackaged as 'The Revie Plan'. Bill Nicholson, the Spurs player, was so heavily influenced by their style it would become a cornerstone of his own approach when he became manager at White Hart Lane.

Contemporary reports suggested Matt Busby believed English teams needed more meaningful competitive matches against

European clubs. This is partly true; though what happened at Wembley had been seen in Manchester United shirts, to some extent, over the past five or six years. There were, as we know, very early reports of United's players (in the press and from the players directly) drifting from their usual positions, causing confusion to opponents, and it is well-established that Busby's brand of football featured movement and deft touches in the manner deployed by the Hungarians.

The synchronicity of the young players coming through the ranks, developed by virtue of their time spent training together, resulted in a blend of quality that was already a tremendous success at junior level. Had English football been wilfully ignorant to a version of the revolution under their own noses? Hadn't Jack Rowley, to name just one, already been accredited with playing in the Hidegkuti manner on at least two separate occasions, against Preston in the 1948 FA Cup run and against Wolves later on? Of course. It just went without a label.

"When I finished playing and went on coaching courses they had invented one touch and two touch games as part of the coaching system," Eamon Dunphy wrote, "it was only then I realised Matt had us playing like that unknowingly."

A little note is necessary – shirt numbers had only been made mandatory in English football in 1939 and because most teams played the same formation, it was considered sportsmanlike to wear the numbers as they lined up on the pitch – save for the centre-half, who wore five, in spite of now playing in the last line of defence. There were variations around the world – such as in Argentina, where a back four would be fielded as it was in 1978 and has the two centre halves in four and six.

Following United's title win of 1952, Stan Cullis' Wolves had become the best team in the country, and while Cullis favoured the strategy of bringing through his own players, his brand of football was very much a long-ball, traditionally English style. Wolves would play a major role in the advancement of European club competition; but before we get to that, let's return to the name mentioned earlier, Jimmy Hogan, he who had spent so much time in Austria and Hungary. We can remember the Sandor Barcs remark about Hogan after the 6-3 Hungary win at Wembley: "He taught us everything we know about football."

So where was Hogan now? He was back in England, coaching the youth team at Aston Villa, via a spell at Celtic. These two spells are notable for two reasons. The first is that he was still widely derided in spite of the respect he commanded overseas. He was hired as coach under Jimmy McGrory at Celtic but many of the players mocked him, hating his discipline; he left less than two years later, in 1950, to take the job at Aston Villa. The young players were receptive to his methods and loved the training, but as soon as they graduated to the Central League team, they found the philosophy was out of the window and long-ball was back on the schedule.

English football had marginalised one of its greatest visionaries. But their loss was Manchester United's gain, in a completely roundabout way. The links to Jimmy Murphy have already been well established. However, Hogan was to have a longer-term impact on Old Trafford thanks to the influence he had on two players. The first player was Tommy Docherty, a young wing-half at Celtic. Docherty described Hogan as 'the finest coach the world had ever known' and once told the BBC: "He used to say football was like a Viennese waltz, a rhapsody. One-two-three, one-two-three, pass-move-pass, pass-move-pass. We were glued to our seats, because we were so keen to learn. His arrival at Celtic Park was the best thing that ever happened to me."

A player at Villa Park was similarly receptive. "Jimmy was completely unique... because everything was done with the ball," Ron Atkinson recalls. "Even a running exercise had to be finished with a pass. At the time in British football that was not known. His standard thing was, 'wherever you are on the field, if we have got the ball we are attacking, and if they've got the ball, wherever it is, we are defending.' He would tell the wing-halves that they had to be like waiters serving the wingers and serving the front players. He had a lovely way of delivering it. All of the young lads used to love playing for Jimmy."

It is clearly no coincidence that Hogan's impression was felt so heavily by three figures who were so influential in delivering some of the best football Old Trafford has ever seen. Likewise, it is probably no coincidence that all three (and you can add Matt Busby) were half-backs, students of the game who were skilled in the reading of it, even if the method of their own conveyance of the message would differ.

A slight diversion from the free-flowing beautiful game; not all revolutions concerned themselves with attacking craft. Austrian coach Karl Rappan had created a system labelled as the *verrou* (translated as 'lock' from French) and this formation was, effectively, a 4-3-3 or even 4-5-1: one forward was sacrificed to be a part of the defensive line. Throughout the 1940s this formation was adopted in Spain and then later in Italy where the philosophy was given its most famous name: *Catenaccio*. Italian coach Nereo Rocca was introducing his version to Padova at the same time as the Match of the Century; Busby described it as 'defensive rubbish'.

English football, meanwhile, remained in shock after their two humblings by Hungary and a new attempt at retribution was made by Wolves, who took on Honved in a friendly in December 1954. The Midlands side had staged a series of friendlies under their new floodlights; when they defeated Spartak Moscow 4-0, the *Daily Record*'s report stated the Russians had been 'hammered and sicked'. The visit of Honved was no joking matter; it was taken so seriously that the second half was screened on the BBC. Honved went 2-0 up inside 14 minutes. With this lead still intact at half-time, Cullis ordered junior players (one of whom was Ron Atkinson) to go out on to the pitch with watering cans to waterlog a surface that had already seen four days of rain. The approach worked – Honved struggled with their pass and move game, and the long-ball tactic of the hosts worked to such effect they turned the game around and won 3-2.

It was a cathartic result for the British press. The *Daily Express* felt it proved English football 'was still the best of its kind in the world' and other newspapers proclaimed Wolves to be 'champions of the world'. These headlines prompted Gabriel Hanot, a French sportswriter, to strongly disagree. "Before we declare that Wolverhampton are invincible, let them go to Moscow and Budapest," he wrote. "And there are other internationally renowned clubs: Milan and Real Madrid to name but two. A club world championship, or at least a European one – larger, more meaningful and more prestigious than the Mitropa Cup – should be launched."

The speed with which Hanot's wish was granted was breathtaking. In March 1955 the idea of the European Cup was formally presented at a UEFA congress and in the following season the inaugural competition was held.

Manchester United, trailblazers as they were, had already claimed one actual European title before that which was bestowed upon Wolverhampton Wanderers. In May of 1954 their junior players competed in the Blue Star tournament in Zurich; they had been invited to participate in 1953, but had already accepted another tour, so Wolves took their place.

One year later Jimmy Murphy, having just enjoyed his second FA Youth Cup win in a row, was in charge of the squad, but Matt Busby was in the touring party and quipped to a journalist, "I think we shall have a good chance of winning – we don't have to play any Hungarians!"

United won the tournament with some comfort, mostly facing Swiss teams and playing them off the park. Their team in the final match of the tour had been:

HAWKSWORTH

BESWICK FULTON

COLMAN HARROP[1] MCGUINNESS

CHARLTON WHELAN EDWARDS PEGG SCANLON

"I am not usually given to boasting," Busby said at the conclusion, "but I can assure you British prestige has taken a terrific leap through the wonderful football of the United youths… it has been a magnificent tour and I can honestly say that my young players have done much to restore continental confidence in the future of British football."

A couple of those players were already in the Manchester United first team; within two years half of the team who won a youth tournament in Switzerland would feature in the team that would be champions of England to such an impressive standard they would be ranked amongst the greatest ever.

---

1   Busby listed this himself, lining Harrop in the half-back line, though it is probable he would have been between Beswick and Fulton

7

THE BUSBY BABES

TAKE ALL OF THE INDIVIDUAL ELEMENTS OF MATT Busby's architecture – his demand for complete control; his insistence that a team should always aspire to play good football; his ability to create a team who could blow opponents away with a number of goals in a short space of time; his hope that the patience and time investment would yield similar footballing results as seen by the Hungarian side at Wembley; his acceptance of one distinct individualist; and finally, his desire for his team to prove themselves against the very best, and you would arrive at the formation of the team that would become known as the Busby Babes.

In 1956 – four short years after the 1952 title win – Busby had dismantled and rebuilt his side, introducing the talent he had reckoned to be valued in the region of £200,000. His boast was proven to be correct. The Babes won the title in record fashion.

In terms of formation the Busby Babes were no different from the 1948 or 1952 teams:

FOOTBALL, TAUGHT BY MATT BUSBY

WOOD
FOULKES JONES BYRNE
COLMAN EDWARDS
WHELAN VIOLLET
BERRY TAYLOR PEGG

In terms of attitude, there seemed to be an almost complete transformation. It would be wrong to describe the earlier Busby sides as workmanlike but those older sides were their own men, fully developed with their own distinct personalities. They were not raised through the Busby way of doing things but, as men who mostly were soldiers, followed commands dutifully. Many seemed to feel as though some form of witchcraft was at play, almost as though it was the manager performing the heroics even though this wonderful brand of football was being played with their own feet and using their own intelligence.

By contrast, almost all of the team who won the 1956 championship were fully indoctrinated in the Manchester United way. They had been coached by Murphy and Whalley; the best education in football, a harsh environment for the rough edges to be knocked off so that players were streetwise enough to handle themselves, make instinctive decisions and develop their own distinct personalities.

If there was one player who was old enough to not be completely deferential to Busby, it was club captain Roger Byrne; he'd been around the first title-winning squad and had experienced characters unafraid to challenge the manager. This did not mean he would wilfully challenge the boss – but he was not fearful of him in the same way Murphy and Whalley had made the others.

James Gibson had once dared to dream of a team completely comprised of Mancunians. That was beyond even Busby and Murphy but they did manage the next best thing, and that was to field a Manchester United team that was almost fully homegrown, and they did it in a season where the team were reigning champions, a measure of their complete superiority. From the 24 players who managed some first-team minutes, only Ray Wood, the goalkeeper, Johnny Berry, the outside-right, and Tommy Taylor, the centre-forward, were signed. No typos here. That means *eight* of the regular first 11 were homegrown, and a further 13 played their part in bringing the Division One trophy back to Manchester. Not only that, they were so much better than the opposition that they won the league by a record margin of 11 points.

Another by-product of the United academy was the impact it was bound to have on the long-term prospects for an unprecedented dynasty of success. Plenty of teams had won consecutive championships, and Huddersfield and Arsenal had won three in a row in the 1920s and 1930s respectively, but only Portsmouth since the war had retained their title. Arsenal's two titles since the war, won in 1948 and 1953, made them the most prestigious club in the country, with a total of seven. Busby's line of thinking was different. He wanted to match that total himself. He reckoned the usual lifespan of a manager at a great team to be five years, after which time he would plummet. "Unless he has made other arrangements," he said, "like thinking ahead, at least five years ahead. All teams are apt to be over the top within five years of reaching it. Buying players piecemeal is at best a chancy business, at worst a financial disaster... In 1946 it was revolutionary even to think about getting boys straight from school. Get them early enough, I thought, and they would be trained according to some sort of pattern; in my case, the pattern I was trying constantly to create at Manchester United, in the first team and any other team, so that if a boy came through as far as his ability, courage, speed and character were concerned, he would fit into the pattern without feeling like a stranger among people painting pretty pictures he did not understand."

The composition of the 1956 team, the product of a decade's work, was compelling. Each of the usual first-choice players were outstanding in the roles which they occupied but, with the possible exceptions of Jones, Colman and Berry, there was a tremendous positional flexibility. Foulkes was possibly not as mobile as Carey but was as strong in defence. Jones was every bit as reliable as his hero Chilton. Berry and Byrne already had championship medals from 1952 to prove their brilliance and Viollet, Taylor and Whelan possessed all the same sort of trickery and goal threat as the central forward three from 1948.

The most indisputable area where there was a distinct upgrade from 1948 was in the half-back line. In fact, even United's reserve half-back line in 1956 – Jeff Whitefoot and Wilf McGuinness – was the envy of any in the country, and that was before you mentioned the names Eddie Colman and Duncan Edwards who, if you had to pick midfields in the pairs in which they came, would arguably be United's best-ever.

The first significant steps to finally introduce the Babes en-masse came, ironically enough, after a *win* against Aston Villa in October 1953. The performance drew criticism from the press and in a friendly at Kilmarnock, Busby brought in a couple of youngsters to shake it up. Legend has it that he wielded the axe with as many as seven new players coming into the team, but it wasn't quite so dramatic; Duncan Edwards, Jackie Blanchflower and Dennis Viollet played in the following week's 0-0 draw at Huddersfield. Three is still not an insignificant number and was of course representative of the greater change. United finished in eighth in 1953, then fourth in 1954, then fifth in 1955. Busby conceded it 'wasn't perfect', but still believed the progress was "a remarkable affirmation that my pattern system was right. The pieces dropped out, the pieces dropped in."

In *Matt Busby's Manchester United Scrapbook,* the manager explained further. "I had made the decision that only the best would be good enough," he said, "I wanted ability beyond question; I also wanted loyalty to myself and the club, players of real character, and lads who would be amenable to discipline, for without that you are headed for trouble."

And he had succeeded. "Busby has built up a precious pride in Manchester United," wrote Ralph L. Finn in his 1965 book *Champions Again.* "He has worked unceasingly to develop this faith between club and player. The *esprit de corps* at Old Trafford is second to none. Everyone associated with Manchester United, from boot-boy to Busby, believes that Manchester United is the greatest club on earth. Unless Manchester United can be a love, a trust, a religion for any boy, Busby doesn't want him. The club is bigger than any one player yet any one player, no matter who he is, is as important to the club as their most famous star."

The generation of young players now at the club had not been through the war as soldiers but they had been through it as children; the residual effects could be seen in their resolve and resourcefulness to not take anything for granted. A big reason for that may have been the still-compulsory national service that every young man needed to take. There was a definite class divide that existed in football, as it did in society. Where more had to be made from less; where a fight to survive existed, so too did a force of personality, shaped by upbringings, families, friends – community. Manchester, but in particular Salford, was less a geographical position and more a frame of mind. The fight to survive wasn't individual; it was communal. It was a brotherhood. And in the survival of the fittest, sometimes you had to be loud to be heard.

FOOTBALL, TAUGHT BY MATT BUSBY

Nobody was more Salford in Manchester United's team than Eddie Colman. Raised on the cobbles of Archie Street in Ordsall, Colman had not been a naturally confident footballer – he believed he was selected to play in a game for Salford Boys at The Cliff to make up the numbers. But he was identified by Busby and Murphy – who couldn't believe he hadn't been spotted by another club – and became a crucial part of the half-back line in the youth team. His partnership with Edwards was so well-established that he effectively skipped the educational process of the Central League due to Edwards' own rapid advance. Colman was the pragmatic mind of the pair, often plugging whatever gaps might arise from his half-back mate's dashes up the pitch. Yet he also quickly blossomed, growing into his own skin and becoming almost *too* confident at one point.

Colman's sense of humour and effervescent charm made him a player all of the club took into their heart. Murphy adored him for representing all the gritty ideals he'd tried to implement; he once said there was 'no better tackler in the game', and indeed, the man-marking job he was once given on Alfredo Di Stefano showed that Busby agreed. To describe Colman in this manner suggests he was economic more than he was talented, but that couldn't be further from the truth. He was known as 'snake hips' because he had a mesmerising body swerve to dodge an opponent. If there was economy in his play, this was thanks to the Busby mantra of keeping the ball moving, and a personal awareness of Edwards' influence.

There were many other local lads. There was Fallowfield's Dennis Viollet, a laid-back ladies man. Geoff Bent, also from Salford, who was a left-back – an understudy to Roger Byrne, but a player who could have starred for any other side in the country. This local influence helped bring the personalities out of the likes of Edwards

(Dudley), Whelan (Dublin), Charlton (Newcastle) and so on. It cemented the local connection, especially as the young players would live a stone's throw from Old Trafford – in the everyday gaze of younger boys who idolised them. A perpetual stream of fishes swimming towards the development streams of The Cliff; or, as Jimmy Murphy might put it, a growing orchard for his one-day 'golden apples'. If these youngsters could not make it on the pitch, they would provide fervent support off it. Even though the vision of Busby was still in progress, by the mid 1950s, the dreams of Gibson, Rocca and Crickmer had been realised beyond even their own comprehension.

Colman's personality is worth returning to only to reference the development of both himself and the team. In the summer of 1955, United were celebrating their third successive FA Youth Cup. The seriousness with which Busby still took that competition was reflected in the fact that Colman – now of age and ability to play in the first team – captained that winning side against West Brom, and Duncan Edwards was also still in the 11, despite being an established member of the first team. Elsewhere, players like Bobby Charlton and Shay Brennan were cutting their own teeth, ready to become the 'senior' members of this youth side for the likes of Kenny Morgans, Mark Pearson and Alex Dawson to follow. Jimmy Murphy's success at that level was unparalleled and the clear improvement of Busby's first team was evidence that, given time, the best youth team in the country could evolve into the best senior team in the country too.

To the bemusement of some domestic sports writers, but to the advantage of Matt Busby, United's brand of football continued to be 'un-English'; the country was falling in love with a team who played football that would be viewed sceptically if the individuals came from Mainland Europe. Busby's natural sensibilities and experience of the way the game should be played, Murphy's passion and insistence for relentless commitment, and their shared belief that the Hungarians had it right, all combined into a club side that was probably even closer to perfecting that ideology that even the Honved team had been.

In his book *Champions Again*, Ralph L. Finn listed all the great English teams and used one word to describe them. Humility, purpose, vision, skill, glamour, brilliance, understanding, achievement, distinction, modesty, lustre, notability, conviction, imagination, stability, wisdom, science, attack, pliability, coolness and class. His one-word tribute to Manchester United was 'invincibility', saying they possessed *all* of the above. Their weaknesses were tolerance and manners (two qualities shown by Everton and Liverpool respectively).

"Manchester United's success should be a lesson for all clubs," he wrote. "If the United formula of no-formula is followed; if individual players are allowed full freedom to express themselves in play; if a side moves fluently as a team, rising like a wave into the attack, flowing back into defence as occasion demands; if the long-ball is used sparingly and mainly as a surprise weapon; if the Scots short-ball pattern of play is employed, not squarely but progressively; if star billing is encouraged as the crowd-puller it is – if all these things, then we could not only have a better league competition but a better England side."

What made United so beloved was those personal expressions. Whitefoot and McGuinness were more than capable at half-back, and more than capable of impressing in a title-winning team in that position. The combination of Colman and Edwards was magic and different even in their pairing. Though not a hard and fast rule, the right-half would generally be the most adventurous of the pair, and the left-half would hold a more disciplined position. But Edwards was a special case. His intelligence and reading of the game made left-half a natural position for him. However, he loved to carry the ball on surging runs, and he would also drop back to defend in times of need; in fact, if there was a criticism of Edwards in his first two or three years in the first team, it was that he tried to do too much. His talent was so great that Busby was happy for his team to include this minor deviation from the pattern. His ability to win a game was so great that Colman was content to show discipline when required, and this in turn improved his own game.

It was the emergence of Edwards as a special talent which introduced a concept that would somehow become a staple of the greatest Manchester United teams. They will be covered in detail but George Best, Eric Cantona and Cristiano Ronaldo are the other three players who fit into this category – and they are mentioned here to express just how exceptional Edwards was, and how exceptional it was that Busby settled on left-half as the best position for him. Best, Cantona and Ronaldo were all forwards. Playing a player who was, for want of a better phrase, free of the tactical restraint of the team, is far less hazardous if they are in an attacking position than if they are in a defensive role.

Edwards had a complete array of skills, but now had a maturity that belied his youthfulness. His reading of the game was peerless and he had become so dominant that he would tackle for fun. He would set what other players would describe as 'tank traps', luring opponents into an area where they thought they had a 50/50 chance of getting the ball, unaware that a 50/50 in the estimation of a mere mortal was already 90/10 weighted in the favour of Duncan Edwards. His shots with either foot were renowned as the most powerful in the country and even if he still carried too much of the team's burden on the rare occasion the Busby Babes were not winning comfortably, his economy of play and decision-making was almost flawless. It's easier to accommodate a player like that, even Duncan Edwards, in such a crucial position when the rest of your team is so talented.

Were there any weaknesses in the Busby Babes? Busby trusted Ray Wood but still had dreams of a more imposing goalkeeper. Byrne and Foulkes had been trained to be the modern Aston and Carey, though it could be said Foulkes was not as mobile as Carey and certainly not as capable of overlapping like Busby's earlier full-backs. Tommy Taylor had scored 50 goals in 77 games for the club even before their title-winning season of 1955/56 and as far as most United supporters were concerned he was one of the very best centre-forwards to have ever played for the club. He was earmarked to be a long-term replacement for Bolton legend Nat Lofthouse in the England side but there were, strangely, doubts in the national press about his ability to make that step up. No doubts for Busby – Taylor was 23, nowhere close to his peak and a player around which the manager was happy to build his attack for years to come.

Taylor served as evidence that the manager would still be happy to pay a tidy sum for a player he felt would fill a void that no other player on the United roster did. "There might well have been a youngster who promised to make the breakthrough," Busby explained, "but even United could not afford to wait maybe two or three years, when one key signing could add the ingredient for continued success."

Still, the United boss was blessed when it came to that dilemma. He had an abundance of half-backs and left-sided players. There were a great number of inside-forwards. He had enough players to switch around and not sacrifice on quality if there was a clashing international or army match, but he could also make changes depending on the opponent or his own fancy. It was, in effect, the creation of squad rotation. The product of 10 years of work and at least five or six of intensive scouting, with half a decade invested in the development of a group of players with a new school on the way through. Through training, through youth matches, through reserve-team matches, the chemistry developed between the players was so strong that almost any combination of 10 outfield players could be trusted to put in a first-class performance. It was a conveyor belt that could continue for as long as the system was in place to produce it.

United were top of the table going into 1956 following a couple of headline-grabbing performances over the Christmas break, where West Brom were hammered 4-1 in front of their own fans and Charlton were beaten 5-1 at Old Trafford on Boxing Day. The Addicks inflicted United's sixth league defeat of the season a day later – but a win against Manchester City on New Year's Eve gave Busby's babes a four-point lead. They would suffer just one more league defeat all season, even keeping four consecutive clean sheets, which would give the impression that United had become miserly and defensive if we didn't know the truth.

On the same day as the derby, there was a reserve game between the two Manchester clubs. United were victorious in that one too, with Charlton, Whelan and Scanlon in fine form. "His (Busby's) reserve team are so good that I wouldn't back the so-called first team to beat them," said one dejected City player. "It's quite true. For 20 minutes I saw this reserve team roll the ball around with the slick precision passing I thought was the copyright of the Hungarians." The identity of this Maine Road star? None other than Don Revie, the man who had been described as a singular, living representative of that brand of football.

In an interview for Tony Whelan's seminal work *The Birth Of The Babes*, Bill Foulkes explained that the Hungarian team was often referenced in training. "Yes, they were talked about," he said. "How to play the Hungarian way and all this. We were told 'watch these players…' They were talked of as the best in the world. This is what we were aiming for." It may have been an external example of a pinnacle, but it ought to be impressed again that United were playing and training this way well before 1953.

In January, Don Davies attempted to describe the way United were playing in his *Manchester Guardian* column: "The extreme youth and ease in ball-play of many of those who now join his (Busby's) club, and the large proportion of them to emerge as capable players, suggest that they are selected largely on the premise that the boy who has developed true ball skill by his early teens is usually ripe for expert development. It is probably significant that Busby and Murphy were both international wing half-backs of constructive bent – players in the position which pre-eminently demands football, blending attack and defence, strength and control, and flexibility in tactics. This helps to explain, too, the balanced linking of defence with attack in the teams they have produced.

"Each player has been encouraged to develop his particular gifts to the advantage of the team. Variety has been achieved without loss of balance, through mutual understanding of the game's problems, upon which the players are encouraged to think for themselves. Most of the successful teams of post-war football have employed a particular style of play… There is, however, no characteristic Manchester United style. Aiming to produce players of all-round ability, the club's planners have sought to place in the team the varied skills necessary to defeat every type of play. Thus, from match to match, defensive formation or attacking method may vary; clearances may be long or short, attacks may be developed along the wings or through the middle."

To return to the team that was more or less the first 11: Wood

/ Foulkes, Jones, Byrne / Colman, Edwards / Whelan, Viollet / Berry, Taylor, Pegg. Other significant contributors who should be mentioned include Ian Greaves, a full-back. Jackie Blanchflower, adept at inside-forward or half-back. Wilf McGuinness was a half-back. John Doherty and Colin Webster played in the inside-forward positions.

Busby was a champion of balance. If one of his full-backs liked to race up the pitch, he preferred the other to be sensible. He would like one winger to be direct and one to have the tricks. Prior to Busby, a team would carry one inside-forward who was a skilful dribbler while the other would be a runner, trying to latch on to chances. All of his inside-forwards at United had possessed craft, a clear influence from watching the Brazilian forwards in Florence when he was in the army. He was inventive with the way he put his team out, and it's fair to say that he was a visionary – what he had achieved with two fantastic teams was beyond the comprehension of the players and the analysts.

And Revie was right – the reserve side were strong enough to challenge in the league on their own merit. In the Central League they scored more than four goals on more than 10 separate occasions, with scores of 7-1, 6-2, 7-1, 6-1, 7-1 and 8-0. The FA Youth Cup was won by United for the fourth year in a row. It could have been argued that at every level, Manchester United's brand of football, this Busby style that had influences of everything he'd experienced, was the most attractive in England.

The victory which brought the Busby Babes their first league title, against Blackpool in April 1956, had two anecdotal quirks. The first, that Busby wasn't even there to see it, as he was back in Scotland with his wife at her mother's funeral. The second was that the title was delivered by two goals by signed players, Berry and Taylor – that dash of experience to get the kids over the line.

FOOTBALL, TAUGHT BY MATT BUSBY

Was Busby so ahead of his time that the football could be indefinable? The traditional analysis of the Busby era comes with a few descriptions – that he pioneered a new wave, a new pathway from youth football into senior football. That his teams were successful, and that they did it using smart passing, clever skill, tremendous team play and no little individuality. But it doesn't get a term. It's not tiki-taka. It isn't gegenpressing. It isn't Total Football. And because it doesn't have a catchy phrase to summarise it – because nobody seemed to think of it – then it often gets missed when discussing the most successful philosophies of all-time. Even catenaccio, this style which seems against everything entertaining football is supposed to stand for, has a legion of support and modern interpretations. It has books, websites, *a wikipedia page* dedicated to it. Football, as taught by Matt Busby, has none of this. The most comprehensive attempts to define it came from some of his most articulate players, and some of the most articulate sports writers of their day, and even they could not summarise it, so they would conclude that there was no defined style.

And yet it was so comprehensive in how much it covered, it was so impressive in terms of how successful it became, and it was so positive in its approach to progressive football, that it deserves at least as strong a mention as Total Football. And it deserves to be mentioned in the same breath as the Hungarian approach – at the very least because Busby was doing that *years* before England were humiliated at Wembley in 1953. Even Don Revie went on record as to identify it as the same brand of football. Busby, however, is perceived as the elderly, kindly grandfather of British football, and not one of the sport's greatest minds in the mould of a Michels, a Cruyff or a Guardiola. Are catchphrases so powerful in the enhancing of a reputation? Do we need to invent one that is catchier than *Football Taught By Matt Busby*? What is more total than Total Football?

As it happens, Busby had his own thoughts on the matter. "I believe my pre-Munich team was the sort of side capable of winning in Europe," he wrote in the 1969's *International Football Book*. "Had it not been for the disaster, others might have been copying a team of United's football whose influence would have spread beneficially through the football league. Call me biased, but I believe this to be true. It has always been my aim to field a team composed of pure ball artistry. That team would have impressed all the imitators."

Let's add another layer of perspective. The comments from Revie were not made at the end of an era looking back. These were comments made about a brand of football right at the offset of a generation; a first team populated mostly of players in their early 20s and late teens and a reserve team mostly in their late teens. Ferenc Puskás was 26 at the time of the Match of the Century. Duncan Edwards was only 19 in the summer of 1956.

Eddie Colman was a teenager, too. They still had four years to reach a similar average age to the Hungarians and even then, their peak should follow that. At this point, with two league titles, an FA Cup and this successful youth system, there was a compelling argument that Busby was the greatest football mind in British history, and that his was the greatest team. And together most of them had barely played two full seasons of top-flight football between them.

They were, though, playing with the experience of a team with at least five years' worth of familiarity – and that's because many of them had enjoyed those extra years together in the youth team, reserve team and every day on the training pitch.

Furthermore, many of these players were now experiencing two years of national service – and therefore could not train with their club during the week. For United to have such a strong groove in spite of this made their triumphs even more remarkable – and suggested an unthinkable peak still to come.

8

COMING OF AGE

THE BABES WERE DOMINANT CHAMPIONS. THEY WON 10 and drew two of their first 12 league games in the 1956/57 campaign, again establishing an early lead they would not throw away. The strong start was necessary, for the club had ambitions on three fronts for the first time. The young players who had grown up on the 1948 FA Cup success were keen to enjoy their own Wembley date, for the national cup still served as the most glamorous date on the English football calendar.

New players graduated into the first team squad. Inside-forward Bobby Charlton was one, making his debut against his namesake club, Charlton Athletic, in early October. He scored twice in a win but still only made 17 appearances over the entire campaign (scoring an impressive 12 goals). United were a goalscoring machine, registering more than 100 league goals, and Busby seemed to be on a mission to see just how attacking he could make a team of 11 players. Mark Jones had been a worthy successor to Chilton but was most definitely a hard, defensive centre-half. There would always be a time and a place for a player like Jones;

but Busby had begun to feel that his team were so powerful that they sometimes might not need that sort of physical prowess.

What if he tried Jackie Blanchflower, usually an inside-forward or half-back, at centre-half? Blanchflower, an amateur boxer in his youth, certainly didn't lack in aggression, but he was more cultured on the ball than Jones. The results didn't suggest any great deviation from the manner of wins or number of goals scored when either of those players lined up in the number five, but it was nonetheless a new approach; as a consequence, only Wood and Foulkes would be seen as truly defensive players.

Only six games were lost in the league and the Charity Shield was won too. Busby's side would go all the way to the FA Cup final but he had certainly set his own eyes on another competition – the European Cup. It was in this tournament that Busby made perhaps his first tactical concession in a United team. Belgian champions Anderlecht were overwhelmed 2-0 on their own ground and 10-0 at Maine Road. United were now back at Old Trafford, but Maine Road was used for European football due to it having floodlights, with Busby still to convince directors that playing continental football could raise enough funds for floodlights at their own ground. Busby described that mammoth second leg victory as "the greatest display of football I have ever seen. They had all the skill in the world, all the confidence in the world, all the ruthlessness in the world. They played as I've always dreamed they could… I want them to be confident. I want them to be arrogant. I want them to tell themselves that they are better than anyone else. Because they are."

After a tight first leg against German champions Borussia Dortmund – won 3-2 – Busby trialled a new plan in the away game. The formation was the same – 3-2-5 – but McGuinness was in the half-back line and Edwards was moved to inside-forward. He was tasked with keeping an eye on any unusual tactical decisions made by Dortmund on their own ground; and in the second half, moved into half-back line, breaking the play up on an icy pitch.

United's line-up in the second half of that second leg therefore looked like this:

WOOD

FOULKES   JONES   BYRNE

COLMAN   EDWARDS   MCGUINNESS

WHELAN

BERRY   TAYLOR   PEGG

Call it pragmatic, call it sensible; it was successful. Edwards put in one of his most controlling performances, dominating the game in his advanced position just as it was hoped he would. United, in a 3-3-1-3, saw the game out 0-0 to qualify for the next round. There they faced Athletic Bilbao, never deviating from the 3-2-5 even when 3-0 down at half-time in the first leg. That match finished 5-3 to Bilbao. At 5-2, Billy Whelan scored a breathtaking solo goal. It was the sort of strike that could reignite confidence in the most testing of circumstances. Individualism had birthed inspiration.

United mustered a stunning 3-0 win in the second leg to go through to the semi-final. With a 1-0 lead at half-time in a raucous atmosphere at Maine Road, Busby insisted that if his team kept their cool, they could blow the Basque side away in the closing stages. In the 70th minute, Tommy Taylor added to Dennis Viollet's goal. The tie was level on aggregate and would have gone to a play-off – but five minutes from the end, Johnny Berry converted an Edwards cross, completing an epic comeback. Henry Rose, in the *Express*, described it as the 'greatest soccer victory in history'.

"Damn silly isn't it," Jimmy Murphy said through tears. "After all these years in the game. But this is my greatest game of football."

And, probably, although he didn't say it, Busby's. His young players had climbed a proverbial mountain that twice seemed insurmountable in the space of 180 minutes. What's more, he had done it trusting that his players were good enough to navigate those significant hurdles largely by themselves, trusting in each other and the system.

This was football taught by Matt Busby; United's refusal to stray from their trusted way of playing. Their refusal to resort to desperation. Their belief that playing attractive football, keeping the ball and themselves moving, and trying daring individual feats would turn the tide. The self-confidence that sometimes required the concession of a goal to sting them into action. The arrogance that sometimes it might require the concession of more than one.

It was football taught by Jimmy Murphy; a never-ending pursuit of goals, the same approach in 3-0 down as in 10-0 up. It was the penny dropping that they didn't always have to look to Edwards, as proven by Billy Whelan's first-leg strike.

It was football taught by James Gibson. A Manchester crowd roaring on a mostly homegrown team to inspire them onto achievements that seemed superhuman; almost greater than the sum of their parts.

It was football taught by Walter Crickmer and Louis Rocca – or is that too contrived? Crickmer in the original vision of the young players. Rocca in the sheer Salford grift, the insatiable desire to get what they wanted. It was all of this, and yet still wrapped up in a presentation of class – a team able to deliver this remarkable turnaround with enough time for supporters to catch their breath, to marvel and applaud before the final whistle.

There was a sense of irony in that Bilbao's manager Ferdinand Daucik was widely thought to be one who deployed the Hungarian approach of drifting forwards in his attack. The Spanish newspaper *Marca* delivered a savage assessment of that – 'mistaken like a pig for a hare'. Another Spanish team – the holders of the European Cup, the great Real Madrid – lay in wait for Busby's team in the semi-final.

Talk of an incredible 'treble' filled newspaper columns. It was clear that a number of elements would need to be in United's favour for the greatest achievement in football to be fulfilled. Individual players stepped up. Duncan Edwards was occasionally still needed to put in a superhuman effort, just as he did against Bilbao, and again in the FA Cup against Everton, scoring the game's only goal. Qualification for the final was secured by semi-final goals scored by Berry and Charlton. There was not quite the same fortune in Europe, when Real Madrid used home advantage and their extra year of continental experience to take a 3-1 win on April 11th, 1957; the last eight minutes of the game were memorable for Duncan Edwards' refusal to accept the game was lost.

Interestingly, for this game, even though Busby had specifically made a visit to watch Real Madrid play, he did not alter his team's approach in the same way he did in Dortmund. He did make a concession; after watching Alfredo Di Stefano, the Scot felt he'd witnessed perhaps the greatest player in the world, and so asked Eddie Colman to man-mark him. Colman had done an admirable job – but he was only 20, at the start of his career, and Di Stefano was almost 31, in the elite category of all-time stars. For the first and only time, United's kids had been overawed by the size of the palatial Santiago Bernabeu stadium.

Before the second leg later in the month, United could seal the league title – captain Roger Byrne now conceded this was the 'least glamorous' of the club's objectives. That feat was accomplished with comfort when Sunderland were defeated 4-0 on April 25th, with three goals coming in the last 16 minutes, a familiar Busby flurry. Just as notable in United culture was the release of a new song, which was aired over the public address system before the game, with the words printed in the match programme. The lyrics included this passage:

Manchester, Manchester United. A bunch of bouncing Busby Babes, they deserve to be knighted. If ever they're playing in your town, you must get to that football ground. Take a look and you will see, football taught by Matt Busby.

An immortal phrase, and one fitting to summarise a philosophy. The early league win gave the manager the opportunity to ring the changes for the Easter Monday game with Burnley that preceded the return with Real Madrid. This game saw one of the remarkable flexes of strength in the Busby era in terms of squad depth. The team which had faced Sunderland read:

WOOD
FOULKES BLANCHFLOWER BYRNE
COLMAN EDWARDS
WHELAN CHARLTON
BERRY TAYLOR PEGG

Against Burnley, Busby made nine changes:

WOOD
FOULKES COPE GREAVES
GOODWIN MCGUINNESS
DOHERTY VIOLLET
WEBSTER DAWSON SCANLON

Dawson and Webster scored the goals that earned the recently reconfirmed champions a very impressive win. And if that wasn't enough, the Central League side – shorn of all the players they would normally play, because they were in the first team – won 2-1 *at* Burnley.

The two elements United needed to succeed in their pursuit of the treble evaded them. The first came in the inability to overcome the experience of Real Madrid. The question was, against one of the truly great teams, whether United's youthful exuberance and quality would just be better, as it had proven domestically, or whether they would have to familiarise themselves with the gamesmanship of European encounters.

By and large they had proven themselves good enough. Good enough to completely outclass a team in the first round with a performance even the usually-reserved Busby had to applaud. Good enough to show a professional edge in controlling a slender lead in difficult circumstances in the next round. Good enough to go to Spain and keep fighting despite a 3-0 deficit to not wilt in the second half. To take that tie back to Manchester and create a new thread of personality for both the club and the team – the Busby Babes did not know when they were beaten. Duncan Edwards had been an individual fire but the rest of them had been set alight against Bilbao.

Three goals down against Bilbao was not the same as two goals down against Real Madrid. The financial reward of the European Cup run had facilitated the installation of floodlights at Old Trafford and so Real's visit was the first European tie under them. On the day before the game, Busby had succumbed to the same sort of skulduggery as Stan Cullis against Honved. When Spanish officials saw pictures of sprinklers on the Old Trafford pitch in the morning newspapers, they threatened to return home unless they were turned off. United agreed – though there was never any indication that Busby would have resorted to long ball tactics. His side had dealt with difficult pitches over the British winter and still played their own inimitable style.

The anxiety of the first European game at Old Trafford seemed to play into the minds of Busby's side. This was the team he selected in arguably the biggest game of his managership to date:

WOOD
FOULKES BLANCHFLOWER BYRNE
COLMAN EDWARDS
WHELAN CHARLTON
BERRY TAYLOR PEGG

One can trace the bold decisions. The Blanchflower selection was made with the admission that United needed to chase the game and so required as many players to build the play as possible. To select a green Bobby Charlton was courageous and the manager was hoping to benefit from the momentum he had enjoyed. Even picking Byrne was now a matter of some discussion; the United captain still carried some damage to his reputation as he had played in the second thrashing of England by Hungary.

If there was a suspicion that United's youthfulness was weaker for their naivety, that seemed to be confirmed by the 33rd minute. The visitors were 2-0 up on the night and 5-1 ahead on aggregate. At half-time, there were no words Busby or Murphy could offer to realistically inspire a four-goal comeback. The last 45 minutes were played in a different sort of atmosphere. The floodlights were switched on, casting a new glow over the pitch, creating a new sense of occasion.

United scored through Taylor and for a brief moment, although there were only 28 minutes left, 62,000 at Old Trafford allowed themselves to dream. So too did the 11 players on the pitch. After all, was it not this team who had rewritten the rule on comebacks? Even though 5-2 seemed unassailable, the goal ignited a new approach from Real – they were going to slow the game down. Edwards became frustrated – Byrne too.

Charlton later observed that Edwards seemed to take defeat as a personal affront. At one point, Real Madrid player Manuel Torres dropped to the floor; feeling he was exaggerating his injury, Edwards and Byrne attempted to haul him over the touchline so the game could continue. Charlton equalised in the 85th minute to make it 2-2 on the night – but his colleagues' frustration was interpreted as a lack of sportsmanship by the domestic press. All accepted United had been well beaten over two legs. Busby admitted he was disappointed but he insisted it was a great game.

And so the first competitive game played in continental competition at Old Trafford ended in a valiant draw, delivered the Busby way. Delivered the Manchester United way. In the 1930s, a correspondent wrote in the *Manchester Evening News*: "Some day some learned professor ought to write a treatise on the psychology of United. No other club can send its supporters to quite such heights of bliss and depths of despair. And there are few other supporters who so enjoy either process."

In many ways, the first European Cup game played at Old Trafford was Manchester United in a nutshell. We've mentioned Busby's team sometimes needed to concede to remember there was a game of football to be won rather than simply enjoyed. They came back, roared on by a crowd expecting miracles. That atmosphere helped them get a result – even though it was not enough on aggregate – but the supporters went home entertained after a breathless game of football. From this point on any great Manchester United side had to have an element of jeopardy about it; a masochistic exercise for both the team and the crowd, but one with a unique allure. Many of the club's greatest triumphs in the future would have this sense of being on a knife edge. The integrity of the defeat seems pivotal.

When faced with a deficit, United continued to play their normal way; they didn't resort to the tactics Wolves had shown against Honved. If they were to succeed, they would do it through their skill, will, and education.

So, the maiden voyage into the European Cup, and Busby's first quest to showcase his team in competitive action against the world's best, ended in defeat at the semi-final stage. The considerable consolation of an FA Cup final against Aston Villa lay in wait – the United manager settled on the same team that played against Real Madrid.

Six minutes into the final, the second element all teams need when chasing a number of different trophies – luck – proved it was not smiling on Manchester United this year. Goalkeeper Ray Wood was injured in a collision with Peter McParland and United were forced to play much of the game down to 10 men. Jackie Blanchflower went in goal and Edwards moved into the centre of defence. Villa, ironically through McParland, scored twice past Blanchflower. United's young team continued to fight, and pulled back a goal through Taylor in the 82nd minute; a concussed Wood, who had been brought on to play effectively as a passenger on the left wing, went back in goal. But United were defeated and had learned a couple of valuable lessons – put into a singular definition, they were not in control of everything in a football match by virtue of their talent alone.

As well as having a peerless and prescient philosophy, Busby was also philosophical when it came to his team's chances in the future. To have come so close to football's version of perfection at such a young age, and to have tasted failure in the forms in which it was delivered, could surely only be a good thing.

To get a sense of how United's quality was assessed in the day, the May 25th edition of the magazine *Soccer Star* made interesting reading. Columnist Graham Payne wrote: "Morris, Rowley, Delaney, Pearson and Mitten were rated as the best club attack since the war. Comparing them with today's bright 'Babes' would be a tough task, but currently, it's likely the former would get the edge – just."

It is necessary to consider these contemporaneous words, written without the benefit of hindsight. They serve as a good reminder of two things – that the 1948 team were greater than most give credit for, and that the 1957 side still had a little way to go to convince that they were the greatest in the club's history. There would be no resting on laurels moving into the following season. The United manager still saw areas to improve while also protecting what he currently had; he rejected a £65,000 offer from Inter Milan for Tommy Taylor (who had been tempted) and put in an advance notice ahead of any other approach – "Duncan Edwards is not for sale."

The Babes had a sluggish defence to their league title in 1957/58, possibly brought on by the ease in which they won five of their first six games, all of them by at least three clear goals. That was how they started the campaign, at Filbert Street, when Billy Whelan hit a late hat-trick. "The way United played the ball from man to man was uncanny," *The People*'s Joe Hulme observed. "They always had a man spare to run into the open space for a pass."

But complacency began to creep in, and opponents no longer were caught out by the United youth. A number of embarrassing results followed. A 4-0 defeat to Bolton and a defeat at Blackpool. A 3-1 reverse at Molineux, a 3-0 home defeat to Portsmouth and a 4-3 defeat to West Brom. United were third in the league, and Wolves were setting the pace. The next defeat, against Spurs at home, did at least have one positive contribution to Manchester United history when part of an ambition was realised.

FOOTBALL, TAUGHT BY MATT BUSBY

GASKELL
FOULKES BLANCHFLOWER BYRNE
COLMAN EDWARDS
WHELAN CHARLTON
SCANLON WEBSTER PEGG

Webster aside, this was a completely homegrown side – 10 out of 11 is the highest number achieved in the top flight in English football history, and some might even include Webster as he was 18 when he joined United from Cardiff (for the pedantry of the writer, however, the fact that Webster didn't play in the youth team disqualifies him). United lost 4-3 on the day; after taking an early lead, they were 4-1 down at half-time.

What were the realistic issues facing the Babes, just two months before their ultimate date with destiny? Let's start with the star man, Duncan Edwards.

Sportswriter George Follows opined that the half-back still hadn't grown out of that need to be everywhere on the pitch. "Every time his side is losing he thunders into his party piece, which is a dramatic version of 'The Charge of the Light Brigade,'" Follows wrote. "But I don't see it as soccer according to the Busby blueprint. In fact, death or glory Duncan is doing it so often that I categorise it as 'X' certificate soccer… It concertinas the play until you can't see the goal for footballers."

It infringes the first rule of football that the ball must do the work. The work is done by Duncan Edwards instead. And it was certainly not a good thing for Manchester United against Spurs. They were three down after Spurs had scored four goals with four shots… something most certainly had to be done. But they had the men to do it. Whimsical Whelan had re-found his wizard touch. Behind him Colman's hip work had Spurs under its spell.

They were using rapiers while Edwards battered away with his bludgeon."

Follows may well have been right. But maybe on one occasion – that occasion being 4-1 down at home – Edwards could have been forgiven for trying too hard. But it is also a fair suggestion to say that in those moments even Edwards needed to trust in the ability of his team-mates, who nearly rescued a result. There were other issues – and not just the distraction of the European Cup and the prospect of another FA Cup run. Eddie Colman had begun to show signs of overconfidence, significant enough for staff to have a word. He was at risk of a spell out of the team.

The number of goals conceded had become a matter of concern for the manager. He was beginning to question his own preference for Blanchflower over Jones and recalled the Barnsley-born defender – his more pragmatic approach led to an immediate defensive improvement. Even that didn't satisfy Busby. He had plans to mould Foulkes into a centre-half, taking a long-term view that he might need a more mobile right-back. And perhaps most crucially, he finally appeared to have identified the man who would revolutionise his goalkeeping position. Harry Gregg, the Northern Irish goalkeeper playing for Doncaster Rovers, was a man of tremendous ability. "I couldn't understand why, if the ball was 70 yards from me, I should handicap myself by 18 yards by staying on the goal-line," Gregg told the author in 2013. "It was basic, common sense to me."

He became the second goalkeeper to be signed by Busby for a world record fee – this time £23,000 was spent. And Gregg, one of the most outspoken men in United's rich history, probably comes as close as anyone to a phrase that could replace *Football Taught By Matt Busby* in terms of describing their overarching methodology.

"I loved what had happened to me," he said. "If I'd been born a rich man, I would have paid to have played for Manchester United. I stood on the Stretford End as a Doncaster player and watched the Busby Babes play. It was like Hollywood. I joined what I thought was the 'Hollywood' of football.

"There were four teams at Old Trafford, the first, the reserves, the A and the B. Around 43 players; this wasn't the 'Busby Babes', it was Manchester United. And out of those 43 players, only four had been signed from the outside. Ray Wood, the England goalkeeper. Johnny Berry, from Birmingham City. The great Tommy Taylor, and then myself. The strength of the club was in what it had developed itself. It was incredible."

Hollywoodball? There might be something in that, if only Salford's sensibilities didn't conflict so strongly with the glitz and glamour of tinseltown.

Now he was inside the dressing room, moving from being a player who had observed what inspired this fantastic brand of football, Gregg could attempt to analyse it. "On a Friday evening we'd have the team meeting – the boss would pin the team-sheet up on the board," Gregg recalled. "'If you aren't good enough lads, you wouldn't be here.' Week after week. The simplicity of it. And then he'd walk out. Jimmy Murphy would be in the dressing room. 'Up together, back together. Up together, back together. God bless.' They were saying different words, but the same thing, really. It was the most straightforward idea. When we have the ball, attack, when they have the ball, defend. You hear all the shit about 4-4-2, 4-3-3, catenaccio and so on. It's been taken over by people who've never played the game."

Gregg, then, was not one to over-analyse. It was what it was. What he added was a goalkeeper of outstanding reflexes, but also, for the first time, an 11th player. That's not to say he would join in the build up play, but he involved himself in the 'up together, back together' approach, by patrolling the edge of his area. This, in theory, enabled United's defensive line to be pushed up by another 20 yards. In Gregg's early weeks, this seemed to have an instant impact, the first two games were won 4-0 and 3-0.

United had done well in the earlier rounds of the European Cup, and were drawn against Red Star Belgrade in the quarter-final. The first leg saw Red Star return to Manchester in a repeat of their friendly years earlier. They had continued to grow in prominence themselves and in Dragoslav Šekularac had one of the most dangerous players in football. The clash was billed as Šekularac against Edwards but once more Colman would be given a man-marking job. For the first leg, United's team now read:

GREGG

FOULKES JONES BYRNE

COLMAN EDWARDS

CHARLTON VIOLLET

MORGANS TAYLOR SCANLON

Indeed, this would be the team that would play the second leg, too – and it earned that right after a well-fought 2-1 win at home.

It was this 11 which played the Busby Babes' last game on British soil while, for reference, the reserve team which won against Wolves on the same day the first team famously won 5-4 at Arsenal looked like this:

WOOD

COPE BLANCHFLOWER BENT

GOODWIN BRATT

WHELAN WEBSTER

BERRY DAWSON PEGG

That was a second string capable of competing in the top flight, even if the half-back line was possibly a little weak. With the first team, Busby had shown himself to be unafraid of making major changes. There were four new faces in the team compared to the side who had come up against Real Madrid less than a year earlier.

After taking a 3-0 lead in Belgrade, United allowed their hosts to draw level and take a 3-3 draw on the night. Albert Scanlon described the first half as the best attacking display of a team he'd featured in, and the second as the best defensive display, in spite of the goals conceded. It was enough for Busby's side to qualify for the semi-final, where they would face AC Milan. It is clear that they still had some issues with complacency. But Gregg's arrival had sparked an 11-game unbeaten run, with some thumping wins, as the team seemed determined to make 1958 a memorable one in their quest to win a treble.

9

MUNICH AND ITS REPERCUSSIONS

THIS BOOK IS A RECORD OF MANCHESTER UNITED history that concerns itself with on-pitch development. That is to say, this is not a book to recount the events of the Munich Air Disaster, which resulted in 23 fatalities, including eight United players: Geoff Bent, Roger Byrne, Eddie Colman, Mark Jones, David Pegg, Tommy Taylor, Billy Whelan, and 15 days after the disaster, Duncan Edwards. Jackie Blanchflower and Johnny Berry both survived but never played again. Three members of United's staff died – coaches Bert Whalley and Tom Curry, and club secretary Walter Crickmer, one of the men so influential in implementing the identity of what Manchester United were supposed to represent.

Matt Busby was gravely injured in the crash. In the short term, Jimmy Murphy would take charge of the first team (he had been absent from the trip to Belgrade, as he had been in charge of the Welsh national team in a successful World Cup qualifier). Joe Armstrong and Les Olive stepped up to share the volume of work that would need to be done in Crickmer's stead. Bill Inglis, one of the team coaches, now had a greater role to play. Murphy also enlisted the help of Jack Crompton, who had been trainer at Luton Town, and now returned to Old Trafford in the same capacity.

It's easy to conclude that Matt Busby was not only a visionary – he was a man keen to evolve. That would be proven in the future, too. But from the time he took charge at Old Trafford, to the time of the Munich disaster, all of that vision was effectively contained in the traditional 3-2-5, or 3-2-2-3, shape.

Busby's team had a goalkeeper, two full-backs, a centre-half, two half-backs, two inside-forwards, two outside-forwards, and one centre-forward. But the role of almost all of those individual positions had been redefined by February 1958. The goalkeeper now had the responsibility of condensing play further up the pitch, enabling his multi-functional outfield team of 10 to suffocate the play and possession.

Full-backs in a Matt Busby team were expected to attack and defend. In another team they might have been expected to be the last line of defence, but in his first great team Busby had converted two-inside forwards into full-backs in Carey and Aston. He had recognised the need for his centre-half to be a strong defensive rock but clearly wanted that player to be confident on the ball too. He had rightly identified the half-back area as the most important to the dictation of a team's tempo and had ensured he had his best player in that area. Even there, he'd bucked the trend, switching the commonly accepted defensive left-half and progressive right to play to the strengths of Edwards and Colman.

The traditional pair of inside-forwards – one schemer, one

runner – had been reimagined, with both players capable of doing all the above. In Charlton, Whelan and Viollet, Busby had an embarrassment of riches in players who were similar but had distinct differences. Charlton could operate wide and had a tremendous shot from distance with either foot. Viollet had a greater nose for goal in the instinct of a predator. Whelan was a mix of the two, similar to Stan Pearson before him. All three were masterful creators. On the wings, Busby preferred to have players of different approaches – a direct player in the form of Berry or Delaney and a tricky player like Mitten or Pegg, for example. His centre-forward would ideally be able to drop deep and hold the ball up or create space for the inside forwards, or, be adept at scoring from any position inside the box. Tommy Taylor was the perfect example of this and not even a world record offer could tempt Busby to part with him. If one was to study the comments earlier in this book about how the United boss would consider his perfect team to look, it is definitely accurate to say he had accomplished that with the Busby Babes.

They had bags of personality, on and off the pitch, especially in the likes of Edwards, Colman, Viollet, Byrne and Gregg. The production line was strong, with an ability to make wholesale changes and remain competitive. The maturing attitude of the team indicated even greater potential – the United players had complained about poor refereeing in Belgrade but still spent the evening partying with the Red Star players. Football was a game to be enjoyed and perhaps they had learned one of their greatest lessons in the humility and sportsmanship of their Yugoslavian opponents.

That – like their potential ability and potential achievements – is forever lost to hypothetical debates, the Busby Babes crystallised in romantic tragedy, immortalised by the contemporary reports that they were already one of, if not the, greatest teams of all-time.

Jimmy Murphy's task in the weeks after Munich was to work out how to continue – once it was decided that he would at all. The club was in a state of limbo, its future uncertain, until Murphy visited Munich and was implored by Busby to 'keep the flag flying'.

The reference was a literal one; the stadium carried a club flag, and the tradition with flags has always been to hang them at half-mast to mark a significant death. Busby was fighting for his life. But here he was, pleading with his colleague to carry on the work they had started; for all Busby and Murphy knew, the plea was to continue indefinitely. The phrase 'keep the flag flying' has entered United lexicon to such an extent that the emotional resonance is almost diluted. It's worth, then, just dwelling on it to allow it to permeate. Murphy pledged to continue, but he did not have a road map; he did not lead the plan in the way Busby had. He hadn't worked with Harry Stafford. He hadn't worked directly with Louis Rocca or James Gibson. But now here he was, fighting for the club's survival in a very recognisable way.

"My first job was to call an Old Faithful 'Uncle Joe Armstrong', our chief scout, to draw up the complete list of players," Murphy said. "I groaned, it read like a team of schoolboys. There was plenty of talent which might – and indeed did – show itself in two, three or four years time. But I needed players, top class players with First Division experience, immediately!"

Clubs offered help, but not in the form of their first-team players. Other players offered themselves if they could – one such name was Ferenc Puskas – and though Murphy seriously considered it, the amount of red tape concerned with signing a foreign player worried him. "Even if everything else was right, it seemed to be a negation of all Matt had tried to build," he said. "His aim was a team of dedicated youngsters who looked upon Manchester United as their club, something they had grown up with, and therefore, almost a part of the bricks and mortar. This was the ideal we set out to achieve and just as it was coming to fruition came the Munich tragedy to wreck it."

The actual measure taken by Murphy was courageous. He signed just two players, Ernie Taylor and Stan Crowther, who he had rated as unsung heroes in their respective teams' FA Cup wins. The rest of the team would be populated by young players who would be asked to step up out of the Central League before they were truly ready. They were being asked to skip a crucial part of their footballing education and to do so in an emotionally overwhelming time.

The team Jimmy Murphy named to face Sheffield Wednesday in the first game after the crash – blank on the team sheet in the match programme:

GREGG

FOULKES COPES GREAVES

GOODWIN CROWTHER

TAYLOR PEARSON

WEBSTER DAWSON BRENNAN

In addition to the new signings, Shay Brennan and Mark Pearson were making their debuts, though undoubtedly the most shocking inclusions were Gregg and Foulkes, who were playing less than two weeks after their survival in Munich. Brennan scored twice on Old Trafford's most emotional night, as United won 3-0.

As is plain to see, there were no tactical variations, and that extended to the reserve team as well in the forthcoming weeks. "Frankly I was astonished by the individual spirit that swept us along on a tide of emotion," recalled Murphy, and though he was referencing the 90 minutes, he could well have been referring to the following 90 days. "The players chased every ball, ran themselves to a standstill until they scarcely had the strength to lift their legs, and tackled with fanatical zeal... this was almost like war-time Britain as the City of Manchester, recovering from seeing one of their teams destroyed, grouped together under an emotional spell. They shouted and chanted as though hurt at the loss of young players they had idolised and now gave voice for the new United team urging them ON....ON....ON."

This makeshift United fought their way through the rest of the league calendar. Wolves were able to win the championship, while Murphy guided United to ninth and just one game was won in the rest of the league season. The FA Cup was a different story, as United's kids – and supporters – seemed to be galvanised by the jeopardy of the knock-out format. Improbably, they marched all the way to the final, where they were defeated by Bolton Wanderers (suffering more goalkeeper misfortune in the concession of a goal when Nat Lofthouse barged Harry Gregg into the net with the ball – goal awarded).

"I shall always feel we didn't do ourselves justice," Jimmy Murphy said, "and this because the young United players took too much out of themselves, mentally and physically, in the hectic weeks after the air crash. They were living on their nerves."

The list of results devoid of context, from Munich until the end of the season, makes grim reading. United were also eliminated from the European Cup after braving travel to face AC Milan; though they did put up a good fight for themselves. But from, and including, the decision to keep going, Manchester United's misfit side – led by Jimmy Murphy – were creating another thread to add to the rich tapestry of what the club stood for. The Welshman refused to surrender everything he and Busby had worked for. He refused to give up on the potential of what was still in reserve. Murphy had been forced to be unapologetic. The players were going to have to play through grief. They were going to have to seek both comfort and inspiration in the overpowering mourning and charged energy from the terraces. Over the period of three months, there was a transformation.

Watching the Busby Babes play, it felt impossible that such skill could be replicated. It felt impossible that the same sort of personality could be found – because it *was* impossible. That's what made those players so unique. In Duncan Edwards, the player who had fought for life longer than any other, United had been blessed with a player who did not believe any cause was lost. It had seemed impossible that he could share this deeply personal trait with an entire club. Munich changed that. It made every single player so appreciative of their ability to even have the opportunity, that a willingness to fight for a cause that seemed lost became a default part of their mechanism. Yes, this was part of Jimmy Murphy's mantra, and these players had all been through this same education. But Jimmy had largely been in the background, and Duncan Edwards was a national figurehead of what this team, this club was supposed to stand for. In death, he gave the club its most enduring trait – which was still present generations later. Of course it is impossible that a team could play with such relentless energy for 90 minutes every time they stepped on to the pitch; the point is that so long as a United team was playing with a clear commitment, there was a resonance and a connection with the support which ran deeper than the average relationship between a supporter and a sports team.

There was one significant quote made by the *Daily Express*, after Colin Webster had scored that last-minute winner to earn United a knockout win over West Brom in the FA Cup on March 6th, the start of a trend which would become an integral part of the club's identity. The reporter was making an observation on how United played under Murphy. "If you play for Manchester United you will NEVER shirk a tackle. You ALWAYS chase a loose ball. No game is EVER considered lost. Get it? And never forget it."

With so many players lost – players who had been through Busby's refinery process – the rawness of Murphy's tutoring took short-term precedence. This was the way the Welshman (with the great assistance of Bert Whalley) had always taught his kids. But now it was the default attitude for those left to deal with everything. Once the overpowering nature of the acute grief was escaped – and this is a reference only to time, because for many the actual consuming of grief was inescapable – United's staff would carry the silent burden that they had to continue. They had to chase the achievements that the Busby Babes would not fulfil.

Ultimately, those players of future generations would not only be striving for those reasons. They were also working hard in gratitude to the effort shown by those players who were forced, in grief, to sacrifice their own careers, in order to step in when the club needed them most. Kenny Morgans, Mark Pearson and Alex Dawson were Manchester United legends in the making. They are anyway, but they share the sporting repercussions of Munich in terms of lost potential, because the burden was theirs to carry, and they carried it with the greatest of dignity.

This group of players would hold itself together until Busby had convalesced and returned to duty later in 1958. Remarkably, they would finish second the following season. By the time of their next FA Cup final, only two members from the 1958 team would remain, and Matt Busby was in the process of his first major tactical shift at Old Trafford.

In August 1958, former manager Scott Duncan, who had

announced his retirement, was serialising his career in the *Manchester Evening News*.

"Matt is fortunate," he said. "He is surrounded by officials, players, and ground staff who do not know the meaning of defeat. I think their efforts since Munich have proved it. Nobody connected with the club throughout its long history has really believed that the Reds would go by the board. There will always be a United, come tribulation or triumph. The club seems to thrive on trouble and lean times."

10

1963: REBIRTH

THE GREAT HUNGARIAN TEAM OF THE EARLY 1950S had fallen victim to time and politics. At the 1954 World Cup, where they were heavily tipped to win, they lost a controversial final to a West Germany team they had defeated 8-3 in the group stage. The Magnificent Magyars were not yet done. Following that tournament they went unbeaten until February 1956, winning 16 of their 19 games. The Budapest Honved team which contained most of these great players faced Athletic Bilbao in the 1956/57 European Cup. After the first leg, which Honved lost 3-2, political tensions erupted, causing the Hungarian Uprising. It was decided to hold the second leg in a neutral venue, and a 3-3 draw was played out in Brussels. Of course, had the Hungarians qualified, their opponents in the quarter-final would have been Manchester United.

The uprising caused an instantaneous break-up of the team, with many of the players moving to Spain. By the time of the 1958 World Cup, only a couple of the great names remained. That tournament saw the emergence of a brilliant Brazil side who had evolved the 3-2-5 into a 4-2-4. A flat back four might have seemed defensive – not so. Yes, one forward had technically been sacrificed to move into defence, but the strategy was all about ensuring opponents were outnumbered. It was almost, in effect, a 3-3-4, because the extra centre-half was intended to carry the ball forward. An Edwards or a Blanchflower as opposed to a Jones. It was an approach which facilitated domination of possession, because the outnumbering could occur in any position on the pitch. 'Up together, down together' needn't mean all 11 players; the two half-backs, now effectively midfielders, could move to create six defenders or six attackers, constantly overloading the five in a WM formation. It helped that Brazil had outstanding individuals who could manipulate spaces for the outside-forwards to exploit.

On their way to the final in 1958, Brazil knocked out Jimmy Murphy's Wales; back in Manchester, nursing his way back to health, Busby was already observing the generational shift that this new formation was likely to bring. Brazil won the World Cup, with talk rightly focussed on their thrilling offensive play.

They were so inventive that Murphy had been forced to consider solutions. "We sat and talked about it," recalled his captain Dave Bowen. "The Brazilians had Didi, Garrincha and this new fella Pele. They could play magical stuff. So we set out to deny them space behind us. We let them have the middle of the park. If they couldn't get behind us they couldn't create chances and we went so near to beating them."

Rebuilding at Manchester United for Busby was both a short term and a long term thing. Despite mixed results, it could not be said that United's players put in anything less than a heroic shift in the two or three years after Munich. Busby returned to deal with first-team duties and Murphy promised to deliver another Youth Cup winning team. He would be assisted by John Aston, who returned to coach the junior players. Realistically, everyone at United knew that replicating the system in its almost autonomous fashion was going to be impossible. Busby and Murphy moved from their 40s into their 50s and for the manager in particular the effects of Munich took their own ageing impact. He had resolved to try and win the European Cup, it became his life's obsession, but it was a silent one; just like Munich, it was never spoken of among the staff or players at Old Trafford. There was just the ominous sense of purpose, and while one might call that a driving force, for years it hung like a dark shadow over the club.

In the players who had died, the players who could not play again, and the players whose developments were impacted so heavily afterwards, United had lost more than a full team. It was impractical to think the club could rebuild this from the bottom up if they wished to remain competitive in the short term. Some compromise on the philosophy would have to be made, at least in the short term, and it was established in the balance. Perhaps it would be best to start with the FA Cup final team of 1963 and unpick it.

GASKELL

DUNNE FOULKES SETTERS CANTWELL

CRERAND

GILES LAW

QUIXALL HERD CHARLTON

Before the deconstruction, it should be noted that not only was this team represented in the 3-2-5 shape in the match programme, it was the even older version of it – so Foulkes was positioned in the half-back line with Crerand and Setters.

The truth was that in practice, it was more like a 4-2-4, with Giles and Law taking it in turns dropping back to partner Crerand or moving forward to partner Herd (more often than not, it was Law moving forward, as he did to devastating effect when he scored the fantastic first goal against Leicester in the final). You could even describe it as a 4-3-3, with Crerand the anchor of the three in the midfield.

Busby wanted a more physically robust back line; the repositioning of Foulkes was successful, and Tony Dunne and Noel Cantwell were signed from Shelbourne and West Ham respectively. The fourth defender was Maurice Setters, a fiery left-half whose ball recovery was among the best in the country. He was signed from West Brom and would be tasked with moving back to make a four when the need arose, as English football slowly got used to these new shapes.

In midfield was Paddy Crerand, recently signed from Celtic as a half-back who could dictate the play. He quickly became so integral that it was said 'when Crerand plays, United play'. He was an intelligent reader of the game and could position himself to intercept balls, without the need to tackle – though he was fierce in that regard too. It was his elegance and range of passing which really made him so important; he had the wisdom to know when to pick a short or long ball and the vision to spot openings that few others could. He would be joined in midfield more often than not by Johnny Giles; nominally the inside-right, he would drop back to connect the play. The other inside-forward was Denis Law, the fiery Scot who Busby and Murphy had tried to sign when he was at Huddersfield. They had to wait until Law had played for Manchester City and Torino before convincing him to move to Old Trafford in 1962 for a British record transfer fee of £115,000. He was an important player not just for his influence in United's future success but also in his significance to the evolution of tactics at both Old Trafford and in the wider game. Law had not found it easy in Italy yet returned to England with a new side to his game thanks to the experience. "I never settled down in Italy," he confessed. "But there was something about the football which appealed to my instincts. They used to excite me because they were never afraid to indulge in spectacular attempts at goal. I liked that."

When Law returned to Manchester, one of the first things that stood out was his confidence heading the ball for someone clearly below six foot. The second was even greater – if he felt the cross was too high for a header, and even sometimes if he fancied it, Law would execute the body throw of a gymnast and elevate his foot high into the air to perform what is now commonly known as the bicycle kick. It would be a few years until Law pulled it off in a game – in the 1967 Charity Shield most remembered for Spurs goalkeeper Pat Jennings scoring a goal past Alex Stepney, Law had equalised with an overhead kick. The entire stadium fell into an instant, momentary hush, unable to quite believe what they had witnessed. So too, presumably, were the officials – the referee disallowed it for foul play. It was reflective of the liberation of Busby to encourage his players to try such things.

Law was a striker in the commonly understood nature of the role but he fancied himself as a box-to-box player. He would often drop deep, but his real damage to opponents was caused either by runs between the opposition lines or his predatory instinct in the box. An observation of the 1963 FA Cup final shows United, in the first half, repeatedly winning possession and outnumbering Leicester in midfield areas, with Crerand often breaking up the play and serving the ball to Giles, who would feed Law. Charlton was comfortable with either foot but often drifted infield from the left to join in with the play. Albert Quixall was a pure right winger (in this shape, but he was renowned as a striker) and David Herd, signed from Arsenal, was a prolific centre-forward.

United's style of play remained faithful to the Busby hallmark, centred around movement of the ball and players. Players were instructed to recover the ball as quickly as possible and then were encouraged to look for openings just as quickly. Ball retention meant deliberation in possession rather than circulation just for the sake of it.

The forward line was so inventive in its creation of space that the full-backs were not often required to overlap in the old manner of a Byrne or an Aston; the space that Quixall or Charlton might leave as they moved from position would be guarded by Giles or Law, with Dunne or Cantwell pushing as high as the halfway line but never so far that they would leave themselves exposed. In defence, Foulkes was most definitely in the Jones mould; Setters would be considered the ball-player of the pair, even if he too had a reputation as a 'hard man'.

United won the final 3-1 – Herd scoring twice to add to Law's marvellous opener. Five years after Munich, Busby had delivered another trophy-winning team. In Gaskell, Foulkes, Giles and Charlton, they had an admirable four homegrown players in the team, though that is evidence of how difficult the rebuild had been – previously the first team would have Gregg, Taylor and possibly Berry for a balance of 9-2 or 8-3 when it came to homegrown players versus signed players.

It was a team of talent, endeavour and craft. But it did not seem as beloved as the Busby Babes nor even as polished as the 1948 FA Cup-winning team – maybe because there hadn't been a genuine infusion of youth. There needed to be a sufficient distance from Munich, so that a wave of young players could be introduced into a club that wasn't burdened by grief in such a profound way.

As early as the first two seasons after Munich, Busby had started to evolve so that all of the teams were playing a variation of this new system, with the long-term plan to move to the Brazilian 4-2-4 – although occasionally, the old-fashioned 3-2-5 was adopted at junior level. In the 1963/64 season, United embarked on a Youth Cup run that would be just as important to future successes as the 1963 FA Cup final win had been to the confidence of the club. That junior side, which won against Swindon in the final to claim the first trophy at this level since 1957:

RIMMER
DUFF FARRAR NOBLE
MCBRIDE FITZPATRICK
BEST KINSEY
ANDERSON SADLER ASTON

There are a number of notable names in there – although of course, by mere virtue of winning the Youth Cup for Manchester United, they are all notable in their own right. Still, it is clear Murphy had arranged his team in the older formation. Contemporary reports of the time mention the older positions – right-half, inside-forward and so on.

Is it possible that they played a 4-2-4 in a subtle change missed by the sportswriters? Yes – George Best, in the inside-right number eight shirt, had a tendency to play all over the pitch. If he was considered one of the forward four, then theoretically it could be said that Kinsey would have dropped back. John Fitzpatrick was just as capable in defence as he was in midfield.

In Willie Anderson and John Aston, there were two definite conventional wingers. Even moving into the 1964/65 season, as a number of these youth graduates began to make their presence known in the first team, football publishers had not caught up with the times.

For United's September visit to Chelsea in 1964, the match programme had their team listed thus:

P DUNNE

BRENNAN   T DUNNE

CRERAND   FOULKES   STILES

CONNELLY   CHARLTON   HERD   LAW   BEST

We will return to this in a moment. Busby had moved into a clear 4-2-4 but using the Brazilian philosophy. Collyhurst-born Nobby Stiles was an integral part of this system. Stiles, an inside-forward in his younger days, had moved to half-back. Eddie Colman was his hero and he also once asked Jimmy Murphy if he could have Tommy Taylor's boots.

As he began to make his own reputation, Stiles was described as a 'mini Duncan Edwards'. Quite so; if Edwards had a way of seeming somehow bigger than his 5'11 frame, Stiles' slender frame often made him seem slighter than his 5'6 body. Not that you could ever miss Stiles on the pitch.

"To me, Nobby Stiles is the ideal 'sweeper up' both in temperament and practical ability," Jimmy Murphy observed. "He is so neat and tidy, spots danger and immediately nips in to stop it. Thus when I see a boy who is a sharp tackler, positions himself cleverly by watching the run of play and spotting where the danger is likely to come, and allies to this snappy interceptions and neat work tidying up and plugging gaps at the back, then I know I am looking at a future Nobby Stiles."

Incidentally, the repositioning of Stiles did prompt an interesting revelation from Murphy. "A good club has to be able to cope with a situation like this where they have a player of great individual talent who has to be slotted into the team and given confidence," he observed. "In this respect Manchester United have as good a record as any for finding the correct position for players... How easy it is to dismiss a young inside-forward struggling to find his form as a failure, when in fact you may have a high class full-back in the making."

Stiles is worth dwelling upon because of how profoundly his role helped United evolve into this shape of the future. He was more like Colman than he would probably have dared believe, but with a greater natural sense of economy; where Colman might have been inclined to dance and move forward, Stiles was content to let the ball do the work. Murphy's comments were published in 1968, so it is interesting to note that he described Stiles as a sweeper; in these days, the sweeper could play behind or in front of the defence, and traditionally Stiles has always been described as a defensive midfielder. His role in this team was just as crucial as Crerand's in terms of how they were able to tick along smoothly. The fact that Stiles was often deployed as that second centre-half reveals much about the infancy of the approach, and how it aligned with Busby's ideals. The manager had clearly placed an emphasis on the individual footballing ability rather than any physical prowess; no 5'6 centre-half was ever selected for their height advantage[2]. We can ascertain that the United boss had recognised a need to evolve, but he would embrace any such evolution in the most positive way possible.

Busby had established a fine balance. There was the right amount of experience linked to the club to the past – Brennan, Foulkes and Charlton from the pre-Munich days. There was an injection of new youth in Best and Stiles. The requisite Scottish class in Herd, Law and Crerand. Reliability in the form of Tony Dunne and John

---

2   As an interesting side note, it should be stated that the average height for an adult male was 5'6 at the start of the 20th century, and 5'10 at the end of it.

Connelly. Where changes were necessary, the manager could now call on promising young talent like Fitzpatrick, Aston, and Sadler – players to present a genuine threat to established starters. The subtle moves paid dividends. Charlton had spent much of his career playing at inside or outside-forward. Now he was in the middle of the pitch and influencing play.

United had needed this time to get back to where they once were, even if things were not quite the same. Where the pre-Munich side had resembled a machine of perpetual motion, the post-Munich side was closer to a collection of individuals selected to play together. That's not a remark of disparagement – the United boss was operating much like any other manager, whilst always trying to ensure they played his brand of football and hoping the work done with the younger players could spark some of that old chemistry.

Things had been so difficult that in April 1963, prior to the FA Cup final, the club had been struggling with a relegation fight. In October 1964, United hit their best run of form since Munich, scoring four at Wolves, seven against Aston Villa, six against Djurgardens of Sweden in the Inter-Cities Fairs Cup, and another six against Dortmund in the same European competition – and, in that run, still managed to fit a win in at Anfield.

What was the difference? The confidence of a cup win. 18 months more chemistry between these players. And the magic stardust added by George Best, a generational talent much like Duncan Edwards who had, within the space of a year, got people musing that he might well be the best player in the division. Best, only 18, was a forward capable of playing anywhere along the front line. He was barely 5'9 and possibly even lighter than Stiles, but his dribbling ability was unlike anything ever seen in the British game. His proper introduction to the team came after a 6-1 Boxing Day defeat at Burnley in 1963 (though Best had made his debut three months earlier) – as most journalists wondered how Busby might fix the defence, he instead presented a new attacking threat in Best and Willie Anderson, the pair running riot in a 5-1 revenge win two days later.

Upon seeing him for the first time, Busby observed Best's 'dislike for passing the ball' and hoped Murphy could coach it out of him. Murphy informed his manager that this was one player who could not be coached. Best was not only good – he was outrageous. In an FA Cup tie with Burnley his boot came off on a muddy Old Trafford pitch. The visitors were winning, so Best was running bootless as he tried to help his team back into the match. He not only set up Law's equaliser, but Crerand's winner a minute later – both with his left foot that had only a stocking on.

Only a matter of weeks later he spent the morning at The Cliff trying to score directly from a corner kick before the team travelled to Wolves in the FA Cup that evening. At Molineux, Best scored direct from a corner. It was wizardry that even none of the Babes had displayed, but Best still seemed to possess that familiar vivaciousness, illuminating the games and making the crowd feel excited once more about seeing Manchester United play. It was as though Best single-handedly restored technicolour to a club that had been enshrouded by a dark grey cloud for six years. Like Law, and like Edwards, Best was personification of the fact that players were capable of dictating tactical shifts. His dribbling style was unusual in English football and hadn't really been seen since Stanley Matthews; it was almost as though Best had brought it back in fashion.

Best's rising stardom made a mockery of supposed ceilings and for a period in the mid-60s he seemed to redefine standards of excellence. As United closed in on their first league title since 1957, they welcomed Chelsea to Old Trafford. The line-up as it would have looked on the pitch, identical to the side that played the same opponents earlier in the season:

P DUNNE

BRENNAN FOULKES STILES T DUNNE

CRERAND CHARLTON

CONNELLY HERD LAW BEST

Best scored an outrageous lob over the goalkeeper, after robbing the full-back of possession – the first of his team's four goals without reply. To pay attention to the detail in the match report is to recognise the subtleties at play.

"Genius, it seems, still will not answer to numbers," wrote Maurice Smith in *The People*. "Not the sort of genius personified by Law, Best, Charlton and co., soccer purveyors extraordinary of Manchester United. To say (Chelsea) were outwitted, outmatched, outfought is to put it mildly. They were outclassed. Men they could never mark – those United players always seemed to have a trick too many up their sleeves – caused as much confusion among the Chelsea numbers-brigade as a stuttering caller would at a bingo session. Foulkes, Tony Dunne and Brennan padlocked the Chelsea attack who have grown up on goals but who hardly got in a real shot here. Crerand and Stiles, the midfield links, had so little to do defensively that they were able to become sixth and seventh forwards. And Law, Best and Charlton spread havoc, there is no other word for it."

Smith's summary suggests Stiles was usually playing further forward and that Busby was playing with a three-man backline. Not so – by now, having used Setters as the fourth defensive player, Busby now identified Stiles as the successor. He was simply so good at it that he was able to play his natural midfield game and move the ball up the pitch.

In fact, Stiles had effectively been in that role since March 1964. Setters had picked up an injury in United's humiliating Cup Winners' Cup exit to Sporting Lisbon, where the team conceded five to suffer their worst European defeat. Setters would miss the game at Spurs the weekend after – presenting an opportunity that Stiles was proactive about. He approached Busby and asked to be considered as Setters' replacement. "Though I've never known for sure," Stiles said in his autobiography, "maybe they (Busby and Murphy) had some input from Foulkes, the former full-back who had built a new empire for himself in central defence. Perhaps they simply reached the same conclusion as I had, noting my speed in the tackle and my ability to read the play. I knew Bill wanted me alongside him. On the practice field, he had registered that I was very quick off the mark."

Stiles also observed that Jimmy Murphy had been integral to the reshaping of the team. "Murphy had done what had always been the core of his work," he said, "the organising of proper defence, the provision of that foundation without which even the most talented team will always struggle to find lasting success."

United's first title for eight years – a remarkable rebuilding job – was effectively confirmed with a 3-1 win over Arsenal on April 26th. In attendance at Old Trafford were Di Stefano and Puskas; the two Real Madrid legends never got to partake in more classic duels with the Babes but had still made many visits to Manchester as the clubs faced each other in a series of fundraising friendlies.

The statistics over the 1964/65 season revealed a significant number: 89 goals scored was nothing new for a Busby team, but 39 conceded was. It was less than half of the goals conceded just two years earlier, while the 16 clean sheets in 42 games was another club record.

How did this team compare with the Babes? The *Daily Express* suggested the title win was 'perhaps Matt Busby's greatest' but that tribute may well have carried the weight of sentiment and the recognition of the personal journey.

But the 1965 side were not as universally beloved as the Babes, as the conclusion to their season proved. United's European adventures concluded with a bad-tempered semi-final with Hungarian team Ferencváros. Pat Crerand was sent off in the second leg, taking the number of United players dismissed in the last two years to ten.

You might trace the seeds of this new fiery side to United to the immediate weeks after Munich. The kids who had been promoted ahead of schedule were finding most opponents naturally unsympathetic as far as competition was concerned. Sometimes the players – and Mark Pearson was one in particular – would become over-zealous. Pearson was the target for Burnley owner Bob Lord's criticism that United had 'Teddy Boys' in their team; a jibe that seems comically tame now, but was felt as a slur at the time. United's fight was actual and not just symbolic, and even though Busby frowned upon incidents that brought the club into disrepute, he still kept a core of these players in his team.

It could not be said that Manchester United's title-winning team of 1965 would be physically intimidating. In Dunne, Stiles, Best, Connelly and Law, there wasn't a man over the height of 5'9. Their aggression and attitude, though, was evidence that in this situation size did not matter.

"On one count only can United be faulted," wrote Clive Toye, when summarising this title-winning side, "and that is that they were involved in too many rough games. I am not saying United were always to blame. But a truly great side does not welcome the smear that went with some of United's performances."

With that attitude came a desire to prove themselves against the very best. The Inter-Cities Fairs Cup was considered the weakest of the European trophies but United now had the opportunity to compete in the big one, the European Cup, for the first time since Munich. Real Madrid had continued to leave an impression on United's young players. In one of the friendly games, Stiles observed Puskas and Di Stefano arguing with each other at half-time because Real were losing 2-0. Although he couldn't understand their Spanish, he understood the common language of football. The Hungarian was telling his legendary pal to calm down. "Di Stefano was saying there was no such thing as a friendly," Stiles said. "There was only a football match in which you always carried your pride."

Best had been similarly impressed by Di Stefano; watching as the best player on the pitch also did the most amount of work, popping up in deeper positions to help his team – this in a friendly match, well into his mid-30s, at a point in his career where his all-time reputation was secure.

The European Cup represented something different to Manchester United now. And those friendly games against Real Madrid had played a significant role in how United had recovered after Munich. In spite of the fundraising nature of the games, part of the appeal of facing the glamorous Spanish side was to see how far United had come in their rebuild. The first friendly games were not competitive. On October 1st, 1959, the Spaniards won 6-1 at Old Trafford. In the *Daily Herald*, Sam Leitch described the style showed by Di Stefano, Puskas, Gento and Didi as 'Football From Outer Space'. A few weeks later, United lost the return game in Spain 6-5. In October 1960, Real won 3-2 in Manchester. The games were beginning to get tighter and United's first win came in December 1961, a 3-2 victory in Manchester – the one where Best was so enthralled. In September 1962 they won 2-0 in Spain, the above-mentioned match where Stiles was left with the same impression. These moments were shots in the arm for the kids coming through, for it gave them a belief that they deserved to be on this sacrosanct stage of football. A confidence that they belonged.

European football had undergone its own transition since United's last participation in the premier tournament. The European Cup was won by Inter Milan in 1964 and 1965, pioneering Helenio Herrera's catenaccio style. In 1963, AC Milan had won the tournament with Nereo Rocco using a similarly defensive strategy. Benfica, who had won back-to-back European Cups in 1961 and 1962, were the last team of true adventure to triumph. It suggested that managers would now have to be smarter. The 1965 final had been the first to feature just one goal. It was an illustration that concentration and a clinical edge were now key.

One note of some significance – in the summer of 1965, Harold Hardman passed away, and Louis Edwards – who had obtained the majority of the club's shares throughout the previous season – became sole chairman. Edwards sought to invest some of the club's money into the redevelopment of Old Trafford, in particular a two-tier cantilever stand that would house over 20,000 supporters. The stand would also contain 34 executive boxes and Busby encouraged the idea, feeling it was somewhat in line with the palatial Santiago Bernabeu stadium of Real Madrid.

As United's first return to the elite progressed, it was evident that Busby was embracing the changes, but he was also clearly keen to allow his team to naturally express itself. The campaign started with a complacent away win against HK Helsinki that saw Herd and Connelly score in the first half hour. Against the Finnish part-timers at home, Busby trialled Best through the middle and selected John Aston Jnr on the left. Best scored twice in a 6-0 win but few conclusions could be drawn. Nor could they from another straightforward win over Vorwärts Berlin. The first leg, played in East Berlin, saw the return of Harry Gregg, who had endured a difficult relationship with luck and injuries since Munich. This misfortune meant he did not have a winner's medal from the FA Cup or league triumphs. Now here he was, playing in front of a new-look four-man defence in Europe. He exuded his natural confidence and kept a clean sheet in victory – the performance prompted a semi-permanent recall. It also prompted another concession – at 33, and with his track record of injuries, Gregg couldn't be invested in in the long term. A new goalkeeper was needed.

United's next opponents in the European Cup quarter-final were Benfica. Inter Milan may have been the reigning European champions but in Eusebio, the Portuguese had the current Ballon d'Or holder. An indication of United's own growing stature could be found in the fact that Denis Law had won the award before him – and, in this year, 1966, Bobby Charlton would win it, thanks mostly to his stellar performance as England won the World Cup, though his 18 goals (including a memorable solo strike at Villa Park) over the season for United would not have hurt.

For the home leg, Busby's approach to Eusebio was to assign Nobby Stiles in a man-marking job. "When I am asked to follow players around I am virtually putting myself out of the game," Stiles later admitted. "It becomes a matter for great discipline but it's not really football." Still, Stiles performed admirably; United won 3-2, and it might have been 3-1, but Benfica's second goal came from a looping header that a Harry Gregg without chronic shoulder pain might have stopped. Benfica had never lost a home game in Europe and United still had nightmares about their previous visit to Lisbon. Stiles had his man-marking job in a team that was the same which had defeated Arsenal to (effectively) clinch the title in April 1964, save for one subtle difference – George Best would wear the number seven shirt, and Connelly would wear 11. This was a change that had occurred earlier in the season, in November, so was not a specific plan for the continent. Connelly and Best could change positions and it was possible that the change was made to reflect John Aston Jnr's emergence, and his definite left-sided status as opposed to Best's tendency to move around.

It is a tale often told that the manager urged his side to play cautiously for the first 20 minutes. Gregg dismissed that as 'nonsense', saying "No Manchester United team I ever played in was told to defend." There was a feeling that United's luck would not be in – some of the players were kicking a ball around in the changing room, and one Pat Crerand pass went astray and smashed a mirror.

Certainly, it seemed Benfica were banking on caution from their visitors. As it transpired, this was naivety on their part – George Best was in scintillating form, scoring twice in the first 15 minutes. The second of his goals featured a slalom run between two defenders, the sort of gravity-defying exploit that only a player of his diminutive frame could perform. Best was mesmeric, going after the defenders with the ferociousness of a lion toying with its helpless prey. United, 3-0 up after 16 minutes, came away with a landmark 5-1 victory.

More than trophies, more than successes, the true beauty of football is measured in moments. Only one team can win a tournament, so the genuine beauty of football has to be measured in the moments on the journey, for what they are and what they represent. If these moments of magic happen in a journey that concludes with success, then we can assign it to fate; if not, then where is it assigned to? Of course it is still fate, because the romance of it all may well be increased by the context surrounding it, but the real beauty is that it happened at all.

United won 5-1 in Benfica in March 1966 but did not win the European Cup. George Best's night in the Stadium of Light was seminal. It established him as a global megastar. His team-mates like Paddy Crerand and Jimmy Rimmer already held the belief that Best, aged just 19, was the best player in England. Now it was clear that he could do what he did in England against the best teams in the world.

The result also re-established United as a major force in European competition. Never before had United won away in Europe in such a dominant manner. It was Matt Busby's greatest vindication yet; the finest victory of his tenure, a peak in terms of performance that even the Babes hadn't managed on foreign shores.

That much is as true individually as it was collectively. Even Duncan Edwards had not made his mark on such a big club game in this way (though he most certainly had for England). It belonged to Best in such a personal way that the win was never ascribed to Busby's tactics or philosophy of football, but of course, it was *thanks* to that philosophy. That was the structure upon which Best's individual star could shine. However, Best was injured in the semi-final against Partizan Belgrade, and United were eliminated, despite facing a team who were not quite as outstanding as the one they had already knocked out. "For Busby," wrote Roger MacDonald in his book *Manchester United in Europe*, "this was a time for agonising reappraisal. Partizan went on to lose to Real Madrid in the final, but neither were equal to United at their best. The truth was that his team, allowed too much to play by ear, lacked the organisation that might have made better use of their brilliant potential. The risks of attacking football, when advocated without regard for the circumstances, were greater than the rewards."

MacDonald's observations are fair though it is worth countering with a couple of points; one, that the 'play it by ear' approach was the precise approach which facilitated George Best to play the way he had. Two, that United as a team had a genuine claim to be the best in Europe, as admitted by MacDonald himself – and he could not have been suggesting that they were in that position in spite of Busby's philosophy.

To have another chance at winning the European Cup, first Manchester United had to win the league title again. That was not a straightforward process. Yes they had great players, but the team was now beginning to show signs of ageing. So was the staff. Busby had been in post for 20 years and could easily have been forgiven if he had seen restoring United to the summit in English football a suitable enough accomplishment after Munich. He was creeping up to 60 years of age, and a new generation of coaches were coming into the game. Many of them were from West Ham, known as the Cassettari Cafe group which included Malcolm Allison, Dave Sexton, Frank O'Farrell and John Bond. The game was changing. Busby had been more prescient than most but time eventually catches up to all and there was at least now time to ask questions. How long did Busby have left as a manager? Could his philosophy still succeed without some form of evolution?

11

1968: REDEMPTION

COULD IT BE THAT MANCHESTER UNITED HAD A TEAM good enough to win the European Cup but not the English First Division? Matt Busby's team finished fourth in 1966 – behind Burnley in third, runners-up Leeds and champions Liverpool. Their mean defence had regressed, conceding 59 goals, even if up front they remained as prolific as ever. Concluding that the answer was in a change of goalkeeper, Busby made another world-record signing. There was some fortune in this – Alex Stepney had accepted a move across London from Millwall to Chelsea. However, the Chelsea owner decided he preferred club legend Peter Bonetti to remain in goal, and Stepney was made available for transfer after making just one appearance.

Busby had started the following season with Gaskell, Dunne and Gregg, but none looked as though they could perform in a team with United's aspirations. Stepney lacked Gregg's imposing character but he was cool, unflappable and reliable – younger readers might say he was the Van Der Sar to Gregg's Schmeichel. One trait they shared was their fondness to start the play, while Stepney would often play outfield in five-a-sides in training.

There were no great tactical innovations from Busby but he did make adjustments. Three more members of United's Youth Cup-winning side became prominent first-team players. Bobby Noble, a left-back with the potential to become the club's greatest, necessitated the move of Dunne to right-back. John Aston Jnr now took Connelly's wing place. And David Sadler, an elegant player who could play in the middle of defence or attack, found himself with plenty of game time due to injuries suffered by Foulkes and Herd. Before the end of the campaign, Herd and Noble were to suffer heavily with injuries that in the former case heavily disrupted his career and in the latter, ended it entirely.

United did win the league, finishing in front of Nottingham Forest and Tottenham Hotspur. Their most common team:

STEPNEY
DUNNE FOULKES STILES NOBLE
CRERAND CHARLTON
BEST LAW HERD ASTON
(WITH SADLER IN REGULARLY FOR HERD AND FOULKES)

One substitute was now permitted, so many teams opted for a goalkeeper on their bench. Others opted for a versatile player who could fill in most positions. Busby had no such fixed rule, with a number of different players all getting the chance. A change would only be made in case of injury. Stepney's arrival instilled a sense of calm to United's defence, matching the club record of 16 clean sheets in the league – even more impressive considering he missed a fifth of the season. However, there was anything but calm in the defence moving into the

1967/68 season, as Busby prepared for a renewed assault on the European Cup.

With Noble injured, young Francis Burns was drafted in. But as the big matches came thick and fast, Busby erred on the side of experience, bringing in the faithful veteran Shay Brennan. Stiles also suffered his fair share of injuries, reduced to just 20 appearances – his number six shirt was usually filled by Sadler, and occasionally by John Fitzpatrick. With Herd injured – and with Law joining him on the treatment table too often with a knee injury – an opportunity presented itself to 18-year-old Brian Kidd, a local youngster who could play across the front line.

In March 1967, Clive Bond – a coach with the Football Association – wrote an article in the FA News magazine where he studied the tactics of the United team that was about to win the league. "Basically," observed Bond, "the system United use is a 4-3-3 with Stepney, Dunne, Noble, Foulkes, Stiles providing the rearguard which is linked by Crerand, Charlton, Best to the front line."

Most onlookers would feel Best was a nominal right-sided player but there was truth in that Di Stefano-esque insatiability to be everywhere on the pitch. In fact, as Bond wrote, Best was "really too gifted a player to wait for service and now finds himself working midfield with Charlton, fetching and carrying, covering in defence, and initiating attacks." There is little doubt that this is reflected in Best's relatively low-scoring start to his United career – scoring four, ten, nine and 10 goals respectively in his first four seasons before five campaigns of 15 goals or more.

Charlton, having started out as an inside-forward and then having spent five years as a left-winger, was now based in the middle of the park, a "fine midfielder with a very high work output… his tremendous speed, coupled with a deceptive change of pace and direction, makes him a hard man to pin down" as told by Bond.

1968: REDEMPTION

When Best was dropping deeper, Herd would move out to cover space on the right, though as Bond put it, he was not 'blessed with the qualities of a flank player'.

In defence, credit was given to Foulkes as a 'most competent and dependable defender, dominating in the air and hard in the tackle, without being a sparkling offensive player' and Sadler was rated as someone who had the potential to become an international centre-half if his positional awareness improved.

"That completes quite a cavalcade of stars," wrote Bond, "and with such talent, United can adapt their basic 4-3-3 system to the needs of the moment. Best or Charlton can move up to make it a 4-2-4. Stiles could easily modify his role to that of a 'front centre-half' or a 'sweeper' and with Crerand playing deeper one has the basis of a blanket defence; so necessary for their two legged European matches. Having watched United over the past three seasons, my major criticism would be that they appear not to have been very tactically conscious.

As a team, they are used to dictating the tactics and when, rarely, they are up against it, they do not seem to have the ability to adapt. Is Denis Law a tactical captain? Are Manchester a tactical outfit? Whatever questions are posed, there can be no doubt that they are a great club side with perhaps the finest club manager of all time."

Inconsistency of selection, thanks to injuries, had some impact on the ability to retain the league title. It was relinquished on the final day of the 1967/68 season, after defeat at home to Sunderland meant Manchester City's win at Newcastle had earned them the championship. By this point, however, there was a considerable consolation waiting for Manchester United, in the form of their first European Cup final.

There were some tactical variations in the run to the final. In fact it seemed as though more aspects of the game were finally catching up with the changes on the pitch. All match programmes listed the teams as lists in 1-11, rather than a 2-3-5 shape.

When United travelled to Sarajevo for the first leg of their second round tie, Busby went with an unapologetically cautious approach, selecting John Fitzpatrick in the number seven shirt – marking the first time he had played a definite 4-4-2 rather than a 4-2-4. United had anticipated a similarly physical encounter to what they had experienced against Partizan, with Sarajevo a little more of an unknown quantity in their inaugural European Cup campaign. Of course, anticipating usually involved getting in the first jab – literally speaking in this match, as United fought their way to a 0-0 draw.

Busby described the match as 'disgraceful' and 'worse than anything we have ever experienced in this competition'. At Old Trafford, Busby's team seemed even more pragmatic on paper, as Burns came in for Fitzpatrick. United triumphed 2-1 on the night – and in the following round, 2-1 on aggregate against Polish side Gornik Zabrze. In the home tie, Busby played a 4-2-4 – footage of this game suggests this was a traditional approach, with Aston pushing high on the left and Dunne pushing high to support him and condense the space. It worked.

In the away game, with a 2-0 lead to protect, some sources suggested Busby went so far as to play a 5-4-1. Is this possible? If so it would have looked like this:

STEPNEY

STILES

DUNNE   FITZPATRICK   SADLER   BURNS

BEST   CRERAND   CHARLTON   KIDD

HERD

This system would have given Fitzpatrick and Stiles some

freedom to move forward with the ball, while neither Best nor Kidd would shirk their defensive duties. A 4-4-2 could also be fielded, and if so it would have looked like this:

STEPNEY
DUNNE STILES SADLER BURNS
FITZPATRICK CRERAND CHARLTON BEST
KIDD HERD

In blizzardous conditions (so bad Busby had considered asking for the game to be called off), arguably the most defensive shape he'd ever fielded as a Manchester United manager just about paid off for Busby, as they lost only 1-0 to qualify for the semi-final where they would face Real Madrid. The repeated absence of Law and Foulkes is noted – but for the first leg against the Spanish club Busby regarded as 'a brother', the United manager had the rare luxury of a near full-complement. When the time came to face their strongest opponent yet, he went with his most ambitious and adventurous team.

STEPNEY
DUNNE STILES SADLER BURNS
CRERAND CHARLTON
BEST KIDD LAW ASTON

That Aston's cross was marvellously volleyed in by Best in the first half, for the first leg's only goal, was a clear reward for that attacking approach. For the trip to Spain, Foulkes was back, but Law missed out, and the slender nature of the first leg win necessitated another pragmatic approach. Between the games, United had surrendered their league title, meaning that once again, realistic hopes of competing in this tournament lay in winning it.

Television coverage of the game had the proposed match

formation superimposed over the team as they lined up for their pre-match photograph on the Bernabeu pitch.

STEPNEY

DUNNE   BRENNAN   CRERAND

FOULKES   STILES

BEST   KIDD   CHARLTON   SADLER   ASTON

It should now be obvious that the telecasters had made an error – they made the same error with the Real Madrid team, listing the side in 1-11 in the old 3-2-5 formations. Miguel Muñoz, their manager, was widely accepted as one of the great football minds of the continent and his success in the 1960 European Cup final – the fifth in a row for the Spanish side – was seen as a landmark. He had played a 3-3-4 formation against Eintracht Frankfurt at Hampden Park and was enthralled, like all in attendance (including a young Alex Ferguson), by his team's 7-3 win. Muñoz's style was almost as undefinable as Busby's, relying heavily on the expression of his star names like Di Stefano and Puskas. But like Busby, the approach featured the manipulation of space and the creation of sharp passing combinations.

There were clearly defined spaces between the midfield and defence to allow those areas of the pitch to regain possession easily. Against Frankfurt, the system had worked to near-embarrassing effect, and largely because of the work rate of Di Stefano, who would drop back from his forward position into deeper midfield pockets, always ensuring his team had a numerical advantage. But Di Stefano was now retired, and Muñoz had eventually followed the trend and used a four-man defence.

In Spain, Busby certainly used a 4-5-1, though he was keen to mix it up. The key to this was David Sadler, who was wearing the number 10 shirt. This was how the team started:

1968: REDEMPTION

STEPNEY

BRENNAN FOULKES SADLER DUNNE

STILES

CRERAND CHARLTON

BEST KIDD ASTON

Stiles' starting role was in front of the defence when United had the ball – and behind Sadler and Foulkes when they did not. Sadler, of course, could move into a forward role to make this a 4-2-4. And Best and Aston could drop back to make a 4-5-1. This time pragmatism didn't work. Busby had even made the call to drop Burns and play Brennan, but his error in the 41st minute allowed Gento to make it 2-0, and give Madrid a 2-1 lead on aggregate. A fortuitous own goal brought United back into it a minute later – but before the break, Amancio lashed in a third.

At half-time, the away dressing room was silent. The team waited for Busby to tear into them. He didn't. They looked at Murphy, who was never shy. This time he did not speak. Just before the bell went to get the players back on to the pitch, the manager finally spoke. He reminded them it was their finest chance of getting to a European Cup final. Why weren't they attacking like they had done all season? Then came the sting. "You're letting me down, you're letting the club down, you're letting the supporters down. Go out and enjoy yourself. It's 3-2 on aggregate. If you get an early goal, you'll win."

Sadler was moved up front. His striker's instinct paid off in the 75th minute when he converted a Best flicked header to silence the crowd. It was 3-3 on aggregate – but Busby was right. United had the advantage, as in 1965, the away goals rule meant that they would qualify for the final if the score remained the same. With only 15 minutes left, the anxiety of the home support fed into the players. United capitalised immediately. Sadler moved back into defence; the shape facilitated one of those defenders to make a forward run if the opportunity arose. Nobody expected the player to do so would be Bill Foulkes, but when Best went on a mazy dribble and cut the ball back, it was Foulkes who popped up on the edge of the opponent's six yard box and, according to John Aston, used the side of his foot 'for the first time in his life' to steer the ball into the corner with all the guile of a Denis Law finish.

The significance of Foulkes, a Munich survivor (and, alongside Charlton, the only player left who had played against Real Madrid in 1957) scoring such a goal made it even more symbolic. With 12 minutes left, Madrid now had to score twice, and they couldn't muster a response.

If United were now feeling like destiny was smiling on them, they had two more reasons to feel a boost – the first that the final was being held at Wembley, and the second that their opponents would be Benfica, whose defenders were still having nightmares about George Best.

Law's knee injury would keep him out of the final – and Busby therefore decided to keep faith with the same system, and same players, he had played in Madrid. The television graphics displayed a 4-3-3 for United:

STEPNEY
BRENNAN FOULKES SADLER DUNNE
CRERAND CHARLTON STILES
BEST KIDD ASTON

This was technically the right shape, with a slight move and another caveat. The alteration was Stiles, who would, for the purposes of a diagram, be in the middle of the three – but in actuality he would be wherever Eusebio was as he was given the task of man-marking him. The caveat? Best would start from the right but had licence to roam. Benfica had a similar approach to man-marking, and at times it seemed as though they used two men on him. "Our defenders spent much time before the game preparing for George," recalled winger Antonio Simoes. "It was straightforward. Stay close. Don't let him get the ball. Our defenders were trying to anticipate the moves that were going to him. We knew if he caught the ball, especially with momentum, there would be a problem."

Those TV graphics showed Benfica in their correct 4-3-3 shape, with Eusebio in the middle of the attack. One area of the United team that was definitely fixed was John Aston, who was instructed to go at the right-back Adolfo. Aston was not a star name in this team but the Benfica side were well aware that danger lurked around every corner. "It was a very strong team," Simoes said of United. "They had four or five extremely good players and then the others were good players who were always willing to work extremely hard. That combination and balance in a team, even today, is the best you can get."

There did seem to be a more defined line between the machine and the stars than there had ever been at United. In Busby's first side there were star names such as Morris and Mitten. In the Babes there were Taylor and Edwards. Never, though, had there been such a pronounced disparity in terms of the headline names and the rest of the team. Best, Charlton and Law were quite evidently the star attractions – though this did not mean United carried a trio of queen bees with eight worker bees. The 'Holy Trinity' were just as integral to the smooth running of the Busby machine as any other player; they worked just as hard for the cause. The difference was, perhaps, time and fulfilment of promise. Best was in the middle of a year where, at the age of just 22, he too would claim the Ballon d'Or. A different thread of destiny might have offered the same fate to Edwards, Taylor and say Viollet or Colman.

It remains the case that the 1968 Manchester United team are the only team in history to field three Ballon d'Or winners, and even if this team were not seen to be quite as fluid as the Busby Babes, then that is surely just an acknowledgement of how exceptional they were and how exceptional that achievement was. Some of the football was as good as any Busby side. The game which decided the league title in 1967, a 6-1 win at Upton Park, was so outrageous that it seemed to surpass even Busby's vision of perfection; Best and Charlton scoring as United were 4-0 up by 25 minutes, and Law adding two in the second half. Law, of course, was missing through injury in May 1968.

How did the tactics for the long overdue European Cup final work? Well, if we accept that with true greatness it is possible for a man-marking plan to work well even if both players play well, Eusebio caused United numerous problems. It can also be said that there would have been further problems, had they not had Nobby Stiles man-marking him. Benfica's attention to Best, too, was largely successful. To rewatch the game now, Best's self-critical evaluation of his contribution seems extreme. He created danger and invoked a level of panic that was admirable considering he often had three Benfica players trailing his moves. And the man-marking presented an opening for either side to exploit if only they had a plan B. United did – John Aston terrorised Adolfo, putting in a man-of-the-match display on the wing.

After a stalemate first half, a breakthrough came early in the second period. Bobby Charlton headed in a fine Sadler cross and the idea of destiny once again crossed the mind of everyone inside Wembley Stadium. Jaime Graca hadn't read the script – and equalised in the 80th minute. In the 89th, Eusebio escaped the attention of Stiles to unleash a powerful drive at Stepney. A lesser goalkeeper might not have held the ball with such authority. It was a save that would be the most significant in the club's entire history. Shortly after, the full-time whistle was blown – extra-time awaited.

Elsewhere in London, printers began to work on a run of programmes for a replay two days later at Highbury. Those programmes would not be needed, but are now a highly sought-after item for collectors.

"I think everybody wanted to win for the boss," Shay Brennan admitted later. "It was his final more than the players." Busby and Murphy talked to their players. They asked them to look at the Benfica players, who looked exhausted. They were there to be beaten – and though United's players were no less tired, they suddenly had a spring in their step.

Early in extra-time, Best drifted inside to receive a long kick from Stepney. Benfica were unprepared. Best now had to demonstrate the sort of clinical edge that had become necessary in the catenaccio era. He nutmegged his marker, and drew the goalkeeper, knocking the ball almost playfully past him, the sight of him diving back in vain trying becoming as iconic as Best's own hand raised in celebration.

All of the great hallmarks of everything Busby had built descended upon Wembley in a wave of tangible sporting emotion. The two most famous players in his team had scored the goals. The second was delivered in distinctive style; it was deserving of the *Hollywoodball* tag given to the club by Harry Gregg, as was the entire story behind this journey. The goalscorers and the best player on the night were three of the eight players in the team who had been developed by the club. It was as close to the Crickmer, Rocca and Gibson dream as possible, and even beyond that, considering that European competition did not even exist in Rocca and Gibson's lifetime.

What remained? Victory, of course. But let it first be served in Busby fashion. Best's goal came in the 92nd minute. Within 60 seconds, Kidd, on his 19th birthday, had made it three when he headed in. In the 99th minute, Kidd fashioned space to cross for Charlton to expertly finish, giving a poetic end for the boy who had listened to half of Busby's first Wembley final on the radio, and then ran out on to a playing field to imagine scoring goals one day for Manchester United. The 4-1 final result, and the way it was delivered, was a complete fulfilment of every dream Matt Busby had envisioned for his club.

Then came the emotion. The acknowledgement of what it meant. The word Munich, never spoke of inside the club when it came to their present-day ambitions. With victory certain, the remaining period of extra-time played out in an overwhelming sense of sentiment, the knowledge that after the final whistle, United's present would face the past, literally, in the form of the families of those lost in Munich at the post-match dinner.

Alex Stepney remarked how Best had embodied the spirit of the Busby Babes both in the way in which he played his natural game and also in the way he scored the 'most important goal in Manchester United history', also remarking on how it was significant that the goal had come exercising the exact freedom Busby gave his players.

"There were so many memories," Jimmy Murphy recalled of the after-match. "Like Mr and Mrs Gladstone Edwards, the parents of Duncan, coming over to my table, 'Big Dunc would have liked this night. He always said United would win the European Cup, and we are so proud he was proved right.' I nodded, I couldn't say a word. My heart was too full just as it was when David Pegg's parents came over to join me and Mr and Mrs Colman. They were so pleased when Nobby Stiles came over. 'Eddie was my hero,' he said, and Mr Colman replied, 'Our Edward would have been so proud of the way you played Eusebio tonight, it was a wonderful performance Nobby.' You see, even in triumph there are always tears."

Embracing Munich in the club's ultimate victory was an admission that it had been a solemn, unspoken part of Manchester United's composition in every game ever since. It had been an evident point in the months after the disaster, with Jimmy Murphy using it to push the club forward, but had become one of those unwritten rules ever since.

It was part of the motivation for Busby and Murphy to continue in the years after the disaster. This became as significant a factor in the club's identity as any team shape, any playing philosophy. It became a reason to win while expressing style; it became a reason to keep going even in times of adversity – *especially* then. Can that be taught? Is it just something that is understood?

It became a reason those qualities should be expressed, especially in European competition. It was a privilege to have that opportunity at all. A privilege not to be taken for granted; and a privilege to follow these players who pioneered the club on their first adventures, so it should be incumbent upon any player fortunate enough to be able to represent the club in European competition to understand their privilege.

There are natural differences between Busby's pre- and post-Munich sides and the most obvious, particularly in these later years, was an evolution of style and the occasional pragmatic team shapes. There was no such concession in the earlier years but that's not to say that without Munich, Busby wouldn't have evolved, because all of the evidence suggests he would have. He changed formations to embrace the changes in the sport but never – as his last missive in the Bernabeu proved – told his team to play in a fashion any less than an adventurous manner befitting of the Manchester United he had built.

It was fitting that Busby's greatest triumph featured tangible elements of everything so exciting, so romantic, so tragic, and so very brilliant about his reign as Manchester United manager. That he delivered a four-goal final 20 years removed from his first – delivered with the same style and ethos, having completely changed the way his team were assembled – was proof enough of his sheer genius.

*****

Matt Busby was knighted over the summer of 1968. He announced his intention to retire in January 1969, and handpicked his replacement – Wilf McGuinness, the United reserve team coach, who had been forced to retire early from playing. Before that, there was one more new adventure even for someone as experienced as Busby.

In 1960, the first edition of the Intercontinental Cup was held, pitting the winners of the European Cup against the winners of the South American Copa Libertadores, and over the following years the matches became increasingly violent. The Brazilian FA even refused to allow their teams to participate after the perceived rough treatment of their players in the 1966 World Cup. United's opponents in the 1969 Intercontinental Cup would be Estudiantes of Argentina.

The first leg was played in Buenos Aires and Busby – aiming to ease diplomatic relations, with a bad-tempered match already forecast in the media – invited his opponents to a reception dinner.

1968: REDEMPTION

They declined – agitating the United manager. The team for this first competitive match against a club outside of Europe was:

STEPNEY
DUNNE STILES FOULKES BURNS
MORGAN CRERAND CHARLTON BEST
SADLER LAW

The villain of the piece was Nobby Stiles, who had been involved in altercations with Antonio Rattín of Argentina at the previous World Cup. Alf Ramsey had described the Argentina side as 'animals' and so the domestic press were keen to remind everyone that Otto Gloria, the Benfica manager, had described Stiles as 'brutal' for his zealous marking of Eusebio. Stiles was repeatedly targeted by the home side, fouled no less than 10 times, and when he retaliated he was the one sent off.

United lost 1-0 and were keen to return to Manchester. A few weeks later, in the return, Busby again went with a 4-4-2/4-2-4. Sadler moved into the back-line, and Kidd came back to play up front. The rematch was even more violent. Law, already suffering with the long-standing knee complaint, was kicked off the pitch and had to come off before the break. By that point, the South Americans had taken a 2-0 aggregate lead – Juan Ramon Veron, father of Juan Sebastian, the future United player – scoring the first goal of the family at Old Trafford.

George Best, who had incited Carlos Bilardo in the first leg with some showmanship, was sent off after fighting with Tato Medina, who was also dismissed. Willie Morgan's late strike was inconsequential. In the tunnel Stepney confronted Bilardo who he felt to be the chief instigator, to the chagrin of Busby, who felt the club had been let down – but only because the goalkeeper had been caught on camera striking his opponent.

So, United had come out losers in this final pioneering exercise of Matt Busby to pit his club against global opposition. He had entrusted them to play their natural way, hoping against a realistic expectation of how the two legs would pan out. He probably anticipated the cynical nature in which the tie would unfold, but did not wish for his team to lower themselves.

To close out the Busby era, his final fling with Europe saw a 2-1 aggregate defeat in the semi-final of the European Cup to AC Milan; that too was bad tempered, and that too saw the United boss disregard any previous caution, and try and go out in style.

This is a tactical and spiritual history of Manchester United and not exactly linear – so it shouldn't be a spoiler to say that the Wilf McGuinness era lasted approximately 18 months and by December 1970, Matt Busby had resumed control on a temporary basis.

Busby's *actual* final game in charge was a 4-3 win at Manchester City's Maine Road, fitting for a variety of reasons; his team hitting a three-goal blast in the first 30 minutes, through Charlton, Law and Best, the latter scoring again in the second half. The team that day:

STEPNEY
O'NEIL JAMES SADLER BURNS
CRERAND GOWLING CHARLTON
KIDD LAW BEST

One final roll with the punches as Busby fielded a 4-3-3, and was still able to deliver a team that played in his inimitable style, still with eight players developed by the club. Matt Busby – Sir Matt Busby, now, so impactful had his tenure been – may have recognised that his own time to be a football manager had been and gone, but he had implemented a structure and a theory, an identity, that would be timeless.

12

SIR MATT BUSBY IN INTERVIEW, 1983

MY FIRST CUP FINAL AGAINST BLACKPOOL WAS ONE OF the great matches, because there was so much talent there, and individuality at the right time, and the players displaying their natural ability, and it created this tremendous thing.

Blackpool were a great side too with Mortensen and Matthews. Mortensen gave them the lead towards half-time. I remember at half-time Johnny Carey saying, 'we should keep playing'. I said, 'yes, if we keep playing, we're going to make chances'. We finished up winning 4-2. So, this was the first trophy. Every time you win something, it's something you're proud of, it's something you feel you get a great deal of satisfaction from.

I realised that football was not only an English game, not only a British game, but a world game. I'd got in mind that we should enter Europe. And despite the opposition from the Football League at the time, the FA understood and they had no objection. Mr Hardman was the chairman and the board of directors decided that we should enter Europe.

The first game we played in Europe was against Anderlecht. It was a new procedure, and it created another side of the game, which was exciting. Of course we won 2-0, which was a good start. When we came back, we played the match at Maine Road because of the bomb damage at Old Trafford. We had an amazing night, and the score was 10-0. We started getting tremendous crowds, probably 60,000 people. We displayed football of the highest quality and scored goals with it.

That was our first experience in Europe, and then the next round was in Dortmund. I always remember it was a terrible night. The conditions the players went through... despite the fact that it was a very big trial for us, we managed to get by. We managed to win, 3-2 here and a 0-0 in Germany. I always remember, at the end itself, [the actor] Albert Finney had flown out because he was a bit of a United fan. He went to the match, I saw him there and it was nice to see that he was interested in the club.

I went to Brussels to see Honved play Bilbao. At the time, I was very interested in signing Puskas. He eventually went to Real Madrid but he was the only foreign player I wanted. Bilbao won the tie and we went there for the first leg. I felt that probably the match wouldn't be played, but nevertheless, the referee decided otherwise. The snow was blowing, and the rain was tremendous. Early on, things went really wrong for us. We were losing 5-2 or something like that.

Liam Whelan picked up a ball in the middle of the field, and he was very clever at feinting... he started going this and that way, and I kept the feeling to myself. Billy, pass it, give it to someone. And, on he went, and sent this one the wrong way, and that one the *wrong way, and finished up by side-footing in the back of the net. So, it made it 5-3, and it made it appear as though we had a slight chance at Maine Road. What an amazing night that was, because we were still two down on aggregate. Despite us having a lot of the game early on, it wasn't breaking kindly for us. We got one goal, two goals and of course, we finished up winning the match. This was tremendous. It was an experience for the players, too, who were in the main very young. They didn't sit back. They went forward and forward and forward all the time.*

And in our next experience, we landed at Real Madrid who were European champions. And this was the test, it was the first test, because actually our team was still very immature, we'd just changed over from the days of Johnny Carey, Stan Pearson, Henry Cockburn and all the rest. This was the first experience for them, and against the great Di Stefano.

I went to see them play Nice. I well remember the match itself and after it, I came back and made a statement, that I had seen one of the greatest players in Di Stefano. And subsequent to that, the two teams got together at the end of the first leg of the semi-final. And Di Stefano came up to me and he says, 'I want to thank you for your kind words'. He said, 'I think I'll make you my new press representative.'

Before the match, we had two or three players with upset tummies, Eddie Colman was definitely one. We had to go on, because at that time it was only one substitute. We held on until late in the game, and then we finished losing 3-1.

You still felt we had a chance, and it was back at Old Trafford and a full house of 60,000 people. We went at them, and then on a breakaway, they scored two quick goals, but we still went at them. We eventually made it 2-1, made it two each, but it was rather just too late. Despite the fact that it was disappointing, I felt that we needed this sort of experience, because the team was very young.

Still, we won the league again. The 1957 FA Cup final against Aston Villa was, I think, one of the great tragedies, because at that time, there was no question who was going to win. I felt it, and on the Saturday morning, I checked up, the players were all right, and I thought, 'This is it'. Sadly, after eight or ten minutes, our goalkeeper Ray Wood was tackled by Peter McParland and fractured his cheekbone. We carried on from there, but it's very difficult to fill a gap when it's a goalkeeper. Jackie Blanchflower came in and did a very, very wonderful job really, but it meant we lost a player. We had to struggle and in the end, we lost 2-1, which is very, very sad, because really, that was the year we should have won the double.

A year later we played in the 1958 FA Cup final, and of course, the disaster had happened, sadly, and Jimmy Murphy had taken over. I turned up at Wembley on sticks and saw the game. It was a great performance, and it was sad to see them lose.

Moving on to the 1963 final, at that time, we were in the process of rebuilding again, and we were having a worrying time in the league. We weren't the favourites. But Law, Crerand, Charlton, Foulkes, all the lads put on a tremendous performance there. It was a great win.

After all the problems we had, that were terribly sad, and always, they are with me, we arrived at the European Cup final. Benfica had some famous players and we had a great, great match. In extra-time George Best dummied the defenders, turning them inside out once or twice, and we finished up winning the European Cup, which, I felt, was wonderful for me, but it was wonderful for the club, and the players, because of the sad moments we had, the fact that we had achieved this wonderful ambition, and achieved this wonderful pinnacle. I felt I had achieved all my ambitions by winning the European Cup.

I've been blessed to work with so many great players and great teams. It is very difficult for me to pick between them because, despite their own natural individual ability, they all played for one another, and in each era they were all the same in that regard. To choose which one was the greatest is the most difficult decision for me to make. I could say Duncan Edwards was the greatest, but so many of the players I've had the good fortune to be with are some of the greatest players you could wish to see. You never hear any mention of Tony Dunne, for instance. There's a number of players of that calibre, who were outstanding, that it's just so hard.

Looking back 30 years, I think probably in the earlier days, players were encouraged to express themselves without fear. I think probably as time has gone on, the defensive side of it has become more important rather than the fact of creating and going with a mind to score goals. In a way it developed into a little bit of a game of fear. I think there was more freedom to play in these early days than there is now. There's good coaching and there's bad coaching. Good coaching is creation and building and encouraging the ability of that player to play. There's no fear about that.

13

HOLLYWOOD OF FOOTBALL

LET US TAKE A BRIEF PAUSE BEFORE WE PROCEED, AND find a concise way to describe the attributes of a great Sir Matt Busby team. The tactical differences between 1946 and 1970 are already explained, however, Busby's intelligence within this should be acknowledged. Whether it was overlapping full-backs and asking half-backs to cover the space, whether it was asking his centre-forward to drop back years before the Hungarians ran riot at Wembley, or whether it was naturally settling on different disciplines for his right and left half-backs, it was clear that Busby was well ahead of his time.

The style of play centred around movement of players and movement of the ball, with an emphasis on chemistry learned through familiarity. The theory of those talented players being younger men loyal to the cause was another sound idea. Time can not be cheated, it cannot be bought, and it has an immense value, as Busby was able to affirm in the mid-1950s. His retraining of talented players into different positions was ingenious, and was some 20 years ahead of the Michels/Cruyff approach to doing the same thing. The occasional switch – such as playing Duncan Edwards at inside-forward and then packing the midfield in the second half at Dortmund – also saw Busby showcase his nous, but United were never better than when they were told to enjoy their game.

The rhythm of the system was so perfect that it accommodated an individualist, be that Duncan Edwards or George Best, who would still work tirelessly as one of the 11 and yet have a unique star quality all of their own.

And, of course, there was then the impact of Munich; where the team were decimated, but continued to fight, and Jimmy Murphy's battle through the grief seemed to introduce a new strain to United's character – that as shown by Duncan Edwards in the semi-final defeat to Real Madrid in 1957. At the time, his refusal to accept the defeat was seen as extraordinary by his team-mates. Following Edwards' death, refusal to accept defeat transmitted itself to the United team as a silent burden. It was never more obvious than in the 1958 FA Cup run when United made it all the way to the final. It was never more romantic than in 1968 when Bill Foulkes stormed up the pitch to equalise against Real Madrid. It was never more poetic than when Bobby Charlton, a survivor of Munich, scored in the Wembley final against Benfica.

Busby's reign as Manchester United manager was unique; he had given to them an identity that could not be replicated because the journey was so extraordinary. It was probably due to the tragedy and the romance that his tactical innovation is not appreciated as much as it should be, but there is no mistaking that his was a philosophy that bore a close resemblance to the Hungarian style well before the Match of the Century. One could argue Busby's approach combined elements of the Hungarian style and that of the Dutch team from a couple of decades later – that there was such a strong emphasis on passing and moving, dropping into different positions, and the tireless work at making sure players were trained in multiple positions, that what he had at Manchester United was, at its peak (1957 and 1968), a combination of the two greatest strategies the game has known. Adding the stardust of the maverick individual and still being able to maintain the same magical flow was possibly the quintessential ingredient, the little bit of Hollywood, as Harry Gregg called it.

It was though, a system impossible to replicate, because that specific journey, and the romance and tragedy of it all, could never be recreated. The challenge for Busby's successors would be in trying to live up to what came before. Could they be their own man? Could Old Trafford be receptive to a new kind of football? If not, why? Well, these were the questions and challenges that would lie in wait forevermore.

14

WILF McGUINNESS

PERHAPS IT IS FITTING TO START THE EXAMINATION of Wilf McGuinness' spell as Manchester United manager with the words of Sir Matt Busby, taken from his announcement to the press in January 1969. Busby informed the assembled journalists that he would retire at the end of the 1968/69 season; and he elaborated on both his decision and his desired blueprint – not necessarily for how Manchester United ought to play, but for the qualities he desired in the actual manager.

"It will come as a great surprise to a great many people that I have relinquished control of Manchester United," he said. "But it will come probably as a greater shock to everybody to know why I have done it. I don't mind admitting that the reason is: I am losing my grip! That is the honest reason after months of heart searching. I have not had enough time with the players, and yet, in soccer, players are the all-essential beings. Therefore a manager must be with them and must live with them and know them. Over the last few months this has not been possible. Therefore it is time for me to go. The decision was inevitable. Manchester United need new blood, a new supply of ideas.

"The big thing now is for Manchester United, which I believe to be the greatest club in the world, to appoint my successor. I have very definite ideas on the subject. He must be: 1 – Young, in his early 30s, up to the absolute age of 45. 2 – He must have experience because Manchester United are not in a position to experiment. 3 – He must be a manager who has proved himself to be a leader, who commands respect. 4 – He must have the human touch. The advice he gives will have to be the best for the players, but, more important, the best for the club. 5 – He must NEVER, EVER, make a promise without ever being able to fulfil his words.

"There is a sixth quality which Manchester United now expect… the man chosen will have to be right in his decisions and though he will be given time to prove that he is right this is a final condition… until he is dreadfully wrong. And I hope my man will NEVER be dreadfully wrong. The man who takes on Manchester United has a difficult job. He must have success in terms of championships or cups, otherwise he is going to be deemed a failure. Frankly, it is not the sort of job that I might have taken on 30 years ago. So, we need a new face, we need new life in the club, we need new blood."

There was a tacit admission that Busby, having moved with the times so successfully, realised time and patience were needed. Having built three great United sides, the outgoing manager knew it was the right moment to give his successor the best opportunity. Don Revie, Jock Stein and Dave Sexton were all rumoured targets for the position, but in April, it was announced that the job would be given to Wilf McGuinness. That job would be chief coach, with Busby staying on as general manager, taking some of the duties that may once have been done by Walter Crickmer. This was a

Busby concept – so how much of what he had originally said, in his six criteria, did the new appointment satisfy? Point one, and possibly point four. Points two and three were not McGuinness' fault and points five and six were arguably the responsibility of the club more than any manager. What is obvious is that even though McGuinness was Busby's choice, he was not the person the outgoing manager was describing when he made those January comments.

Busby also acknowledged the projected scale of the build. "Manchester United are not just a football club but a kind of institution," he said, "So many things need attention that I felt my move to general manager was a step in the right direction."

Another change to the footballing structure was Jimmy Murphy's position. How he would be deployed was unclear – but it wouldn't be as assistant manager. "It was no surprise," Murphy admitted after Busby's announcement. "Matt and I talked it over for a long time. The new team manager will be in a tracksuit working with the players … the new man can count on my full backing. The years cannot take away knowledge and this is where perhaps I will be able to help most."

The announcement of McGuinness' appointment came on April 18th. He had been forced to retire at the age of 22 but had always shown strong leadership skills so had been hired as a trainer assisting Jack Crompton with the reserve team. The English FA appointed him as youth team coach and training assistant to Alf Ramsey for the 1966 World Cup. Now only 31, McGuinness had supreme confidence that he was prepared to take the job.

He elaborated on Murphy's position. "He didn't fill a specific role," he admitted, "but he was always on hand, imparting his wisdom, talking to the scouts, giving his opinion on young players, generally helping to make sure that things ran smoothly."

Still, McGuinness admitted that he didn't utilise that experience as much as he should have. He retained Jack Crompton as trainer and felt the players had 'given their all' in the first pre-season. McGuinness made no instant changes though he had advised Busby in the previous season that Jimmy Rimmer was worthy of a chance. Rimmer was given a run of games, and Alex Stepney was dropped, immediately causing a minor issue.

McGuinness' first game in charge was at Crystal Palace. The team that day:

RIMMER

DUNNE FOULKES SADLER BURNS

CRERAND CHARLTON

MORGAN KIDD LAW BEST

There were no profound changes; United came from behind twice to draw 2-2. That was a disappointing start, and losing 2-0 in the first home game to Everton was even worse, but a 4-1 home defeat to Southampton induced early alarm bells. Bill Foulkes, now 37, made the last of 688 appearances as he was given a torrid time by Ron Davies. McGuinness, having worked with the reserve team, knew there wasn't a strong enough replacement, but felt young Paul Edwards was the most ready.

The headlines for the following game at Everton centred around the dropping of Charlton and Law, although Dunne was also a big name absentee. McGuinness insisted Law was injured, but admitted Charlton was dropped for tactical reasons.

"The centre of the pitch had been a pretty frantic place, very crowded and with everything moving at 100 miles an hour, and I felt Bobby had been bypassed," McGuinness explained. "I went for a completely new formation. This involved Don Givens as an out-and-out spearhead, with Brian Kidd playing just behind him, and a midfield of Morgan, Crerand, Best and Johnny junior, in which the two wingers, Willie and John, played deeper and narrower than usual... I didn't mention to Matt my intention of changing virtually half the side, and when I did let him have the line-up he made no attempt to interfere. But I had talked it over with my trainers, Jack Crompton and John Aston senior, who agreed that some sort of drastic action was needed."

STEPNEY

FITZPATRICK EDWARDS SADLER BURNS

MORGAN CRERAND BEST ASTON

KIDD

GIVENS

It wasn't just a disaster because the game was lost 3-0 – it was that all of the goals came in the first 25 minutes, suggesting a significant issue in the middle of defence. Busby, as general manager, was in charge of transfers. He suggested Ian Ure, and the Arsenal defender was signed for £80,000. McGuinness expressed concern that since the physio Ted Dalton had passed away, neither Laurie Mawson, or Laurie Brown, who succeeded Dalton, had the requisite experience to identify the seriousness of injuries. Ure had chronic knee issues and although his introduction to the team saw an immediate improvement, soon enough he was struggling, as was Stiles, and as was Law.

There was some progress. McGuinness went back to a familiar 4-2-4, with Crerand and Charlton in midfield and Best starting from the left. United even won 4-1 at Anfield just before Christmas, inviting critics to ask why they couldn't play like that every week. Privately, McGuinness still dared to dream that he would one day win the Intercontinental Cup as Manchester United, holding that as his ambition as it was 'the one peak which even Sir Matt Busby had not scaled', and would of course mean that the club had won another league title and European Cup.

The league title would have to wait, but McGuinness seemed to have better luck in the cups. There was an unfortunate semi-final exit to Manchester City in the League Cup and then an epic battle with Leeds went all the way to a second replay at the same stage of the FA Cup. Billy Bremner's early goal settled in favour of Don Revie's team; and team is an apt word, for it was the manner of their cohesion which had many observing that Busby's approach of encouraging expression of individuals was outdated.

The first replay had been played at Villa Park and was preceded by controversy when George Best had taken a lady to his room on the day of the game. As it was a breach of club discipline, McGuinness discussed the matter with Busby, who asked if he still wanted Best to play in the match. The coach said yes – but Best played poorly – and when the news of the incident leaked, it did not reflect well on any party.

United finished eighth after McGuinness' first full season in charge. He had made no significant changes in shape, although he had tried a couple, and no significant changes in personnel, although again he had not been completely shy in that regard. The summer of 1970 was spent with United linked to a whole host of names. Malcolm Macdonald, Don Davies, Mick Mills and Colin Todd were just four names McGuinness coveted, but in the end, he was told that finances were too tight.

That summer, the fifth edition of David Meek's Manchester United Football Club book was published. In it, Meek praised McGuinness' 'bold sweep' of transfer-listing Denis Law and Don Givens, giving nine players free transfers and signalling Foulkes' retirement. Meek wrote of youth being 'no handicap' for the manager. "The biggest question mark placed against his appointment," he wrote, "was concerning these not-so-young players and whether he could command the respect of men who were his contemporaries."

There was some suggestion this was an issue. Willie Morgan never felt convinced and in dropping so many of his pals, McGuinness had possibly alienated players who would not be naturally inclined to be allies.

Internal restructuring over the summer saw McGuinness given a vote of confidence with the role of 'team manager'. Joe Armstrong retired at the age of 76 and John Aston Snr became chief scout. Bill Foulkes was placed in complete control of coaching for all the young professionals and amateurs, a sort of proving ground to succeed Jack Crompton. Laurie Brown was officially made the physiotherapist, Ken Merrett was named Les Olive's assistant, and Ken Ramsden was appointed manager of the ticket office.

October 1970 saw United's 3000th competitive game. And it was a memorable one. The League Cup fourth round tie went down in history because of George Best's 70th-minute strike, where he evaded a thigh-high challenge from Ron Harris and rounded the goalkeeper to score one of Old Trafford's greatest goals. United were through, and would beat Crystal Palace in the quarter-final, but were eliminated again at the semi-final stage – this time by Aston Villa over two legs. Even more frustratingly, Brian Kidd had given his team the lead in the second leg at Villa Park, the team for which read:

RIMMER

FITZPATRICK URE SADLER DUNNE

CRERAND CHARLTON

MORGAN KIDD LAW BEST

As for the changes in between the games – Charlton, Crerand,

Dunne and Law were four big names who were all dropped and recalled, and Brennan, Stiles, Foulkes and Stepney three who completely fell out of favour. Brennan and McGuinness were best man at each other's wedding and it would not have been a pleasant conversation for the team manager to inform his pal that his time to leave had come. The same could be said for the conversation between McGuinness and Matt Busby the day after Boxing Day 1970. United had drawn 4-4 at Derby County, an entertaining match no doubt, but the team were now languishing close to the relegation places in the league.

The board decided Matt Busby would take charge of the first team once again. His objective? To gain a respectable position and "to get Manchester United playing like Manchester United again."

McGuinness was offered his old job of reserve team manager, which he initially accepted, before deciding before the end of the season that it was not the right decision.

Is 18 months a strong enough sample size to truly analyse a footballing philosophy? Let us consider the observations of David Meek. "Sir Matt was striving for continuity when he promoted McGuinness," he wrote. "His policy has always been to try and keep the organisation of Old Trafford with the family... in the end the idea went sour, but it was much nearer succeeding than most would give credit for. It needed just one lucky break in one of the three semi-finals to have given McGuinness a team spirit that reaching a final would have created."

That much is true; and the idea of a young coach coming into a team that had more success than any and trying to assume authority was always going to be difficult. Maybe if he had been backed with another significant signing it may have made a difference in a semi-final and then a final. That might have inspired a little more confidence from those senior United players.

By all accounts McGuinness' way of playing football was heavily influenced by Busby – McGuinness regarded Busby as a deity, a respect that continued long after 1970. Even in his autobiography, when most observers felt Busby's signing of Ian Ure was too involved, McGuinness accepted that was part of his responsibility, and insisted that there was no interference with the team's style of play. His tinkering with the system had not been successful, but it did at least prove he was a modern coach with different ideas. More than anything, with the McGuinness reign, it seemed to be a desertion of luck at the crucial moments that defined the tenure rather than a coach out of his depth. Crucially, it is worth noting that this hierarchical idea was Busby's, and that there was nobody on the staff better placed than McGuinness to be the chief coach. There could have been nobody who loved Manchester United more, nobody who understood the journey of the club more, and no young coach on the staff better educated and therefore better prepared for this particular role in this particular set-up that Busby had created.

After the manager had left, one player anonymously told the *Sunday Times* that McGuinness had 'no personality' (though as anyone who has ever had the fortune of spending time with the man will attest, this could not be further from the truth). "He did not understand that the team he was controlling needed handling in a special way," said the player, "I believe that we would have been screwed even if Wilf had a million squid to spend."

David Meek opined that 'with that kind of attitude it was hardly surprising that there was not a total commitment from all the players', and there seems to be some truth to that, especially considering the quite transparent fact that it had been Busby in charge of the transfer policy. One might say that United and the hierarchy – if it was Busby or Edwards – were just as responsible for the poor 18 months in that they never gave the manager full control, they continued to make huge decisions without his genuine consultation, and yet it was he and not they who paid the consequence.

In the time before the end of the season, Busby admitted: "Apart from Munich, I don't think I have had a period of heavier pressure." A clear indication that things had to change. Busby recognised that too, deciding that the permanent successor would have to come from outside the club and would have to be given full control.

15

FRANK O'FARRELL

THE MAN SIR MATT BUSBY ORIGINALLY APPROACHED to become Manchester United manager after Wilf McGuinness was Celtic boss Jock Stein. The Scot had enjoyed tremendous success in Glasgow, winning six consecutive league titles, five league cups and, most significantly of all, the 1967 European Cup, breaking Inter's stranglehold on the trophy. Busby had been tipped off by Pat Crerand that Stein had interest in managing in England so a meeting was set up. In it, Busby insisted that many of United's long-serving staff members should be kept on. The 49-year-old Stein had reservations about this but had also gone into the meeting needing to be convinced anyway as his family were settled in Scotland. Upon realising that he wouldn't even have the full control as a manager, Stein rejected the offer.

We could take another full book looking at the number of people who were linked to the job and how their philosophy would have fitted in at Old Trafford. When Celtic defeated the notoriously defensive Inter Milan to win Europe's biggest prize, they did so, according to Stein, "playing football. Pure, beautiful, inventive football" in a straight 4-2-4 formation, coming back from a 1-0 half-time deficit to win late on.

Back at Old Trafford, there were a number of factors that made Frank O'Farrell seem a sensible choice after Jock Stein had rejected the opportunity. Born in Cork, he had those Celtic connections, and he was also a renowned former wing-half of international reputation. At the age of 43, he fit neatly into Busby's wishlist, and had been raised through that famous West Ham academy, when Ted Fenton's wish of developing 'not only good footballers, but good men' seemed to marry perfectly with what was going on at Old Trafford. Fenton encouraged the players to spend as much time together off the pitch as possible in order to discuss their own ideas of playing football and was one of the domestic coaches to embrace the Hungarian way of playing the game.

After retiring as a player, O'Farrell had built his reputation at Weymouth and Torquay United before being appointed manager of Leicester City in December 1968. He opted for former West Ham team-mate Malcolm Musgrove as his assistant. Leicester had been relegated at the end of that first season, ironically enough at Old Trafford in what was originally intended to be Matt Busby's last game in charge. But O'Farrell rebuilt the Foxes, taking them to the 1969 FA Cup final, and in 1971, taking them to the Second Division championship and back into the top flight.

What was his philosophy of football? O'Farrell inherited a team that played with a target man, Andy Lochhead, and played a traditional long-ball style. He did not make a major change until the start of the 1970/71 campaign, at which point he moved to a 4-2-4 after signing two combative midfielders, Willie Carlin and Bobby Kellard. The Leicester manager often complained about the state of the Filbert Street pitch, insisting it hindered his team from playing the sort of free-passing movement he wanted them to.

O'Farrell's Leicester were a counter-attacking team that was rapid on the break, thus relying heavily on their wingers, Ally Brown and Rodney Fern. Counter-attacking, by its very nature, is a reactive strategy, but still proactive as it demonstrates intelligent game management from managers who might usually be the underdogs.

O'Farrell became popular with the Leicester support and was very approachable; after securing promotion with a 1-0 win at Bristol City, one supporter, Pete Johnson, waited after the match to thank him. "I shook his hand as he was about to get on the team bus," Johnson recalls. "He thanked me for my good wishes on Leicester City's promotion, and hoped that he had brought enjoyment to the supporters. He wished me a safe journey home."

One can imagine how a man who acted with such dignity would have felt when he discovered the truth about the offer to become manager of Manchester United. That he considered the offer at all was only because he was out of contract at Leicester and waiting for a new proposal; he insisted if he had been under contract, he would not have considered an invitation to manage elsewhere. But out of contract he was, and when Matt Busby made an unofficial offer of £12,000 and a five-year contract, O'Farrell played dumb and asked his chairman, Les Chapman, if he could speak to United. That formal meeting was attended by Busby and Louis Edwards at a lay-by on a 'little B road' between Manchester and Derby. When O'Farrell asked Busby to repeat the offer, and Busby said £12,000, Edwards interjected to say the proposal was supposed to be £15,000.

Nonetheless, O'Farrell accepted the job; he was informed that a new office was being built for him at Old Trafford, down the corridor from the manager's office. "Never one to not state my case," O'Farrell later explained, "I said I needed Busby's manager's office because that's where people would expect to find the manager."

It was agreed; and Busby also relinquished his 'general manager' title, joining the board alongside Louis Edwards' son Martin. Malcolm Musgrove would follow O'Farrell, meaning a more permanent answer had to be found for Jimmy Murphy – he was paid five years' salary and formally given a scouting job.

O'Farrell was not about to make huge changes right away, and he attributed that approach to starting management at a much lower level. "It helps to learn the business," he said. "The first time you pick a team and leave someone out who thinks he should be in is a problem and there is too much to learn. You have to learn to use authority, to manage people, to make decisions, to spend money. I think it best to acquire a sense of values when you are spending £250 on a player before you might be faced with spending £250,000."

O'Farrell insisted he had no 'preconceived ideas' over any individual at the club and described effective communication as one of the 'most important things'. "I want to get my way of doing things over as quickly as possible, " he said. "If someone beside you already knows your ways, it is a tremendous advantage. Malcolm Musgrove and I have this partnership. He knows I expect a high degree of dedication. Football has never been more competitive and the sooner the machine at Old Trafford is ticking over at our management level, the sooner the players and the team will tick over as well."

United had finished eighth for a second year in a row and while it could be said that the players who had started to replace the outgoing European Cup winners had shoes that were too big to fill, those remaining from that triumph were proving just as big a headache. Brian Kidd reacted angrily to Busby's return, feeling that he was being humiliated after being left out of the team completely for the trip to Crystal Palace in April.

"Does Sir Matt think he can trample all over me until a new manager takes over?" Kidd complained. "If he does, he can think again. I have got my pride… A move can be the only solution for me. Sir Matt has completely washed all my feelings for Manchester United out of me and I can tell you that takes some doing."

Kidd was recalled before the end of the season – scoring in a 3-2 win over Ipswich, Busby's last official Old Trafford match as manager. The home crowd were beginning to become unsettled and demanded transfers, but Busby's brief return and the resurgence in form suggested that much better could still come from this squad. This in spite of Kidd's open desire to leave, Best's increasing issues with his personal life, Law's injury problems, and Charlton's age (he was now almost 34 and had just made his 664th appearance for the club, bringing him to just 24 behind Bill Foulkes, the club's record appearance maker).

The O'Farrell and Musgrove approach to training was not a case of reinventing the wheel. There were no significant changes beyond the simple fact that the pair did not have a previous association with United, so the existing players were keen to impress their new manager.

In fact, the most notable change came about as a consequence of George Best being, if you can believe it, too good. On the indoor sessions on the shale surface at The Cliff, nobody could get the ball from him – so a rule was introduced that players could only have two touches. Best, ever the inventor, would use his second touch to play the ball off the legs of an opponent to beat the rule!

O'Farrell's first match as United boss was at the same venue as McGuinness' last, and yielded the same result – a draw at Derby. This time he could play his favoured 4-2-4 from the off.

FOOTBALL, TAUGHT BY MATT BUSBY

STEPNEY
O'NEIL   JAMES   SADLER   DUNNE
GOWLING   CHARLTON
MORGAN   KIDD   LAW   BEST

Over time, the shape of this team would change slightly, with Morgan dropping back to form a midfield three, and Kidd, Law and Best interchanging in a fluid front three. The front three were not told which position to pick up, the only rule being that if one player drifted, then another should pick up the vacant space to maintain the shape. Significantly, the United players were not instructed to play a counter-attacking style – the emphasis was always about them imposing themselves on the game.

This had not really changed from the Busby or McGuinness days and even when attention was dedicated to opponents, this too was familiar for the players, with the drills generally being set plays and instructing the best headers of the ball to pick up the best headers on the opposition team.

United went 2-0 up at the Baseball Ground before surrendering the lead in the second. Due to crowd trouble at the end of the previous season, United were ordered to play their first two home games at a neutral venue (Stoke and Liverpool were chosen), meaning it wasn't until the seventh game of the campaign that O'Farrell took charge at Old Trafford. In that match, Best scored the only goal against Ipswich – coming direct from a corner – but his first impression on his new manager had not been as positive.

Before a ball had even been kicked that season, Best had been on a television show speaking about how women would throw themselves at him. When quizzed on this, O'Farrell was flummoxed that a football manager would face such questions. In his second game, a 3-2 win at Chelsea, Best had been sent off on an evening described as 'soccer's night of shame' with numerous red cards and crowd incidents. The increase in red cards was due to new, tougher rules clamping down on bad tackles – although Best was sent from the field for apparently swearing at the referee. He protested his innocence and Morgan covered for him at a hearing, meaning United's best player escaped punishment; and how O'Farrell needed him.

Over the next few weeks, Best was in outrageous form, a purple patch to match any in his career. A couple of weeks after the corner against Ipswich, Best hit a seminal hat-trick against West Ham. Two weeks later he scored a memorable solo goal against Sheffield United. Three weeks later, he scored the only goal of the game at Newcastle, prior to which he had been the speculated target of an IRA threat at the match. And, in late November, he scored another remarkable hat-trick in a 5-2 win at Southampton.

An entertaining 3-2 win over Nottingham Forest a week later, in which Law scored and Kidd scored twice, put United five points clear at the top of the table. It prompted a December article in the *Daily Mirror* celebrating United's return to glory and O'Farrell's status as the best coach in the country. A diagram examining the team's adaptation since the start of the season was shown, which had the team laid out in a 4-3-3. The most notable aspect of that was Morgan, who had "successfully converted from a winger to a midfield player at the start of this season." Law was said to be 'revitalised' on the right of attack whilst Charlton had 'benefited from O'Farrell's decision to strengthen the middle of the field'.

All of this was true, and even Kidd seemed to be enjoying himself, with the introduction of 17-year-old Sammy McIlroy adding extra unpredictability in the front line. However, despite United's free-scoring forwards, the defence seemed to be an issue.

United had shipped 24 goals in 20 games and in eight of those had conceded two or more.

Best's form invited more attention on and off the pitch. December was a difficult month where the pitches and the aggressive tackles took their toll on his mood, causing him to drink more and miss training. O'Farrell took an immediate hard line, dropping Best for the home game with Wolves in January. But the visitors won 3-1, proving this was not a chance the manager could take. Best was recalled, but with the cracks beginning to show, United's form dropped.

A 5-1 defeat at Leeds was alarming and after the match Jack Charlton remarked that United players were 'glamour boys left behind by the legend', while United conceded they would have to invest in the transfer market.

One player for each end of the pitch was brought in. Aberdeen's forthright young captain Martin Buchan arrived to help shore up the defence, and Ian Storey-Moore, the thrilling winger, was signed from Nottingham Forest to both relieve some of the attention on Best and to help O'Farrell move to a 4-2-4. The boss still occasionally used the three-man midfield – notably at Coventry, in a great game where all of United's goals came from outside the box in a 3-2 win – but did also toy with the quite bold idea of dropping Morgan to play his preferred shape and have Best operating from the right. The 4-0 win over Crystal Palace on March 25th, 1972, saw United line up like this:

STEPNEY
O'NEIL BUCHAN JAMES DUNNE
GOWLING CHARLTON
BEST KIDD LAW STOREY-MOORE

The second half of the season saw a collapse that was so dramatic that United finished in eighth for the third season in a row. This was still a fairly competitive league, so their swing from being five points clear saw them just 10 behind eventual champions Derby in one of the most entertaining seasons in British football history.

At one point, it seemed as though O'Farrell might preside over one of the most entertaining seasons in Manchester United history, but those days were long gone by the time the summer rolled around. No new players were brought in ahead of the next campaign, despite the sales of Alan Gowling, John Aston and Francis Burns, while a whole host of other names were put up for sale. George Best provided another issue – absconding to Marbella where he announced his retirement, only to reverse his decision a few weeks later.

"The job is so big it's hardly true," Malcolm Musgrove admitted over the summer. "Yet Frank O'Farrell will measure up. He is the ideal choice. His greatest quality is his honesty, yet you don't pull the wool over his eyes."

The 1972/73 season started with O'Farrell trying a midfield pair of Charlton and Morgan. Ipswich won 2-1 at Old Trafford with their players commenting on how unfit Best looked. But it was Law who was dropped for the trip to Anfield, with the manager reverting to a pragmatic three in midfield – Liverpool taking a 2-0 lead early on and never giving it up. Another bombshell days later – Charlton was left out with Law for the trip to Goodison. Sadler was moved up front but United's midfield of Morgan and Fitzpatrick could not hold off Everton, who also won 2-0. The 4-3-3 was in play for consecutive goalless home draws with Arsenal and Chelsea.

It wasn't until mid-September, in a League Cup second round replay with Oxford, that United were able to register their first win of the season, and it took a further week and half for the first league win – coming against champions Derby. One of the goals scored in that 3-0 win came from Wyn Davies on his debut; the veteran former Manchester City player was shortly joined by Ted MacDougall, the coveted Bournemouth striker.

Davies was very much a short-term squad booster, but MacDougall was a risk; at the age of 25, he was expected to hold his own alongside Best and Storey-Moore and be a long term replacement for Law. MacDougall scored in the next win, over Birmingham, and both he and Davies scored in a victory at home to Liverpool. But by November 11th, these were the only four wins of United's season to date.

Malcolm Musgrove suggested the team were not working hard enough. "Our play is flat because we are not looking to get in behind defenders," he said. "We don't support the man on the ball as well as we should."

Including the new signings, this was the team for the Liverpool match:

STEPNEY

O'NEIL SADLER BUCHAN DUNNE

BEST MORGAN CHARLTON STOREY-MOORE

MACDOUGALL DAVIES

It was certainly an adventurous team and perhaps suited playing at Old Trafford. But the same team took to the pitch in the following week's Manchester derby with very different results. A 3-0 defeat at Maine Road placed immense pressure on O'Farrell, and a 2-0 defeat at home to Stoke a few weeks later had United third from bottom. Best skipped training – O'Farrell placed him on the transfer list. However, by now, the United manager was suspicious that there was a growing number of people with an unhealthy influence. "The whole structure of the club and the greatness of the stature loomed larger than ever to him," David Meek wrote. "He felt there were too many people on the fringe of the club who had been missing the glory of the old days. They had become almost a pressure group and O'Farrell suspected they had more influence than him with the board… O'Farrell believes in coaching and modern techniques. He will tell you that it was this approach that had taken United to the top of the division the previous year."

Meek observed how O'Farrell felt other teams had 'left United behind in terms of running, effort and team-work'. It was perhaps more complicated than that. O'Farrell had believed strongly in the virtue of communication but, from December 1971, had retreated, creating a distance between himself and the squad. Paddy Crerand suggested he 'came as a stranger and left as a stranger'. The board's observation was that he was 'too remote' and the difficulty of George Best's situation left no party coming out of it well.

David Meek felt compelled to write a defence piece of the United manager in his *Evening News* column, titled 'Be Fair To Frank', explaining how McGuinness had been sacked after just 18 months and how he didn't want the same to happen to O'Farrell.

United lost 5-0 at Crystal Palace and there was no hiding place. It was one of the worst performances in the club's post-war history, and though O'Farrell claimed to have been taken by surprise, few were genuinely shocked when he was sacked in the following days. Best was also 'sacked' at the same time, though he seemed to pre-meditate this with a letter of resignation. Malcolm Musgrove was also relieved of his duties and, to some shock, so too was John Aston Snr.

The appointment had been United's first experiment in bringing in an 'outsider' and expecting them to adhere to a philosophy, as outlined by Busby himself in January 1969. Those values would not be dismissed but Busby's words made it clear there must be some form of compromise. So how close was O'Farrell to the United way? It has to be said that going forward, the tactical tweak did indeed seem to inspire some of the best football United had played since their title-winning team. It was cavalier in the way that it placed such emphasis on United's goalscoring approach, and the 4-3-3 shape liberated Best, which had originally worked magnificently.

Once the old problems resurfaced, O'Farrell did not have a solution. It is often fairly pointed out that Buchan and Storey-Moore were astute signings, and had those players arrived eight weeks before Christmas instead of after, it might have made a difference.

There was no resistance to O'Farrell's and Musgrove's methods. The concerns only began to surface when the players observed O'Farrell's reaction to criticism in the press and they started to question whether he had thick enough skin to handle the job. It was a fair question to ask; O'Farrell had never quite got over his initial mistrust of Busby and there was an infamous altercation where his wife Ann scolded Busby at a club event after Busby had questioned the dropping of Bobby Charlton. The O'Farrell reign, particularly after the complaint of McGuinness having 'no personality', seemed to indicate that the manager of Manchester United not only had to be a master tactician, *and* enjoy success, he was required to have some of the showmanship of some of his players. Busby was never flamboyant but he was incredibly charming and, perhaps most pertinently, never hid.

Tactically, United had no rigid history to follow so no defined history to stray away from. It could be said that they traditionally played with width and always to entertain; it could be said that the best United teams showed a lot of movement, and of course it was a part of the fabric of the club that they should play a number of their own players. Taking those games against Liverpool and Manchester City as samples, O'Farrell had fielded four homegrown players and brought in McIlroy.

United's need for senior improvement was more urgent and, for whatever reason, they hadn't been as aggressive in acquiring the best young players in recent years. That could have been due to the restructuring or the slight marginalisation of Armstrong and Murphy; whatever the reasons, United were not the hotbed of youth development they had once been.

As the manager retreated, the players became less trusting of his ability to turn around a difficult situation. They became decreasingly confident of his authority at the club. So too did the board – although his first two signings showed promise, the latter two seemed to indicate poor judgement.

Willie Morgan said "even McGuinness was closer to the players than O'Farrell… Frank wouldn't bend from the formula he had adopted at Leicester" while Stepney explained, "Frank seemed to go against the experienced players and some lost their respect, especially when he started treating them like children."

The decision to relieve him of his duties was a critical moment in Manchester United history. It was the second admission in three years that problems not caused by the manager were still too big for that manager to solve, and perhaps, for the first time, an admission to the footballing world that the next man would have to be given carte blanche to make wholesale changes, as unpopular as they might be.

And while there was no indication of a power struggle, Busby was still a permanent fixture at the club and it was no secret that O'Farrell was not completely enamoured by his former manager's influence.

"He had a big influence in the boardroom," O'Farrell said. "At a function Matt told my wife that I was 'an independent sod' and why didn't I go to see him. So I did. He started finding fault with one of my signings, Martin Buchan, which I disagreed with. He also said that I shouldn't have dropped Bobby Charlton. I knew he had gone to see Matt. It was an impossible situation. Manchester United wasn't going to be rebuilt until George Best, Bobby Charlton and Denis Law, who had all been great players in their day, all left Old Trafford. We needed to rebuild but you can't do that overnight. I wasn't given the chance."

Ultimately, O'Farrell would have similar complaints as McGuinness. Both men would find allies and defenders of their tenures, with the argument being that they were not given either enough time or enough power to succeed. Furthermore, at the critical moments, when it seemed some backing might allow the manager to navigate a difficult spell, the club made the decision based on results, focussing on the more immediate results than the bigger picture. That was football, after all. For the club to be able to truly get out of the mess they were in, it would have to be the board learning a lesson – that the short-term results would have to be a secondary concern against the long-term health of the team.

16

TOMMY DOCHERTY

THERE CAN BE NO DOUBT THAT THE WAY THINGS ended with this particular reign shaped the perception of the era as a whole for certain individuals, and Tommy Docherty himself was no exception.

Docherty was sacked in the summer of 1977 for having an affair with the wife of the club's physiotherapist. The relationship between him and the club never fully healed, which was a shame, because not only did Docherty breathe new life into Manchester United, for a long time it seemed he was made for the club – and, more than that, that he believed it too.

Certainly, soon after his appointment in December 1972, David Meek was under the impression that Docherty had wanted the job for '25 years' and to this writer in 2017, Docherty did indeed admit: "I always felt I'd like to follow Sir Matt Busby. He was a great manager." There was one story often told by the man himself that after getting the job he walked out on to an empty Old Trafford pitch and hummed the Freddie and the Dreamers line, "You were made for me."

Tommy Docherty was the 44-year-old manager of Scotland and, following the tradition, a former wing-half of international acclaim. He had grown up in the Celtic youth system before moving to Preston. He then transferred to Arsenal, and then Chelsea, where he became player-manager. He was unable to prevent a struggling team from getting relegated, but rebuilt them and not only got them promoted, he made them contenders for the league title and won the League Cup.

In that victory, seven players had come through Chelsea's youth system. 'Docherty's Diamonds' played in a thrilling fashion, the manager innovating with overlapping full-backs even in the new four-man defences. In one game he picked a full-back, Eddie McCreadie, to play up front – it was a gamble that paid off, with McCreadie scoring the winner. Docherty seemed to have something of a Midas touch.

All good things come to an end. Docherty's larger-than-life personality was loved by journalists but often invited controversy. The FA reacted harshly to events on Chelsea's 1967 pre-season tour to Bermuda where Docherty was said to have complained excessively about the local officials. In October, the FA banned him from all football matters for a month. The club were in a bad run of form and the board called a meeting; anticipating he would be sacked, Docherty brought a crate of champagne to the meeting and announced his resignation.

He had short-lived stints at Rotherham, QPR, Aston Villa, Porto, and as assistant manager at Hull, but restored his reputation in a year with Scotland's national team, winning seven from 12 matches. In December 1972, he was at Selhurst Park to watch a number of his Scottish players in Crystal Palace's match with

Manchester United. At half-time, with United 2-0 down, Docherty spoke with Matt Busby and Louis Edwards.

"How do you fancy becoming Manchester United manager?" Busby asked Docherty.

"You've got a manager."

"We won't have on Tuesday."

Busby had sought the advice of Denis Law and Willie Morgan, who both gave positive recommendations, and within days, Docherty was the new man at Old Trafford. His first game in charge was a 1-1 home draw with Leeds but the first time he picked the team was, like his two predecessors, for a game at Derby County.

STEPNEY
O'NEIL   SADLER   BUCHAN   DUNNE
MORGAN   CHARLTON
KIDD   MACDOUGALL   DAVIES   STOREY-MOORE
SUB: YOUNG (FOR DUNNE, HT)

This imbalanced team lost 3-1 at the Baseball Ground. It required only days for Docherty to convince the board to provide him with transfer funds. Just as he did at Chelsea, the manager signed George Graham to add experience in midfield. Full-back Alex Forsyth followed. Then Jim Holton, a physical centre-back. Lou Macari, the highly-rated Celtic forward. All of them Scots – on Macari's debut against West Ham on January 20th, an incredible *eight* Scottish players were in United's first team.

One Englishman who was brought to the club in Docherty's early days was Tommy Cavanagh. Busby had convinced Docherty to have Pat Crerand as his assistant, but Cavanagh, who had played with the new United manager at Preston, was to come in and oversee training. Cavanagh accepted without even asking about his salary. Docherty knew his old pal would not fear any of the egos at Old Trafford. "I wouldn't be messed about," Cavanagh recalled of his time managing at Brentford. "We had one very well-known international who used to think he was a cut above everyone else. I told him to train on his own and when he asked why I told him that we all appreciated that he was too good to train with the rest of us. In the end I had him in tears asking to be allowed to train with us again. If it is ever necessary, I have my own little ways of cutting players down to size."

This sort of abrasive attitude worked best for a coach and not a manager and before long, Johnny Carey had hired him as his assistant at Nottingham Forest, where he remained for six years. "I have no designs on the manager's job," Cavanagh said. "I think the job of trainer has been belittled in recent years. This is an expert's job. I love football and I love footballers. People have said I am a hard man, but you don't get the players complaining how I treat them. Of course I want my players to fight and play hard. Strength allied to skill, is one of the phrases I use most often. I cannot stand negative football. I am sure that both myself and Tommy Docherty feel that there is no substitute for class. The one thing we will not do is turn the United players into robots. They will be encouraged to play football at all times."

John Aston Snr's departure meant Norman Scholes was appointed chief scout after an association with the club that went back 22 years. Bill Foulkes kept his job as reserve team manager, with increased responsibility. "Probably at most clubs the manager picks all the teams, certainly the first and second sides," Docherty explained. "That is not the way I work, particularly when I have someone like Bill Foulkes in charge of the reserves. It is his job to push these boys. He sees them every week and so he is the best man to select the reserve team."

Later in 1973, Frank Blunstone, a former Chelsea winger, would join the staff, where he ostensibly became Docherty's assistant, and officially so when Pat Crerand left a few years later. Blunstone helped Foulkes with the reserve team and also worked with the junior players at the club.

Docherty's philosophy of football was, of course, moulded significantly by Jimmy Hogan at Celtic. He had grown up playing in the old 3-2-5 but was very much a modern manager and independent thinker. "I was brought up with wingers at Preston, with the great Tom Finney and Angus Morrison," Docherty said; a simple statement that outlined how he would prefer his United team to play. One problem – George Best was gone, Ian Storey-Moore had suffered cruel luck with injuries, and Willie Morgan had been converted into a midfielder.

For that game against West Ham, United lined up in a 4-3-3:

STEPNEY
YOUNG BUCHAN HOLTON FORSYTH
MORGAN GRAHAM CHARLTON
LAW MACARI MACDOUGALL
SUB: DAVIES FOR LAW 55

The game ended 2-2, with Macari, in Law's number 10 shirt, scoring a late equaliser (Law was in the unfamiliar number four shirt, and Graham was in 11, showing that the old days of numbers relating to positions were well and truly gone). Docherty used the 4-3-3 shape and the players responded by playing some good football and creeping, ever so slightly, out of relegation danger. Safety was guaranteed with a 1-0 win at Leeds – the club's seventh win from 11 taking them as high as 12th.

It was the best that could have been expected with what Docherty had inherited. "I felt we did have some good young players who weren't getting a chance," he said. "There was no future in what we had in the first team. I felt those players were there and they were just waiting for someone to take a chance. A lot of players were past their sell-by date and had their place at the club on sentiment."

Well, some of those would soon be gone. Bobby Charlton, days after his 600th league appearance for the club, informed Docherty he was going to retire at the end of the season. Denis Law, whose knee injury was now so debilitating that he couldn't train, was given a free transfer by the new manager in controversial circumstances. Docherty was unimpressed with O'Farrell's forward signings and both MacDougall and Davies were sold.

One face who left the club in December 1972 did return, when George Best was convinced to pull on a shirt again by Matt Busby, who visited his former player in hospital when Best was suffering from thrombosis. Docherty signed another Scot, Stewart Houston, to add more physical presence to his defence, but did try to bring some young players through.

Brian Greenhoff, Arnie Sidebottom, Clive Griffiths, Paul Bielby and Peter Fletcher were all given chances, with varying degrees of success. Sammy McIlroy – whose life seemed at risk following a car crash just after Docherty took charge – was given the chance to play through his recovery as his lungs healed. When United played Chelsea on November 3rd, 1973, this was the team:

STEPNEY

BUCHAN GRIFFITHS JAMES YOUNG

MORGAN GREENHOFF GRAHAM

KIDD MACARI BEST

With six players developed through the club, United came back from a 2-0 deficit to score 88th and 90th-minute goals and snatch a draw. Old Trafford responded – but the inexperience told on the road, and inevitably those away defeats, narrow though they often were, eroded confidence. Best – by now suffering from the early stages of alcoholism that was effectively misdiagnosed as 'drinking too much' – was not training often, though he had lost weight. He no longer had his spritely speed; in spite of his trickery, he was now almost a mere mortal. When QPR made an offer for him, Docherty felt there was a convenient way out – but when newspapers carried pictures of Best in his nightclub, Rangers manager Gordon Jago pulled out of the deal. Best was dropped for an FA Cup game with Plymouth and walked out of the club for the final time.

That match, and the previous home game with Ipswich, were United's only wins from late October all the way through to the start of March. They were in a relegation dogfight. But Alex Stepney had kept 12 clean sheets so far, and in nine other games conceded only once – not a dreadful record from 35 games.

Stepney and Kidd were now the only players remaining from the European Cup-winning team; a significant turnover in less than six years. The incredible experience of the spine of Foulkes, Stiles, Crerand and Charlton was completely gone. The players brought in, such as Buchan and Macari, would have to take their brief experiences with the likes of Charlton and Law and combine it with their own standards and Docherty and Cavanagh's philosophy of football to create a new, modern, Manchester United way.

If history was repeating itself, time was running out for Docherty's approach to yield positive results. Even if safety could be salvaged again, would that be enough to convince the United board that the club were moving in the right direction? Docherty had one last roll of the dice. Another member of the Tartan Army. George Graham's experience had not helped, so Docherty tried to add some in the front line, in the form of Wolves forward Jim McCalliog.

McCalliog certainly did help. He did not carry the burden of

McIlroy or Kidd or even Macari, and his natural confidence took some of the pressure away. Gerry Daly, of similar build and style to McCalliog, also had a laid-back way about him, and the pair helped to inspire an upturn in form. Daly scored in a 3-1 win at Chelsea where United's continued attempts to play good football finally found reward. A late equaliser in a 3-3 draw with Burnley kept the momentum going and a 2-0 win at Norwich built it even more. McCalliog then stepped up, scoring three goals in two wins over Newcastle and Everton. The shape against Everton was beginning to look like a team Docherty wanted to build:

STEPNEY
YOUNG BUCHAN HOLTON HOUSTON
MORGAN GREENHOFF MCCALLIOG DALY
MACARI MCILROY

When McCalliog scored a penalty at Southampton it may have seemed insignificant – but before that point, the regular taker had been goalkeeper Alex Stepney, who had scored two before Christmas before missing one and realising that it was too risky to be caught that far upfield. McCalliog took responsibility at the Dell, though he was surprised when Willie Morgan nudged him forward. But the Saints equalised, and another four-pointer ended with United taking just one, and feeling deflated. Defeat at Everton three days later left United virtually condemned to the drop.

They now needed to win and have other results go in their favour – neither happened, and so, in an infamous match against Manchester City, Denis Law scored the sort of classy goal he had registered so often in a red shirt, only now in sky blue. His back-heeled strike and haunted trudge off the pitch would become the image of the moment. Manchester United were relegated and one

Sir Matt Busby: a colossal figure in Manchester United history.

Johnny Carey with the FA Cup in 1948 – Busby's first trophy.

United beat Arsenal 5-4 in February 1958, the last UK game before Munich.

The Babes line up in Belgrade, unaware of the horrors to come on the way home.

Bill Foulkes skippers the side days after surviving the crash.

Busby leads the Reds out for the 1963 FA Cup final against Leicester at Wembley, which would become the landmark first trophy since Munich.

George Best slays Benfica in 1966 and announces himself to the world.

Wembley, 1968: Busby watches on before captain Bobby Charlton meets his Benfica counterpart. A 4-1 victory would prove Busby's crowning glory, winning the European Cup a decade on from the devastation of Munich.

The victorious Reds parade the trophy through the streets of Manchester.

Tommy Docherty's swashbuckling side win the 1977 FA Cup.

Bryan Robson beats Barcelona on a heady Old Trafford occasion in 1984.

November 1986, and Alex Ferguson meets fans at his new club...

Ferguson leads United to the 1993 league title, ending a 26-year wait. Steve Bruce's heroics against Sheffield Wednesday (below left) prove pivotal.

Pure footballing perfection against Wimbledon in 1994...

David Beckham takes the acclaim as United beat Arsenal in April 1999.

Kings of Europe in 1999 and 2008 as the trophies keep coming for Sir Alex.

Opposite: One of the great Old Trafford goals as Wayne Rooney goes airborne against Man City in 2011.

George Best's 1968 strike v Benfica was one of the great United goals...

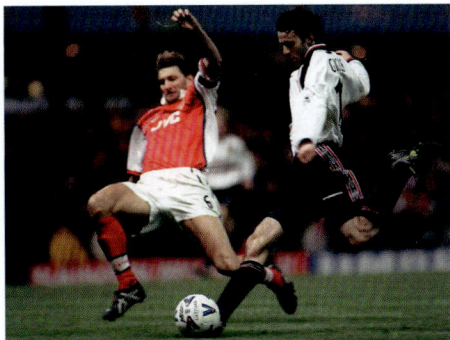
... as was Ryan Giggs's dramatic FA Cup effort against Arsenal in 1999.

Federico Macheda emerges from the bench to beat Aston Villa in 2009...

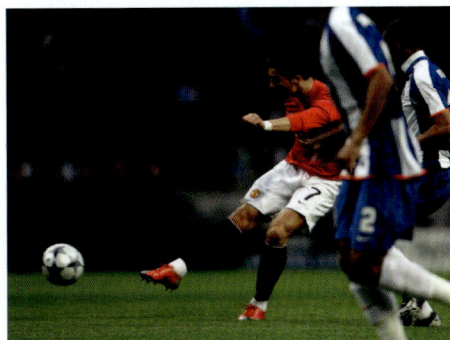
... while Cristiano Ronaldo lashes home against Porto in the same year.

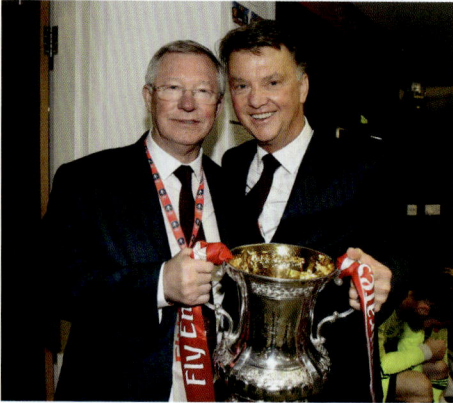

2016 FA Cup winner Louis van Gaal with the now-retired Sir Alex Ferguson.

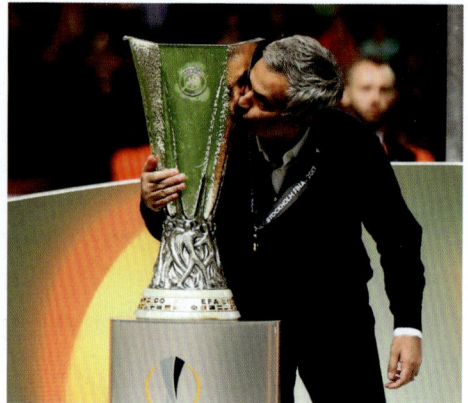

Jose Mourinho wins the 2017 Europa League amid tragedy in Manchester.

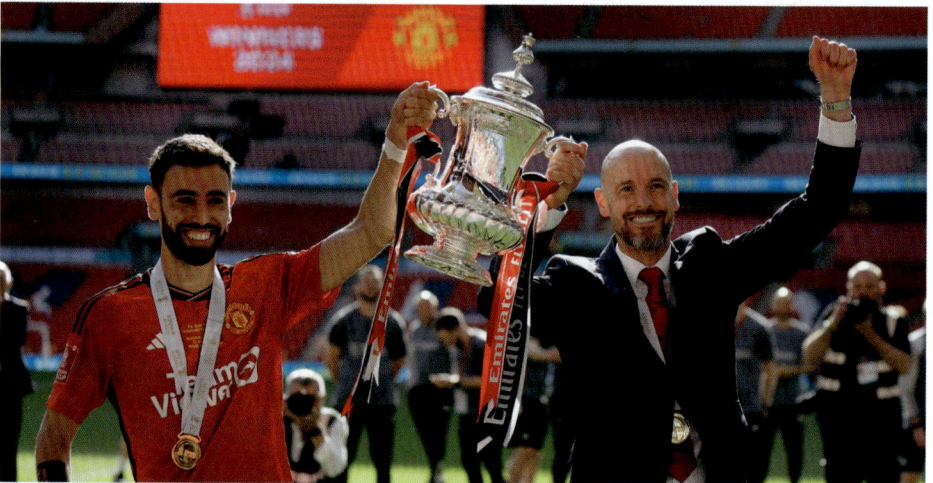

Bruno Fernandes and Erik ten Hag after a glorious FA Cup final in 2024.

The influence of Sir Matt is still felt to this day.

of their legends had symbolically performed the execution, less than a year after being unceremoniously kicked out of the club.

Docherty expected to follow, his 18-month reign concluding with the relegation of the club. But the board, led by Busby, decided to try a different approach. They had given the manager the duty of moving on Best, Law and Charlton. Sadler and Dunne had followed. So too did Brian Kidd, despite saying Docherty had 'brought him back from the dead'. Perhaps better had been expected of the players he had signed – but Busby and the other directors felt sufficiently encouraged by the style of football to give the manager a chance to take them back into the top flight.

"The full force of United's attack has yet to be seen," David Meek opined. "Docherty fought the relegation battle with a mainly 4-3-3 set-up. For he was robbed by injury of the player (Storey-Moore) he wanted in order to switch to an attacking 4-2-4 side."

Docherty confirmed that in the summer of 1973. "I have always believed in wingers, but I am not a great believer in numbers and systems. I consider that players should be mobile enough to keep a set pattern changing all the time. But eventually I do want United to play with two wingers. I think it makes for exciting football and pleases the crowd."

He would at least be given the time. And it was Docherty's time to be presented with champagne at an odd moment – Busby handing the manager a case as a show of faith.

When Busby commented over the summer, it seemed the board were accepting culpability too. "When I came out of management five years ago," he said, "I really did want the managers who have followed me to have full scope, just as I had. Sometimes things develop that you can't stop, and once they begin to go wrong, then other things follow... towards the end of last season though I saw things come into the side which have given me great heart."

Proving his belief that no major changes were needed, the manager signed just one player, Stuart Pearson, as a replacement for Kidd. Pearson was used to life in the lower divisions and Docherty felt he would put away some of the chances his team were creating.

Pearson and Macari started atop Docherty's attempt at a 4-2-4; there was not a natural balance in the traditional form as Daly, from the left, would drift infield, but the United manager felt that the quality in his team would be too strong for Second Division opponents, even if those teams would be putting in an extra special effort. "United are coming to Bolton and we will want to beat them, simply because they are United," Wanderers boss Jimmy Armfield admitted at the start of the season.

And so the process began. Willie Morgan was initially appointed team captain, describing Docherty as 'magic', but Martin Buchan was emerging as the leader of this squad – which now had an average age of 23 – and was eventually handed the armband. United's form was strong – winning at Leyton Orient, Cardiff and Millwall, and winning their home games with some comfort. They responded to their first defeat with a win and then six consecutive clean sheets. Confidence came from the wins. Then came the goals. The team were so entertaining that Match Of The Day, for the first time, screened a Second Division game as their main match – United's home game with Sunderland, which lived up to the billing as Docherty's side won 3-2.

The young team were beginning to feel befitting of the shirt, and a generation of supporters who had become enamoured with the 1968 side and were now old enough to travel to away games were developing a special connection of their own. The sold out grounds were a testament to both the novelty of England's most famous club coming to some unfamiliar venues, and also the strength of their travelling support. Police were unprepared – in this early age of hooliganism, trouble was never far away, and many local businesses would close down in anticipation of the Red Army descending on their town or city. United's young players loved it.

Tommy Cavanagh spoke of this spell in 1989 and recalled it with fondness, giving an insight into his approach to training. "There was a time at Old Trafford when things were bad when we first went there," he told Tom Tyrrell. "All of a sudden, Tommy and I looked at one another and said, 'We've got a team'. It comes to you that way. All your hard work's starting to show. And that's the satisfaction. It's been interesting in more recent years talking to some players like Stevie Coppell and Lou Macari where we talk about what it used to be like and they might complain. But I just say, well, I didn't do you no harm. They're very appreciative. Footballers know what you're trying to do for them. I know they hate your guts one day. But, when they calm down, they know."

The first half of the season saw such an improvement that the team were able to overcome the setbacks – a bumpy run of form, a broken leg to Jim Holton which would play a huge part in bringing an abrupt end to his career – and secure promotion with some comfort. McIlroy, Macari and Pearson were outstanding, forming an understanding that thrilled the fans.

Late in the season, Docherty acted quickly on the advice of Jimmy Murphy to sign Steve Coppell from Tranmere. Coppell was a right winger – or a right-sided midfielder – and so Morgan, who had been moved back out wide with United finally now getting players to do the job in the middle, was switched to the left for the visit of York City (now managed, incidentally, by Wilf McGuinness).

This game, on March 29th 1975, finally saw Docherty field a 4-2-4 formation with players of the required skillset to play it. The team also featured Brian Greenhoff at centre-back – he had first deputised in that position at Chelsea the previous season, and was now there due to an injury suffered by Steve James.

STEPNEY
FORSYTH GREENHOFF BUCHAN HOUSTON
COPPELL MCILROY DALY MORGAN
PEARSON MACARI

United won 2-1, an understated victory, with the afternoon more remarkable for the implementation of what would finally become Docherty's established shape. Five of the last six games were won as the club closed out their season in style. And United then went on an arduous post-season tour to Australia and the Far East, barely even catching a breath before they were back for pre-season preparation (just 40 days break between the last game of their post-season and the first game of their pre-season tours).

United signed Tom Jackson to add some midfield steel – in Coppell, McIlroy, Daly and Morgan, Docherty had players who would work hard and run, but no natural tacklers. Jackson started in midfield in the First Division and Docherty persisted with the 4-2-4 almost as above, only with Daly on the left and Morgan dropped.

It was in November 1975 when the most significant signing of the Docherty era was made; Gordon Hill, another Murphy recommendation, arrived from Millwall (incidentally, another old name joined the scouting staff – Johnny Carey, Busby's first captain). Hill was an attacking left winger, a player who certainly made it a 4-2-4 and not a 4-4-2. And this was the case in games at home or away; be it against Sheffield United or Liverpool, for better or worse. The ethos had dripped through the club and confidence coursed through the veins of every player and staff member.

Tommy Cavanagh's pre-match ritual was to scrunch up the opposition's teamsheet and throw it in the wastepaper basket in front of the United players, to symbolise that it didn't matter who they were playing against.

The cavalier approach was adopted at every level. "We play attacking football with our junior team," recalled Frank Blunstone. "We play with wingers and we go for goals. My main duty is to bring the youngsters through to first-team level, so we can play the style I choose. I can get my teams playing the way I believe must eventually be adopted at all levels if football is going to survive as entertainment. At youth level I don't go to watch an opposing team with the idea of making plans to stop them. I am more interested in imposing our style on them."

Docherty heralded the work done by his youth coach. "I consider the system is now back to where it was when Sir Matt was manager," he boasted. "You will see young players coming through to the first team again. We are bang on the right lines, thanks to changes at scouting level and the appointment of Frank."

Whilst this might have been a premature declaration – numbers breaking through didn't notably increase – it showed Docherty was conscious of the club's reputation and he was a champion of the same philosophy. It was his on-pitch philosophy, however, which had most people talking. With Coppell and Hill settling in quickly on the wings, Docherty's major decision was how to construct the spine; so Daly was preferred to Morgan in the middle, the manager feeling Daly and McIlroy worked well in tandem. The groove was magnificent and Hill's addition in particular was spectacular because the cocky Londoner would try the outrageous, either in attempting to beat a man or score a goal. It was the sort of flamboyance United supporters hadn't seen since Best. This new dimension made United very attack-heavy but Docherty went at it full-tilt, in a manner not observed since Busby's pre-Munich side where Blanchflower had been trialled at centre-half. But that was then, in a time of 3-2-5. These were days of organised defences and counter-attack strategies. It shouldn't have worked so well, but, perhaps like all new and bold strategies – much like Holland's early iteration of Total Football at the 1974 World Cup – perhaps it was the newness and the boldness which made it work.

While the midfield didn't really have a tackler in it, the same might be said of the centre of defence in the absence of Jim Holton. Brian Greenhoff had effectively moved into that position, and even though Docherty would often attribute that decision to a stroke of fortune (he would reference an FA Cup tie at Wolves which had forced him to move Greenhoff back) he had been more or less playing in that role for most of the season.

United took everyone by surprise with their electric form back in the First Division. A combination of factors were working for the club; the first was that Docherty celebrated his three-year anniversary in the job in December 1975. That meant he had enjoyed twice as long as both of his predecessors, so had more time to see the benefit of his ideas. Timing was another factor. Docherty had to have his three years when he did in order to be able to move on the number of legendary players, and you almost feel that it was necessary for some sort of decline to occur to make it acceptable for those players to be moved on.

The drop in division, while never a good thing, did come with consequential benefits. A young team was able to mould and develop its confidence – its arrogance – and how it did so.

If a feature of relegation was a drop in quality of opposition, then it was nowhere near as pronounced as it would be today, while every single away game carried the atmosphere of a cup tie, with a feverous home crowd desperate for a win. At Old Trafford, United still attracted the highest gate in the country in league football, bringing in an average of 47,781. Once they were back in the top division, this inexperienced side had the ego boost of opponents treating them like they were a proper Manchester United team and they rose to that level of expectation.

It was not a perfect team. We'll come on to that. But there are always two standards with a football team, the first being its own potential and the second being its comparative quality against opponents. United's lack of physicality, and their youthfulness, sometimes cost them dearly in crucial away games. Defeats at QPR and Liverpool in the early part of the first season back up represented the difference between the three clubs at the end – United finishing in third, three points behind the London club and four behind the Anfield-based champions.

There were still other factors, not least because United topped the table after those defeats. One defeat at home to Stoke at the end of the season proved pivotal; Docherty lamented the supreme form of Peter Shilton, a goalkeeper he had coveted, and would have felt his team might have had a cutting edge at the other end of the pitch with the guile of Stoke's front man, Jimmy Greenhoff.

Another goalkeeping decision had cost United dear earlier in the campaign. Docherty felt it was an area that could be improved upon, and whilst he could not get Shilton, he did sign Paddy Roche. The Irishman was called in to replace Stepney after a defeat at West Ham, but conceded three goals at Anfield, four at Maine Road in the League Cup, and another three at Arsenal in the space of two cursed weeks. United had performed admirably, overachieving to finish third, but a reminder of their inexperience came when they lost to Second Division Southampton in the FA Cup final in 1976.

Still, with Coppell's industry on the right and Hill's magic on the left, as well as the style and craft in the middle of the park,

Docherty had built a Manchester United team that was the most entertaining for many years. The energy in midfield and the workmanship of the frontline meant the tempo of the team was relentless, and sometimes the crowd would pray for half-time only to catch their breath. Opponents would find it absurd that United could keep going at the same pace for the full match – but 20 of their 85 goals scored through the 1975/76 season came in the last 20 minutes of games, proof that they remained just as strong later on.

Over the coming months Docherty would make another offer for Shilton – Stoke's financial situation made them more agreeable to discussions. The deal broke down over Shilton's request for £100 a week. When Docherty discussed it with the board, Busby insisted there was no way they would pay such a salary for a goalkeeper, which seemed a contradiction to the fact that he had broken the world record three times to bring in a goalkeeper. There was more joy, however, with a proposal for Jimmy Greenhoff – and roughly a year after Hill arrived to be told he was the 'final piece of the jigsaw', that piece in fact came in the form of the elder Greenhoff brother, for a fee of just over £100,000.

Greenhoff's arrival required the Doc to find a new home in the team for Lou Macari – and, liking his aggression, the manager felt it would be a good fit to go alongside McIlroy. In November 1976, Manchester United finally had the team that would forever be associated with Tommy Docherty. This makes it an opportune time to dig into the psyche of the manager, much as we did when dissecting Busby and Murphy's vision of a perfect Manchester United team some 30 years earlier.

First of all, what value did Docherty see in Shilton? What did he want from his goalkeeper that Stepney wasn't providing? "I just thought he was a better goalkeeper than Alex, without wanting to be disrespectful. I thought he would have let in fewer goals. I think the most important quality for a goalkeeper is coming for crosses. Distribution is important, too, because there was no point catching the ball and just blasting it upfield."

When it came to his full-backs, Docherty wanted them to be: "Good defensively. Quick. Good going forward and quick at getting back. I never considered the risk of them being high up the pitch because they were making the other wingers play as full-backs. I'd always played that way at Chelsea, too. I remember reading one newspaper report that said one of our goals had been disallowed because both of our full-backs were offside. I was very much a fan of full-backs overlapping."

Of course overlapping full-backs was not a new thing even at United; it had been one of Busby's very first experiments. One thing Docherty could take full credit for was to completely do away with the old 'stopper' centre-half.

"You would have a stopper and a sweeper," Docherty said. "We ended up with two sweepers. If there was a stopper of the two, it was Martin, but they complemented each other so well and the longer they played together, the better they got. Martin got better on the ball, so you never worried about them carrying it. You'd be quite happy for them to come into the opposition half and play. Buchan was a good defender. Exceptionally quick. He wasn't a great passer, so we instructed him to move the ball on as soon as he could. He didn't like that – being Martin, he thought he was great on the ball. I didn't think Brian Greenhoff would ever make a good centre-half, I have to be honest. Cav only ever had praise for his ability. Good on the ball, good in the air and a great passer. He maybe lacked a little pace but he read the game so well. Managers today don't play two defenders like that because they're frightened of losing the ball. But if you're frightened of it, you end up not wanting it."

Perhaps bravery would have been a more apt description of this team if there was a true list of accolades to show for it; but in the absence of a big trophy haul, we have to consider it more the fearlessness of youth. That's no less courageous in a spiritual sense – to suffer the humiliation of not only a slump, but relegation, to recover and then win the hearts of the supporters with scintillating football… well, those players who experienced that full journey showed a tremendous amount of character.

It had been a shared journey, creating an emotional bond, a certain pride. Those supporters had shown faith in the tough times, and were now rewarded with the best football being played anywhere in the country. There were older fans – those old enough to remember war, to remember Munich. And then there were the younger fans, those who remembered Munich and the recovery. They remembered the introduction of George Best and the transformative impact he had. There were some too young to remember that, but they had lived through the European Cup win with Best as their hero. They had watched their team fall and were now experiencing their latest rise. It was almost a rite of passage, and the youth in the team was reflective of the vibrancy on the terrace.

Nowhere was that better represented on the pitch than in United's midfield. There were no six footers – in fact, anywhere in the front six come to that – and none of the physicality of Edwards or passing class of Crerand, but there was something different. Any of Docherty's front six could play in the forward positions, and all did at some point, including the regular stand-in for the starters, Gerry Daly. There were defined roles for the six players in midfield and attack, and Pearson and Greenhoff were definite attackers, so although they would drop deep enough to allow for forward runs, they would not drop deep enough to cover the defence.

"I played 4-2-4," Docherty explained. "I would play Macari and McIlroy, and Gerry Daly, in the middle. Daly and McIlroy were not aggressive players, but Sammy would run all day. He had a Rolls-Royce engine. He had great stamina and a good passing range. If we had bite in the middle it came from Macari. It could well have been a risk to play them both. We should have had a good tackler, a dirty bugger in midfield, but we never did.

"But it was about how *we* played. We dictated the pace of the game. When we cleared the ball, we wanted to push the play up the pitch as quickly as possible. Not only did that put us in a stronger position to attack, but it made it tricky for the opposition to attack without getting caught offside. Stamina and energy were key attributes, because when we lost the ball I wanted the players to be like flies around a sugar bowl, but I felt that having a team that picked itself also helped develop that consistency. They talk about the pressing game at Barcelona. Cav and I did that at United. When you lose the ball, press and get the ball back as quickly as you possibly can."

In this age where teams were playing four and even five men in defence, it seemed ludicrous to have a strategy where eight of your outfield players had an inclination to attack first. Buchan and Houston were the exceptions but even Buchan would, as Docherty confessed, be encouraged to disregard caution and have a go. Houston, on the other hand, was facing competition from Arthur Albiston – and while Albiston would not regularly get past Hill on the left, he did provide higher support, giving Docherty the potential for almost complete high compression. "It was almost suicidal when you think about it," Sammy McIlroy said. "It shouldn't have worked as well as it did."

A main reason for the success was the constant danger of the wingers. Coppell's crossing was metronomic, while Hill's ability to create and score from out wide was exemplary. His performance in scoring two goals in the 1976 FA Cup semi-final against Derby County was one of the most memorable of the decade.

"When a winger has the ball, your team are already on the attack and the opposition is worrying," Docherty said. "I loved the wingers to take on full-backs because they hate it. They're the players I enjoyed watching most. I liked them to be quick and I liked their delivery to be strong and whipped in. As Cav used to say in training, 'Violence! Smash the ball against their faces!'

"The reason for that is that I always used to play with forwards of 5'8 or 5'9. We wanted the ball to be a bit wet, a bit greasy, so we could smash the ball all over the place. If you lob or float a cross, good defenders can anticipate it. If you hammer it hard and low, it's much harder to defend. The ricochets often work in your favour. Hilly was great at that. We knew Coppell was prepared to work harder than Hill so we had that balance deliberately. Jimmy Nicholl was always happy to come forward so we always had a threat on the right too. Coppell was brave, quick, he would never get involved in any skirmishes."

It brings us to the forwards – Pearson and Greenhoff. "Pancho was brave and strong," Docherty explained. "Jimmy was a beautiful, delicate and elegant player. They were both fantastic at holding the ball up. It was worth the money for Greenhoff just so I could watch him play. Pancho would do the angled running behind Jimmy, Jimmy would come deeper. When the ball went up to either of them, no matter how hard or how ferocious it came at them, it stuck. Their touch was always immaculate. We had a regular pattern for build-up that we worked on. Stepney to Houston. Houston to Hill. Hill straight into Greenhoff or Pearson, and one would always be open to get the ball. Sometimes if the ball was on, Houston could bypass Hilly. On the right, Stepney would get the ball higher up the pitch to Coppell, and Jimmy Nic would already be going for the overlap."

Jimmy Greenhoff's arrival seemed to settle United into a perfect groove. Once Macari and Buchan had recovered from their injuries, and Docherty was able to field his team the way he wanted to, they went on a fantastic run of form, winning 12 out of 15 games, and scoring three times in five of those. The goals came from all over the pitch – Hill, Pearson, Macari, and Jimmy Greenhoff in particular proving that United could strike from anywhere.

Those earlier injuries had exposed the lack of true squad depth, and a poor run undermined any genuine chance of a league title push, but after elimination from the UEFA Cup (where Ajax and Juventus were both beaten at Old Trafford, before the latter triumphed on aggregate in Turin), attention turned to the FA Cup, as Docherty had promised to 'bring the cup back to the finest fans in the world'.

Against Leeds United in the semi-final at Hillsborough, Docherty fielded his strongest team:

STEPNEY

NICHOLL B.GREENHOFF BUCHAN HOUSTON

COPPELL MCILROY MACARI HILL

PEARSON J.GREENHOFF

Sheffield had been Hill's happy hunting ground a year earlier; now Coppell and Jimmy Greenhoff made hay, both scoring before the quarter-hour mark to send their team back to Wembley.

The opponents in the 1977 FA Cup final were Liverpool – in the early stages of their redefinition of domestic dominance. They'd won the league in 1973, 1976 and 1977 to become the most successful team in English football history. Bob Paisley had inherited the manager's job from Bill Shankly and was building a team capable of running roughshod over the rest of the league. They prepared for the FA Cup final hoping to do what Busby had never been able to accomplish – the treble of League, FA Cup and European Cup.

Paisley played a 4-4-2 and wasn't renowned as a master tactician but, like Busby before him and even arguably Docherty, was probably hugely underrated in that regard. Liverpool had a style of their own – United's junior players would often joke as they rose through the ranks that their Anfield rivals had players of almost identical physical composition, be it in the youth team, reserve team or first team – down to the haircuts!

Liverpool had some tremendous individuals but they had mastered the art of defence, playing a physical game and, when taking the lead, often suffocating a match thanks to the back pass rule – in these days, a goalkeeper was still allowed to pick up a pass from a team mate, leading to insufferable moments of frustration for opponents. In players like Ray Kennedy, Jimmy Case and Kevin Keegan (and later Kenny Dalglish), they also had no little class at the other end of the pitch. This was not the Italian door-bolting method; but it was efficient and economic, reliant on the value of experience, which of course was one advantage they had over United.

The final, then, would be a battle of quality and nerve. Docherty was forced to make one change from his preferred team, as Houston had suffered a broken leg, so Albiston played. United found the same issue as they had with Southampton a year earlier – Wembley, on a hot day, is a big pitch – too big a pitch for their wingers to inflict their usual damage. Games at Wembley were usually won and lost in midfield and so Macari and McIlroy were required to exhaust every ounce of energy.

It was a fascinating tactical battle because, by default, the circumstances played into Liverpool's favour. The play was slower, the capability to strike impulsively was hugely reduced, and United's only real chance was to impose their frenzied style in either short bursts or smaller pockets of the pitch and hope that they would not be caught out by a clinical and organised opponent.

The breakthrough came in the 51st minute, with Greenhoff flicking the ball on for Pearson. He struck it early, catching out Ray Clemence at his near post. Liverpool equalised within two minutes – Jimmy Case scoring a fine goal from the edge of the box. But before the game could settle down again, Docherty's chaos theory reaped dividends. Macari and Jimmy Greenhoff harassed the defenders and the ball dropped for Macari to shoot at goal. It was going well wide – but the ball struck the thigh of Greenhoff, only the wind of fate directing it into the Liverpool net.

The champions fought back but Buchan and Brian Greenhoff were magnificent – the latter winning the man-of-the-match award, holding firm, demonstrating a sense of authority that seemed to grow over the 90 minutes. Docherty won his first major trophy, the FA Cup, and although it took more resilience than their usual flair, it was this key fact that seemed the most promising aspect of their victory. Liverpool would go on to win the European Cup a few days later, further emphasising the heights United could hit.

How could this team have played with a Shilton? What if they had a more physical presence at the back or in midfield? Or how about if they had a 30-goal a season striker, or another wide man to offer a different threat to Coppell and Hill? Some of these questions would be answered – but not *under Docherty*, who was sacked just weeks after the victory when news of his affair was exposed. And it is under Docherty that is the key phrase because no manager before or since, and you can include Busby himself in this, played with such a wilful disregard for the identity of the opposition.

Docherty introduced his own way of doing things, though crucially many of the ideals he held were shared by the club's historical identity. He didn't just arrive at Old Trafford and try to live up to what had gone before; he had modern ideas and was clearly in tune with modern formations. He heavily favoured attacking football. He favoured the concept of bringing through a core of young players, not necessarily because of their connection to the club but because of the loyalty those players would show the manager who gave them their chance. He understood that United had to compete for the biggest prizes.

He fulfilled all of the criteria Busby himself had outlined as desirable for a manager of Manchester United, and also one that arose as a consequence of the subsequent lean spells – the necessity for the manager to be a force of personality; almost like a statesman, a politician, the public face of the club. It was this factor, ironically, which would count most against Docherty's successor. The Doc could not boast a reputation as a tactician in the same way as Dave Sexton, and truthfully, he never really claimed to be one. His was a philosophy, almost a chaos theory, and one almost gets the feeling that it couldn't have worked with 11 other players. That is why this 11, and Gerry Daly, David McCreery and Stewart Houston are all included, are crystallised in a certain sense; their Old Trafford careers before and after the summer of 1977 asterisked due to the extremely different attitudes of their managers.

How close was Docherty to football taught by Matt Busby? As close as one could get, in the modern circumstances. The possible exceptions were the ability to coach his players to be multi-functional and the number of homegrown players in the regular side. In the FA Cup final, Jimmy Nicholl, Arthur Albiston, Brian Greenhoff and Sammy McIlroy started, while David McCreery came off the bench. Four starters and five in total might not have been the eight or nine Busby could boast, but it is a number that compares favourably with most successes in the club's history aside from that.

Docherty himself was a product of the times. Raised as a player through the era where Busby as a debonair diplomat was the public face of soccer, introduced into an era as manager where George Best's personality became the most prominent aspect of the sport, in a time where liberation and expression were encouraged and wisecracking and sarcasm were becoming hugely popular social mechanisms. He truly was made for Manchester United – controversy and all.

17

DAVE SEXTON

HISTORY DECREED IT WOULD NOT PLAY OUT AS desired, but the decision of Manchester United's board to turn to Dave Sexton after Tommy Docherty seemed a prudent one at the time. In fact, Sexton seemed the natural choice to inherit this United squad and take them to the next level.

Sexton was from the West Ham school; and while Frank O'Farrell, another graduate of that class, did not succeed at Old Trafford, time had proven that the problems were so deep that perhaps he never stood much of a chance. Most of those old Hammers were now prominent names in British football management and Sexton was no different. He had ironically been given his first chance in coaching by Docherty at Chelsea, and then inherited the Stamford Bridge job from the Doc after a short spell away from the club. He then took over at QPR and achieved a second-place finish in 1976; in fact, their very first goal of the season, against the soon-to-be champions Liverpool, was the goal of the season as voted by Match of the Day viewers. Finished by Gerry Francis, what was most impressive was the slick and inventive passing beforehand featuring the likes of Frank McLintock, Stan Bowles and Don Givens.

The new man was a polar opposite to Docherty in terms of personality – definitely from the O'Farrell mould to wonder why the press might be so interested – but, unlike O'Farrell, had at least good experience of the cut-throat world at the top of the First Division to not be too surprised by it.

Prior to Docherty's sacking, Sexton had already decided to leave QPR, saying that because they had failed to win a trophy, it was best if he moved on. He was close to accepting a role at Arsenal as an assistant to Terry Neill when developments at Old Trafford changed things.

Of course, Sexton had already been considered for the big job at United when Wilf McGuinness was sacked; the softly-spoken Londoner had turned down a job with Ajax during his time at Loftus Road. Docherty had rated Sexton so highly that he once suggested he'd be a great England coach; the incumbent Three Lions manager Ron Greenwood selected Sexton to coach the Under-21 side.

He clearly had the pedigree and so, in theory, he had the capability to take a young United side to the next level. He could arrange them and give them the discipline to challenge Liverpool, fittingly in the club's centenary season.

It is no secret that the way Sexton saw the game of football was quite different to the way Docherty saw it. The Londoner was an admirer of Rinus Michels and the Dutch team of 1974, fascinated by the methodology behind it. But he was not merely a football fanatic, he enjoyed many different sports and felt there was something which could translate across many disciplines. Where Docherty built by instinct and feeling, Sexton preferred to be deliberate and methodical.

His fundamental belief was that counter-attacking was the most effective way to play, and would liken it to boxing. "The initial retreating action is neither negative nor defensive," he said in his coaching book *Tackle Soccer*. "Quite the opposite. I believe the counter-attack to be the most effective way of penetrating the opposition's defence. The first thing I do when I go to a club is explain the meaning of the spirit of counter-attack to the players. The process takes time and patience."

Sexton felt footballers were 'two-thirds' developed – that they knew football was a game of attacking and defending, but the missing third was the act of regaining possession. He spoke about a football team as a unit of individuals, and of the key to success being creating smaller units within the bigger team unit. He believed in a team controlling possession of the ball, just like the Dutch. "Never let players forget the importance of moving the ball," he said. "It's the only way to run a game... Pass and run football is impossible to stop if it is played correctly."

He had a clear vision for how he saw training. From July through to October, the emphasis would be on ball skills, passing and team play. From November to January, the focus would be on stamina training, and then as the season reached its climax, more ball work would be reintroduced. "I'm talking about the outline rather than the entire schedule," he elaborated. "Every week, do shooting practice, crossing the ball, attack against defence, all the essential parts of play. Don't push these to one side just because the pitch becomes muddy." He felt that a sportsperson who had trained harder than they'd have to work in a match would have a psychological advantage over another who didn't train so hard. He favoured an old military saying: "Defeat requires an explanation – victory covers a multitude of sins." To that end, there would be no angry recriminations in the heat of the moment after a loss. He felt the strongest conclusions could only be reached once the dust had settled.

So – how did Sexton's team look? How did he want them to play football? When it came to goalkeepers, he had no set idea. Busby had been ahead of his time in terms of what a goalkeeper brought to the side, and Sexton did stress that a goalkeeper 'was not a separate entity' to the rest of the team, but he would speak about how to make the best out of the qualities of the individual he'd inherited, rather than, for example, saying he would prefer a Harry Gregg to a Ray Wood. He wanted a goalkeeper who could do the basics well – be safe with his hands and good under pressure, to have a strong positional sense, and to be a good kicker, but did not express a preference to one who stayed on his line or one who joined in the play.

It was a similar story when it came to defenders. Sexton believed all marking systems could be exploited by good coaching. At Chelsea he had always used man-marking but after travelling around Mexico watching the World Cup in 1970, came back convinced that zonal marking could bring an extra dimension to his team's chances of succeeding in Europe. So his pre-season was spent instructing his defenders to mark space instead of following opponents. Though it took some time for them to get used to it, particularly the centre-half John Dempsey, by the end of the season, the value was proven – Dempsey scoring the first goal in the European Cup Winners' Cup final win over Real Madrid. In spite of this, Sexton did eventually revert back to man-marking, clearly feeling that such deviations were better employed as an element of surprise.

Sexton did express one more interesting, original thought: "Never be so single-minded in defence that you become incapable of adjusting to new situations… don't sit back with four defenders marking two forwards while the opposition take control in midfield. Push a defender into midfield to even the contest. It's all a matter of what to do with the spare man at the back."

If such vision seems progressive, then it has to be said it was hardly put into practice during the four years Sexton was Manchester United manager – that could be because the balance of the team was so top-heavy that it would be too much of a risk. Sexton believed that concentration and discipline were the key elements of a strong defence and thought the midfield played a big part in protecting them. Wingers should come back – if only to give the opponent an extra problem to think about.

The new United boss indicated he would be almost as hands off with the strikers as he would with the goalkeepers. He felt a good striker was born, even if their technique could be improved. He seemed to have his strongest ideas based around what his midfield should look like. "The midfield cover every inch of the pitch," he said. "They support the defence when it is under pressure… and support the forwards when they are attacking. So our link-pin must have bags of stamina as well as natural skills, tackling bite, heading ability, good control and vision and the ability to score goals as well as create goals. Not all midfield players will possess all these qualities… but all these qualities must be evident in your midfield unit. At Manchester United, Sammy McIlroy is the ideal all-purpose player. He can work hand-in-glove with the back four, spray passes about and has the pace to get away from defenders for a shot at goal."

When it came to wingers, Sexton clearly seemed to favour a wide man who had a plan rather than one who would play on instinct. "The difference between scoring and not scoring a goal can come down to which player keeps thinking the longer," he said. "The art of total concentration is not easy to master. The winger whose brain keeps ticking over all the time will be aware of the possibilities from the moment he sees the full-back dither."

Sexton added he would often change things up in training. "Nothing can be worse than monotony," he said. "Try to vary your routines. Spring the occasional surprise on the players. When they turn up expecting a tough, stamina-sapping session, kick off the training shoes and watch a coaching film… when they roll in expecting a five-a-side session and a build-up match-chat for the coming game, run their legs off with a cross-country slog."

None of the above sounds particularly negative in theory, but the significant issue Sexton faced when taking the job – and inheriting all the staff who'd worked with Docherty – was that everyone else was so used to that way of business, that *anything* else would have seemed negative by comparison. United's players looked to Tommy Cavanagh as Sexton tried to encourage the concept of counter-attacking to a team who were only used to imposing themselves on opponents. Cavanagh was game, but the players could see that he did not quite have the same conviction as under Docherty. The condensing of the play, the speed and instinct of their first-touch football and their harassing to achieve ball recovery were all hallmarks of this great side and, as far as some of the squad were concerned, Sexton either wanted to micro-manage or to understand what they were doing naturally to the extent it was disturbing their rhythm.

Furthermore, Sexton favoured a 4-3-3 as he believed it gave him better support in different areas, but he could not practically achieve that with the players he inherited, so he hoped to strike a balance with a flatter four in the middle. That meant asking Gordon Hill to consider working back more – something even his own team-mates didn't want. Hill was shown videos of how Hungarian wingers worked hard out of possession. The theory, again, was sound. But it demonstrated a profound misunderstanding of the squad and its personalities, even though he was a coach who strongly believed in the value of treating players as human beings. Asking Hill to curb his instincts was to instantly reduce his effectiveness as a player.

Hill wasn't the only player to suffer a difficult relationship with the new manager. Stuart Pearson struggled, as did Brian Greenhoff; two 'sweepers' was one too many for Sexton, and attempts were made to find another home in the team for the Barnsley-born player. Greenhoff insisted he was happy to play anywhere, but such tinkering with the system was only likely to create difficulties. Sexton had, after all, inherited a team with an average age of around 24, and they had just won the FA Cup. The manager had not been sacked for failure, so his successor was going to give it a fair amount of time before wanting to make his own purchases.

A spate of injuries exposed the thin nature of the squad – there was no convincing replacement when Buchan or Jimmy Greenhoff picked up a knock – and an ill-fated plan to play a friendly in Tehran, for which the players required injections, was said to play a part in a humbling 4-0 defeat to Porto in the European Cup Winners' Cup.

That match did precede a famous night at Old Trafford which almost saw an unlikely comeback against the Portuguese side; with attack the only option, United went 4-1 up, almost luring the home crowd into believing the impossible could happen. Some of the old spirit was invoked, with many thinking of Bilbao in 1957. Ultimately, it would be reminiscent of the vain attempt to recover the deficit to Real Madrid later in that same season, but it did seem as though the club was displaying some form of muscle memory; remember those quips about Busby's side needing adversity to truly get going?

DAVE SEXTON

Try as they might, they could not. Sexton signed Gordon McQueen to add height at the back, moving Greenhoff to right-back, and Joe Jordan to add height at the front, moving Pearson out of the team altogether. He then shockingly sold Hill – Tommy Docherty had become manager of Derby, and was attempting to poach as many of his former players as he could. The transfer was deeply unpopular with supporters. That the sale came after United had won just once in 14 games, Bilbao in 1957, with Hill top scorer at the time, compounded matters – the manager was inviting pressure.

Sexton tried to move to a 4-3-3, having struggled with his version of Docherty's 4-4-2 system all season – his team for an end of season trip to Bristol City read:

ROCHE

NICHOLL MCQUEEN HOUSTON ALBISTON

COPPELL MCILROY B.GREENHOFF

PEARSON JORDAN GRIMES

Through injury or selection, five players were changed from the team which had won the FA Cup less than a year earlier, as the club stumbled to a hugely underwhelming tenth place finish. Over the 1978/79 season, Sexton moved back to a 4-4-2, signing Mickey Thomas to replace Hill, and Gary Bailey to replace the now-veteran Alex Stepney.

Thomas in for Hill was perhaps the most pronounced example of the difference between Sexton and Docherty, and, perhaps, Sexton and his understanding of the United way of doing things. Thomas was a hard worker and a popular lad but scored just twice over his first full season; his style also resembled Coppell's, in that they were both workaholics down the flanks rather than unpredictable wizards. Busby, as we know, would always like to have one of each.

Sexton was likeable but tried to avoid confrontation. Players would feel they were not getting a straight explanation when they were dropped, and not being given a fair chance to get back into the team. If he did make the team, any of its players, or any of the units within the team, any more functional than under Docherty, then projected against the bigger picture it was a futile argument because regression was clear. United finished mid-table in Sexton's second season and the football was so dour that in one game a female supporter hit out at the manager with her shoe.

It wasn't just that the football was poor – defeats were heavier and more comprehensive in their nature. The entire mindset of the club had changed, and the change was so instant that it destabilised the United team and incentivised their opponent. Results in the first half of that second Sexton season made grim reading – a 3-0 defeat at Ipswich, a 3-1 loss at home to Bristol City, 5-1 at Birmingham, 3-0 at Everton, and at Bolton. Christmastime was particularly distressing for United fans – a combined gate of over 145,000 for consecutive home league games against Liverpool, West Brom and Arsenal saw United heavily beaten in all three. The club were languishing in ninth place – and they were fortunate to finish there as they won just six of their remaining 19 games.

It was a reflection, then, on how powerful the FA Cup remained as an indicator of progress. There was no telling what a good FA Cup run could do for a team's confidence. It was Busby's first trophy. It was the 1963 win which seemed to inspire new belief in the post-Munich team. McGuinness' brushes with semi-finals were used as what-ifs when it came to how his power and control would be perceived in the dressing room. If Sexton could win the FA Cup then he might earn a stay of execution. United overcame Liverpool in an entertaining semi-final that went to a replay;

the decisive moment came from Thomas pinging one of those measured crosses, for Jimmy Greenhoff to head in.

In the final against Arsenal, United played okay, but were punished at key moments.

BAILEY

NICHOLL MCQUEEN BUCHAN ALBISTON

COPPELL MACARI MCILROY THOMAS

JORDAN J.GREENHOFF

Observing the game, it's not clear the players had necessarily been told to be pragmatic. Sexton's approach wasn't overly cautious; for example, for throw-ins high up the pitch, the full-backs would come forward to take them. McIlroy and Macari could never have their natural game repressed. Coppell and Thomas seemed to be part of a definite flat four in midfield but still went forward. Considering Docherty's trophy was won displaying some of the pragmatism the team didn't usually show, then some compromise would be necessary; still, United were 2-0 down at half-time.

They were still 2-0 down in the 80th minute and would have to gamble. When McQueen scored in the 86th minute, it sparked a panic in the Arsenal backline. McIlroy took advantage of some desperate defending, dodging a couple of tackles to snatch a remarkable equaliser in the 88th minute.

At that moment, Brian Greenhoff, who had been warming up, was instructed by Tommy Cavanagh to take off his tracksuit bottoms quickly to get on before Arsenal kicked off again. Sexton, employing that cool head, stopped the substitution, saying "We'll make it in extra-time." Famous last words. With emotions still running high, Arsenal threw a cross into the box; Bailey came for it but missed, and Alan Sunderland had a fairly easy task to finish, breaking United's hearts less than 60 seconds after drawing level;

all in the time it would have taken for Sexton to take some of the sting out of the game.

Following the match, Sexton exuded dignity, congratulating Arsenal and describing his pride that United had taken part in such an entertaining final. It brought to mind two similar statements in defeat – the first by Matt Busby, who congratulated Joe Mercer on television after Manchester City won the league in 1968.

The second was by Tommy Docherty in 1976 where he had vowed to bring the FA Cup to the supporters the following year. Football had changed a lot in 11 years; with hooliganism on the rise throughout the previous decade, there was much more confrontation between fans of rival clubs, much more tribal defence of your own, and United's supporters – who had endured the jeers of their rivals through their descent – were not in the mood to entertain the congratulating of a rival after such a soul-crushing defeat, even if doing so revealed much about Sexton in a positive way.

United's best moments in the Sexton era had arguably been when the team seemed to require shock therapy to play – for a brief moment in time – like they had in the Docherty era. The board kept faith in spite of the defeat and Sexton, instead of heeding the message, doubled down on his pragmatic approach. In the summer, Ray Wilkins was signed, a player who definitely fitted the job description of an actual central midfielder. His considered use of the ball was a contrast to the pass, move and find pockets of space approach of McIlroy and Macari, but there was no reason why it couldn't be complementary and, to be truthful, it was, and also facilitated a flexible 4-3-3 shape.

A handsome win over Nottingham Forest in December 1979 with this team showed how dynamic they could be:

DAVE SEXTON

BAILEY

NICHOLL MCQUEEN BUCHAN HOUSTON

COPPELL WILKINS MCILROY MACARI THOMAS

JORDAN

(MACARI PUSHING FORWARD)

This flexible system helped United score three goals before the half-hour mark; it serves to show there were positive moments, there was good football and there was some benefit to investing faith in the manager. Such excitement was rare, though, and there was a nagging feeling that a lack of quality in key areas was still the issue preventing United making a title challenge. Unfortunately for Sexton, these were generally the areas in which he had brought players. The same team which won against Forest lost easily against Liverpool in the next game and when the Merseysiders visited Old Trafford for the return in early April, they were six points in front with seven games left. An away win would effectively seal the title – United were in second, but their lack of goal power had proved significant, with just 50 goals scored in 35 games.

McIlroy was suspended, so in came Jimmy Greenhoff, who had been suffering from injury problems so bad that this was only his second appearance of the season. Sexton switched to a 4-4-2 and United came back from 1-0 down to win 2-1. Greenhoff scored the winner – but the game was perhaps more memorable for a display of how United's offside trap worked. Or didn't. As United attempted to launch a counter-attack, all of their players rushed up the field. They were almost on the halfway line when the ball fell to Alan Hansen, who flicked the ball over all of them and raced through the crowd. Not one home defender anticipated it, and Hansen gathered the loose ball to find himself in space at least 15 yards in front of an opponent. Hansen tried to be too cute and played the ball to Dalglish – he somehow put the ball wide, but the exposing of the poor defensive organisation almost three years into the job effectively undermined one of the few improvements Sexton was supposed to have made.

Sexton did seem to get the hint about what might be needed to lift the crowd – giving Andy Ritchie, a young homegrown striker, a chance. He took it, scoring a hat-trick against Spurs and provided the team with an extra dimension in a 4-4-2 which enabled Jordan to score a few more goals too. Ritchie's youthfulness galvanised the crowd – United won six on the bounce, so in their last game, they actually still had a mathematical chance of winning the title, as Liverpool had drawn a couple of games. They had to win at Elland Road and hope Paisley's side lost their home game with Aston Villa, and then again at Middlesbrough three days later. But United lost to Leeds, and Liverpool defeated Villa, and the wait for a league title at Old Trafford moved to 13 years. However, a second placed finish, following a cup final – this was progress, and Sexton was kept on, in spite of earlier comments he had made along the same lines as the ones he'd made at QPR about offering to resign if United didn't win a trophy within three years.

"We did well last year because everyone played to their full potential in an unselfish way," Sexton wrote in his programme notes for the first home game of the 1980/81 season. "We have proved what can be achieved if the players are prepared to work for one another."

Four goalless draws from the first 11 league games came in spite of Sexton's private concession that he would have to play 4-4-2 and do away completely with his three-man midfield. Andy Ritchie hadn't scored since his hat-trick against Spurs and in six of the last seven games he played, the team had failed to score – so he was deemed dispensable, with Brighton making an offer. The transfer helped to fund Sexton's big move for Garry Birtles, the Nottingham Forest striker. He had helped Forest win the European Cup. Aston Villa would also win the biggest trophy in the game in the next couple of years, making that two teams who were with United in the Second Division to do so – an indictment of how everything had stalled at Old Trafford.

A look at the team Sexton picked to face Coventry at Old Trafford on November 8th, 1980:

BAILEY
NICHOLL JOVANOVIC MORAN ALBISTON
COPPELL MACARI MCILROY THOMAS
BIRTLES JORDAN

United drew 0-0, and registered another couple of goalless draws before the turn of the year. The industry in the middle of the park was neutralised by the system they played in; two defenders behind them who were definite defenders, one target man in front, and another anchored to the front line as he anxiously awaited his first goal for the club. Ray Wilkins returned from injury and Sexton's first response was to drop McIlroy for the FA Cup third round replay at Brighton. That game saw Birtles score his first goal, as United won – but this was only brief respite. Forest eliminated United in the next round and the team went on a run of five games without scoring. That made it 15 games from 33 in the league where United had failed to score. The club were languishing in ninth place on March 7th, but had played one or two games more than the six teams beneath them.

McIlroy was called in to replace Thomas on the left, the closest Sexton came to conceding that his pragmatism was partly responsible for the team's dour season. It was obvious that he would be dismissed, but he was reportedly saved by an intervention;

an emergency meeting of First Division chairmen was called in February where it was reported a pact had been made for no more managers to be sacked, following a record-high number of dismissals.

United's representative in this meeting was not Louis Edwards, but his son, Martin, who had recently taken ownership of the club following Louis' death. The decision had been taken nonetheless, so not even a remarkable conclusion, where United won their last seven games in a row, could save the manager. The team sheets from that run of games are interesting because in 1-11 they read (give or take one name, this was from Sexton's final match against Norwich City at home): Bailey, Duxbury, Albiston, Moran, McQueen, Buchan, Coppell, Birtles, Jordan, Macari, Wilkins.

Sexton was definitely employing a different shape as we can tell by the lack of width on the left. A back five could definitely be constructed from this system but Sexton had instead decided to use Coppell as part of his front three.

BAILEY

DUXBURY MCQUEEN BUCHAN ALBISTON

MORAN WILKINS MACARI

COPPELL JORDAN BIRTLES

United won that game 1-0 – Jordan scoring. The new shape helped the side record five clean sheets from those seven wins, and an eighth-placed finish, but it wasn't enough and Sexton was relieved of his duties days after that last game.

Birtles remained without a league goal but Jordan scored seven from the last nine games to invite offers from overseas; AC Milan were the club who won his signature, a lucrative move for the physical forward who had divided opinion ever since his arrival. There was no doubt he added a presence but even some of his new team-mates were shocked when, early into his Old Trafford career, he fractured an opponent's cheekbone with his elbow. Jordan did prove to be popular with supporters but he would inevitably be perceived as one of those players who personified a shift away from the Docherty era into the Sexton era, therefore associated with a transition to dour football.

This was always the risk when a new manager comes into an existing set-up that has been successful. A new manager has his own ideas and his own vision of how to improve a team. Docherty's team were so personally associated with him that you almost get the feeling that any disruption of the groove was likely to result in some form of implosion. Does that give the impression that regression was inevitable? It didn't have to be that way. Like the McGuinness appointment, there were many theoretical reasons to support the decision to recruit Sexton. His hiring was not linked to Docherty's firing; so, someone had to come in. Dave Sexton was as qualified as any, was a tremendously respected coach, and had proven at QPR that he could take over a squad with potential and take them to further heights, playing attractive football.

It was clear that he favoured a three-man midfield and counter-attacking football and it is fair to say that both of these elements created a ripple that, whether subtle or substantial, was significant enough to disrupt the fluency. Sometimes that's all it takes.

In the interest of fairness let's bear in mind McIlroy's assessment of Docherty's way – that it was 'suicidal' and 'shouldn't have worked'. One response to that is that it possibly wouldn't have worked for much longer without a plan B. Another is that it was too attacking, to the extent that anything would be seen as defensive by comparison. So we have to present a balance, in the form of a player and a coach.

Mick Duxbury, a young player given his chance in the team

by Sexton, remembered being shown videos of how Franz Beckenbauer brought the ball out of defence. He recalled the first thing the United boss said to him. "When Stevie gets the ball, go past him."

And Frank Blunstone, who one would feel could definitely be neutral, said Sexton "was always an attacking coach. He was the first person to get full-backs to attack."

So he lacked the success and the entertainment on the pitch and, off the pitch, according to Gordon Hill, "left reporters wondering what to write in their columns after press conferences, whereas with the Doc they were wondering what to leave out." One thing he could not be accused of was a neglect of the youth system, with many getting a chance, and many also crediting Sexton's experience as helping to galvanise a flagging system. By his final team, though, only a couple of players in Sexton's first XI had actually come through the youth system – and only one, Duxbury, through him.

Opinion, conjecture, comparison; sometimes the numbers speak for themselves. Sexton inherited a side with an average age still three or four years away from its peak; his final team featured just three who had won the FA Cup and many of the star names from that team were gone from the club altogether. The ones who seemed to typify the cavalier or specific nature of Docherty's football were the first to fall – Hill, Brian Greenhoff, Pearson – and if you are keen on observing trends then here's another. You will recall the controversial sale of Johnny Morris in March 1949 – a world-record fee was commanded for the youngest member of Busby's first trophy-winning side. Since that point, the youth system had proved a boost to the club's bank balance, with hundreds of thousands of pounds over the years being earned by developing players and moving them on. Usually, these transfers would take place when United deemed the player was not going to play a big part; so, more reasonable asking prices were negotiated, as a way to thank the player both for their service and to allow them to ask for a higher salary.

It puts into context, then, that Hill (although not developed by United) was sold for a club-record fee of around £250,000. When Brian Greenhoff moved to Leeds 16 months later, his fee eclipsed even that. Sexton was given the full backing of the board to make these unpopular decisions. At some point, there was even a concession that the gung-ho football might have to be sacrificed for a more stable and consistent push for the championship. But the second place of 1980 was followed by eighth place, and even though the defence was mean enough to concede just 36 times, the attack could only score 51, their lowest since relegation.

Joe Jordan's abrasiveness is sometimes misconstrued; United did need a more dominant force up front. You could also argue that they needed all of the attributes that Sexton identified in new players – the conscientiousness of Thomas, the height of McQueen and the grace of Wilkins, for example – but the prevailing feeling was one that these qualities should have been a plan B or plan C for a very effective plan A that he inherited. Tactically, Sexton was most certainly of his time. As he proved at Chelsea and QPR, there was no fundamental flaw in his system that made it unattractive. Those teams played fine football and, in QPR's case, became the best and most attractive side in the club's history.

When you have a squad of players who have become so indoctrinated in a way of playing, and are so invested in their relationship with the manager, this can be counterproductive when a new coach arrives. They become resistant, apprehensive about new ideas. United's players in the main still tried to go along with the new way, but even when the new manager brought in replacements, there was no genuine improvement. You could argue Sexton was a better coach than Docherty, but not a better manager for Manchester United, and ultimately, that was the defining factor.

Was the Sexton era football as envisioned by Matt Busby? No – but considering the circumstances, it is difficult to know how else the club could have handled the matter after the sacking of Tommy Docherty. So it would be unfair to simply categorise the appointment as a mistake. All in all, Sexton had four years, which was long enough to make his own impression. He most certainly did that.

18

RON ATKINSON

MARTIN EDWARDS WAS NOT ABLE TO HIRE AN immediate successor to Dave Sexton. He believed he had, in the form of Lawrie McMenemy, but the Southampton boss decided to remain on the south coast. It forced the Manchester United chairman to go back to the drawing board but he was turned down by Bobby Robson and Ron Saunders – so the club went on their post-season trip to Malaysia in the summer of 1981 with Jack Crompton serving as caretaker manager.

Edwards was in charge of the effort to rediscover some of the club's identity and he was cognisant of what would be required. "Supporters always appreciate a player coming through, they got behind him perhaps even more than someone who was bought in," Edwards said, speaking about Busby and the MUJACs. "I think homegrown players give you more… is it romantic or overplayed? Perhaps sometimes, but you can't deny there is a synergy there."

It was important for Edwards to make the right appointment with it being his first hire since becoming chairman. The ownership of the Edwards family had not been popular – the success in the early part was naturally attributed to Busby and supporters had become disenfranchised by the number of dismissals over the previous decade or so. Louis Edwards had been very close to Docherty, and the decision to relieve him of his duties was taken with reluctance. It was then at least clear that the younger Edwards knew of the club's history and was conscious of the traits a United manager must possess.

The man who finally got the job was Ron Atkinson, the manager of West Brom who had a good record at Old Trafford, famously winning one game 5-3 in December 1978.

West Brom had a distinctive connection with United – they were the team Jimmy Murphy had spent most of his playing career with. They were league champions in 1920, and five-time FA Cup winners – the most recent of which, in 1954, was widely thought of as being the best team in their history. They were coached by Vic Buckingham with his interpretation of the Hungarian game. In 1971, Don Howe introduced a more defensive style at the Hawthorns, which proved to be unpopular. In 1975, he was sacked and replaced by Johnny Giles – previously, of course, of United. "Giles was the one who changed the system back to short passes, patient build up, but with licence to attack with pace in the final third," explains West Brom historian and author Chris Lepkowski, "but Atkinson was perhaps the manager who encouraged the side to attack most since the day of Buckingham."

At the Hawthorns, Atkinson facilitated the 'Three Degrees' (Brendon Batson, Laurie Cunningham and Cyrille Regis, three Black British footballers who were named after the pop group) as he attempted to make the club everyone's 'favourite second team'. Everything seemed to be about presentation – even as Cambridge manager, he drove a distinctive white Jaguar, and when he was interviewed by Martin Edwards and was offered a Rover, Atkinson responded, "I want a car, not a dog."

Upon his hiring at Old Trafford, Atkinson explained his priority was "to win, but I want United to play positively and attractively – and I certainly don't envisage sweeping the current players out." Atkinson also explained that he felt his immediate responsibility was to establish United as a European force again – even mentioning that before referencing the league title.

The club permitted Atkinson to make some sweeping changes, however – to the staff. Tommy Cavanagh and Laurie Brown were let go, and Mick Brown, Brian Whitehouse and Jim McGregor came in (the latter as physio, after Jim Headridge was initially appointed but then died of a heart attack one morning at The Cliff). Harry Gregg, the goalkeeping coach who had been brought back to the club by Sexton, walked of his own volition due to a previous disagreement with Atkinson. Jack Crompton retired from the game. Syd Owen, the youth team coach Dave Sexton had trusted to take over from Frank Blunstone, was replaced by Eric Harrison. (In an interview in 2019, Atkinson told the author that he had privately considered offering Sexton the job as youth team coach but didn't want to offend him. Sexton would go on to work with Atkinson in a similar role at Aston Villa a decade later.)

United knew they would have to spend big to back the new boss, especially as Joe Jordan had gone. Frank Stapleton, the Arsenal striker, was brought in, as was right-back John Gidman, and Atkinson made no secret of the fact that he was desperate to sign Bryan Robson, the all-action midfielder he had coached at West Brom.

Atkinson's first game as manager came against Coventry City – managed by, of all people, Dave Sexton, who had been offered a job there. 'Big Ron' used a 4-2-4 (just as he did when he started at West Brom):

BAILEY

GIDMAN   MCQUEEN   BUCHAN   ALBISTON

COPPELL   WILKINS   MACARI   MCILROY

STAPLETON   BIRTLES

Gidman was a definite attacking full-back who would overlap. McIlroy was tasked with being an out-and-out left winger. Atkinson, who was from the Docherty school when it came to facing the media, was never short of a quip or two, and wasn't completely sold on McQueen or Wilkins. He had remarked about McQueen's tendency to run with the ball and how, when he was West Brom manager, he would instruct his players to allow it. He had also described Ray Wilkins as 'The Crab' due to his sideways passing. But changes would need to be made in other areas – Buchan and Macari were in their early 30s, McQueen was 29 himself, while in Albiston, McIlroy and Coppell the manager had inherited three consistent performers who were approaching their peak. Disaster was to strike Coppell in the 1982 World Cup, when he suffered a knee injury which induced a premature end to his career in 1983 – an indication of his consistency being that he still holds the record for most consecutive appearances for the club, from 1977 to 1981.

The first game was lost, with Sexton getting some revenge in a 2-1 win. There was still a significant conclusion to be taken from Atkinson's debut in spite of defeat. Another change had occurred in English football – at the same meeting where the chairmen convened to agree not to poach managers from fellow clubs, a rule change was introduced, to award three points for a win from the 1981/82 season. This was made to encourage teams to attack, particularly away from home. Was there any notable change? Over the season, goals-per-game in the top flight went down marginally from 2.66 to 2.54 and attendances fell by almost nine per cent – an indication that supporters, many of whom were voting with their feet due to growing hooliganism, would need more than this to be wooed back. United saw a drop, too, of three per cent, in spite of sacking Sexton.

In fact, in Atkinson's first year, it could be argued the football was no greater – at least if you looked at the numbers. A total of 23 clean sheets were kept in the league – a new record, with just 29 goals conceded. United had scored just 59 goals, too. But they finished third, a definite improvement – and, despite favouring a system with wingers, Atkinson regularly used a three-man midfield, thanks mainly to his success in the signing of Bryan Robson and Remi Moses. Robson, at £1.5m, was a new club record – causing Sir Matt Busby, who had already expressed concern at Birtles coming for £1m, to resign from the board.

Atkinson was unperturbed – Robson was, in his mind, 'solid gold', and perfect for the style of play he wanted to implement. "Fans love aggression," he said. "They love flair, they love quality, but they love aggression. They love people who can tackle, and players like Robson, who had it all."

What Robson had, he felt United lacked. "When we played United we used to think they had a lot of weaknesses," he said. "You could get about them in midfield. We had good pace up front at West Brom and we knew that United defenders did not like to be disturbed by players who ran the channels. We knew Martin Buchan didn't like to leave the middle... we would always say if in doubt, let big Gordon McQueen have the ball."

Atkinson spoke of introducing 'high-intensity training' and wanted to see his players enthusiastic, remembering the way he had been brought up by Jimmy Hogan. At this point it should be made clear that the shared history of Docherty and Atkinson was purely coincidental – there was no knowledge or investigation about their way of playing other than the fact everyone could see both managers clearly liked to play attractive football. And neither Docherty nor Atkinson were truly aware of how Busby and Murphy had been influenced by the Hungarian way of playing.

When United visited Anfield on October 24th, Atkinson played this team, which was laid out in this fashion according to television graphics:

BAILEY

GIDMAN MORAN BUCHAN ALBISTON

MOSES WILKINS ROBSON COPPELL

STAPLETON BIRTLES

Commentator Martin Tyler explained how the industrious Coppell had been placed on the left to track the forward runs of right-back Phil Neal – an odd player to man-mark, one might think, in a team including Kenny Dalglish. It was a strategy that showed tactical intelligence Atkinson was never really renowned for – allowing United to make a compact middle three, and providing space for their own full-backs to move forward if the opportunity arose. In the last minute, Albiston did just that. He made a smart run and played interchanging passes before rolling the ball into the net to give his side a win.

The success of the strategy convinced Atkinson he could do without Sammy McIlroy, and so, after his sale of Mickey Thomas, he was left without a natural wide left player, forcing him to play a 4-3-3 at times. In the later part of the season, young Alan Davies proved that opportunity was just as important as talent – his capability as a left-sided attacker gave him a chance ahead of players such as Clayton Blackmore and Mark Hughes, both of whom were probably ahead of him in terms of ability. Norman Whiteside, a few years younger than Davies, was even tried, as Atkinson used the conclusion of his first season to see if there were internal solutions.

He was unconvinced, and so moved to sign Dutch playmaker Arnold Muhren on a free transfer from Ipswich Town. He seemed to be a perfect fit for United with his Total Football background, having won two league titles, a European Cup, a European Cup Winners' Cup and an Intercontinental Cup earlier in his career with Ajax. At Ipswich, he'd been part of the successful UEFA Cup-winning side of 1981, and so came to United as a 31-year-old with tons of top-class European experience.

Muhren recalled that there was a building pressure at the club to win the league after 15 years without it. "The pressure was high but I felt different," he told *Red News*. "Maybe the ones who were playing at United for a longer period had some problems with it as they all wanted it so desperately for themselves and the supporters, but if you cannot cope with that pressure it goes at the cost of your performance."

The ability to deal with that transition was not helped by the loss of Buchan and Macari, who moved into the reserves in their final moments with the club, allowing for Moran and Whiteside, to name just two, to establish themselves. The new pair were very popular but, as rookies, required time and patience. Whiteside's qualities enabled a potential move to a 4-4-2, but debate raged over his best position. His whip on the ball was so impressive that he could play wide (though Muhren had resolved that issue), his ability to strike a ball was so sweet he was an improvement to most front lines, and his tenacity made him a perfect midfielder. He was a generational talent from the same lineage as Best and McIlroy.

United again finished third in 1983 but qualified for both

domestic cup finals. Bryan Robson was missing from the first one, the League Cup final (the first in United's history) against Liverpool. Atkinson lined up with a 4-4-2:

BAILEY

DUXBURY MORAN MCQUEEN ALBISTON

COPPELL MOSES WILKINS MUHREN

STAPLETON WHITESIDE

There was no great pace in the side, just one survivor from the last cup final United had won, and just three from the last they had played in. A team built by three managers of different mindsets, although each of them believed in the same ideologies, which really seemed to prove that it's all in the teaching. Docherty's approach had been all about imposing the game through self-belief. Sexton believed in the value of instructional coaching, the sort of improvement technique that generally works better with younger players. Atkinson was probably more of the former than the latter, and would like to get involved in training sessions to show exactly what he wanted.

Successful coaching depends as much on the players as it does on the managers. It took Docherty a while to get things his way. Sexton inherited a side that was almost wholly under the Docherty spell. Atkinson had all this to deal with and the added pressure of a long wait without a league title, and the idea that United had not quite done things in the Busby way since 1970. In his first cup final, Liverpool were able to exercise their considerable experience to win in extra-time.

Two months later, however, United were back at Wembley, to face Brighton in the FA Cup final. Brighton took it to a replay, but Atkinson's side won that comfortably – 4-0, in fact, with Muhren becoming the first Dutchman to play and score in a club game at Wembley. One big difference between the League and FA Cup finals was Bryan Robson's absence from the first and presence in the second – he had quickly established himself as the bedrock of this team in a way that no midfielder had since Duncan Edwards. He had inherited the captaincy from Martin Buchan and led by example, covering every blade of grass and serving as a constant threat. In the FA Cup final replay, he scored twice, and a new era was born.

Team against Brighton:

BAILEY
DUXBURY MORAN MCQUEEN ALBISTON
DAVIES WILKINS ROBSON MUHREN
STAPLETON WHITESIDE

Incidentally, Coppell's career had more or less succumbed to injury, in spite of his appearance against Liverpool. Alan Davies was given a chance on the right in the final. However, it seemed clear that a ready-made replacement for Coppell would be necessary. There were no obvious players in the youth system and there were no obvious players available on the transfer market. Atkinson compromised, signing another veteran, Arthur Graham, who was definitely more at home on the left. But the emergence of Mark Hughes and Whiteside's versatility gave the United boss scope to experiment. What happened midway through the following campaign, however, was one of the more bold tactical shifts in the club's history.

There was a clear recognition of a lack of pace and width in the team. Atkinson had been frustrated trying to play Muhren from the right and Graham from the left. He began to trial a different shape, one that would make the most out of all the ability he did have to call upon. This was the team that won 5-0 at Luton in February 1984:

FOOTBALL, TAUGHT BY MATT BUSBY

BAILEY
DUXBURY   MORAN   HOGG   ALBISTON
WILKINS
MOSES   MUHREN
ROBSON
STAPLETON   WHITESIDE

Atkinson had created a variation of what would become known as the diamond. Johan Cruyff would be credited as the pioneer of this shape when he became manager of Barcelona in 1988, using the tactic to dominate the centre and still have cover in wide areas, a counter to the 4-4-2 formation which had almost become adopted universally now. But this was also the system used by Atkinson for various stages throughout the 1983/84 season, though perhaps it was more of a flat three in midfield, with Moses and Muhren helping the full-backs, who were asked to support the attack in an approach that was identical to the one the manager had used in his previous job.

Atkinson had often used this shape at West Brom, though Robson had played as one of the three deeper midfielders. What the diamond, or the 4-3-1-2 system, did bring was a multitude of threats. Moses and Robson had energy and dynamism; Moses was comfortable winning the ball and moving it on. Robson, as the head of the diamond, was given licence to attack – his ability to carry the ball and shoot from distance and also to arrive late in the box both threats to which opponents had little answer. Muhren conducted his wizardry from a more central position, and Wilkins could shine in his responsible ball-recycling role. Because teams were unprepared for the number of players in the centre, and because the approach played to the strengths of United's best player (and, at the time, Robson was acknowledged as one of the greatest players in the world), the change resulted in a blistering run of form. Five at Luton, three goals against Aston Villa, another four against Arsenal – United were top of the table in mid-March and finally looked as though their league title hoodoo would end. They had a favourable run of fixtures and had already taken a morale boosting late draw from Liverpool, the main contenders, in January.

After the win against Arsenal, United then faced Barcelona in the Cup Winners' Cup – and, after losing the first leg 2-0, came on to the Old Trafford pitch to a roar of almost unreasonable expectancy similar to that heard against Porto in 1977.

Team against Barcelona:

BAILEY

DUXBURY   MORAN   HOGG   ALBISTON

MOSES

WILKINS   MUHREN

ROBSON

STAPLETON   WHITESIDE

Hope came through Robson, with a goal in the 21st minute. In the second half, with expectations building, United came out in frenzied fashion – Robson levelled the tie in the 50th minute, and less than 60 seconds later, Frank Stapleton made it 3-2 on aggregate, sending the home fans into such a frenzy that the noise is renowned to this day as the loudest ever heard at Old Trafford. Barcelona had Diego Maradona, rated as the best player in the world, but he was marshalled well by Hogg, and Robson dominated this game from start to finish, making it one of the most memorable in United history. It reignited the feeling that anything was possible. Especially with their captain.

Disaster struck when Robson, then Muhren, suffered injuries to keep them out of a crucial part of the run-in. A defeat to Notts County and draws with Watford and West Ham without the pair were crucial, and United's momentum was lost. Defeat to Juventus in Europe was hard to stomach. They finished fourth in the league, somehow, six points behind Liverpool – from their last eight games, 17 points from 24 were dropped, the remarkable decline clear to see.

United were labelled a one-man team, and whilst unfair, Atkinson had not exactly shied away from it. He had indulged in the sort of temptation Busby had always resisted with Edwards, making him the figurehead of the team, creating a system that could not be as effective with any other player. But the 4-0 win over Arsenal, and the following midweek win over Barcelona – seminal though it was – were no consolation for missing out on a championship again. Frank O'Farrell's start made people excited; Tommy Docherty's side seemed to feel the closest; Dave Sexton's 1980 position was as close to the finish line as anyone had come. And yet the feeling in mid-March 1984 was the first time since United won the title in 1967 when it felt as though they were the commanding leaders and the best team in the country at a truly crucial part of the season. And it was the manager's tactical shift that had the transformative effect, even if the focus was obviously all on Robson within that system.

By the time United kicked off the next season, they had a brand new formation again – and one which resembled something more like the latter-day Docherty era:

BAILEY

DUXBURY MORAN HOGG ALBISTON

STRACHAN MOSES ROBSON OLSEN

HUGHES BRAZIL

Atkinson had splashed out on three more stars in the summer of 1984, partially funded by the sale of Ray Wilkins to AC Milan.

Alan Brazil, who he had wanted to sign prior to Stapleton, came, although it seemed as though the severity of a back injury the striker suffered had been misunderstood, making this signing doomed to failure. Much more successful were Gordon Strachan and Jesper Olsen. Strachan was energetic, clever and adept at nipping into spaces; Olsen was pacy and tricky. Both were good at beating players though had a tendency to frustrate by occasionally overplaying. Nonetheless, proper, natural width was restored, and a threat from both wings which was arguably even more adventurous than Docherty's side was countered by the change in dimension in the middle, with Moses and Robson much more physical than Macari and McIlroy.

Up front, Mark Hughes had broken through to the instant adulation of the United supporters; he was an all-action forward, really unlike anything the club had ever fielded. You could go as far as to say Hughes was unlike any other forward to ever play in England. He scored goals, but he wasn't a traditional attacker in the conventional sense of a target man, a runner, or anything else, really. He could hold up the ball with strength that defied his 5' 10 frame, could link up the play, was good on the ball, able to strike with either foot and more than anything had a sense of timing, a sense of knowing where to be.

Atkinson's style of football engaged the fans and many of the players enjoyed working with him. Others felt he involved himself too much in training, and that much training was unplanned. "We went to Heaton Park, which was a regular occurrence with United, but was always well planned out," Mick Duxbury recalled of pre-season training. "However on this particular day, we went to do some running and there was a woman with a pram – he was just telling us to run around the woman! Thoughts then occurred, what happened if she wasn't there, or even if she moved as we were running? There was no respect for how she'd feel with 30 blokes bombing towards her, and I didn't think she'd be on the pitch on the Saturday either."

After four successive draws to start the season, United demolished Newcastle 5-0; Whiteside already in for Brazil, as Atkinson's side boasted as physical and intimidating a spine, certainly in midfield and attack, as the club had ever fielded. They were still capable of the odd implosion – doubts over Hogg and Bailey's ability at the top level, and Moran's durability, meant the strong forward line was undermined by a soft centre of defence with no combination ever lasting – the league appearance charts noted Hogg 29, McGrath 23, Moran 19 and McQueen 12. McGrath had such talent that he could be one of the greatest ever – fantastic on the ball to the extent he was sometimes played in defensive midfield, great in the air, and so good in the tackle that he developed a certain showmanship, drawing the crowd into a sharp intake of breath and allowing a forward to think he had a chance before robbing him. He was almost miraculous – but *was* too good to be true, as he often picked up injuries, before later succumbing to an alcohol issue that impacted his recovery from knee problems.

The defensive problems contributed to seven league defeats by January 12th, and that coupled with the early draws put paid to a chance of winning the league. But United were generally better, more rounded, better defensively when boasting a fit selection, unpredictable up front and now at least boasting another potential dimension in Robson's repositioning – should Atkinson be tempted to use it, although he didn't.

United made it to the 1985 FA Cup final, overcoming Liverpool in the semi-final – Robson scoring a memorable goal – to face Everton, who, in an echo of the 1977 final, had won the league and were due to play in the Cup Winners' Cup final against Liverpool the following week.

BAILEY
GIDMAN MCGRATH MORAN ALBISTON
STRACHAN ROBSON WHITESIDE OLSEN
HUGHES STAPLETON

It was another tight encounter that seemed destined for extra-time until Kevin Moran became the first player to be sent off in an FA Cup final in the 85th minute. Atkinson's side held off the champions until the end; his necessary reshuffle meant Stapleton moved back into the defence, and then Duxbury was brought on for Albiston. The grit and determination was evident. But then came the moment of class, when Norman Whiteside created a small pocket of space, out of the eye-line of goalkeeper Neville Southall, to score a sensational curled shot into the corner. It was the only goal of the game – winning Atkinson his second FA Cup, and making him the most successful post-Busby manager. Another tactical triumph for Big Ron, but this time, no reward of taking United back into Europe, due to the ban on English clubs after the Heysel disaster on 29th May 1985, when Liverpool and Juventus faced each other following the European Cup final in Belgium and 39 supporters were killed in crowd trouble.

Four years in charge, a team built in his own vision, and an FA Cup win against the best team in the land, it now seemed as though Atkinson had the opportunity that Docherty never did. He added to his team in a conservative manner, acquiring only Peter Barnes, at first, to add some depth on the left side.

United's form in this 4-4-2/4-2-4 was so exceptional at the start of the following campaign that they not only won their first 10 games, they compelled respected *Guardian* columnist

David Lacey to ask if the club had ever 'had a better quartet than Strachan, Olsen, Whiteside and Hughes', which was high praise – not just because Bryan Robson was still seen as the best player in the country.

Then the wheels came off. Injuries to Robson and McGrath deeply hurt United's spine. Albiston, usually so durable, spent time out. So too did Moran. Gidman. Olsen. Try as they might, a groove could not be restored, and that was in spite of Atkinson splashing the cash to bring in Chris Turner in goal, Colin Gibson in defence, and Peter Davenport and Terry Gibson up front.

United's form collapsed, although Atkinson maintained the same team shape and the same approach, always hoping his team had a strong enough lead to turn it around. By February, their perfect start had completely been derailed, and Everton had gone above them to lead the table. By mid-April, United were lucky to recover form in their last four games to finish fourth and not sixth – an absolute disaster.

Atkinson reportedly offered to resign in the last league game of the season, but he started 1986/87 in charge. The writing was on the wall, though, as Robson missed the start of the campaign with a shoulder injury picked up at the World Cup that summer. But there is underperformance without your talisman and there is losing six of your first eight league games – and, when Atkinson saw his team heavily beaten in the League Cup by Southampton in November 1986, he found himself out of a job.

Injuries were of course a major reason for United's failure. They happened at the wrong times as well, highlighting the difference between succeeding and not succeeding. However, towards the end, Atkinson also seemed to be suffering under the strain, making gambles by bringing in players on short-terms deals or loan. Although he had given a fair number of homegrown players a chance, these gambles alienated both those younger players and the senior players who were left out. This meant an increasing problem with discipline, and it did not help that Mick Brown, Atkinson's assistant, didn't command the same respect as Jimmy Murphy or instil the same fear or affection as Tommy Cavanagh.

At youth-team level, Eric Harrison – who, alongside Bryan Robson, would not only be described by Atkinson as his best signing, but would also prove to be very beneficial in future years to Atkinson's successor – had taken the team to two Youth Cup finals, their first since 1964. From the 1982 team Hogg, Garton, Blackmore, Dempsey, Whiteside and Wood all made the first 11 under Atkinson. From the 1986 team, Walsh, Martin and Gill all enjoyed a fair number of first-team games. United's youth team continued to play with wingers in a 4-4-2 shape. There was an obvious pride at the relative success of their achievements but the emphasis was on the progress of the individuals, and therefore, just as it had been in the Busby days, players were tried in different positions.

For the most part, Atkinson was charismatic and genial with the press; even after his dismissal, he was happy to be interviewed in a fairly nonplussed way at home, wishing the club all the best. That night, he held a 'farewell party' at his house, where the divide in the squad was clear in those who did, and those who did not, turn up. There certainly could be no accusation that the profile was too big for him in the same way it was said about O'Farrell and Sexton, nor could it be said that his philosophy of football did not resonate with the club and the support. It was thrilling, it was always dedicated to attack and finding ways to win. Those wins were earned through individual brilliance, fine team play and, sometimes, managerial wits. He had managed a turnover of two managers' squads and built one in his own image. Tactically he was more than simply astute, there was evidence to suggest he was innovative.

His assistant, Mick Brown, did not give many interviews, so it is difficult to fairly assess him in comparison to Jimmy Murphy or Tommy Cavanagh or Frank Blunstone or even Malcolm Musgrove, but he did speak about his time at Old Trafford shortly after becoming assistant at Bolton in 1987. He was asked if he felt Ron Atkinson was finding it difficult to adjust to life away from the spotlight of Manchester United. "I think anybody does," he admitted. "There's nothing bigger than that. It was a thrill and a joy. Something which I'll always treasure. If you've worked with anybody, and you've seen how much heart and soul they put into it, you leave something behind with them. And that's very much my feelings towards United. The Bryan Robsons of this world, the various trials and tribulations that he's had over the years, and how he's fought back, he's a role model for everybody else. And it's very satisfying to see all those kids coming on now and making a name for themselves. So I take great pleasure out of that."

There are other reasons cited for United's failure to win the title. Some players, like Clayton Blackmore, felt the pitches in winter did not help the team play its natural game. Others felt the rules were still more inclined to reward pragmatic football and that Liverpool were better at that approach. Some United players were beginning to feel as though the efforts they were seeing opponents put in against other teams did not quite match the cup final atmosphere they seemed to be playing in every week. And then there was the significant alcohol culture in the game, though it was part of football outlook everywhere, and it didn't harm Liverpool or Everton, the dominant teams of the decade.

In terms of British culture versus European culture, the welcoming of foreign players had coincided with an era of dominance of English clubs in Europe. From 1977 to 1984 the European Cup was only won by a non-English team once, giving weight to the theory that English football was not only the best but also the standard bearer in terms of pioneering change. This was the other element counting against Atkinson; he, like Sexton and Docherty, was competing against at least four clubs who were enjoying their best spells in history in Aston Villa, Everton, Liverpool and Nottingham Forest. They once had lean spells, and sometimes Manchester United were winning trophies in those periods.

United's lean spell in terms of a league title had lasted almost two decades – and despite two very entertaining teams that had come very close to the club's historical identity, it was clear that another hurdle must be cleared in order to truly achieve that goal.

19

ENTER ALEX FERGUSON...

ALEX FERGUSON WAS THE MAN CHOSEN TO SUCCEED Ron Atkinson – of course, we all know the story, and a book of this nature could focus only on the eras of Busby and Ferguson and still feel complete in terms of how it defines Manchester United. However, as Ferguson told the author in 2016, "To know your future, you must know your history" so the stories of the other managers are no less important in the tapestry of the club.

Ferguson's era covered more than 26 years, the stories of which cover many books, interviews and records. The best way to summarise it here is to take a journey that has several stops down the road. Before we set off, let us briefly discuss why Ferguson was hired, what he immediately brought to the role and the first few years.

Rewinding all the way back to when Ferguson was a ten-year-old boy, he recalled his first true education in football being delivered by a man named Mick McGowan. Ferguson was playing for a local team called Harmony Row. "We just wanted to get the ball out and play," he remembered, "but he kept on about passing and movement." So far, so Scottish. Ferguson was present when Di Stefano and Puskas inspired Real Madrid to destroy Eintracht Frankfurt at Hampden Park; a lesson in movement and hard work from the forward players.

There were three things that stood out to Martin Edwards and Bobby Charlton (now on the United board) about Ferguson when considering him for the job. The first was obvious – the success he'd enjoyed at Aberdeen. He'd broken the domestic stranglehold of the Old Firm and even overcome Real Madrid in the European Cup Winners' Cup final. He believed in the introduction of young players, which of course was important to United's past. Perhaps most distinctively there was the memorable sight of Ferguson on the pitch after the 1983 Scottish Cup final, which Aberdeen had won – on live television, their manager labelled the performance a disgrace, an indication that he held a standard of his own that wasn't dictated by the level of the opposition or even winning the game.

Once at Old Trafford, Ferguson was not afraid to make big changes. Archie Knox followed from Aberdeen as his assistant. Eric Harrison was kept on and over time the manager provided assistance for him in the form of club legends Brian Kidd and Nobby Stiles. He inherited some good young players, and was willing to use them, but the scale of the necessary transition was so severe that it would need at least one full turnover of players. Bryan Robson aside, even if individually many of the players would feel good enough to play in a title-winning team, collectively they had not proven it. There were plenty of other factors, such as addressing the drink issue and showing a ruthlessness to move on players he had signed once they had contributed as much as they could.

Ferguson survived criticism from supporters, the controversy of a failed takeover, and press speculation that he was on the verge of the sack before delivering his first trophy, the 1990 FA Cup.

Through it all he demonstrated bravery. First, by going where others feared – to directly embrace the input and influence of Busby and Murphy. To be fair, Murphy had been brought back into the scouting fold consciously by Docherty, while Atkinson had tried to include Busby after his resignation from the board. But neither seemed to make as concerted an effort to personally engage with the pair as Ferguson did. In the early stages of 1989, Ferguson then bucked the trend of Atkinson and even Docherty to address short-term problems with short-term signings, by throwing in a number of young players who had barely played. There was no success that season, but the memory of games against Liverpool and QPR remained a bright light from the early Ferguson years, a reminder that the United support would come alive to back their own boys. Lose those games and the manager's position might have been even more precarious. In the early years, Ferguson predominantly played a 4-4-2, just as he had at Aberdeen for their major successes. In fact, his first FA Cup final team was similar in composition:

LEIGHTON/SEALEY

PHELAN BRUCE PALLISTER MARTIN

WEBB INCE ROBSON WALLACE

MCCLAIR HUGHES

...similar in that it was a 4-4-2 with an industrious winger capable of moving inside on the right, and a more traditional, pacy winger on the left, something that of course was familiar to United fans too. In the three-and-a-half years since Ferguson had become manager he had turned over the 1985 side almost completely – only Robson remained (even Hughes had been sold and bought back) while of the others, only Lee Martin, the player who scored the winning goal in the replay, was inherited as a youth player. Furthermore, there was a turnover of talent that the manager had been trusted with to get to this stage. Viv Anderson and Mal Donaghy were now no longer in the first-team picture, neither was Ralph Milne, and Jim Leighton served as collateral evidence that Ferguson wasn't afraid to make such a call between a cup final and a replay.

The new manager had made United much more resilient. Steve Bruce and Gary Pallister were such a tremendous partnership that the idea of Robson ending his career as a sweeper was put to one side; with Paul Ince, and Brian McClair and Hughes up front, there was such a physical spine now that United could no longer be bullied on the road against the lesser teams. Evidence of this was found in the run to the 1990 final, as the club played every tie away from home. Robson and Ince were box-to-box – Bruce the archetypal stopper, Pallister the sweeper. Neil Webb was arguably the best passer in the team, and Mike Phelan had an engine to overlap to create space for Webb. Lee Martin could overlap on the other side, though Danny Wallace was more unpredictable and could drift infield. Up front, Hughes' qualities have already been outlined, and McClair, signed as a goal-hanger, had proven to be much more – he could drop into midfield and showed great comfort on the ball.

United, as stated, won against Crystal Palace in the replay. But it was 12 months later, when they faced Johan Cruyff's Barcelona in the Cup Winners' Cup final, that one of the first truly compelling tactical battles in generations transpired, certainly as far as Manchester United were concerned. It was portrayed as the English against the Dutch and Spanish, traditional British style against the technical Total Football. The revered Cruyff was now making his early steps into management, and had adapted the 4-3-3 he'd played in under Michels into a 3-4-3, the idea of manipulating space to dominate in numbers at the forefront of his mind.

"If you have four men defending two strikers, you only have six against eight in the middle of the field: there's no way you can win that battle," Cruyff said (and we might remember Sexton said similar). "We had to put a defender further forward. I was criticised for playing three at the back, but that's the most idiotic thing I've ever heard. What we needed was to fill the middle of the pitch with players where we needed it most." Sometimes, the abilities of players make those tactical switches straightforward, and Ronald Koeman had already played that way for the Holland national side (prompting Bobby Robson into a tactical shuffle in the 1990 World Cup).

Ferguson embraced the challenge – and realised the tactics would need to be right. "Word reached me that [Cruyff] had been making inquiries about me so he was obviously wondering about my ability as a tactician," Ferguson said in his book *Six Years At United*. "I enjoy a good managerial battle of wits and I tried to read what he would do. I worked out that he would play with one centre-back to leave Ronald Koeman to choke things up."

SEALEY
IRWIN BRUCE PALLISTER BLACKMORE
PHELAN INCE ROBSON SHARPE
MCCLAIR
HUGHES

Instead of counteracting this by overloading different areas, as other managers might have done, Ferguson decided to do something out of the box – and ask Brian McClair to man-mark

Koeman. The original plan had been to play McClair from the right and pack the midfield, but the change was pivotal in determining the result. Through the pace of Lee Sharpe on the left and the endless energy of Phelan, United had enough threat out wide to cause problems – and Alexanko, the Barcelona centre-back, did not at the age of 35 possess the same mobility as Mark Hughes. It helped United score twice, particularly in the events that led to their second goal, as Hughes exploited space to draw the goalkeeper out, round him, and then score from an improbable angle thanks to the improbable power he could generate in his thighs.

A late scare provoked by a Koeman goal kept the game tense but United held firm to win their first European trophy since 1968. Ferguson had triumphed over Cruyff, using nous while still not straying too far from his own approach. The full-backs were changed from a year earlier, as Denis Irwin had proved to be an instant hit and Blackmore's run of form was just too much for Martin to deal with. Phelan was preferred to Webb – Webb had issues with injury, but Phelan's work rate would likely have tipped the scales in his favour anyway. Sharpe, for the first time since Gordon Hill, was a winger who possessed so much pace and penetration that opponents were genuinely concerned about them getting in behind the defence. Incidentally, there had been another cup final in-between times – United coming up against Sheffield Wednesday, now coached by Ron Atkinson, who made a specific and successful plan to stop the ball getting to Sharpe in the League Cup final.

If only there could be another Sharpe. Well, if Atkinson had taken the Docherty model of two out-and-out wingers to another level with Strachan and Olsen, then Ferguson went further still, bringing Ryan Giggs from the youth team and signing Andrei Kanchelskis. In those three, United had arguably the three quickest players in the country; Ferguson suddenly found himself with three wingers, arguably the most precious commodity in the sport, of the highest speed and highest class.

Further smart signings followed. Paul Parker, one of the country's best man-markers. Peter Schmeichel, a goalkeeper with an immense frame and possessor of a powerful throw, gave the team a physical presence in goal they'd not had since Harry Gregg's heyday. Later in 1991, United contested the European Super Cup with old friends Red Star Belgrade, recent winners of the European Cup. The game was played over 90 minutes at Old Trafford (it was usually a two-legged affair, but political unrest in Yugoslavia caused UEFA to intervene). The Super Cup was created in 1972 as a way to, in the mind of Dutch sports writer Anton Witkamp, determine who was 'definitely' the best team in Europe.

With Sir Matt Busby in attendance, United, then, could claim to be just that when coming out 1-0 winners thanks to a Brian McClair goal. But there was no doubt that Red Star had put on a technical masterclass and were perhaps denied by the poor state of the Old Trafford pitch. Ferguson was compelled to pay tribute. "They certainly have the talent and the imagination," he said. "Most of the football came from Red Star. They strung us out and they deserved more. They have players of true quality… especially Dejan Savicevic, who has that imagination which all the great players have."

With the confidence boost of believing they could beat the best (and why not, considering Barcelona would go on to win the 1992 European Cup?), United's players believed themselves to be the top side in the country. They almost won the league in 1992, but two cup runs had caused a fixture pile-up. The League Cup was won for the first time in the club's history, but the league title evaded the grasp of Manchester United once again, after a calamitous week (and a bit) where Ferguson's side played four games, with players dropping like flies. Final surrender came at Liverpool – the Anfield side had now moved to 18 league titles, leaving United's seven looking meek by comparison, and the great north-west rivals were able to enjoy further taunting their foes by virtue of the fact that the title-winners this time around were Leeds United. The Yorkshire club, in fact, held the contract of the man who would prove transformative to Ferguson's fortunes.

He was celebrating six years at the club in November 1992, longer than any Busby successor, and already more successful than any of them with three trophies. There was a fourth which arrived in May 1992 – albeit at junior level. Ferguson's aggressive restructuring at youth level, including a massive scouting revamp which was reminiscent of Busby's earliest days, had attracted some of the best young players in the country. David Beckham, from London, was captivated by Manchester because his dad was a huge United fan. Keith Gillespie, from Northern Ireland, was another promising winger. But United also managed to get the cream of the crop locally too – Ryan Giggs and Nicky Butt, followed by Paul Scholes, Ben Thornley, Chris Casper and Gary and Philip Neville.

This group of players won the club's first FA Youth Cup since 1964:

PILKINGTON

O'KANE CASPER NEVILLE SWITZER

DAVIES BECKHAM BUTT THORNLEY

MCKEE GIGGS

With the likes of Gillespie, Scholes and Robbie Savage still in the wings, this side had the same sort of liberation as the early Jimmy Murphy (who, sadly, had passed away in November 1989) sides. The midfield and front line in particular had plenty of character

– there was something of Eddie Colman in Butt, while pinning Davies, Beckham, Thornley and Giggs to specific positions was as fruitless an exercise for an author writing a book as it was for opponents knowing who to mark. These were players who were developing an interchangeable quality. Butt was definitely not afraid of a tackle but, to some extent, watching the youth team of this era was not a million miles away from watching the Docherty team, albeit with a dash of the old Murphy relentlessness, thanks to the hard nose of Eric Harrison.

Giggs, like Edwards and Best before him, was already starring in the first team while winning a Youth Cup medal. At times it seemed like he would be the final piece in United's title-winning jigsaw – but that honour went instead to Eric Cantona, who signed just before Ferguson's sixth anniversary for a fee of £1m. The transfer was a gamble – Cantona came with a history of controversy, there was discussion over how influential he'd really been in Leeds' success, and United seemed to require a striker to deliver 30 goals a season. Yet, just like Jimmy Greenhoff, sometimes the unexpected opportunities yield the greatest results.

SCHMEICHEL

PARKER BRUCE PALLISTER IRWIN

KANCHELSKIS INCE ROBSON/KEANE GIGGS

CANTONA HUGHES

For expedience, we'll include the signing of Roy Keane, who arrived around eight months after Cantona. This was the most settled team United had fielded since the 1977 FA Cup final win, or the easiest 1-11 to rattle off. Or at least that should be the easiest team sheet to read – as in 1993, the Premier League (the new name for the top division in England) introduced squad numbers so names were included on shirts too. That was a superficial change;

in 1992, one of the most significant alterations to the game since the offside rule in the 1920s occurred, when goalkeepers were forbidden from picking up a back pass from a team-mate.

Schmeichel, better with his feet than the average goalkeeper, and an established starter of counter-attacks already, was almost the perfect goalkeeper for this. He still had his dependable defenders in front and Irwin's ability to play on either side softened the blow of Blackmore's hernia issue; Parker claimed the right-back spot, and though not as proficient an attacker, he could nonetheless join in, and his diligence meant United were never outnumbered at the back. Ince and Robson, and later Keane, were like three Rottweilers in the middle, players who found the mere idea that an opponent might want to dominate the middle of the pitch a personal affront. They could defend and attack, providing a potent threat around either box, causing a constant headache for opponents. Cantona and Hughes were happy to play in front of the opposition – defenders notoriously hate forwards who want to get in behind them, but they must detest even more the sight of two players so capable of causing extreme harm in front of them.

A ball up to Hughes would be held until it was played back to Cantona, Ince or Keane, who would bomb forward. A ball up to Cantona would see the Frenchman instantly scanning right or left to see which of Kanchelskis or Giggs was setting off, destined to win the race behind any full-back. Both wingers were adept at running with the ball in front or behind defenders – Kanchelskis more deadly if he could get behind, Giggs with a tendency to give a marker 'twisted blood' if he had the temerity to defend.

Cantona, meanwhile, went from *enfant terrible*, exiled from his own country at the start of 1992, to third place in the Ballon d'Or list of 1993 as he inspired United to win their first league title for 26 years. His contribution was immeasurable. Ostensibly a striker, the Frenchman could often disappear from a game only to pop up in an area where he could inflict the greatest damage. His brand of craft and ingenuity was hitherto only seen in a United shirt when George Best wore one. Like Best, trying to define Cantona as a player seems reductive – to some, Cantona tops any all-time player poll without question, to others, he might not even make their all-time United team, but nobody would ever doubt his status as one of the most important players to play for the club, nor would anyone diminish his role in that first era of proper dominance since the mid-60s.

It is probably no coincidence that Cantona's arrival made United more of a European team than at any time since 1968 – so what exactly does that mean? Well, from 1968 to 1993, United enjoyed periods of entertaining football, but even the most gung-ho Docherty sides were confined to a 4-2-4, and when the midfielders and strikers traded positions, it would usually be strikers dropping in to fill areas left by marauding team-mates.

Cantona was the second striker in a 4-4-2, but dropped so deep that the shape could be described as a 4-4-1-1 or 4-2-3-1, such was the frequency with which Kanchelskis and Giggs moved forward. It may be a push to describe Cantona's positioning as similar to that of Nándor Hidegkuti in the Match Of The Century in 1953, but the inverse movement of Cantona to make it more about the play and less about the finish had a significant enough impact that we could describe it as one of the great tactical innovations of the early 1990s in British football. It was the most flexible and unpredictable set-up since the late 60s, and possibly explains why the 1993 side seemed more like a Busby side than any since the great man retired.

20

ONWARDS AND UPWARDS

HAVING FINALLY WITNESSED HIS BELOVED TEAM reach the summit of English football again, Sir Matt Busby passed away in January 1994. He had watched, thrilled, as the past seemed to play out in front of him; Ferguson, after some time, making success with what he had inherited, laying the foundations for future success, and building a league-winning team. A team that entertained and that could handle any sort of encounter.

In constructing this side, Ferguson had created the origins of a monster, so far as the rest of the league was concerned. Cantona's magic at Old Trafford coincided with the creation of the Premier League, BSkyB's sponsorship and weekly televised games, around-the-clock sports news, an image clean-up post-Heysel and Hillsborough – Cantona himself had walked straight into the national vacancy for a figurehead after Paul Gascoigne had won the hearts of the nation at the World Cup in 1990. But Gascoigne was now winning Italian hearts with Lazio, and English football was equally captivated (even if the *love* was not quite as universal) with Cantona. United's value as a club rose exponentially in the years Cantona was there. The confidence of the team in 1991 blossomed into outright arrogance after Cantona inspired title wins in 1993 and 1994.

Resilience turned into impenetrable physicality; if so-called lesser teams tried to win with aggression, they were quickly found wanting. There was a spell of games in the 1993/94 campaign which were amongst some of the greatest in the club's history. It was triggered by a goal scored by Mark Hughes at Sheffield United in the FA Cup, where almost every outfield player was involved in the build-up, moving around patiently with the craftsmanship of an elite watchmaker, playing their game at their own will. This synergy continued in the fifth round at Wimbledon, a traditionally over-physical opponent specialising in cup ties. Cantona, victim of a thigh-high challenge by Vinnie Jones, shrugged it off to later score one of the greatest goals of his career. Later, Denis Irwin scored after a similar passing move to the one at Bramall Lane. "You usually get half a dozen matches every season when the whole team are 100 per cent on song and on top of their game," Ferguson reflected, "and Wimbledon caught us on one of those days." Sheffield Wednesday did, too, on two separate occasions – losing 5-0 at Old Trafford and 4-1 in a League Cup tie. The football was so multi-dimensional that in the two-year spell between 1992 and 1994, it was already fair to ponder if it was the greatest United side of all time.

How could they prove that? By winning the European Cup. The issue United faced was in UEFA's rule on foreign players allowed in their competitions. It was a three plus two rule, the two referring to 'assimilated' players – players who had lived in the country for five years. It provided a headache for Ferguson, as six of his 1994

FA Cup final side were impacted by the rule. He was never able to field that side fully in Europe, and they were eliminated first by Galatasaray on away goals in 1993, and then in the group stage thanks mostly to embarrassing defeats away to Barcelona (4-0) and Gothenburg (3-1) in 1994.

Spanish outlet *El Mundo Deportivo* ran a pre-match assessment over Ferguson's tactical approach: "Alex Ferguson uses the classic 4-4-2. The offensive vocation of his team forces defenders and midfielders to exert strong pressure on the rivals in their own zone. This makes the creative task of the opponent extremely difficult."

The Nou Camp mauling was a chastening experience but, with Cantona suspended and Schmeichel absent, there was a caveat – and so the masterclass of Stoichkov and Romario, whilst painful, was seen as one that exposed the weaknesses of the ruling more than it did the weakness of the United team.

Time then began to take its toll, while other factors began to play a part. Ferguson felt Paul Ince had shown positional indiscipline and, when the Londoner's attitude became a little too out of control, he was deemed expendable, because the manager had Nicky Butt and Paul Scholes coming through, as well as Brian McClair. Andrei Kanchelskis started to become an issue due to his agent and a disputed injury – when Everton made a club record bid, it made sense to move him on. Mark Hughes left, too, and although all three were tough blows due to their popularity as players, it did help Ferguson's rebuilding plan, as he sought to work around the foreigner rule.

David May arrived as a versatile defender. Darren Anderton, the tricky Spurs winger, was targeted to replace Kanchelskis, but the move fell through, as did an attempt to sign the Nottingham Forest striker Stan Collymore, though Ferguson was able to acquire an English forward in the shape of Andy Cole. An out-

and-out striker, Cole did not instantly seem compatible with Cantona (who spent nine months out of the game for an infamous kung-fu kick which effectively derailed United's hopes of retaining the double in 1995). David Beckham, who had to step in to replace Kanchelskis, quickly amended his game. Never the quickest, he had envisioned himself as a Glenn Hoddle-style playmaker, but an opening was his and he had to learn to play as a winger. It was a chance he seized, as did Gary Neville, a centre-back in the youth team, when Paul Parker suffered injury issues.

The 1995/96 season really was reminiscent of the first title win of the Busby Babes, as both Neville brothers, Butt, Beckham, Scholes and Giggs played a hugely influential role, and many other youth team players made appearances (another Youth Cup win had followed in 1995). Their chemistry, natural ability and confidence illuminated the league, even if Schmeichel and Cantona provided headline-grabbing acts with their own remarkable form. There was a sacrifice of physicality – and you might even argue overall quality from the 1994 side – for industry and energy. The one issue Ferguson seemed to have was with the confidence of Cole, and so, in the latter stages of the campaign, Scholes was often preferred as a strike partner for Cantona. Cole scored in the last league game of the season, as United regained the title – so he was recalled for the FA Cup final against Liverpool.

SCHMEICHEL

P.NEVILLE   MAY   PALLISTER   IRWIN

BECKHAM   KEANE   BUTT   GIGGS

CANTONA   COLE

Prior to the game Ferguson held a meeting with Schmeichel, the entire defence, Cantona and Keane – an indication of just how prominent the young Irishman had become. He spoke of his concern about Robbie Fowler's scoring prowess and Steve McManaman's dribbling ability.

Liverpool were pioneering a style of their own – a 3-5-2 system with wing-backs was being used by Roy Evans, and so Ferguson's decision to address this was not so much a concession but more, just as with the 1991 final against Barcelona, an inquiry into how the team could handle the threat and maintain a shape as close to its natural form as possible.

"Eric suggested that Roy Keane should sit in front of the back four," Ferguson recalled, "with a three-man midfield ahead of him which would alleviate the worry of Collymore dropping off our centre-backs… we set about practising this way of playing."

Keane was man of the match, dominating the play and nullifying any threat from Liverpool. Five minutes from time, Cantona scored a perfect volley through a crowd of players – if you pause time, the penalty area looks so congested it resembles an L.S. Lowry painting – to exact what he, and United, felt was poetic retribution after his penance. In front of Keane, the work-rate of Beckham, Butt and Giggs had been exemplary, and once Scholes was on the pitch, he made it five outfield players from the club's youth system.

So this was three titles and three FA Cups for Ferguson, with three more trophies along the way. He had survived two periods of turmoil – a rocky spell in 1989 and the summer of 1995 where he let Hughes, Ince and Kanchelskis go – to effectively make himself bullet-proof. The prudence of developing six players, some of whom were burgeoning on the world-class bracket, made Martin Edwards' decision to reconstruct areas of the ground at the expense of lavish transfer fees (though he did sanction £6m for Andy Cole) a sound investment for the club.

In fact, the completion of the North Stand was a major step towards a realisation of a dream shared by Busby and Gibson in the 1940s. Old Trafford had undergone some transformations over the years; the post-war restoration, the installation of floodlights. Ahead of the 1966 World Cup there was another redesign to expand, implement cantilevering and remove pillars. The initial vision when Old Trafford was built saw talk of 100,000 people being able to watch Manchester United play. It wouldn't quite reach that figure, but the various expansions increased capacity to just over 55,000, then to just under 68,000, to, in 2008, a modern record of 76,013. Martin Edwards' tenure is primarily notable for the hiring of Alex Ferguson, but it is no less significant that he ensured the club boasted one of the most iconic stadiums in the world. Its domineering size represented the unenviable task away teams felt, adding to the daunting prospect of playing against a great team.

Back to 1996. A decade into the job, Ferguson could soundly claim to be the manager with the most success in the club's history aside from Busby. It was a vindication of both of his own work and the value of patience; it took Busby, after all, a decade for his fruit to blossom into a title-winning team. The proof of success was found just as much in the introduction of other young players as much as the major stars – no fewer than 12 homegrown players were given games throughout the season. That is not to say every player was a guaranteed success but it was, perhaps, no coincidence that United's greatest successes were coming after a commitment had been made to a manager.

Make no mistake, the first title-winning team was a complete representative of everything Ferguson stood for. Physically resolute, not to be bullied, and multi-functional – he had four key attributes he wanted to see from his team. Pace, power, penetration and unpredictability.

The club's past had been fully embraced; Ferguson ensuring

Busby was always prominently placed during any celebration, as he was in Rotterdam in 1991 and as he was at Old Trafford when United picked up the Premier League trophy against Blackburn in 1993. Yes, it was Ferguson's way of doing things too, but he was not hiding away from the club's history – in fact, in hiring Kidd (who had become his assistant) and Stiles there was always a reminder of past standards. The Youth Cup win, the two titles, the first title with the kids en masse in the team – no longer was the past a burden. It was a responsibility, but it was also an incentive. A motivation. And it was no coincidence that a group of young players were able to deal with it before their sporting maturity had been truly reached, because they were already well-versed in representing the club through the age levels.

Attention and success brings jealousy. The Busby Babes were loved enough in an era where there was infinitely more sportsmanship and Munich brought the eyes of the world on the club. Some resentment followed for the romantic conclusion to Busby's journey in 1968 with three players who had won the Ballon d'Or. It was a script Hollywood couldn't write. United were the team everyone wanted to beat, an amplified feeling when they went into the Second Division and back into the First. They were attracting the biggest crowds in the country and played in the most revered stadium in the land. The size of Old Trafford emphasised the feeling of occasion as well as sporting encounter. The elements combined to induce what United's players often perceived as a greater effort against them than opponents.

Mick Duxbury recalled a weekend in the 1980s when United were playing away and were able to watch Liverpool at Luton. He remembered being shocked at the relatively tepid atmosphere and spoke of how it strengthened his feeling of privilege of representing United. In Roy Keane's autobiography he criticised the attitude of Swindon and Norwich players, wondering why they didn't show that commitment every week. In 1996, Ferguson had made a public reference to the trend after watching his team battle to break down a ten-man Leeds United who had a defender in goal after the sending off of their goalkeeper. He criticised Leeds players for cheating their manager Howard Wilkinson, provoking an infamous rant from Kevin Keegan.

For a generation, many good footballers who came to United were just not prepared for the culture shock of an opponent playing as if it was a cup final every week. Even managers had struggled with this. Not Ferguson, with his own standards set higher than even that. It was the best possible attitude to cultivate an environment where the players could accept this and respond positively to it. Not only had they done that, by and large there had been a gracious welcoming of the generation of young talent which succeeded many of them. The youngsters learned about the physical resolve necessary in the first team, introduced sensibly alongside the likes of Bruce, Parker, Pallister, Ince and Robson. It gave them a mental edge – when trailing Newcastle by 12 points in January 1996, it wasn't just a credit that United were able to pull them back to win the title. It's that they had done it by March, and moving into May, they were already in control of their own destiny. Yes, the form of Schmeichel and Cantona had been crucial. But so too had that of Keane, Scholes, Butt, Beckham and Giggs. They were forming the heartbeat of the team, the area of the side that could have been responsible for a collapse if they did not have the mental capacity to handle sport at the highest level.

It was helpful that they were introduced into a team that possessed those attributes. Did they play football the Busby way? Well they played with pace, flair and unpredictability – and now with an added layer that even Busby didn't have. Fergie Time was a phrase coined some time after the events of April 1993, when Steve Bruce scored two late headers to turn a 1-0 defeat to Sheffield Wednesday into a 2-1 win. The victory was crucial in generating momentum for the first title but it also set in place another element which would become a tactical tool. United's refusal to accept defeat saw them also score late goals to salvage draws against Blackburn in 1993 and Oldham in the 1994 FA Cup semi-final. In these days where injury time was an arbitrary amount decided by the referee, there was a paranoid school of thought that if Manchester United were losing, the game would just be played until that was not the case. It played into the psyche of referees and opponents.

Training was not specifically altered to address this but Ferguson and his coaches were, nonetheless, conscious of it, and it became part of game management. Conservation of energy and showing patience when opponents were expecting panic were vital to keeping confidence levels high and inducing fear in opposition. It became a self-perpetuating aspect to United's game, something *they* didn't even control, and yet made a game a captivating experience for the neutral, and an anxious experience for the leading team, even if they were 2-0 up against United with 10 minutes to go. The likelihood of them pulling back a situation like this was not high, and yet, the fear was real. This was not necessarily a trait of Manchester United under Matt Busby (the 1957 Bilbao game, and 1968 Real Madrid tie aside) but it did bear the hallmark of Duncan Edwards and Jimmy Murphy; the idea that no game was lost and that United played to their own standards anyway, a standard that meant you played with a commitment to win until the whistle went. In all honesty – this was a Ferguson trait, relentless as he was, but the idea of tying it into the club's fabric was something the manager was already conscious of.

Having finally assembled a team that could play all the time under the foreigner rule, said foreigner rule was abolished in the wake of the Bosman ruling – which stated players could move across Europe at the end of their contract without their old club receiving a fee. This was a monumental moment when it came to tactics, diet, and essentially all foreign cultures being introduced into the British game.

Some clubs resisted and others embraced it, leading to a unique era where the positive sensibilities of one culture mixed with another, and the prevailing philosophies still remained fundamentally attached to the domestic countries. Ferguson was one of those to take advantage, making no fewer than five signings – Karel Poborsky, Jordi Cruyff, Ronny Johnsen, Ole Gunnar Solskjaer and Raimond van der Gouw brought varying degrees of European experience to the table. The Premier League saw something of an explosion – Chelsea signed Gianluca Vialli, Gianfranco Zola, Roberto Di Matteo and Frank Leboeuf, Arsenal signed Patrick Vieira and Nicolas Anelka (and added a French manager, Arsene Wenger), as big names and big prospects flocked to England. Middlesbrough acquired Fabrizio Ravanelli – a demonstration that even middle-of-the-road clubs in the Premier League had the financial clout to attract some of the best players in the world.

On the first day of the season David Beckham scored from the halfway line against Wimbledon. No tactical plan here – just sheer confidence and ambition, and a goal that propelled a player into super-stardom in a manner that hadn't been seen since George Best's night in Benfica 30 years earlier. Beckham became the poster-boy of English football, right at the time when Manchester was in the global eye.

In the late 80s and early 90s, numerous musical acts from the city had gained worldwide appeal. Two huge movements in the music scene – Madchester and Britpop – created a platform where acts from Manchester, from the Stone Roses to Oasis, achieved fame for their songs and attitude. So Manchester's personality was almost perceived by the world as a braggadocious swagger, as demonstrated by Liam and Noel Gallagher – and with Manchester United's successful team being built around local young players, they were included by association in the pop culture phenomenon that had exploded.

When Beckham started dating Victoria Adams of the Spice Girls – then the biggest pop act in the world – the consequential impact made footballers celebrities more so than ever before. Beckham's goal, United's success, and Manchester's place as the cultural epicentre of this revolution accelerated the profile of all involved.

Of course, there are other associated factors and events, but the topic of this book is to study the tactical and cultural evolution of Manchester United. Madchester and Britpop played a subtle role in the mid-90s, but significant enough to mention.

There was no sudden tactical deviation on the domestic front but Ferguson went into his third Champions League campaign feeling he would have to make some adaptations. There had already been some experiments. In January 1996 he had tried a three-man defence, although this was mostly due to a defensive injury crisis. In the 1993/94 Champions League, Ferguson had played a 4-5-1 in some games in an attempt to deal with the foreigner rule, but it had never appeared natural, even if United had scored a fair amount of goals.

Concerned about the experience of Cole or Scholes to lead the line, Ferguson tried a 4-3-3 to gain some control in the middle of the park against the European champions Juventus in their first group game in September 1996.

FOOTBALL, TAUGHT BY MATT BUSBY

SCHMEICHEL

G.NEVILLE JOHNSEN PALLISTER IRWIN

BECKHAM BUTT GIGGS

POBORSKY CANTONA CRUYFF

Ferguson compared Juventus' style to Wimbledon in that the ball was often played to the front players and then the build up would begin. "Don't get me wrong," he wrote in his book *A Will To Win*, "they put in the long diagonal ball, but it's not in the air all the time. They work very hard, close in behind you and don't let you out of your own half. We have to make sure we are always in close contact with each other. Our two wide players have to respond to where the ball is. If the ball goes out to Poborsky on the right, then Jordi Cruyff must move in from the left, to become a striker in support of Eric Cantona. Vice versa if the ball comes left… the midfield players must judge their runs sparingly so that we have a grip on midfield. That's my gameplan, but the most important thing is that they must not come in at half time regretting the first half. I tell them: 'You have got to express yourselves. You have the ability and this is the platform we have all been waiting for.'"

At the Stadio Delle Alpi, United's young team suffered as they tried to get to grips with the cynical play of the Italians. Prior to the creation of the Premier League, Italian football was perceived as the pinnacle of Europe.

Italy won the World Cup in 1982 and hosted it in 1990. Gazza's tears and relocation forged a stronger connection and Channel 4's weekend show, *Football Italia*, only strengthened the British fascination. The glamour aside, there still remained the aggressive and close-to-the-bone gamesmanship, particularly from Uruguayan defender Paolo Montero. And there was the bottom line – yes, there was some glamour, but the Italians were here to win and not indulge or even invite an entertaining game.

Fergie's 'Fledglings' were awestruck in the first half; Alen Boksic scored after 34 minutes and the Italians applied a stranglehold they would not relinquish. "Eric Cantona… spent much of last night with his back to goal," reported the *Guardian*, "gazing down the pitch at what Juventus were doing to Ferguson's tactical plan."

After that 1-0 defeat, it was back to a comfortable 4-4-2 against Rapid Vienna at home, and the same again in Fenerbahce, with both matches ending in a 2-0 win. With those encounters proving comfortable, Ferguson trialled the 4-3-3 shape again at home to the Turkish side in the return, hoping that it would be more successful so he could also use it in the return against Juventus. Giggs and Pallister were injured, so in came May and Keane. United's performance suggested that it was the system and not the opposition that was the problem – Cantona was once more isolated up front, meaning that not only did United lack composure in the middle, they also did not create many openings. They had played directly into the hands of the opposition manager, Sebastiao Lazaroni. The Brazilian had prepared for the wingers and a 4-4-2 but United had unwittingly nullified their own strength. "Neutralising Cantona was fundamental," Lazaroni told the author in 2022, "playing compactly, avoiding giving spaces and exploiting the counterattacks, these were our goals. We had a lot of happiness in that game."

With 20 minutes to go it was clear the plan wasn't working. Ferguson took off the wide men and focused his play down the middle. But the anxiety in their play invited adventure from the opponents – Elvir Bolic shot from distance, the ball took a huge deflection off David May, and United's 40-year record of never being beaten in European competition at Old Trafford was gone.

"It was the perfect example of the naivety British teams so often reveal in Europe," Ferguson later complained.

The problems with that system, and the fact that qualification from the group was still undecided, convinced Ferguson to play to his strengths. A 4-4-2 was pitted against Juventus. The first half contained some of that naivety, with the Italians scoring a penalty, United's midfield of McClair and Butt struggling to dominate the experience of Deschamps and Zidane after Keane had moved into defence following an early injury to Phil Neville, while even Cantona was misfiring.

"At the break, all I ask them is whether they want to win the game or be second best," Ferguson recalled. "I remind them how we've been speaking all week about imposing ourselves… but oh, what a glorious second-half performance. This is Manchester United, the Manchester United I love, playing the kind of football that makes everyone want to watch us. It is so exhilarating."

Giggs was outstanding, a constant threat, but his team couldn't muster a breakthrough against the deadlocked Italian defence, and despite playing well, lost 1-0 again. Ferguson was afterwards left to consider how the Cantona 'of old' would have scored one of the five chances he had, but had been left pondering the Frenchman's state of mind in recent weeks – at a testimonial match at Norwich, he'd overheard Cantona telling young players to "make the most of it while you are with Manchester United, because there's nothing like it. When you leave it's the end of life as you know it."

Cantona remained a major part of Ferguson's European plans. He was in his familiar role in a 4-4-2 at Rapid Vienna and was instrumental, creating and scoring, as United secured qualification to the quarter-final – where they would face Porto. In-between times, a suspension to Cantona had provided another twist in the tale. Ferguson had been forced to play Solskjaer and Cole up front at Arsenal and their performances as traditional strikers provided a goal apiece in a 2-1 win, and a certain penetration through interchange, pace, and movement that just wasn't always possible when losing one of the forwards and using Cantona as the playmaker.

Faced with the choice, the United manager decided to shoehorn both the above approaches into the same team when Porto came to Old Trafford in March 1997:

SCHMEICHEL

NEVILLE MAY PALLISTER IRWIN

BECKHAM JOHNSEN GIGGS

CANTONA

COLE SOLSKJAER

"It could be cat and mouse," Ferguson said, "but I want to set the pace in attack… Porto normally play 4-3-3 and they may find us difficult to handle if we play like this. We've been studying videos of them for the past two weeks, and Les Kershaw and Jim Ryan have seen them play four or five times. A lot of people have been involved in the planning for this tie."

The United boss described the way his team played as being 'beyond my wildest dreams'. Giggs and Cantona were outstanding in a 4-0 win following a team-talk where Ferguson had told them that if they didn't believe they were the best, they were at the wrong club. When Cantona, Cole and Giggs combined, particularly in the second half, Old Trafford was electric. The verve and liberation of the attack married with the industry of the midfield made for one of the very best performances of the Ferguson era.

It also proved two things – the first, that Ferguson seemed to acknowledge his team were at their best when concentrating on their own strengths. The second, that he placed a great emphasis on preparation for the opposition in a way that few of his predecessors ever had. When the latter took precedence over the former, it usually ended with a poor result – but with a healthy balance of the latter in a strategy focused on the former, like against Barcelona in 1991 and Porto in 1997, it could yield strong performances and results. It was unerringly similar to how Busby had approached European football.

In Porto, Ferguson sacrificed one striker and played a holding midfielder to achieve a 0-0 draw. In Dortmund in the first leg of the semi-final, the United boss went with a 4-4-2 and the team played well enough to win, but lost– luck deserting them at both ends of the pitch with the Germans winning 1-0.

The same set-up as against Porto lined up against Dortmund at Old Trafford, with a key difference – Butt was in instead of Giggs, who was suffering with a stomach bug. Early on, Dortmund scored to stun Old Trafford and take a 2-0 aggregate lead with an away goal in the bag. United needed three – they could not even score one, their frantic loss of composure evident as a European Cup final was so close and yet so far away. The 1997 Premier League title win – their fourth in five years – felt strangely underwhelming.

That summer, Cantona retired, and was replaced by Teddy Sheringham. The England international liked to join in the play but was still more of a traditional striker than Cantona. Success in the league meant another crack at the Champions League – though, for the first time, United could have finished second and still qualified as UEFA extended the competition. This would move from two teams to three to four entered from top countries into the Champions League in the space of a decade.

With Sheringham in his team, Ferguson played a straightforward 4-4-2 at home and in Europe. Beckham was now an established right-winger with Gary Neville able to overlap. Paired with Juventus in the group stage again, by the time they visited Old Trafford on October 1st, Ferguson was reeling from the recent injury to Keane that would rule his new captain out for the full season. Without him, United put in a stirring performance to defeat the Italians 3-2, Giggs topping off another great performance with a late goal. Ferguson's side went on to win their first five group games, rendering their return in Turin a dead rubber, but the United boss still fielded his strongest side to see how far they had come. A 1-0 defeat to a late Filippo Inzaghi goal did nothing to dampen the growing belief that playing in their natural fashion was the best way forward.

Injuries played havoc with United in the quarter-final against Monaco; Schmeichel and Giggs were out, Gary Neville had to come off, and of course Keane was already missing. Ferguson went with a 4-3-3 at home after a 0-0 result away, hoping Sheringham might act like Cantona in the Porto game. Instead, as against Dortmund, United lacked the penetration of a runner like Giggs from midfield. Monaco scored early on – and though Solskjaer did level in the 53rd minute, the French side were victors on away goals.

21

1999 AND
ALL THAT

ALEX FERGUSON WAS FORCED TO RECONFIGURE HIS squad in the summer of 1998. He was concerned about squad depth, and wanted some more unpredictability in his forward line. In came Dwight Yorke, the Aston Villa forward. Jesper Blomqvist, the talented Swedish winger, arrived to ease the burden on Ryan Giggs. Finally Jaap Stam came in to replace Gary Pallister. Ferguson was not about to change the 4-4-2. He strongly believed that in his midfield he boasted the match of any team in Europe, and furthermore, believed Arsenal's double triumph of 1997/98 was due to their own brilliance and United's terrible fortune with injuries, rather than any tactical failure.

Were there any great tactical shifts across the continent? No revolutions yet – when United faced Juventus, the Italians had used a diamond midfield. Barcelona and Bayern Munich were drawn against Ferguson's side in the 1998/99 Champions League group stage and they both had different approaches. Barca, under

Louis van Gaal, played a 4-3-3 at the Nou Camp, though with Xavi sitting deep and Giovanni and Rivaldo high in front of him, it might as well have been a 4-1-5.

German television had Bayern Munich's line-up at Old Trafford looking a little too ambitious – a 2-1-3-1-3, which in practice was more like a 4-3-3, with one of the midfield 'three' being Lothar Matthaus, a veteran sweeper tasked with occupying a space anywhere between his goalkeeper and midfield. Ferguson stayed firm, determined that his team should play in their most comfortable fashion. It made for a thrilling group stage – and even though all of the matches against Barcelona and Bayern Munich were drawn, the conclusions were reached in all manner of entertaining ways. "The two 3-3 draws with Barcelona might not be cited in any coaching manual dealing with defensive play," Ferguson said, "but their openness and positive spirit made for wonderful entertainment."

He was more considerate about the opposition when it came to the knockout stages. Inter Milan were the quarter-final opponents and Ferguson admitted he'd been thinking of ways to handle the Brazilian sensation Ronaldo for weeks. Ronaldo was the best player in the world and had been in blistering form for Inter in the 1997/98 season, but controversy had surrounded the build up to Brazil's 1998 World Cup final appearance – the forward seemed a shadow of himself on the day and struggled throughout the following season. Ferguson was cautious but pressed ahead with two different tactical plans. He'd noted that Inter were weak in the middle of defence and therefore susceptible to Beckham's crossing – Italian teams had grown so accustomed to being fearful of Giggs, that this still carried the potential to be a surprise. Inter also played with two players who were effectively number 10s, so would crowd the middle. "It was important that, when our attacks broke down and we regrouped," Ferguson said, "we should surrender the wide areas and close off the centre-midfield, again denying them their favourite avenue of penetration."

The gameplan worked perfectly – two first-half goals from Beckham crosses to Yorke established a lead that United were able to professionally maintain over the following 135 minutes of the tie. Ferguson admitted he was hoping that Juventus would be drawn as the opponents in the semi-final, out of a growing feeling of confidence after their head-to-heads. They were. The Italians had been learning, too, and had recently changed their manager – Marcelo Lippi was replaced by Carlo Ancelotti, who had subtly different ideas to his predecessor. The diamond shape Lippi favoured was discarded and a more proactive midfield suffocation, aided by the signing of Edgar Davids, caught United on the hop – forcing Ferguson to address it after just 45 minutes of the first leg. Juventus had the lead at that point; United's manager conceded they were lucky it was just one. Beckham was moved to make a more compact midfield and Giggs snatched a very late equaliser to rescue a 1-1 draw. It could have been worse.

Giggs' goal was merely the latest late late show put on by the club since the turn of the year. It was the fifth time in 1999 United had rescued a result in the last 10 minutes and the third time they'd done so in the last minute. The team hadn't been beaten since December in any competition and this in spite of coming up against not only Juventus and Inter Milan but also Liverpool and Chelsea in the FA Cup and Arsenal in the league. Arsenal were the next opponents in the FA Cup semi-final, and they took the tie to a replay, which was decided by a Giggs wonder goal in extra-time, when he dribbled past numerous Gunners players and smashed a fierce drive into the net. It evoked memories of Best in his pomp, an instant contender for the greatest goal in the club's history, and a telling reminder of the club's ethos that within the patterns and systems there was always room for individual brilliance. "It's uncoachable," Ferguson told the *Sunday Times*. "What we saw was the ultimate expression of the natural gifts he has always had."

When asked how much of a headache this extra fixture had given him, Ferguson dismissed the interviewer, merely expressing how the supporters would be talking about that game for years. He was right. He had reached a pinnacle at that point, possibly without realising it – most connected with the club, and many neutrals, rank the replay as the greatest game in the history of English football. It featured the two best teams in the country, attacking each other at will, playing with freedom in an attempt to prove that one was better than the other. The confidence boost of winning in the fashion they had was worth twice the energy they would have conserved by not playing the game.

With a month to go until the end of the season, an FA Cup final to contest and two more trophies to fight for, for Ferguson the test was to maintain consistency and confidence without derailment. It was no time for formation gambles. In Turin for the second leg against Juventus, United lined up in a 4-4-2, despite an ankle injury to Giggs and the obvious temptation to pack the midfield. Ferguson's side still had to score a goal and they needed to be set out in a manner ambitious enough to do so.

What happened in Italy was, in Ferguson's view 'the greatest performance ever produced' by any team he had managed. Juventus took an early lead then scored again in the 12th minute and suddenly a molehill looked like a mountain. Before the away side even had time to let panic manifest, Roy Keane met a corner with a perfect header to make it 1-2. What followed was, according to Ferguson, 'the most emphatic display of selflessness I have seen on a football field', the manager going so far as to say it was 'an honour to be associated with such a player'. The selflessness came after Keane was booked for a trip on Zidane and so would miss the final should United get there; at a moment where indiscipline could consume, the Irishman channelled his disappointment to nullify Zidane and Davids for the next hour. Yorke equalised before half-time – giving United the advantage on away goals. The only time the club had been this close was in 1968, where Matt Busby had taken to urging his players to play like Manchester United in the second half.

Ferguson was calm. He did not have to deliver any such team talk. He felt confident there was only one winner in the match, never mind the tie. He was right. The team were only consciously thinking about what was in front of them. After the press criticism of the previous years, and what possibly lay in store if they threw away this advantage, they were right to think selfishly. Of course the following hour was about much more than that. You would have to travel back 40 years to uncover the true significance. For Fergie's Fledglings read the Busby Babes. For Juventus read Real Madrid. For three years of epic head-to-heads, remember the devastation of Munich and what it prevented. Looking back on this 90-minute match in Turin is to consider the realistic journey the Busby Babes were on and the educational process of overcoming an established great opponent. The first step is being somewhat cautious, over-awed. The second is learning and going toe-to-toe. Ferguson's team had been afforded what fate denied the Busby Babes. The opportunity of fulfilment. Still riding the crest of a wave from a week earlier, the manager was right – Cole scored late on to make it 3-2, giving his team a definite lead, and giving them a final at a venue they'd already visited this season and an opponent they'd already faced.

Munich was the burden of Busby's side for the 10 years after the disaster. It was the moment in time scarcely spoken of, only for it to be confronted and embraced once the final whistle blew at Wembley in May 1968. The burden since was not Munich, but Busby's legacy. Winning a league title. That had already been accomplished, and even Busby hadn't managed a league and FA Cup double, never mind the two that Ferguson had achieved. In fact, when it came to the cold hard science of trophy count, Ferguson had already surpassed Busby by the time the European Cup final rolled around.

As United prepared to face Bayern Munich at the Nou Camp they did so with Peter Schmeichel, Denis Irwin and Ryan Giggs in their team. Prior to the 1990s, Bill Foulkes was the most decorated man in the club's history with six major trophies. Schmeichel and Giggs already had nine, and Irwin eight (only missing the ninth thanks to a ludicrous suspension for the 1999 FA Cup final). Ferguson was celebrating his third league and FA Cup double in six years after wins over Spurs and Newcastle respectively, and was hoping that destiny had one more favour to provide. As a manager, Busby won eight major trophies at Old Trafford. Ferguson was already on 10 but it was obvious that the 11th would forever be significant in terms of how he was viewed in the footballing world.

SCHMEICHEL
G.NEVILLE JOHNSEN STAM IRWIN
GIGGS BECKHAM BUTT BLOMQVIST
COLE YORKE

The suspension to Keane was the crucial kicker although Scholes would naturally have been the next in to replace him, so his absence too was a source of frustration. Ferguson was unsure whether to have Beckham in his normal position and use Giggs through the middle, but felt the number seven was probably a safer bet for more economic use of the ball. Bayern lined up with Matthaus in the same sweeper role and Ferguson went into the match more in the hope that Beckham and Butt could compete than with the expectation that they could set the pace. The manager praised Beckham's display, calling him 'the most effective midfielder on the park' as he covered every blade of grass in the manner of his hero, Bryan Robson.

Bayern scored early on from a set play. It was not the first time United had been behind against a huge opponent renowned for their defensive strength. After all, they'd just been behind twice to Juventus at separate times in their semi-final. They were familiar with Juventus, though. It had taken six games but they were now more than their match. The problem is United didn't have another three games to get their act together against Bayern – they had 84 minutes.

At half-time, they'd failed to get going. Now it *was* time for a team talk. Sheringham recalled the missive: "[Ferguson] said look, you've seen that trophy on the halfway line. If you don't win this we won't be able to touch it. You might not ever get this close again. So make sure you give everything in your power… don't leave anything out there."

United were in the game and had chances. Bayern did, too, on the counter, and in striking the woodwork twice had the more memorable of the openings. Ferguson made his substitutions. First Sheringham came on for Blomqvist. United now moved into a 4-3-3, Sheringham just behind Cole and Yorke (you might refer to Cantona's performance against Porto and believe that it informed Ferguson's gamble here).

Bayern responded by making two changes – the second, bringing Matthaus off with 10 minutes still to play, seemed strange; yes, he was 38, but it seemed like a premature opportunity for him to be soaked in applause when his job was not yet complete. The lost experience proved vital – Ferguson rolled the dice, bringing on Ole Gunnar Solskjaer – the player who had scored a last-minute winner against Liverpool in the FA Cup in January, when United had been losing in the 87th minute – for Cole. Those sort of victories were supposed to be once in a lifetime.

The sport had moved on to the point where now the crowd and both teams were made aware of how much time would be added on. Three minutes. United, pouring everyone forward, won a corner; a sign of their gamble that Gary Neville was on the left wing, winning it.

The rest is legend, and owes little to tactical masterminding.

Beckham's corner is half-cleared. Giggs scuffs his shot – Sheringham rolls it in.

United regain the ball from kick-off. Solskjaer bursts on the left and wins another corner.

Now you can almost sense it. It is as inevitable as the passing of time itself.

Beckham. Sheringham. Solskjaer.

The reward for bravery and boldness was the greatest pinnacle that can be achieved in football.

It is records like this book that connect the threads – that attempt to convince you it was meant to be because of what happened before, and is somehow connected to it because of that history.

Is all that occurs just random? After all, there are as many reasons to justify that train of thought as there are to suggest it is all linked.

Manchester United's success of 1999 was not achieved with any great tactical innovation, but it was not achieved in spite of a lack of it. Alex Ferguson had proved multiple times that he could make those changes if necessary. But even if it was coincidental, it was still strongly reminiscent of how Busby had his second great team playing. Those Babes had broken through into an accomplished team and were establishing their own legacy. Busby was not breaking ground with a tactical shape – like 4-4-2 in the 90s, the 3-2-5 or 3-2-2-3 was the formation of the day.

The zenith Ferguson had reached had been a product of 13 years of hard work and patience. It was taking a young team, nurturing them and encouraging them to improve even after scaling unthinkable heights. It was removing the glass ceiling, the common perception that being the best was about being better than your opponent, and refocusing it on a realisation of personal and collective potential. *Of course* the nature of the final victory in 1999 was superhuman and seemed supernatural. It is only too tempting to attach it to sentimental threads because there was always an obvious intention from the club, in its conscious and subconscious acts, to make Munich and Wembley – both in singular events and the journey from former to latter – these larger-than-life events in the history of Manchester United. Poetry, as Busby described it. Those moments and accomplishments were crystallised and rightly so. It was incumbent on the team to live up to it. That they did so on Sir Matt Busby's birthday, showing the fighting spirit of Duncan Edwards and Jimmy Murphy, and indeed all of the lost Babes, was absolutely symbolic and undoubtedly tied to Ferguson's deliverance of the message that the past was important to what the club represented in the present.

This can be misconstrued and turned the other way, where criticism is levelled at a team who don't keep going in the same way. This is missing the point. It's not this factor that keeps a Manchester United team from being a proper Manchester United team. It's this factor which distinguishes the truly exceptional.

The burden is heavy, and often regarded as a privilege; with some teams and eras, it is clear to see that even with great players, the burden was too much. In others, even when the accomplishments were not as stunning as 1956, or 1968, or 1999, then you could still see a team who could carry it as a liberating privilege.

Imagine the psychological burden of being a footballer. You fight through hundreds of wannabes to make it as a professional footballer. You climb past hundreds more to make it in the top division. If you're at Manchester United, you're one of at least 600 professionals in the top flight, and one of around 30 at Old Trafford. The club you play for has a reputation of being the best in the country, playing the most entertaining football, delivering that with young players developed by the club, and you're one of those players – oh, and should you have the fortune to play in Europe, you are also not only at the club who served as pioneers, you're also at the club with one of the most notable air tragedies suffered during a European trip. You have to not only put in the hard yards but *show* that you are. You have to live up to it – not only in volume of accomplishment, but nature of it, be that in entertainment or white-knuckle deliverance, and even if you do all that, it still might not be quite good enough to earn you the same adoration as someone who came before you.

The key to success was found in incorporation and not imitation. The more successful managers came into United respectful of the past but not weighed down by it. They did it their own way. If it connected with the club's historical way of doing things then great, but it still seemed to be a coincidence. For Docherty and Atkinson the important thing appeared to be to play well and to win. That was the same for Ferguson, too – it had taken until January 1989 for him to discover just how alive Old Trafford could become when getting behind a nucleus of homegrown stars. When it came to the first league-winning team, only Ryan Giggs was a bonafide starter who had been developed by the club. Of course this quickly changed – in the Champions League final squad, four starters and a further three substitutes were products of the youth system.

In 1958, Jimmy Murphy had decided to continue bringing through young players even when the temptation was to add a whole raft of senior players. Busby, on his return, was clinical and rational, and realised that to achieve success sooner, he would have to establish a more neutral balance. This was the pattern followed for generations; and Busby's own comments about the demands on a Manchester United manager made it clear that success was now a fundamental requirement: "*He must – and I repeat must with all possible emphasis – have success in terms of Championships or Cups, otherwise he is going to be deemed a failure.*" This factor was placed in front of developing young players and in front of playing entertaining football as the all-important. It should be noted that these latter two factors were never implicitly stated by Busby – he was not to dictate the philosophy of another manager – but the expectation of the crowd made it clear that there were demands made by the club.

So it is possibly taking into account the above element which separates the 1994 and 1999 sides in the memory of most. The 1994 team are beloved but the 1999 team seemed to eclipse that – yes, because they delivered a European Cup, but not because they played more entertaining football. Mostly, though, because these were young lads reared through the club – many of them local – and so it made the connection deeper. It belonged to Manchester more, and inevitably, felt closer to the club's historical identity. Because of that, it resonated with the support. Because the support were so fanatical, it brought that vital extra percentage from the players – which manifested itself in the most remarkable fashion time and time again in the space of five months in 1999.

22

GOING GLOBAL

THE YEAR OF 1999 CONTAINED ONE MORE MAJOR success for Manchester United: the Intercontinental Cup. This was, as you will recall, the trophy Wilf McGuinness coveted in his charming naivety, the one he had targeted which would see him accomplish something even Sir Matt had not. United's opponents would be Palmeiras of Brazil.

BOSNICH
G.NEVILLE STAM SILVESTRE IRWIN
BECKHAM BUTT KEANE SCHOLES GIGGS
SOLSKJAER

Palmeiras were coached by Luis Felipe Scolari, who was perceived as so unpredictable many were suggesting a physical fight might break out between him and Ferguson. The United boss concerned himself with the on-pitch battle, as he had noted the Brazilians were playing 4-2-2-2 and brought the width from the full-backs. He decided to pack the midfield himself, to ask his wingers to make those full-backs defend, and to ask one of the midfielders to make supporting runs. As the game got underway, the United staff were shocked to see the Palmeiras strikers drifting wide, causing a headache for the English side's full-backs. "Our pre-match script was in tatters," Ferguson admitted. "We tried to communicate instructions but were too far from the touchline to be heard. I was in torture during most of those 45 minutes as Palmeiras made a string of chances."

Still, part of the plan worked perfectly – 10 minutes before the break, Giggs teased his marker and put in a cross. There at the back post, making a late run, was Roy Keane. Once he could ask his wingers to be more cautious, Ferguson felt the second half went much more comfortably, with his side winning 1-0, becoming the first British team to lift this trophy. To continue the theme of romance, to see Keane be the matchwinner considering his Nou Camp absence the previous season was just. "I have always seen Manchester United as having an affinity with the Brazilian way of playing," Ferguson said, "with the emphasis on flair and the willingness to take risks. That result ranks with the most satisfying I have been able to accomplish."

There would, strangely enough, be another chance to compete against Brazilian opposition just a few weeks later, in the inaugural FIFA Club World Cup tournament, which pitted clubs from multiple continental confederations against each other in the format of a mini-Champions League. If the concept sounds right up Matt Busby's street then it's fair to say Alex Ferguson did not share the same view, commenting that he felt the club were 'pressured' to take part in an act of patriotism, and no little politicking, to help the FA's case to host the 2006 World Cup.

United's group included Rayos Del Necaxa of Mexico, Vasco Da Gama of Brazil, and South Melbourne of Australia. Ferguson played a 4-4-2 in all games, trusting in his side's natural ability, admitting that he felt the competition didn't invoke the same intensity as the Intercontinental Cup had but that they were playing to win all the same.

"I have never known that simple bit of luck mean more in football matches than it did in the conditions at the Maracana," Ferguson said of losing the coin toss, to determine which end of the pitch they would kick towards in the first half, in both of the first two games in the huge famous arena. Necaxa and Vasco, teams more familiar with the climate, chose to attack the half of the pitch which was exposed to the sun. Temperatures reached 100 degrees Fahrenheit, causing issues for the United defence, while the opponents had it more comfortable in the shade. United were able to get a 1-1 draw in the opener, despite David Beckham's red card, but were given a lesson by the home team Vasco – a game most remembered for Edmundo's outrageous piece of skill to outfox Gary Neville. Elimination was still an embarrassment.

Having returned from what Keane admitted was a 'holiday' in Rio in January 2000, United's first game back was against Arsenal in the Premier League. They had three games in hand over the teams around them and Leeds, who had a four-point lead, hadn't really taken the opportunity to establish a strong advantage. United played through the game as if still suffering from jet lag before Keane started to exert his influence in order to get a result, after the concession of an early goal. "Yes, I did get in amongst the Arsenal players," Keane recalled, "but the message was for our own lads – me included – more than Arsenal." The players responded – a draw was rescued. A few weeks later, United won at Leeds, and then steamrolled their way to the title, winning their last 11 games and scoring 37 goals in the process, concentration fully restored.

Success was not quite as straightforward when it came to retaining the European Cup. Real Madrid were the opponents in the quarter-final and, after accomplishing what on paper looked a decent 0-0 draw in Spain playing a bold enough 4-4-2, the same system found itself 3-0 down by the 53rd minute at Old Trafford. The Spanish had the craft and ingenuity in crucial positions and most importantly of all had the clinical class of Raul up front. United roused themselves – Beckham and Scholes with consolations as Old Trafford roared them on – but lost on the night and on aggregate.

Ferguson felt it was a simple matter of Real Madrid being destined to qualify. "That conviction is only strengthened by the memory of the formation they assumed after the kick-off," he said. "They were playing a system that did not deserve to be successful; three central defenders, two wing-backs, three men up front, Steve McManaman as a floating player (although mainly on the right) and one central midfielder in Fernando Redondo. 'Give us a break,' I thought to myself. 'That can't work.'"

Ferguson responded by changing his system and going to a 4-3-3 – but only at 0-3, and he said he 'could kick myself for delaying the change'. "One of the forceful reminders delivered by that defeat was that consistent success in Europe would be more readily achieved if we improved our capacity to defend against the counter-attack," he surmised. "They (opponents in Europe) are liable to go all out for the jugular only a few times in a match, and the suddenness of those isolated thrusts can catch you off guard."

Ferguson's resolution in this matter wasn't a pragmatic one – he did not instruct his side to become more cautious. Rather, he intended to make his team more clinical – they had missed numerous chances against Madrid, with Ferguson feeling his side would win that game seven times out of ten. To redress the balance, he made major moves in the transfer market, but it would take another year, another league title (his seventh, thus overtaking Bob Paisley's record of six) and another European exit before he did so.

The stand out result in the 2000/01 campaign came in February, where Arsene Wenger was forced into public surrender of the title after seeing his Arsenal team crushed 6-1 at Old Trafford. Ferguson had employed a sports psychologist, Bill Beswick, on the behest of his assistant Steve McClaren (who had succeeded Brian Kidd in 1998), and Beswick believed the performance was a consequence of Ferguson and Keane's relentless personal standards.

Ferguson had now won three titles in a row but was desperate to win another Champions League. Ruud van Nistelrooy, a striker predicted to be the world's best, arrived from PSV – a year later than planned due to a knee injury – for a club-record £19m. A few weeks later, one of the world's supreme playmakers, Juan Sebastian Veron, signed from Lazio for £28.1m. Ferguson admitted he never imagined he would spend so much on a player – but he had publicly announced his intention to retire in 2002, and the European Cup final that year was held at Hampden Park. What a potential venue for a climax to what was now the greatest managerial career in football.

Ferguson felt these signings made his team favourites in the continental competition, and they indicated a projected shift, particularly in European games. The club now boasted a surplus of immense talent in the middle of the park – Keane, Scholes, Butt, Veron – and four into two wouldn't go. An injury and suspension to Keane in the early part of the 2001/02 campaign did not provide an immediate answer for what Ferguson would do with a full complement but the visit of Lille for a Champions League group game did.

BARTHEZ
G.NEVILLE   BROWN   BLANC   IRWIN
BECKHAM   KEANE   VERON   GIGGS
SCHOLES
VAN NISTELROOY

Before this, Veron had played in the midfield two but behind two traditional strikers – mostly, usually, Cole and Van Nistelrooy in the early weeks. The Argentine had been in sublime form, scoring and creating. Nicky Butt was moved to say he felt Veron was "so unbelievable, I thought I'd never play for United again." In fact, United were playing with such a cavalier attitude that even when they faced defeat – like they did in a 4-3 setback at Newcastle – they were still receiving plaudits for their adventure. This culminated, of course, in the game at White Hart Lane when United were 3-0 down at half-time. Beckham was inspirational as United scored five times in the second half.

With the introduction of the new signings apparently successful, the United boss then started to tinker, feeling perhaps they had been a little too attacking – whilst also accounting for a settling in period for French international defender Laurent Blanc, who had hastily been brought in to replace Jaap Stam. In the 4-4-1-1, United's form lurched from erratic to desperate, the team rarely having the control the manager had hoped for. In an attempt to accommodate all of his star players, Ferguson even moved Keane into defence for the visit of Chelsea in December:

BARTHEZ
BROWN   BLANC   KEANE   P.NEVILLE
BECKHAM   VERON   SCHOLES   FORTUNE
COLE   VAN NISTELROOY

Chelsea won 3-0. Ferguson concluded that he would have to return to his traditional system, with square pegs in square holes. Hopes of trying to establish a new approach were undermined by a succession of injuries in the heart of defence. By the time United finally got going in a 5-0 win over Derby that was the first of nine in a row, they were fielding their 13th different centre-half pairing of the season in just 26 games.

The erratic start led to United finishing outside of the top two for the first time since 1991, head-to-head defeats against Liverpool and champions Arsenal accounting for their places above Ferguson's side. He had already reversed his decision to retire: there had been two names in the frame to replace him. The first was Martin Edwards' choice, Arsene Wenger – after a couple of meetings, Wenger pledged his future to Arsenal. The second was the choice of Peter Kenyon, the new chief executive – England manager Sven-Göran Eriksson. Neither were close enough to accepting the job to make even a hypothetical conversation about it worthwhile.

In Europe, United failed at the semi-final stage against Bayer Leverkusen. Bayer's shape was extremely unusual – a midfield diamond, with one of the two strikers put into midfield, the shape looking like a 4-1-3-1-1 set-up.

With the desire to regain the title burning bright, Ferguson conceded he wouldn't be able to play the same way as he had in the 2001/02 season. He had made personnel changes – Andy Cole and Dwight Yorke were sold. Diego Forlan and Rio Ferdinand were brought in. United played a 4-4-2 throughout the 2002/03 season, using a 4-4-1-1 on the odd occasion and usually only when injuries forced the matter – as they did when Arsenal came to Old Trafford in December.

BARTHEZ
G.NEVILLE BROWN SILVESTRE O'SHEA
SOLSKJAER VERON P.NEVILLE GIGGS
SCHOLES
VAN NISTELROOY

Despite having Beckham, Butt and Keane missing, United's performance was notable for its grit and hard work – and United won 2-0. The most glaring change that can be noted is the repositioning of Solskjaer on the right wing. The Norwegian had spent most of his career as a notable 'super sub', a player renowned for observing the flow of the game and studying where he might cause most damage if he got on.

Overall, 29 of his 126 goals for the club came from the bench. Another sign of his intelligence came in the reason for his redeployment; it takes a truly fine forward to be capable of providing the service they would love to receive, and Solskjaer had a knack for playing good crosses from the right. United had the best in the business when it came to that, but Solskjaer's consistency in the role ultimately made Beckham expendable. It's not quite right to say Beckham was dropped from the team completely towards the end of the season but he was for two key games – the trip to Arsenal, which was drawn 2-2, and the visit of Real Madrid in the Champions League. In this quarter-final second leg, Real had a 3-1 win from the first game, and with Scholes suspended, Ferguson opted for a 4-5-1 which could look like a 4-3-3:

BARTHEZ
BROWN FERDINAND SILVESTRE O'SHEA
BUTT KEANE VERON
SOLSKJAER VAN NISTELROOY GIGGS

Real Madrid were at the start of their Galactico era. They normally played a diamond, but Raul was injured so the likes of Zidane, Figo, Ronaldo and Roberto Carlos were assembled in an extremely progressive 4-1-4-1 shape that had Claude Makelele working overtime in holding midfield. In the 12th minute, they scored on the break through Ronaldo. It did not stop United from pushing. It was 3-2 to Real on the night, and 6-3 on aggregate with Ronaldo completing his hat-trick in the 59th minute, when Beckham was brought on for Veron and United moved to their 4-4-2. Beckham scored twice – so on the night his side won 4-3 – but United were out and, by July, the number seven had moved to Madrid.

Ferguson did regain the Premier League title but he had already set in wheels the motion of building another great team. As he did so, English football underwent its own transition. Before that, Arsenal's greatest team enjoyed their greatest achievement, when Wenger's side won the Premier League without losing a game in 2004. Tactically there was nothing innovative; Wenger was largely credited with eliminating the drinking culture in the English game though there is enough evidence to say other managers, Ferguson included, were already taking a hard line on this prior to the Frenchman's arrival in 1996. Likewise diet, though this was a cyclical and cultural thing. For example, when the Busby Babes were at their peak, Busby had sought the advice of dieticians who put steak on the pre-match menu! In the 21st century, pre-match meals were lighter and more appropriate for the conditioning of an athlete, which is what footballers were becoming. And for that Wenger can be credited – at the time, his team boasted Thierry Henry, the player most regarded as the best in the league.

Henry might not have been as technically fantastic as his teammate Dennis Bergkamp but he had a fearlessness, a capability of scoring from anywhere within 30 yards, and most of all he possessed blistering pace. Wenger's side were physically intimidating at their best but even he couldn't have claimed to have the sort of profound impact on English football as two imports in 2004 – and not necessarily for the better.

Jose Mourinho was hired as Chelsea manager in the summer of 2004, a year after they had been taken over by Russian billionaire Roman Abramovich. He would spend almost £100m in his first year in charge, completely transforming a team who were qualifying for the Champions League and instantly making them dominant champions. Mourinho favoured a 4-3-3 system with wingers and if not, then a diamond midfield, both approaches established to suffocate the play.

Liverpool, at the same time, hired Rafael Benitez, a similarly cautious coach who appeared to favour ambitions of not losing rather than having a team playing an entertaining brand of football. "Our manager wasn't bothered about the game as a spectacle whereas Alex Ferguson and Arsene Wenger probably were," Liverpool legend Jamie Carragher told the author. "We were content to draw a game 0-0 even if it was at home because the approach was that we weren't going to leave ourselves open."

Benitez and Mourinho had this reputation prior to coming to England but the summer of 2004 seemed to serve as a generational shift in the game thanks to Euro 2004, when Greece pulled off a shock tournament victory thanks mostly to a cynical and unapologetic rearguard action with their 4-3-3 shape. The influence this had on the increase in more cautious football can't be understated. Goals per game in the Premier League dropped year-on-year, from 2.66 per match in 2003/04 to 2.57, 2.48 and then 2.45 in the following seasons.

Wenger would persist with the honourable belief that his

was the right way to do things but his team first had its natural dissolution and then any attempt to rebuild was often undermined by Chelsea's success – their star players would agitate for moves, and Arsenal were never quite able to establish their position at the top of the table.

For Ferguson, losing was not an option. If adaptation to the new competition was the way to do things, he was going to embrace it, even in his mid-60s. He had to first overcome the departure of chief executive Peter Kenyon, who appeared to have exercised his existing contacts to negotiate deals for Chelsea with players who had been strongly linked with a move to United. Didier Drogba, Arjen Robben and Michael Essien were three players reported to be close to moving to Old Trafford before Kenyon's defection to Stamford Bridge.

Chelsea were now operating with a blank cheque. United, on their own dime, could have competed without breaking a sweat. The Cantona years and the early Premier League era had seen a boom, with the club now valued at over 20 times what they were worth back in the Football League days. A £623m takeover by BSkyB was blocked by the Department of Trade and Industry in 1999 – but no such intervention prevented the Glazer family's takeover in 2005, and so 40 years of ownership by the Edwards family came to an end. But just because United could compete, it didn't make it fiscally responsible to do so, especially when going head-to-head for a player, and so that just meant identifying the right players became a much cuter exercise. Acquiring players almost became a matter of cat and mouse – for example, sometimes even strategically waiting until a rival club were heavily stocked in an area before making your own move. This seemed to be the case for Wayne Rooney's arrival in 2004 and then in the moves to sign Patrice Evra and Nemanja Vidic in 2006.

FOOTBALL, TAUGHT BY MATT BUSBY

As Ferguson's tenure reached the two-decade mark, there were numerous coaching and structural changes behind the scenes. Steve McClaren had left his post as assistant to manage Middlesbrough and then England. He was replaced by Carlos Queiroz in 2002. Queiroz was an innovative Portuguese coach who specialised in the sort of professional pragmatism United had often lacked; it had been a part of the club's charm going back to the Busby era that they would make life difficult for themselves in games, particularly in Europe. If Ferguson wanted to win another Champions League, he would have to look at those percentages – the details where his team could improve. Conceding early goals in ties as his team did against Juventus (more than once), Dortmund, Monaco, Bayern, Real Madrid – this would have to change.

On the coaching staff were Mick Phelan, a valued lieutenant who had been associated with Ferguson for long enough to be aware of his exceptional demands, and Rene Meulensteen, who had worked his way up from a post in skills development with very young players at the club. Meulensteen was appointed in 2001 after regulations changed regarding how early young players were allowed to train with football clubs. They were still only allowed to sign apprentice terms at 16 but clubs had been, for a while, permitted to hold nursery academies where children as young as six could train.

As coaching techniques had become more established and related more to traditional cognitive development than merely recreational, the idea of having more young players equipped with strong technical basic skills before even leaving school was encouraged by the Football Association. Meulensteen was given the opportunity to implement his theory of football over an impressionable age group who were being indoctrinated in the 'United way'. The Dutchman's belief in equipping the young boys with all the tools they would need for professional football would prove to be crucial over the following generation.

Another United old boy on the staff was Brian McClair, who was in charge of the youth team as they won the Youth Cup in 2003. The side played a straightforward 4-4-2 although Lee Lawrence, a left-back, remembers they would occasionally trial a three-man defence where he would be asked to play wing-back. This was no different to how it had been for generations – fluid systems more or less mirroring the first team, which more or less mirrored the most common contemporary formation in football. Regulations on registering young foreign talent were always changing and the club were ahead of the curve with that. In the mid-90s they established links with Belgian club Royal Antwerp where United's young players would get some experience of playing abroad. Then a few names started to come to Manchester – Mads Timm, Gerard Pique, Markus Neumayr, Jami Puustinen and Giuseppe Rossi – and in 2004, Francisco Filho was given the job of youth team manager, having had tremendous success with the French Football Academy at Clairefontaine. He was in charge for a year or so before Paul McGuinness took control. McGuinness, steeped in the club's history as he was, would pointedly discuss that history whenever he felt it could be advantageous.

There appeared to be an increased awareness of Munich stemming from the 40th anniversary in 1998, when the club had held a testimonial game. The commemorations every year now became more of an event as more of the survivors passed away, and its very presence was incorporated into the dialogue of the club, in order to educate young players. Bobby Charlton would be involved with preparations around the team. It was probably the right time to embrace the tragedy in a more prominent way to prevent the significance of it being diluted.

23

FRESH
THINKING

AT FIRST-TEAM LEVEL, ALEX FERGUSON DEALT WITH A number of issues in the years after his 2003 title win. The maturing of Wayne Rooney and Cristiano Ronaldo, which took a couple of seasons, and likewise with squad players such as Darren Fletcher and John O'Shea. A suspension to Rio Ferdinand which robbed him of half a season. The long-term absences of Paul Scholes and Roy Keane – the latter leaving suddenly in acrimonious circumstances in the winter of 2005. The goalkeeper issue which had never been satisfactorily resolved since Peter Schmeichel's exit. Then there was the bumpy acclimation of Patrice Evra and Nemanja Vidić. Throughout the period from 2003 to 2006, United won two trophies, playing mostly a 4-4-2 formation, using Cristiano Ronaldo as a stereotypical winger and Wayne Rooney and Ruud van Nistelrooy as the manager's preferred strike pair.

The summer of 2006 brought the first major change in that area. Van Nistelrooy – still a world class striker – was sold. His quality around the box and his peerless ability to convert crosses was not in doubt, but United were evolving into a team that broke with speed and penetration and it seemed logical to make Rooney and Ronaldo the focus of those attacks. Ferguson had been able to sign Edwin van der Sar to finally serve as a consistent number one, and Park Ji-Sung, a mobile and energetic forward player, arrived as a squad player who would become crucial to strategies in future games.

When the whole world was crying out for Ferguson to sign a Roy Keane replacement, the United manager opted for a different sort of player entirely – Michael Carrick, who was more like Ray Wilkins than Bryan Robson.

In November 2006, as Ferguson marked the conclusion of his second decade in charge, this was the team he named to face Portsmouth at Old Trafford:

VAN DER SAR

G.NEVILLE FERDINAND VIDIC EVRA

RONALDO CARRICK SCHOLES GIGGS

ROONEY SAHA

Saha was a conventional striker but less of a target man than Van Nistelrooy; the Frenchman was exceptional at linking the play. Saha and Rooney were also aggressive from the front, setting a defensive tone to retrieve the ball. There was, again, not a tackler in midfield – but unlike the breakneck speed of the Docherty era; there was culture and consideration. The centre of defence featured the traditional sweeper/stopper combination and in Rooney and Ronaldo, United had two of the three most highly-rated young players in the world (the other being Lionel Messi at Barcelona).

The win over Portsmouth was one of 10 from 11 games in the early autumn – United started the season well, a definite diversion from their recent league starts. Ferguson had often used a line that was a variant of 'our form kicks in at the turn of the year' to plant the seed in the mind of opponents, but Chelsea under Mourinho had redefined what strong starts were. They were relentless and in both of Mourinho's first two seasons, their lead looked to be unassailable by the time the new year kicked in. They were miserly to the extreme, winning 10 games 1-0 and keeping an astonishing 25 clean sheets in Mourinho's first season. United didn't play Chelsea every week, so their resolve had to come in developing a similar level of consistency, doing as well as they could in head-to-heads, and hoping Chelsea would drop points somewhere.

The pragmatic era of football had reduced the requirement for tacklers. Ball retrieval would come from interceptions and the old form of tackling had evolved into a matter of reading the pattern of play, anticipating where you could get the ball before your opponent. Ferdinand in particular had mastered this art, and Scholes and Carrick seemed well-versed in it too, though Scholes was almost lovingly renowned for often being late in the tackle. From the moment you had retrieved the ball it was all about retaining and recycling; but it was your intent once you had it which set you apart. Chelsea and Liverpool were experts at controlling a 1-0 lead but United would never be able to play that way, nor would Ferguson ever have wanted to. His acceptance of pragmatism had only come from his ability to adapt to ensure his team were able to compete, and his trust in Carlos Queiroz – who specialised in preparing teams in this manner.

United kept a considerable amount of clean sheets of their own – 16 – as they won the league title for the first time in four years in 2007. It was, however, a game against Roma in the quarter-final of the Champions League which prompted the next big tactical experiment.

FRESH THINKING

VAN DER SAR
BROWN   FERDINAND   HEINZE   O'SHEA
CARRICK   FLETCHER
RONALDO   ROONEY   GIGGS
SMITH

United, having lost the first leg 2-1, were keen to catch their opponent off-guard whilst also not doing their traditional trick of conceding early. The deeper midfield of Carrick and Darren Fletcher served as a reliable screen for the defence. Ronaldo and Giggs were pushed a little further forward, and alongside Rooney, the trio were given the freedom to switch positions. The work-rate of Giggs and Rooney, and front man Alan Smith, also allowed for the forward runs from midfield of Fletcher or Carrick. The Italian side were simply unprepared for the devastation they were about to suffer.

After 19 minutes it was 3-0; Carrick, Smith and Rooney all scoring. But the star of the show had been Cristiano Ronaldo, exploiting his liberation to wreak havoc in the channel between Roma's left-back and left centre-half. His penetrating runs were terrifying the visiting defence and he got goals he fully deserved in the 44th and 49th minute. A second from Carrick, and Evra's first European goal for the club, made it 7-1 on the night.

"Top games of football are generally won by eight players," Ferguson said in his second autobiography. "Three players can be carried if they're having an off night and work their socks off, or are playing a purely tactical role for the team. But half a dozen times in your career you achieve perfection where all 11 are on song."

Perfection – remember Ferguson's earlier statement that it occurred five or six times a season? By 2013 he had a revised list, much shorter, to mark the duration of his career. Roma was on it. Wimbledon in 1994. The 6-1 against Arsenal in 2001 – and the 6-2 win at Arsenal in 1990. That was four. Busby had described the 1948 FA Cup final and the 10-0 win over Anderlecht as his moments of perfection. There were never any such overt descriptions made by other managers but we can use the criteria of Busby and Ferguson to conclude that there was possibly only the 3-0 win over Barcelona in 1984 that belongs on the list. That is not to say other matches, those matches which *define* a manager's era (such as, for example, Derby County in the 1976 FA Cup semi-final), don't deserve a mention; Ferguson himself didn't include the 1999 FA Cup semi-final replay, or Turin a week later, so we can define perfection as a footballing display so complete that the opponent was dominated. Seven perfect games in United's post-war history? It's an interesting discussion. We'll come back to that.

The system used against Roma worked so well, it seemed a shame that it wasn't used more often. For the semi-final against Milan, Ferguson recalled Scholes, who had been suspended, for Smith, and moved to a 4-3-3. Both Ferdinand and Vidic were absent for the first leg – and Milan scored twice before Wayne Rooney's dramatic late winner gave false hope. Vidic was rushed back from a broken collarbone a week later but Milan, inspired by Kaka, gave a harsh lesson, winning 3-0. Without Ferdinand, Evra and Neville, it was destined to be an uphill task anyway, so one could not describe it as a tactical error. It was clear Ferguson needed to add to his squad, and he did so over the summer, gambling that he wouldn't suffer another injury crisis in his defence, and going top heavy. It was the classic Busby twist – when everyone was expecting defensive reinforcement, Ferguson instead doubled down on attack. In came Nani to take pressure off Giggs on the left; Anderson and Owen Hargreaves, to bolster the midfield; and then Carlos Tevez, who was so alike to Rooney that Ferguson felt he was almost replicating Cole and Yorke.

In the early part of the 2007/08 season, Ronaldo was sent off against Portsmouth – in his absence, Rene Meulensteen worked with him personally to discuss increasing his goal output. They worked on maximising the areas he should get into and the areas of a goal he should target; the overall message being to stop trying to score a perfect goal – try and score as many as possible, and the perfect goal would surely arrive. A subtle change occurred in United's play, as can be tracked in the team that faced Newcastle United in January 2008.

VAN DER SAR
O'SHEA FERDINAND VIDIC EVRA
RONALDO CARRICK ANDERSON GIGGS
ROONEY TEVEZ

Tevez's energy and selfless play matched that of Rooney's; they were both adept at scoring and playing as a striker, but their flexibility worked perfectly for a system that accommodated a floating player like Ronaldo. In fact, Ronaldo almost played as a centre-forward, creating a nightmare for opponents. In the above team, the 11 could easily become a 4-3-3 with Giggs coming narrow. This was, in fact, the system United would adopt for the rest of the season, with considerable success. The Premier League title was retained.

With a 0-0 from the first leg of the Champions League semi-final in Barcelona – where United had played 4-5-1, Rooney and Tevez wide of Ronaldo (who missed a first-half penalty) – Ferguson and Queiroz then worked on an industrious 4-4-2 to play in the return, in the absence of Rooney and Vidic.

FOOTBALL, TAUGHT BY MATT BUSBY

VAN DER SAR
HARGREAVES   FERDINAND   BROWN   EVRA
PARK   CARRICK   SCHOLES   NANI
TEVEZ   RONALDO

It was one of the few times in Ferguson's history where a greater emphasis was placed on nullifying the opponent than on playing the team's natural game. That in itself was a risk. Old Trafford was electric but the vibrancy was very different as the home crowd watched their team play cat and mouse in a way the club never had before. They'd need an early goal to settle the nerves – and it arrived, through a fantastic Paul Scholes volley. The energy in the wide areas, in the front line and the calm in the middle of the park were a fantastic blend. Barcelona did have their moments, but so did United on the counter, and though the game is rightly regarded as a rearguard effort, a match that finished 1-0 could just as easily have ended 2-0 or 1-1. The approach was successful – United were in the Champions League final.

Ferguson was later to reflect on the strategy, feeling it had put the fans through hell and himself through torture. "What we did," he said, referring to the first leg, "was to deploy Tevez off the front and Ronaldo at centre-forward, so we could have two areas of attack… we still found it hard, of course, because Barcelona monopolised possession for such long periods and in those circumstances your own players tend to lose interest."

It was a lesson for the future – perhaps – but United did have the final to play. That was against Chelsea, in Moscow. Ferguson played a 4-4-2, with Hargreaves on the right of midfield, and Ronaldo on the left – this was to exploit the shorter height of Michael Essien, who was moonlighting at right-back for the London side. It was again another direct tactic that hit the mark – Ronaldo scoring a

328

header after 26 minutes. But Chelsea (now under Avram Grant) responded with a goal through Lampard and began to exert control in their 4-3-3. Ferguson responded by pushing Rooney wide right and bringing Hargreaves narrower, and believed it put his team in control of the game again.

It was time for the theatre that Manchester United provides more than any other club. Giggs – who had scored in the previous game, a 2-0 win over Wigan Athletic which had secured the league title on his 758th appearance for the club, therefore matching the all-time record set by Sir Bobby Charlton – came on and almost scored a dramatic winner in extra-time. The game went to penalties. Ronaldo, whose strike had been his 42nd of the season, missed his spot-kick – and so, with the last of Chelsea's penalties, John Terry had the chance to win it. He slipped, hit the post – and in the sudden death kicks, Giggs scored his, meaning if Anelka missed, United were champions of Europe again. Van der Sar guessed right to save – and Ferguson, nine years after the first time, had his hands on the most coveted trophy in the club game again.

Success breeds confidence, and for the 12 months they reigned as European champions, United certainly played with that swagger. Ronaldo was named the best player in the world and lived up to the billing. Dimitar Berbatov and Rafael and Fabio Da Silva were added to the first-team squad, creating an intense competition for places that was possibly the strongest the club had seen since 1957. One key change occurred in the staff – Carlos Queiroz left, so Mick Phelan was promoted to assistant and Rene Meulensteen to first-team coach. Phelan and Meulensteen encouraged Ferguson's desire to ensure his team always played on the front foot and the result was one of the greatest seasons in the club's history, and almost the best.

Meulensteen recalled the time Ferguson called a meeting with him to discuss what he saw when he watched the best Manchester United team. They would ideally press from the front – and if they had to defend, then they would defend narrow, compact, and always with a strategy to counter. In possession he wanted his team to show rhythm and move the ball in one or two touches, trying to use as much unpredictability as possible. His four most important attacking principles – speed, power, penetration and unpredictability. "If that doesn't work," Ferguson smiled, "we gamble!"

Meulensteen himself had grown into his role and was seeing youngsters he'd worked with play in the first team. His philosophy of football – holistically rooted in Johan Cruyff's vision of Total Football with movement of players, and methodically inspired by Wiel Coerver's belief that skills could be taught to young children – was having such a distinct impact on United's senior squad that their fluidity and multi-functionality was possibly at its most true, in the most perfect sync, since 1957. Meulensteen had a crucially strong intuition regarding the rhythm of the team's play.

The Club World Cup had now succeeded the Intercontinental Cup and United took on Gamba Osaka of Japan in the semi-final and LDU Quito of Ecuador in the final – Rooney scored the goal that gave United the title of best team in the world for a second time. The formation was 4-4-2 with Ronaldo starting in his false wing position – when Vidic was sent off, Tevez came off for Evans, making it a 4-4-1 or a 4-3-2.

With such a strong goalscoring threat United were always capable of causing damage, but it was in defence they set records this season – Edwin van der Sar keeping 14 consecutive clean sheets in the league (United kept 24 all told in the league and a remarkable 39 in all competitions). This was not reflective of their strategy – scorelines of 4-3, two 5-3 and a 5-2 showed their willingness to play open football, and gamble – but instead of their incredible quality.

Even with this quality, the great teams need luck. United suffered an injury crisis to their strikers in early spring, and Ferguson was happy to turn to Federico Macheda, a 17-year-old Italian rookie. He scored in his first two games to restore some confidence to a wobbling team and instigate a 13-game unbeaten run which saw them win the 2008/09 league title – their 18th, drawing the club level with Liverpool.

Macheda's memorable match-winning introduction against Aston Villa had such a connection to United's fabric that we'll discuss it at length a little later. A few weeks later all of the senior strikers were fit – and thrown on to the pitch at half-time with the team down 2-0 against Spurs. Ferguson had started with a 4-4-2 but in the second period had a front two of Berbatov and Tevez supported by Ronaldo from the right and Rooney from the left. No tactical masterplan was necessary – just the pure thrill, the pursuit of goals. Ronaldo, Rooney and Berbatov delivered them, as United scored five times in the space of 22 minutes to have the game sewn up with 10 minutes still to play.

United's potency was proven by the number of goals scored by their top stars – Ronaldo with 26, Rooney with 20, Tevez with 15 and Berbatov with 14. A League Cup had been added to the pile of trophies after a penalty shoot-out win over Spurs, but the same method had been used to separate Everton and United in the FA Cup semi-final, with Ferguson's team finally tasting defeat in a cup tie.

Another was to follow. At this juncture it's important to make a note about the analysis undertaken so far in this book. Research around tactical innovations has been centred around Manchester

FOOTBALL, TAUGHT BY MATT BUSBY

United in a forensic way and then cross-referenced against football more generally. So, for example, Matt Busby and Jimmy Murphy were not the only British coaches influenced by the Hungarian style of play. Tommy Docherty and his players may have likened their style to the 21st century Barcelona but it is clear they are talking about energy and harassment rather than ball retention. There is no outright claim that Ron Atkinson invented the diamond formation, only a point that it was more or less that system used in 1984 (and earlier than that with West Brom), some time before Johan Cruyff popularised it with Barcelona.

These points are made because there is theoretical evidence that supports the idea that Manchester United and Cristiano Ronaldo were responsible for the creation of their own biggest rival. There is certainly evidence to say United were at the front of the trend – and that trend is the usage of Ronaldo, the team's most talented player, in a false starting position. Up until 2008, Lionel Messi's goalscoring tallies had been what you might consider normal for an extremely promising young player. In 2008/09, Messi's numbers more than doubled to the extraordinary level they would stay for the remainder of his career. What changed? One obvious factor was Pep Guardiola, who replaced Frank Rijkaard as Barcelona head coach. Was it just a coincidence that Messi, who played from the right just as Ronaldo did, was now given the same licence to roam as Ronaldo had?

Ferguson admitted he was more determined to be adventurous against Barcelona in the 2009 Champions League final than he had been against them in the 2008 semi-final, but conceded they were 'beaten partly because of that change in emphasis'. Another fatal flaw in planning was asking Giggs to mark Sergio Busquets in a similar way that McClair had been asked to do with Koeman all those years ago. Giggs picked up a stomach bug, affecting his stamina.

FRESH THINKING

VAN DER SAR
O'SHEA FERDINAND VIDIC EVRA
ANDERSON CARRICK GIGGS
PARK RONALDO ROONEY

It's all ifs and buts – United's greatest lament was the suspension to Darren Fletcher after a strange red card in the semi-final win over Arsenal. Fletcher had become a crucial part of United's midfield in big games and he would have probably been in the team in place of Anderson. In retrospect, you might theorise starting Tevez instead of Giggs and giving Park the man-marking job. Hindsight never won a single trophy in practice, only in theory.

United started well, with Ronaldo coming close on a couple of occasions – but Guardiola quickly noticed the joy that Evra was having down the left, and switched Messi from the right to the centre, telling Samuel Eto'o to track the United full-back. Ironically enough, Eto'o, from the right, cut into the United box moments later, and scored. In Ferguson's second autobiography he remarks that Messi remained as a deep-lying striker for the rest of his career from that moment but it is likely the change was already happening at Barcelona due to the fact that his goal tally had increased so much – he could thank the work of Eto'o, just as Ronaldo had Rooney to thank.

Barcelona dominated the ball from that point and scored a second on the hour mark – Ferguson brought on Tevez but it made his team just more susceptible to being suffocated in midfield. For the first time in their history, and at the fourth time of asking, United had lost a European Cup final.

In the post-mortem, Ferguson insisted he would have a different plan if coming up against the same opponents again. He later reflected on Ferdinand and Vidic, observing that at their age they preferred to defend the space but against Barcelona you needed centre halves who would 'drop right on Messi' and force him wide.

In the summer of 2009 both Ronaldo and Tevez departed Old Trafford, rupturing the fantastic gameplan of this team. A new approach had to be created and the attack was built around Rooney. Ronaldo's replacement was Antonio Valencia, a more direct winger in the mould of Steve Coppell. Throughout the next season, Ferguson played a 4-3-3 more often than not; a February trip to the San Siro provided a typical insight to how the team were set up.

VAN DER SAR

RAFAEL FERDINAND EVANS EVRA

FLETCHER CARRICK SCHOLES

NANI ROONEY PARK

There was a unique twist in the Champions League games, or indeed other big games, where Park played. Off the ball against Milan he was tasked with man-marking Andrea Pirlo. He did the job superbly in both legs – United won 3-2 in Italy, and Park even scored in the 4-0 home win.

With Rooney in superb form, United looked on course to retain their league title and qualify for another European final – but the striker was injured against Bayern Munich, missed crucial games, and all Ferguson had to mark the season was the retaining of the League Cup.

Joining the following summer was Javier Hernandez, the diminutive Mexican striker. When Rooney picked up an injury at the start of the season, and Valencia broke his leg against Rangers in the Champions League, Hernandez played alongside Berbatov in a traditional 4-4-2 formation. It was Berbatov's form which caught the eye, with a hat-trick against Liverpool and five goals against Blackburn, but it was still the Bulgarian who often found himself the odd man out more when Rooney returned. Playing the traditional shape, Rooney was in inspiring form as a deep-lying number ten, scoring the crucial goals that delivered the club their 19th league title – taking them above Liverpool in the all-time hierarchy of English football. The 4-4-2 was used all the way through the Champions League, too, as United made it to their third final in four years.

No such luck in the FA Cup, with defeat to the newly-rich Manchester City in the semi-final. But it was the game against Arsenal in the sixth round which brought most attention from a tactical point of view.

VAN DER SAR

BROWN SMALLING VIDIC EVRA

RAFAEL GIBSON O'SHEA FABIO

ROONEY

HERNANDEZ

This strange line-up, consisting of no fewer than seven defensive players, was sent out with the intention of United's Brazilians stopping the passing channels of Samir Nasri and Jack Wilshere – the basic plan being that if they couldn't get the ball, they couldn't dictate the play. It worked a treat, with a bewildered Arsenal unable to cope with the energy and movement up front. It was, perhaps, not a gameplan that would have been wise to use again against a truly elite team, but Fabio and Rooney scored to give Ferguson's side a remarkable 2-0 win on the night.

The Champions League final in 2011 was at Wembley, and provided a rematch with Barcelona. And, despite Ferguson being conscious of the requirement for energy down the middle, it could not be said that Ferdinand, Vidic, Carrick and Giggs were blessed in that regard at this stage in their careers – certainly not when it came to ball retrieval.

VAN DER SAR

FABIO FERDINAND VIDIC EVRA

VALENCIA CARRICK GIGGS PARK

ROONEY

HERNANDEZ

Park, on the left, could provide the engine, but Barcelona were a team at the peak of their powers, masters of ball retention, against a team with few players equipped to get the ball from them.

"The frustration of playing against a team that plays tiki-taka (the Barcelona style) is that in essence it is a negative tactic," explains Fabio Da Silva. "The purpose is to wear the opposition down. Not only are you tired from trying to win the ball back but when you do you might be in an unfamiliar area to begin an attack. Your frustration at not having the ball for so long has a big impact on your decision-making, so you are more rash and impulsive, and therefore much more likely to give the ball away. You've fallen into their trap, and if you have just one player out of position they open you up to create a chance. The most important qualities are patience and composure, but it's very difficult when you are in the heat of a cup final and you don't have the ball for long periods."

After conceding an early goal to Pedro, United got in at half-time at 1-1 thanks to a fine Rooney strike. Ferguson admitted to making an error, perhaps lost in the momentum of the equaliser, and momentarily forgot Barcelona were usually at their strongest just after half-time. United over-committed – Messi scored, and then David Villa added a third. The United manager described the preparation for the game as 'the best I've ever seen' but was forced to concede that for once he had been on the receiving end of one of those perfect performances.

Meanwhile, a 2011 FA Youth Cup win was delivered by Paul McGuinness with a team that included the likes of Paul Pogba, Jesse Lingard, and the most highly-rated prospect the club had on their books since Giggs, Ravel Morrison. In the first leg of the semi-final, Chelsea were 2-0 up at Stamford Bridge – McGuinness' team-talk concentrated not on the idea of giving the ball to Morrison, but reminding his players that the home side would have been anxious at the legacy of Manchester United always coming back into games when it seemed they were out of it. "Don't let them down," the coach urged – his players recovered to 2-2, and although they'd lose the game 3-2, 10 days later United won 4-0 at Old Trafford. Victory over Sheffield United in the final was straightforward in comparison.

24

EXIT FERGUSON

SIR ALEX FERGUSON RETIRED IN 2013, AFTER WINNING a 13th league title – Manchester United's 20th. It was delivered mostly by the goalscoring boots of Robin van Persie, who played atop a traditional 4-4-2 that was used throughout the season. With the veteran experience of Giggs, Scholes (who had come out of retirement after six months on the sidelines), Ferdinand, Vidic and Evra, this was not a vintage Manchester United with the bombastic pace and physicality of 1994, the telepathy of 1999, or the movement of 2008, but it was possibly the side which represented Ferguson most – numerous comebacks and late winners and a professional resolve to ensure defeat was simply not an option after the heartbreaking title surrender on the last day of 2012, when Manchester City won the league with the last kick of the season. United were relentless in their quest to regain the title and an 18-game unbeaten run over winter ensured the Premier League title did indeed return to the red half of Manchester.

Having already privately decided to retire, Ferguson was the only man in the stadium who knew the defeat to Real Madrid in early March would be his last European match at Old Trafford. He was so furious with the decision to send Nani off – with United 2-1 up on aggregate only to lose 3-2 – that he refused to speak to the press afterwards.

With 27 major honours, and another 11 if you count the Charity Shield and European Super Cup, Ferguson had completed a legacy that established him as not only Manchester United's greatest manager, but the best in British football history and possibly even the global game.

It is obviously not a matter of whether or not Ferguson was able to deliver 'football taught by Matt Busby', more a case of asking just how comprehensively was it delivered? (One might be tempted to ask if Ferguson himself had reinvented the club's philosophy. Your writer might, too, but must add this comment made by Ferguson in 1992. "You look at that man and you say, well, anything you've achieved is just endorsing Sir Matt Busby's indelible print in this club. He built this club. The vision he had has inspired me to make sure that we're trying to approach as near to it as we possibly can." This is a critical statement when it comes to understanding the heritage of the club.)

There was entertaining football delivered by Ferguson's numerous different rebuilt teams; three teams that stand a good argument to be the greatest in the history of the domestic game; four FA Youth Cup wins; two European Cups.

No, he was never quite able to reach the miracle of 11 homegrown players in a team but he did manage nine in a League Cup game against Crewe in 2006. He also handled a dilemma Busby never had to face because of Munich – that being how to handle a great group of young players a) when they reached their peak and b) when they had to be replaced. He did so masterfully, understanding the right time to make the changes. David Beckham's sale was a watershed moment because there was no doubting he still had plenty to give, but the decision to move on the most famous player in the world was reminiscent of Busby's sale of Johnny Morris in that it laid down a marker about just who was the boss.

Perhaps the most important conclusion is that Manchester United's identity was not based on a specific formation. It was possible to achieve success – *success* defined by winning and entertaining football – using a number of different formations. It was possible to achieve that being bold and by incorporating a little pragmatism. The greatest successes – those that yielded most trophies and also represented pinnacles for the club – were achieved after an investment in a long-term process was followed. The teams of 1957, 1968, 1994, 1999 and 2008 (and to a lesser extent 1977) reached their heights thanks to a patience that placed faith in times of adversity and even valuing that adversity in terms of improving the team.

If it wasn't through a specific shape, then there were still common hallmarks. All of those teams were reliable in defence, physically strong in midfield and had electricity on the wings. The 1957, 1968 and 1999 teams had a strong core of players developed by the club – it cannot be a coincidence that these are the three teams probably most beloved.

Another trait shared by the very best Busby and Ferguson teams was their multi-functionality. Let's journey back to Don Davies' assessment of the pre-Munich side.

"There has been no move towards any form of stereotyped 'Manchester United' football. Each player has been encouraged to develop his particular gifts to the advantage of the team, so that the dash of one, the shooting power of another, the speed of a third, the long passing of a fourth have been exploited in harness with the ranging of a fifth, the mobility of a sixth, the plodding steadiness of a seventh. Variety has been achieved without loss of balance, through mutual understanding of the game's problems, upon which the players are encouraged to think for themselves... there is, however, no characteristic Manchester United style."

Perhaps there was, and it contained all of the above, there was just no term to describe it. It was a style that was – at its best, capable of delivering proficiency in all the beautiful arts of the game and handling all the not-so-beautiful aspects of it.

Busby's brand of football was celebrated and yet perhaps suffered at the hands of the British game's early intellectualism; there was such a resistance to what the Hungarians did in 1953 that it seemed English football was incapable of recognising what was happening within its confines. Instead there was an insularism, as could be traced by the reaction to Wolves' win over Honved.

And then as the veiled xenophobia subsided and different styles of football and footballers from foreign shores were perceived in an exotic and romantic way, there remained a projection that the British sensibility prohibited it from producing such a refined style. You will be familiar with keywords associated with Ferguson's reign as Manchester United manager. Trophies, success, power, control, aggression. Fury. Hairdryer. When these are used as leading attributes it almost feels undignified to suggest it was sophisticated and multi-dimensional. That they could pass any team off the park if they wanted to play a football match, but also roll their sleeves up and not back down if a more physical confrontation was on the cards.

The battle with Arsene Wenger's Arsenal sums up the matter. Wenger was seen as the aristocrat, his vision of football deemed more artistic. Ferguson was a force of personality and his teams had a winning attitude. But a faithful observation of that era just doesn't back that up, and this is not to say Wenger was not all of those things, rather to say Ferguson was too. He was just more adaptable.

There are stories from the training camps on both sides. Ferguson's keenness to mix it up. Wenger's insistence to train and play the same way regardless of the opposition. There are incidental points, such as key injuries to key players, for example when Roy Keane's absence had a damaging impact on United's capability to win seven or even eight titles in a row. There are the head-to-heads where Ferguson's side went hell-for-leather and played wondrous football, notably the 1999 FA Cup semi-final, the 1999 league win at Highbury and the 6-1 in 2011. There was the period where United were in transition and Arsenal were reigning league champions having won the title as the Invincibles, only to lose to United home and away in real scraps. There was the regeneration of both clubs and how they dealt with Chelsea's wealth – how Ferguson built another great side that tore Arsenal to shreds in a thrilling Champions League semi-final in 2009. There was an almost sad footnote to the rivalry when Ferguson watched his team score eight past Arsenal, and showed Wenger the response any true winner hates most of all – pity. And yet, Wenger would be portrayed as the manager who believed in beautiful football and Ferguson would merely be cast as the winner. If it is possible for the greatest manager of all time to be done a disservice, then he was at times in this comparison.

Because Ferguson's teams could evolve, and because he didn't adhere to one singular vision of how to play the game, he is a victim of reductive analysis in much the same way as Busby was.

This is no fairytale reimagining. Ferguson's way of doing things meant that naturally he didn't fully involve himself in one singular style. That was the compromise. He couldn't fully commit to a form of tiki-taka and so his teams could not perfect the art. He couldn't fully commit to a form of catenaccio and so there was always the risk that his team might be caught off-guard by a team playing that way. If he didn't have his best 11, or if his team were in the midst of a transition, it might mean having to apply a different tactic to beat a different team.

There is also no objectively perfect way to play. Some people enjoy catenaccio and the art of good defending. Even tiki-taka has its critics as being too negative. Tiki-taka and the Manchester United way are not completely dissimilar; both have their roots in Hungarian football and place their major emphasis in the movement of the ball, the movement of the players, and the outnumbering of opponents by manipulating spaces.

Ferguson's application of that strategy wasn't quite so forensic but it did adhere to the general philosophy. Like everyone else, he applied his interpretation of it – crucially, plugging it into the history of the club, always embracing it, because the idea of fighting for something bigger than just you or even your team could only help in terms of incentive.

A Scottish manager. Players developed by the club. Winning the European Cup for the first time on Sir Matt Busby's birthday when defeat looked certain? Winning it for the second time 50 years after Munich when all seemed lost? Just like the club's first European Cup triumph in 1968, there was a sentimental, intangible and yet incredibly real sense of romance and tragedy, elevating the successes to mean much more than they might have done if they stood on their own. That's the element of the Manchester United way which remains as unfathomable, as unquantifiable, as it ever was.

25

DAVID MOYES

THERE WAS BARELY ANY SPECULATION REGARDING who might succeed Sir Alex Ferguson in 2013, because he had handpicked his successor – David Moyes, of Everton. There was, however, speculation that Manchester United could suffer as they did in the post-Busby era. Moyes had done a fine job at Everton, keeping them competitive around the top six despite not having much money to spend. He was not associated with any notable philosophy. His teams often played direct football, uncompromising in aggression, and he was renowned as someone who could get better results than the sum of a team's parts might suggest.

It most certainly wasn't all Moyes' fault, but his spell at Old Trafford was almost like an experiment in everything that could go wrong, going wrong. It was also like the past repeating itself in a condensed period of time. From the moment he took his first press conference and admitted 'the blood drained' from his face when Ferguson told him he was the man picked to follow him, it seemed the job was too big for him. Natural decisions, such as the one to bring in his own staff in Steve Round and Jimmy Lumsden, came back to bite as Mick Phelan and Rene Meulensteen, two men crucial to the smooth running of the playing side of the club, were let go.

The new manager didn't seek the advice of senior players on the way their conditioning was handled, overusing some veterans to the point they were burned out, and dropping other players like Rafael, who had been first-choice in the previous season. Moyes was also hindered by David Gill stepping down as chief executive as Ed Woodward, an executive with little experience in handling transfers, was hired to follow him. It made for a difficult summer of transfer negotiations and only Marouane Fellaini, who played for Moyes at Everton, came in. Fellaini was better as a target man than a ball-playing midfielder but in midfield is where he played.

The existing players were, much like during the McGuinness era, unconvinced by a man who had won nothing as a coach, and United's early season results and performances were unrecognisable from the team who had won the title the previous campaign. West Brom won at Old Trafford for the first time in a generation. Embarrassingly for Moyes, so too did Everton, and a few days later, Newcastle, after the manager had urged his team to 'make it as difficult for them as we possibly can'. Where one can draw a line between the bullish and reserved personalities between some United managers, and how that contributed to success and failure, it's clear to see on which side of the divide Moyes seemed to fall. Youngster Adnan Januzaj made a bright start but was then overused when the experience of Giggs was wasted on the sideline.

Early sympathy was afforded – perhaps Ferguson had retired at the right time, the cynics said, his team's form about to nose-dive – but results and performances continued to suffer and the prevailing thought was that the decline shouldn't be so pronounced.

Champions League qualification suddenly looked a remote hope for a club who hadn't finished outside of the top three for over two decades. Salvation in the cups? Moyes was less fortunate than McGuinness, suffering a League Cup semi-final defeat and an FA Cup third-round defeat, both at Old Trafford. Moyes responded by spending a club record fee of £38m on Juan Mata, at the same time as offering the club's biggest ever contract to Wayne Rooney. Both players operated in the same area of the pitch.

A 2-0 defeat in Olympiakos and a soul-shuddering 3-0 loss to Liverpool, which could have been double that amount, at Old Trafford, put Moyes on the brink of the sack in March of his first season. United had suffered bigger home defeats in the Ferguson era but this was, by a distance, the worst performance at the Theatre of Dreams for two or three generations.

DE GEA

RAFAEL JONES VIDIC EVRA

MATA CARRICK FELLAINI JANUZAJ

ROONEY

VAN PERSIE

In an emergency, Moyes reverted to experience, calling in Giggs and Ferdinand who were outstanding in a 3-0 win over Olympiakos which would, in any other season, have seemed like a routine win. It was merely a stay of execution. United were humiliated at home by Manchester City, knocked out of Europe by Bayern Munich, and when Everton made it mathematically impossible for United to qualify for the top continental competition the following season, Moyes was sacked on April 27th, 2014.

The relative brevity of his ten-month spell makes it difficult to draw firm conclusions. There are some who felt he should have been given longer – he did have a six-year contract – and some who felt the writing was on the wall much earlier than April. He played 4-4-2 for the most part and there did not seem to be any specific gameplan in terms of patterns or style; even the two players he bought in seemed suited to specific, contradictory styles, and were made to try and fit inside a 4-4-2.

Moyes later admitted he should have retained at least one of the older coaches to keep an established link with the squad but it was too little, too late. Ryan Giggs was named as interim manager, and Louis van Gaal was hired as the next permanent manager, with his job to start after the World Cup in Brazil, where he was coaching Holland. In the meantime, a huge transition was already underway. Giggs retired, Ferdinand and Vidic left, and Evra had more or less agreed to go. Moyes had tried to do things the right way but never really seemed to have his finger on the pulse of what the club was, in terms of its size, the specificities of the team, and the pressure that was on a Manchester United manager. He wouldn't have expected that every word would be scrutinised in a way it hadn't been at Everton, but the fact of the matter was it was now part and parcel of the job – the job he had lost.

26

LOUIS VAN GAAL

IN LOUIS VAN GAAL, MANCHESTER UNITED WERE NOT hiring a shrinking violet. Here was a man who had coached the famous Ajax team of the 1990s – they of the youth academy including Edgar Davids, Patrick Kluivert, Edwin van der Sar, Marc Overmars, Clarence Seedorf and Ronald and Frank De Boer who would win the European Cup – as well as Barcelona and Bayern Munich, before coaching the national team. He was manager there when British football took heed and started to emulate their approach to permitting clubs to train players from an earlier age. At Ajax, Van Gaal created a team with fantastic interchanging of movement, executed in a way that it resembled a machine – he had a way of playing football, a 'philosophy', that he strongly adhered to.

"It is an attacking, technical and tactical philosophy," he said, "you can show your qualities more than ever. The vision, then the team and then who fits in that profile that I make from all positions in my system: 1-4-3-3… Age is not important. The vision comes first which is a step by step framework on how to implement the football philosophy of the coach. Too often coaches go about trying to implement a style of play or system without first identifying the philosophy. I don't think that the system is the most important thing. The important thing is philosophy and that's always the same… the philosophy binds players with trainers and coaches."

Van Gaal preferred a 4-3-3 (though United players would find he seemed determined to move to a three-man defence) that would have one stopper and one sweeper in the backline, a holding midfielder and a creative midfielder, wide players who were capable of playing through the middle and linking with play, with a target man who could always serve as an outlet. Another of Van Gaal's strengths was walking into a squad who might not have the players with the skills he'd prefer and successfully implementing his system. Which was just as well, as apparently, the Manchester United way was not on the agenda at the interview stage. "When I was accepting the job," he told the *Guardian* in 2019, "we never spoke about the system Manchester United played with, or about a philosophy."

Van Gaal was taken aback by this, as before he'd taken any other club job this had been one of the main points of discussion. He was a man credited for technical coaching and tactical innovation; at the World Cup in 2014, he played three at the back with wing-backs, and when Holland beat Spain 5-1 there was some serious optimism back in Manchester. Later in the competition he substituted his goalkeeper in extra-time, with the substitute proving pivotal in the penalty shoot-out to help the Dutch reach the semi-finals. Did he have the Midas touch?

It certainly seemed so in pre-season. New staff came in – Round and Lumsden out, Albert Stuivenberg and Frans Hoek in. Ryan Giggs was named assistant. Van Gaal introduced the boldest formation shift in the club's entire history, experimenting with a 3-4-1-2 and a 3-5-2 in friendly games. The response was emphatic. United looked vibrant, full of movement and completely reinvigorated as they defeated LA Galaxy 7-0, Real Madrid 3-1 and Liverpool 3-1 in three of their five warm-up games. When it came to the real thing, however, things did not go quite so smoothly.

Team v Swansea 16th August, 2014:

DE GEA

JONES   SMALLING   BLACKETT

LINGARD   FLETCHER   HERRERA   YOUNG

MATA

ROONEY   HERNANDEZ

It was a mess on many levels as United lost an opening-day fixture for the first time since 1972. Lingard was injured – Januzaj came on and switched with Young. Swansea scored moments after the change. At half-time, Hernandez came off for Nani, making the shape 4-4-1-1. Rooney equalised – but Swansea scored again to take a famous win. Van Gaal later said that he felt the club's commercial interests had precedence over the on-pitch events, explaining he felt exhaustion from the summer trip to the USA played into the poor early league performances.

The manager sat down with former United captain Gary Neville, now a broadcast journalist, to explain his approach, saying that Giggs would often provide analysis of the opponent, Stuivenberg would analyse and Van Gaal would ultimately decide on the tactical plan. He likened the process the players were undertaking to him learning to drive on the other side of the road in a new country. "We need time to build up a new team, and that cannot be in one day," he said. "It's a process. All my teams in the beginning were not good. They have to switch from instinctive to thinking brain. It's very difficult. I train in another way to the former coaches, and that's difficult. (I play 3-5-2) because it's more easy to defend. You have to defend the space and the player who is coming into it. When you play like that it's always less than 15 metres (between the three centre-backs). And there are always wide players. And they are always free when they move well, in the right tactical way at the right tactical time. When I play with three strikers, they are also wide.

"When you play with full-backs, they are also wide, but they cannot always go. When you play with three defenders, they (the wing-backs) can always go. Both at the same time. That is a risk, but I am a risky coach. Then you have to switch the play. And you know that all the wide players are free. Now, we have to look more for the free player... And I have said everything about how I am... they have hired me for my philosophy. They have said that. I think I shall be supported."

Van Gaal persisted with the 3-4-1-2 but performances and results were not ideal. A number of players were signed in a short space of time, to add to Ander Herrera and Luke Shaw who arrived before Van Gaal started work. Marcos Rojo and Daley Blind followed – Angel Di Maria, man of the match in that year's Champions League final, signed as the club broke their transfer record again, spending £59.7m. Radamel Falcao, a fantastic striker who had suffered a career-threatening injury, signed on loan with an option for a permanent transfer. It was a brand new era, with so much English league experience lost, specifically in defence, and replaced by only one player who had played for one of the very top European clubs.

"I met with them (Ed Woodward and the Glazer family) in Brussels," Van Gaal told *FourFourTwo* magazine. "They asked me about everything, including my vision and how I would want to organise things, and said they would meet my needs for new players. I inherited an old team that hadn't been refreshed for some time, and wanted to rejuvenate with players who would bring the same kind of quality. But to get the ones I wanted proved very difficult."

After the transfer deadline and the first international break, United played QPR at home, and fielded a diamond. They won 4-0 and kept the same shape at Leicester a week later – Van Gaal dropped Mata, who had been playing his best football since signing, to start Falcao. United's front line looked excellent at times but at the back the inexperience came at a significant cost. A 3-1 lead became a 5-3 defeat in an extraordinary collapse.

United's players were struggling with the changes in training. Van Gaal was autocratic, demanding, and restrictive – defensive players in particular were not allowed any freedom, leading to one confrontation in a Monday morning video analysis where the manager criticised Rafael for crossing a ball first time instead of taking a touch – even though it resulted in a goal.

The manager was always said to favour a three-man defence so tried it again at Arsenal – and this time it worked, United winning 2-1. Over the following weeks Van Gaal had his team play in the following formations: 4-3-3, 4-1-2-1-2, and 3-4-1-2, the changes oddly helping the team develop some consistency as they won six in a row. The 3-4-1-2 remained in fashion until an insipid home defeat to Southampton where United failed to register a shot on target. It seemed to resonate with the manager, who finally settled on a four-man defence for much of the rest of the season.

There was a run of games where United were due to face Spurs, Liverpool and Man City – and Van Gaal tried another new shape for a crucial period which would determine whether the club would get back in the Champions League.

LOUIS VAN GAAL

DE GEA
VALENCIA   JONES   SMALLING   BLIND
CARRICK   HERRERA
MATA   FELLAINI   YOUNG
ROONEY

There was nothing intricate about this – the tactic was blunt – get Young on the ball, get an in-swinging cross for Fellaini to either go for goal or knock down for Rooney. Staggeringly, it worked, as United won all three big games (Mata scoring a brace at Anfield, one a spectacular scissor kick) to more or less secure a top-four spot. Di Maria was now barely used and seemed set to leave. "I always ask a player where he wants to play," Van Gaal said. "For him it was wing, wide and mostly left. I started with him there. He was not performing that well, to a level you could expect from an £80m player. I have to see if another position is better for him. I have played him left winger, as the ten, second striker and on the right. Then the critics say he is having to play in too many positions. I gave him all the chances to perform well."

Still, the minimum objective had been accomplished – United's top four status necessary for the lucrative financial rewards, with Champions League qualification now deemed crucial for the operational normality of the *megaclubs* – and it seemed as though there was a solid enough foundation upon which to build. Van Gaal was credited in some circles as being the man who had created the structure upon which Barcelona and Bayern Munich had enjoyed their modern successes and the theory was that he would spend one or two more years in charge before Giggs, his assistant, took the job.

Well, that was the plan. An underwhelming transfer window saw Di Maria depart, Falcao's loan move not made permanent and Rafael, Hernandez, van Persie and Nani all leave for around £6m in total. The incoming transfers were not inspiring – Morgan Schneiderlin could hopefully fill a hole in midfield, but opinions were split over Bastian Schweinsteiger, Matteo Darmian, Memphis Depay and Anthony Martial, though the latter enjoyed a superb debut against Liverpool. He scored twice against Southampton, too, as Van Gaal seemed to settle with a 4-2-3-1:

DE GEA
DARMIAN SMALLING BLIND ROJO
CARRICK SCHNEIDERLIN
MATA ROONEY DEPAY
MARTIAL

Their 3-2 win at Southampton made it six goals from their last six shots on target and, like Frank O'Farrell's side, it was clear that something would have to give. Defensively United remained fairly sound, but the goals dried up. When the defence became leaky before Christmas, pressure started to mount on the manager. Van Gaal had already been forced to admit to journalists that he had been confronted by Carrick and Rooney about training routines. Then the club were dumped out of the Champions League and into the Europa League in the first of four consecutive losses – Wolfsburg, Bournemouth, Norwich and Stoke proving to be a formidable quartet. Jose Mourinho's recent dismissal from Chelsea prompted the press to speculate he would take over at Old Trafford. Van Gaal hit back in press conferences, saying he felt he had been 'sacked twice' before Christmas – and a strange energy around the club began to take hold.

Supporters were infuriated by the quality of football – two dismal Old Trafford performances against Southampton, where the Saints again won without facing a shot, and Sheffield United, where Van Gaal needed a last-minute Rooney penalty to scrape through in the FA Cup, had fans either pulling their hair out or falling asleep. But they remained strangely attached to Van Gaal because of his fractious relationship with the press and, after an injury crisis necessitated the call-up of more young players, there was a galvanised atmosphere around the club for a short period of time.

A number of young players started to get games – Lingard, Andreas Pereira, Cameron Borthwick-Jackson, Guillermo Varela, James Weir, Timothy Fosu-Mensah, and this in addition to Tyler Blackett and Paddy McNair and a couple more. Most notably, Marcus Rashford was called into the side as an emergency starter following the withdrawal of Anthony Martial before a Europa League game – Rashford scored twice, and was kept in the team to face Arsenal at the weekend, where he scored twice again in a win where the home crowd was completely engaged. When Van Gaal theatrically fell to the floor after a back and forth with fourth official Mike Dean, the supporters loved it. Rashford's dream start continued when he scored the only goal in the Manchester derby and then a fine goal in the FA Cup at West Ham.

In the FA Cup semi-final Van Gaal named a 4-1-4-1, or 4-3-3, to face Everton – a game won in the last minute by Martial. So United had their first FA Cup final since 2007 to look forward to, and their first final since Ferguson's retirement, but it was already heavily rumoured that Van Gaal would be sacked anyway – the club had failed to qualify for the Champions League again, also suffering a Europa League exit to Liverpool. The young players had done much to elevate the spirit of the club, possibly because they were largely given exemption from Van Gaal's strict instructions.

Those looking for positive omens noted the opponents in the

FA Cup final were Crystal Palace – the same team who faced Ferguson's side in his first final. The line-up featured Rooney in the deeper midfield role that he'd occupied for much of the season.

DE GEA
VALENCIA SMALLING BLIND ROJO
CARRICK
FELLAINI ROONEY
MATA RASHFORD MARTIAL
(4-3-3, OR EVEN 4-1-4-1)

Another omen – Lingard scored the winner in extra-time, the first time since Lee Martin in 1990 that a young player developed by the club had scored the winning goal in a cup final. It was a fine strike, caught sweetly on the half-volley from the edge of the box. This was not to be the start of a glittering era of success though – in fact, many people were already aware it was the end of the Van Gaal reign. It had been leaked to the press that Jose Mourinho had accepted an offer to replace him; and in 2016, that news was now instantly spread around the world. As Van Gaal lifted the trophy, most of the football world was aware he was already out of a job.

There are many ways in which, in theory, Van Gaal's philosophy was shared by United. But theory is the key word. The difference in interpretation of Total Football comes down to freedom versus structure. "Van Gaal has a good vision of football but it is not mine," Johan Cruyff once said. "He wants to gel winning teams and has a militaristic way of working with his tactics. I don't. I want individuals to think for themselves."

The proof could be found in the way Van Gaal wanted specialists for positions, whereas the variation of the tactic that was deemed more aesthetically pleasing was where players could switch positions.

LOUIS VAN GAAL

In fairness, Van Gaal did seem to believe in that theory: "The system should be based on positional play, lines and triangulations that will allow the correct cover of the field in the different moments of the game." In practice, however, that cover at Manchester United was largely achieved by players staying within their confined parameters.

Van Gaal had previously encouraged teamwork, and allowed for weaknesses of a player to be compensated and strengths of another to be emphasised. Bound to their specific areas, the system made United much harder to beat than under Moyes – keeping 24 clean sheets in Van Gaal's second season – but fairly predictable, perhaps until the unexpected emergence of young players. With so many young players given a chance it could be said that Van Gaal was in touch with the club's identity. That could be fair, but he had a track record of this anyway. The matter is complicated a little because of the implementation of transfer windows which had been active since 2001. Faced with the injury crisis in February and March, Van Gaal could not 'pull an Atkinson' and make a couple of stop-gap signings.

Dismissal came as the club failed to qualify for the Champions League and although it was suggested that the poor football contributed to the decision, the overall philosophy of his successor suggests that the choice was dictated by results. Mourinho had won league titles in all of his five previous management positions.

So, like Moyes there is a split over whether Van Gaal could have delivered major success if he had been given more time. A quick summary indicates no – some of the youngsters were definitely over-performing and there is only so long that could compensate if a player just didn't have the ability at that level.

Could there have been more success? Yes, of course. One trophy could have been followed by more. But it was the standard of football which was concerning most for supporters. Even if the youngsters were good enough, it would mean everyone in the squad fully investing in the way Van Gaal wanted to play. And, from the evidence, the two best periods were in the pre-season, where style of play had a greater introductory impact before the strictness came in – and the period in early 2016 when the kids came in; again, the spell of time where Van Gaal's way was not imposed with such rigidity.

The latter stint was the only real time the crowd connected to the quality of football and that was almost contrary to the direction of the manager.

In his clear directive to remove instinct and to implement theory, Van Gaal had much in common with Dave Sexton. *Do as I say* didn't work the first time at Manchester United, and it didn't work the second time. There is no question that Van Gaal was an excellent coach – Wayne Rooney even rated him as the greatest he had played under, though this could be attributed to the player's falling out with Ferguson.

But the fundamental conflict with the natural United way of expressing yourself through your instinct would inevitably create an incompatibility in the event he was not successful. He did qualify for the Champions League, he did have to deal with the biggest turnover of senior players in the club's history, and he did finish with the FA Cup. If Jose Mourinho hadn't been available then there is every chance Van Gaal may have been given another year. A concession was apparently made – style could be a secondary consideration, so long as Mourinho could guarantee success.

The Louis van Gaal era was not close to football taught by Matt Busby, the simple premise of instruction over imagination was too great a chasm, and his tactical and holistic approach was so unique that it really had no connection to the past of the club, the contemporary game or the future of either, but the mere attempt to see if it worked was probably a move of which the great old manager would have approved.

It was the most tactically diverse period in the club's history, and yet it only went to prove that United's own insular tradition of wide players and instinctive style was more important than many accredited. Van Gaal's regimented, dictatorial style also alienated members of the squad, severing the link between the past – Ferguson's era – and the present for good.

27

JOSE MOURINHO

WHETHER OR NOT YOU FELT HE WAS THE RIGHT MAN for the job, there was no denying that Jose Mourinho was as destined to manage Manchester United as one man could be. It could be said that the way it all ended was equally inevitable. There were probably at least two previous occasions where Mourinho could have been hired. The first was in the summer of 2013, and the second just after his sacking from Chelsea in 2015, when Louis van Gaal felt that the press were putting his job on the line.

Few expected Mourinho to deliver entertaining football. Those few would have cited Mourinho's first months at Chelsea where Arjen Robben and Damien Duff played on the wings, and the 2011/12 season at Real Madrid where the club broke a goalscoring record, netting 121 in the league, and Cristiano Ronaldo scored 60 in all competitions. The idea was that he could come into United, a team with a historical reputation for being entertaining, and simply add that winning obsession missing since Ferguson. That mindset was playing wilfully ignorant with his reputation for controversy which saw each of his managerial reigns since leaving Porto end in some form of acrimony, and a diminishing sense of what success was. At Real Madrid he had been forced to watch an admittedly great team struggle in the same league as the greatest Barcelona side of all time.

Still, it was the decision taken by United, with the hope that his charismatic personality would instantly serve as a sticking plaster over the damage done by failing to qualify for the Champions League. It did. Mourinho established a close link with the super-agent Mino Raiola and brought in three of his clients – Henrikh Mkhitaryan, Zlatan Ibrahimovic and Paul Pogba, who came back to the club for £89m after leaving on a free transfer four years earlier. The echoes down the corridors of time bellowed once more in an evocative flex; Alex Ferguson had once gone on record with some unflattering thoughts of Raiola, and one couldn't help but think of Busby's resignation from the board in 1981 in protest of a new transfer record.

Mourinho had played a 4-3-3 in his first spell at Chelsea, a 4-1-2-1-2 at Inter Milan, a 4-2-3-1 at Real Madrid, and the same formation in his second tenure at Stamford Bridge. This was the approach he used from the start at United, with his first home game against Southampton in August 2016 looking like this:

DE GEA
VALENCIA BAILLY BLIND SHAW
FELLAINI POGBA
MATA ROONEY MARTIAL
IBRAHIMOVIC

It could not be said that United played well, particularly struggling with midfield cohesion, and that was exposed against

Manchester City in September when Pep Guardiola, who had just taken over at the Etihad Stadium, led his team to a 2-1 win at Old Trafford. A week later United collapsed at Watford despite Mourinho already deciding to make it a more compact three in midfield, dropping Rooney back.

For the next big game, at Anfield in October, Mourinho reverted to a 4-2-3-1, putting Pogba wide left, calling up Herrera and dropping Rooney. United took a 0-0 draw but earned criticism for their negative set-up. Mourinho had tons of experience of achieving good results at Anfield, mainly via picking a pragmatic team to kill the atmosphere. United were still a little too pragmatic for most supporters' liking. This was, however, Jose Mourinho in big games away from home. This is what the club had signed up for. The same set-up lost 4-0 at Chelsea. Numerous reshuffles were tried before the manager plumped for a 4-3-3 for a few games, including this encounter with Spurs in December:

DE GEA
VALENCIA   JONES   ROJO   DARMIAN
HERRERA   CARRICK   POGBA
MKHITARYAN   IBRAHIMOVIC   MARTIAL

A tight 1-0 win was the first of six in a row, and it seemed like a corner had been turned. In a few too many games, United's starting shape was too cautious, playing into the hands of sides happy to set up deeper. Burnley, West Ham, Hull City, Bournemouth, West Brom and Swansea all got draws at Old Trafford without ever really looking too stretched – *even* Burnley, who faced 37 shots on goal. Still, the draw with Swansea in United's 34th league game was the club's 25th in a row unbeaten, setting a new club record – and yet they were still struggling to get into the top four.

Early in the new year, Liverpool had visited Old Trafford, with

Ibrahimovic equalising late on in a 1-1 draw that brought familiar questions about style of play. "I didn't think the game had super quality," Mourinho reflected. "We didn't reflect the qualities we have and Liverpool have – but it was very emotional, intense, aggressive. We fought until the last second. They were clever. They took their time, they know how to control the emotions of the game. I have a problem with my neck because I was always looking to the left in the second half and I saw so many yellow shirts in front of me I thought, 'Let's go for it'. We lost two points when we wanted all three. We were the team that attacked and Liverpool were the team that defended – let's see if the critics are fair."

Liverpool manager Jurgen Klopp dubbed United a 'long ball' team, adding: "We were here to win the game, which is why we are not 100 per cent satisfied." For clarity, in the game, United played 53 'long balls' compared to Liverpool's 35. Over the season to date, United had played 510 and Liverpool 478. Liverpool were most definitely not a long-ball team, even though, little over a year later, Manchester City's Fernandinho and Roma's Daniele De Rossi described them as such.

In February, United won the League Cup, and Mourinho's muted celebration seemed to be in reference to it being the least important of the club's targets and also the generally poor performance in the final.

They were one point behind the top four with six games remaining. They were also in the latter stages of the Europa League, which offered an alternative route into the Champions League for the winner. Mourinho made a gamble – he would rest players in the league, feeling there was a better chance of succeeding by winning the European competition. Defeat at Arsenal and Spurs, and a fortuitous draw at Southampton, ended hopes of qualifying for the Champions League via the league, as Mourinho prioritised

Europe. It appeared the gamble had paid off when United won against Ajax in Stockholm to claim their fifth major European trophy in the Europa League final.

```
                    ROMERO
      VALENCIA  SMALLING  BLIND  DARMIAN
          FELLAINI  HERRERA  POGBA
         MATA  RASHFORD  MKHITARYAN
```

Further vindication came in the form of the goalscorers, Pogba and Mkhitaryan, both having been brought to the club by Mourinho. United were not great in the final but there was an emotional atmosphere due to a terrorist attack at the Manchester Arena two days earlier which killed 17 and injured more than a thousand, including many children. From the moment the second goal went in in the 48th minute, United controlled the tie with the professional expertise usually associated with a Mourinho side.

This victory was an important moment in Mourinho's reign, in Manchester United history, and for the context of this book. After the match the manager was questioned on his strategy. "We always thought that we could win the Europa League and we are very happy," Mourinho told BT Sport. "We played intelligently, we did it in a comfortable way. We were much stronger than them. If you want to press the ball all the time, you don't play short. If you are dominant in the air you go long. There are lots of poets in football but poets, they don't win many titles. We knew where they were better than us, we knew where we were better than them, we tried to kill their good qualities and exploit their weaknesses. We did that very well and we totally deserve the trophy... we preferred to reach the Champions League this way than finish fourth, third or second."

Poets don't win titles. What did Busby say in 1967, when saying what he loved about the game? "A sense of poetry."

One year in, and many were encouraged by what they had seen. Two trophies and Champions League qualification was evidence enough. Now people wanted to see if Mourinho could align himself with the club's identity. There were hopes that his decision to name the youngest team in United's Premier League history on the final day of the season, giving three players their debuts and playing eight homegrown players in total, would not be just a gimmick.

In the summer, Mourinho's transfer strategy seemed focused on moving back to a 4-2-3-1. Rooney left, after becoming the club's all-time record goalscorer, and Ibrahimovic had a long-term injury and the decision to retain him at the club only came late in the day, so Romelu Lukaku was signed to provide goals. Nemanja Matic came in, his sensible midfield play judged to be perfect for Pogba to serve as playmaker alongside. And Victor Lindelöf was signed as a sweeper to Eric Bailly's stopper.

In the opening seven league games, United scored four goals on four separate occasions, drawing 0-0 at Anfield again in the eighth, meaning the club had matched its best start to a Premier League season. The match got the managers bickering again. "I'm sure if we played like this, you could not do this at Liverpool. Obviously for United it is okay," Klopp sneered. "It's quite difficult when a top-class team like United has that defensive approach. I think United came here for the point and they got it."

Mourinho's response was that he felt Liverpool were too afraid of his team's counter-attack. "They play with a very strong midfield, with three real midfield players, we only had two," he said. "I was waiting for them to make an offensive change, to try more, but he never did it."

Post-match criticism reflected the instantaneous nature of

modern football coverage. Klopp developed a reputation for complaining about opponent's tactics if his team didn't win but he also complained about the weather – the wind, snow and sun all culpable, long grass, God, even penalties awarded to Manchester United in a game Liverpool lost at Southampton. Still, wider criticism of Mourinho's style was fair, and most certainly in the context of a book like this. Even Van Gaal understood United had to go to Liverpool and try to win (and did, on both of his league visits) – so, although this was part of Mourinho's natural way, it was clearly abrasive to the United ideology.

Still, few could argue with the start he'd made to his second season. If they were up against a normal opponent then this would have been more impressive – but Manchester City were doing even better, largely thanks to a colossal investment of £200m – over £150m of which was spent on new full-backs and a new goalkeeper, presumably because the £166m spent the previous year didn't solve those issues.

When City visited Old Trafford on December 10th 2017, they had won 14 and drawn one from their first 15 games – their 2-1 win over Mourinho's side gave them an absurd 11-point lead, causing the United boss to admit their chances of competing were 'probably' over. It would be unfair to say that Mourinho was 'failing' in the conventional sense of the word, but this was a manager who had already succeeded at Chelsea with a similar financial advantage to his new opponent so was not in a position to complain.

Three consecutive draws over Christmas pushed United further away but Mourinho persisted with the 4-2-3-1, signing Alexis Sanchez to play from the left and creating a headache as the form of Rashford and Martial from that side had been a highlight of the campaign. The manager was given a new three-year contract, the first since Ferguson to be granted a new deal; a strong show of faith that the club were happy with progress.

A Champions League exit against Sevilla was followed by Mourinho facing the press to defend his record *against* United at Old Trafford in the competition. Still, a second-place finish with 81 points was by far the best accomplishment in five years, and though City registered 100 points, there was still a cause for internal improvement if all parties remained on the same page. Towards the end of the season, United's form tailed off and Mourinho was unable to arrest the slide even though he went with a more cautious 4-3-3 at Wembley against Chelsea in the 2018 FA Cup final.

DE GEA

VALENCIA SMALLING JONES YOUNG

HERRERA MATIC POGBA

LINGARD RASHFORD SANCHEZ

The entire back five had been signed by Ferguson, two of them as wingers; a damning indictment of the transfer policy since. Even Mourinho's star striker signing, Lukaku, was on the bench. Herrera was given a man-marking job on Eden Hazard but by the 21st minute the Belgian had already escaped that attention to win a penalty from Phil Jones, which he then scored. Changes only came in the 73rd minute but a flat United were defeated.

United under Mourinho had never really entertained but they had been functional and in their 4-2-3-1, with 4-3-3 used for big games, seemed to be moving in the right direction. It made the following implosion seem unnecessary from all quarters; Mourinho felt he was not given appropriate backing in the transfer market, signing just Fred, Diogo Dalot and veteran goalkeeper Lee Grant in summer 2018.

FOOTBALL, TAUGHT BY MATT BUSBY

A succession of defensive horror shows included this strange shape at the start of the season against Tottenham at home:

DE GEA
HERRERA SMALLING JONES
VALENCIA POGBA MATIC FRED SHAW
LINGARD
LUKAKU

A 3-0 defeat might have been even worse and Mourinho seemed to show signs of cracking under pressure as he demanded 'respect' from journalists after the loss. A few weeks later he played the same system at West Ham, this time with young Scott McTominay in place of Herrera, with exactly the same outcome – three goals conceded. One year on from a record-equalling best start, United now had their worst start since Moyes, and even since 1989 due to goal difference. The formations never seemed likely to be used in the long-term, nor did they seem the best fit for the players Mourinho had available – in early October there was mounting speculation that he would soon be out of a job.

It was suggested that Mourinho's pragmatic approach was out of fashion, with the game already moving into its next era. Tactics were now universally accessible and could be studied on a computer. Those advances – as well as the popularity of football simulation video games – introduced more words into the football dictionary to intellectualise the game. A playmaker could be an *enganche* or *trequartista*. A defensive midfielder might be a *carrilero* or *mezzala*. This analysis evolved to describing players by numbers. A number six would be expected to be the holding player in midfield. A number eight could play box-to-box. Those descriptions seem awfully familiar; after all, in what number shirt would we expect to find Duncan Edwards or Liam Whelan? At its heart, the sport could still be simplified and understood. The challenge for anyone wanting to go toe to toe with Manchester City was also as ostensibly straightforward. Who could challenge a team with the best players, the most resources and a top coach?

Klopp's 'gegenpressing' – a tactic based in the art of winning the ball back as high up the pitch as possible – only started to feel truly successful after two years of him being in charge at Anfield. It was a different system entirely to that used by Guardiola, and made for a great spectacle whenever Manchester City and Liverpool came up against each other, with Liverpool's high intensity often forcing City to play in that same way.

Mourinho's approach differed in an obvious holistic sense, but again in a way that conflicted with the very fabric of the Old Trafford tapestry. Pragmatism worked when it was an added layer to a normally attacking approach, like in 2008. But when it was the key strategy there was something disjointed about it. Old Trafford didn't respond well to such an approach. If defeat should come, it should come in the concession of an early goal that provokes the team and the crowd into life. Real Madrid 1957, Porto 1977, Real Madrid 2000, and so on. Not 2-1 to Sevilla after a compact defensive system laboured for 77 minutes at Old Trafford. It should even come as it did against Barcelona in the 2009 and 2011 Champions League finals, before it should come like that.

United's supporters had no particular loyalty to a specific formation. Of course there was an affinity with wingers and if it was possible for a team to include two wingers then all the better, but it wasn't necessary. A new generation would probably attach themselves to a new shape, so long as it was entertaining to watch.

The success of Mourinho's system, like Klopp's (and like most managers), relied heavily on the subscription of his players, but as results and performances dipped in the autumn of 2018, it was clear that the relationship was strained. If we recall the moment where an anonymous player made a comment on Wilf McGuinness to the press, it was notable by its rarity – in the days of agents, large squads, social media and 24-hour news coverage, such discontent is so commonplace that it's impossible to verify its veracity. Particularly for Mourinho and Manchester United in this period, it was so rife that it was clear there was no smoke without fire – the end was nigh. In a European game against Young Boys, Rashford missed an opportunity – Mourinho turned to the stands, folded his arms and shook his head. After the next game, at Southampton, the *Telegraph* alleged that the manager described Pogba as a 'virus' who 'killed the mentality of the good honest people' in the squad.

Ahead of his third trip to Anfield as United manager, in December 2018, Mourinho admitted his team was 'far' from the way he wanted it to be. He had reportedly been furious with the failure to sign at least one defender, and it seemed a race against time – could the manager make it through to January and convince the club to provide him with more funds?

Including the subs, at Anfield United fielded two players who had been bought by Ferguson (and two who had been youth players since those days), five signed by Mourinho, three by Van Gaal and two by Moyes; all of this in an unfamiliar 3-4-1-2. It was more Mourinho's squad than any other but it was still a mess and two of the highest-profile signings of the latest era, Sanchez and Pogba, didn't even get on the pitch. There was little discipline in the display, United shipping three goals and facing 36 shots, a record since Opta started recording this data in 2003. They finished the game 19 points behind Liverpool before Christmas, and had already conceded more goals in the league than in the entire previous season. Mourinho was duly sacked within 48 hours, after two and a half years in charge.

JOSE MOURINHO

Faithful analysis of his era shows how much Manchester United's identity has been influenced by Sir Alex Ferguson's achievements. Memory tells us that the last five or six years of his reign, although they featured some thrilling football, contained the most pragmatic football of his era. This has facilitated a misnomer that pragmatism is necessary to succeed in the modern game. The truth of the matter is that even Ferguson would have faced criticism if his teams had played without entertaining. In this case, entertainment is meant in the truest sense and not being entertained *because* of the win itself. United knew what they were getting when they hired Mourinho. If he had been hired much earlier, say 2013, he may have delivered greater success. His methods were not completely archaic when it came to tactics but the relationships he established with his players were fragile.

Success? Well, there were two trophies and a Community Shield, though unfortunately not trophies which served as a springboard for better things. The most exciting football came in the first few weeks of his second season when Pogba and Lukaku seemed to work well in tandem before both dropped, and to say it was entertaining to watch in comparison to the swashbuckling days of Busby, Ferguson, Docherty, Atkinson or even early day O'Farrell would have been generous.

Tactically Mourinho was largely sound with two significant issues – the first being a persistence with a 4-3-3 in home games against weaker opponents. The second was playing midfielders in defence, a tactic never likely to work and, in the case of McTominay at West Ham, an approach with potential to set back a young player's career. Ironically enough, McTominay was the one true success of Mourinho's flirtation with the youth system. The club still boasted a proud record – every matchday squad had featured at least one player developed through the club – and Mourinho did not end that record despite the feeling that he may well. Rashford played more times for him than any other player and Lingard played the best football of his United career under Mourinho.

It seemed strange that someone as theoretically incompatible as Jose Mourinho should feel so inevitably destined for the United job; maybe it was a simple force of personality, which he most certainly possessed. In the end, it was that personality which seemed to expedite his own departure. United's embrace of something new under Van Gaal and Mourinho had unwittingly aggravated a fault line, and the club was instantly searching to reclaim its sense of self. With his poets remark, Mourinho seemed to admit his approach was almost entirely contradictory to the personality of the club. To him, the pursuit of winning was all that mattered; under Busby and even under Ferguson, winning mattered but it mattered much more if they played with adventure and imagination.

If he was able to determine that winning a trophy in 2017 meant more than finishing second then maybe it's a peek into the psyche that enabled United to overcome Chelsea back in 2007; the attitude that again gave weight to the idea he just didn't understand the nature of the club. To say it didn't matter if the club finished sixth or second if not first has some truth, but it impacted the psychology of games and also factored into the approach of the opposition. The club were not in a position to pick and choose what games they turned up in, and any manager who couldn't understand that was always doomed to ultimate failure – even if failure included a deal of success along the way.

28

OLE GUNNAR SOLSKJAER

MANCHESTER UNITED'S POST-FERGUSON TRAVAILS were now so reminiscent of the post-Busby era that many analysts were keen to try and compare the reigns of the successors. The issue was that none could truly be like for like, and all had their own complex reasons for not working out. When Ole Gunnar Solskjaer was hired as interim manager in the days after Jose Mourinho was fired, the intention was only that a familiar face might steady the ship and lighten the dark mood around the club. Solskjaer had coached the United reserve team, managed Molde in Norway and tasted Premier League management with Cardiff, where he was relegated, before returning to Molde – it was not a CV that made him an obvious candidate for permanent choice.

Ahead of his first game as caretaker in December 2018, Solskjaer spoke of how he saw his responsibility. "It's about getting every player to be their very best," he said, "speaking to them on the training ground, getting through our philosophy and principles of how we want to play. They are quality players so it will be easier to get players expressing themselves… You play with courage, go out there and express your skills, he (Sir Alex) said go out and express, take risks. The last game he had as a manager was 5-5, and I want the players to be similar, be the kids that love to play football and go out in front of the best fans in the world."

DE GEA
YOUNG JONES LINDELOF SHAW
HERRERA MATIC POGBA
LINGARD RASHFORD MARTIAL

United won 5-1 at Cardiff – the first time they'd scored five in the league since that final game of Sir Alex. Form over the following weeks was remarkable – United won at Spurs, at Arsenal, and at Chelsea, all playing a variation of the above system, Solskjaer occasionally pulling the odd surprise, such as using Lukaku wide right against Arsenal, or starting Lingard through the middle at Spurs. In his first 17 games, Solskjaer won 14, and with each one a case was growing for him being named permanent manager. There were definite issues, the results more consistent than the performances; but, when Solskjaer boldly played a 4-4-2 away at Paris Saint-Germain for the second leg of a Champions League tie he was 2-0 down in – this in spite of an injury crisis, as he claimed 'mountains are there to be climbed' – a mountain was indeed climbed as United controlled much of the game and went through thanks to a dramatic last-minute penalty by Rashford. The result prompted the United board to offer Solskjaer a three-year deal – and, from that moment, form immediately collapsed, United losing eight of their last 12 games to fail to even qualify for the Champions League.

Solskjaer seemed to favour a move to a 4-2-3-1 and he did so after signing Harry Maguire, Aaron Wan-Bissaka and Dan James over the summer of 2019. The new manager was tasked with reducing the inflated wage bill and Fellaini, Herrera, Sanchez and Lukaku were all moved on in fairly symbolic moves.

A poor start to the season, where United won only three times in their first 12 games, saw Solskjaer already under pressure. At a crucial moment, United's form picked up, inspired by a fabulous win at Chelsea in the League Cup where Rashford scored a stunning free-kick.

ROMERO

LINDELOF MAGUIRE ROJO

WAN-BISSAKA MCTOMINAY FRED WILLIAMS

LINGARD RASHFORD JAMES

The change in shape was an experiment, and one of the most pragmatic United had fielded. Solskjaer mostly reverted to the 4-2-3-1, finding faith in the following side, which played at Manchester City in December 2019:

DE GEA

WAN-BISSAKA LINDELOF MAGUIRE SHAW

MCTOMINAY FRED

JAMES LINGARD RASHFORD

MARTIAL

This system required the two midfielders to offer disciplined protection while the front four used their pace and link-up play to break through the opponent. It worked to devastating effect against City, Rashford and Martial scoring inside of 30 minutes; but it was a strategy less successful at home, due to the two midfielders not being progressive enough, the forwards not being as effective when asked to play in front of defences, and no creative link. Pogba was injured and Mata was often brought on in times of struggle, but it was clear this was a system best used in away games. Solskjaer had at least navigated his team out of a slump, unlike the apparent terminal declines of his three predecessors, this thanks to his strong man-management skills.

After a January wobble, where United lost at Arsenal and Liverpool in the league and were so blown away in the first half against Manchester City in the League Cup semi-final that it seemed they were as far away as ever from matching their local rivals, Solskjaer signed Bruno Fernandes to serve as playmaker. It had an immediate impact on form and when United next faced City, on March 8th 2020, at Old Trafford, Solskjaer used his 3-4-1-2 shape – this time having success again in a 2-0 win. His success against Guardiola seemed, like Klopp, to be in finding a contrasting workaround, and not just setting up with a system designed to frustrate. Where Guardiola wanted his players to suffocate the space, Solskjaer wanted his to find it. "Quick, attacking football with pace, power and personalities," Solskjaer described it; almost identical phraseology to that used by Ferguson to Meulensteen.

That would be the last league match before the coronavirus pandemic caused a halt to most global sport. It was June before football returned, and this on the condition that the matches were behind closed doors.

United played in their 4-2-3-1 formation and enjoyed a fabulous run of form, winning six from eight unbeaten games and scoring five in one game and three in three others. The club were in a comfortable position to qualify for the Champions League via the league, and despite some low moments – leading to concerns about Solskjaer's inexperience – there was some optimism that in the bigger picture they were at their healthiest point since 2013.

Reservations included the idea that Solskjaer had become

tactically inflexible, reliant on the 4-2-3-1 because Fernandes had been such a revelation, though there was not a natural replacement for him in the squad. Furthermore, many were curious about the impact playing in empty stadiums was having on players, teams, and patterns of games – broadcasters eventually included audio feeds of simulated crowd noise to avoid the games looking like glorified training sessions. As far as United were concerned, it meant the removal of that white-hot intensity that generally accompanied every away game, a unique atmosphere that can make or break a player, and also the anxiety of home games – the vast emptiness also contributing to a strange environment for away players too.

United finished third, and suffered elimination in the semi-final stages of both the FA Cup and Europa League, naturally inviting thoughts of Wilf McGuinness' misfortune.

A quirk from that Europa League run occurred in November 2019 and is worth mentioning. United travelled to Kazakhstan to face FC Astana in the group stage. They were already going through to the knockout stages and so Solskjaer named this team:

GRANT
LAIRD TUANZEBE BERNARD SHAW
GARNER LEVITT
CHONG LINGARD GOMES
GREENWOOD

SUBS: MELLOR, RAMAZANI, GALBRAITH

Nine homegrown players started as United named their youngest team to play in European competition. A further three came off the bench to make it the highest number of homegrown players to ever play in one game for the club. Like Mourinho's approach against Crystal Palace, however, there was no feeling that many of these names would be given sustained chances in the team.

The pandemic meant that the following 2020/21 season would begin behind closed doors, with decisions on whether spectators could attend again taken periodically. Solskjaer's plans for building his squad were impacted by the pandemic and the financial consequences in wider football, and a number of players arrived late in the transfer window due to an erratic start to the season which included a 6-1 home defeat to Spurs – now managed by Jose Mourinho – and prompted a little panic.

That was the story of the season, with some highs and some shocking lows, and even though Solskjaer did occasionally try a diamond shape in an attempt to accommodate Fernandes and new signing Donny van de Beek, he usually reverted to the 4-2-3-1. In January 2021 United were the team best-placed to challenge City for the league title – the first time they'd been in such a competitive position since the Ferguson days – but didn't strengthen the squad and dropped crucial points. Injuries contributed to a drastic slump, but United finished second nonetheless, an improvement on their previous season.

Solskjaer also beat the McGuinness curse, qualifying for the Europa League final against Villarreal in Gdansk, where he played a 4-2-3-1. Instead of selecting McTominay and Fred, his go-to reliable midfield, the latter was dropped to find a place in the team for Pogba, at the cost to the functionality of the whole system.

DE GEA

WAN-BISSAKA LINDELOF BAILLY SHAW

MCTOMINAY POGBA

GREENWOOD FERNANDES RASHFORD

CAVANI

Changes were not made until extra-time; United drew 1-1, and Solskjaer appeared to make a number of substitutes late on specifically to prepare for penalties. The drama went all the way to sudden death, all the way to the goalkeepers being forced to take them – and De Gea, who hadn't stopped a single one, saw his effort saved, a night of dreadful luck rounded off fittingly.

For the following season, Solskjaer signed Raphael Varane, Jadon Sancho, and then late in the transfer window brought Cristiano Ronaldo, now 36, back to the club. If he intended to play his 4-2-3-1, some questions were posed – would Sancho play from the right, where United needed a player, or from the left, where he was most effective? Was Ronaldo still mobile enough to play in the middle on his own – and what would that mean for the likes of Edinson Cavani, Rashford and Martial? And how would the midfield dynamic work, considering it was still not strong enough to dictate the pace in big games? The answers – Sancho played in a number of positions, as did all the above players, as Solskjaer looked to find a solution, and the midfield dynamic rarely did work, Pogba still ill-suited to any midfield combination and not dynamic enough moving with the ball.

There was also a concerning drop in the performance levels of some individuals. In a run of 10 games, United played seven at Old Trafford, the standard of performances declining at such a rapid rate that it was hard to believe this was a team who had finished second. Solskjaer persisted with his 4-2-3-1, perhaps realising that tinkering with it might result in more harm than good. There was also a tendency to try and play out from the back, which the goalkeeper and defence seemed ill-suited for. These grave signs manifested themselves in two of the worst performances by a Manchester United side that Old Trafford has ever seen.

Against Liverpool, United supporters were stunned into silence as the visitors scored twice in the first 13 minutes, and twice more before half-time. The midfield was so deep that they would have been on top of the centre-backs if not for the centre-backs dropping back to the edge of the six-yard box themselves. Four became five and then United's crowd had to watch Liverpool take pity for the last 40 minutes; a similar story played out against Manchester City in the next home game, even though Solskjaer had switched to a 3-5-2, with Guardiola's team taking a seventh-minute lead through a Eric Bailly own goal and never looking threatened at any point afterwards. Solskjaer moved back to a 4-2-3-1 against Watford – United were crushed 4-1, and the manager was out of a job. At half-time, with the score 0-2, it was reported that some players were in tears with the inevitability of another change on the horizon.

Rarely is a manager sacked because they are successful. There are still a number of contradictions in Solskjaer's reign because of his inexperience at the top level and the fact that he still showed more tactical nous, particularly in his first months as caretaker, than many expected. Like Wilf McGuinness, it could be said that just because you embody the spirit of the club, it doesn't necessarily make you the best-placed person to demand those standards as manager. But, *like* McGuinness, there is a strong enough argument to say that he was the best-placed person, if he had received the backing he needed.

For a period, when the crowd were there, they were seduced by the romance; the idea of Solskjaer being successful created a strong emotional bond that made many reluctant to turn against him or even voice discontent in the way they did under Van Gaal and Mourinho. Like McGuinness, he needed luck in the cups and it abandoned him, and that could have made the difference in terms of giving him the sort of power a manager should have. And yet there was sometimes a little too much naivety – perseverance with systems that didn't work, delays in changes until it was too late, too much faith placed in players with none of the ruthlessness shown by Busby or Ferguson.

The football, when it was entertaining, featured clever movement and a quick tempo. With most teams adopting two deeper midfielders, defences were much more compact. Much of contemporary football was focused around patient build-up and the necessity to break through defences because teams did not like to offer space behind. It couldn't be said that Solskjaer's squad didn't have the players who possessed that imagination, but at United's level, players were required to have constant concentration, which was not Pogba's strongest point, or boundless energy, which wasn't Mata's, leaving too much of the responsibility on Fernandes. Consequently, the risks that Fernandes would take to create a chance could often be seen as careless surrendering of the ball. That approach also required a midfield to be comfortable maintaining possession, and the club had not had a player truly adept in this regard since Carrick. If the required qualities are not available in a squad, then answers must come either from new players or from managerial wit. If you don't have a team capable of maintaining possession, then they need to at least be reliable at the back and clinical up front. There were only periods where this was the case for United.

Solskjaer, like the three men before him, showed no disregard for youth, ensuring there was always a healthy presence in the team and squad; as someone who had coached the reserve team, he was aware of the pathway at Manchester United. He had also overseen a restructuring at junior level as the club had lost its way since Ferguson's retirement – too much emphasis was placed on the short-term success of the first team and the instability and changes of philosophical direction played a not inconsiderable impact.

There was, then, a touch of the McGuinness *and* O'Farrell about Solskjaer; lacking perhaps the rub of the green, the feeling of complete authority or conviction, and good moments never quite followed up with that crucial moment of success that would have tipped momentum in his favour.

29

RALF RANGNICK

CARETAKER AND INTERIM REIGNS HAVE MOSTLY BEEN avoided in this record for a reason; they are, generally, much too short to draw any true conclusions from. Solskjaer's was an obvious one to include because it lasted more than a few games, and Ralf Rangnick's spell lasted around six months, so it is worth studying.

Rangnick was seen as the 'godfather of gegenpress', and credited (somewhat generously) with having influenced then-Liverpool boss Jurgen Klopp and Thomas Tuchel, who was now manager at Chelsea and had won the Champions League after just a few months. Gegenpress, under Rangnick, was a high counter-pressing attacking system, demanding huge stamina and then quality on the ball to create chances in moments where they seized possession. Rangnick, at 63, was coming into the English game at a similar age to Louis van Gaal, but with nowhere near the elite experience of the Dutchman, though he was largely credited for the work he did with Red Bull's nest of clubs, notably at RB Leipzig. The traditional demands of that style of play were at odds with what many deemed to be the lethargic performances of United players. It would take some turnaround to be successful.

In his first press conference, Rangnick was asked how long it would take to get his ideas across. "I think to gain control on games has got to do with playing proactively, no matter if we have the ball ourselves or if the other team is in possession," he said. "It's about helping the team to play together, it's about togetherness, it's also about team spirit… It's not about playing pressing or counter-pressing for pressing sake, it's about control. This is the major target."

This time around it was clear from day one that Rangnick would only be an interim manager. As he would reportedly stay on as consultant, there was speculation that the permanent manager would have some form of existing belief in the system. However, the two names in the frame were Mauricio Pochettino and Erik ten Hag, both of whom had different ways of playing.

Still, United fans were ready to see something new, so long as there was structure and desire. They got at least one of those things in Rangnick's first game in charge, against Crystal Palace.

DE GEA

DALOT LINDELOF MAGUIRE TELLES

MCTOMINAY FRED

SANCHO FERNANDES

RASHFORD RONALDO

For 35 minutes United supporters saw their team press high up the pitch but the novelty soon subsided; a late goal from Fred gave Rangnick a winning start, but an indifferent run of form in the new shape forced the German interim to try something new for the league trip to Aston Villa in mid-January.

RALF RANGNICK

DE GEA
DALOT LINDELOF VARANE TELLES
FRED MATIC FERNANDES
GREENWOOD CAVANI ELANGA

This seemed a decent approach – Matic was a sensible holding man in the middle while Fred and Fernandes were able to make attacking runs and create space for the wide forwards. Wide forwards was now a more fitting description than wingers. There was a growing preference for inverting, so players would be on the opposite side to their natural foot, cutting inside.

United went 2-0 up at Villa Park – Fernandes benefitting from this liberation – before Villa staged a late comeback to draw. It was another formation Rangnick persevered with before reverting to the 4-2-3-1 – illness and injury necessitated the reintroduction of the 4-2-2-2 with two midfielders, Fernandes and Pogba, serving as the front two against Manchester City. "United gave up," Gary Neville said on commentary of the 4-1 defeat. "In a derby… in any game, it's unforgivable. I can forgive mistakes, but not running back, not trying to tackle – there are players out there who shouldn't play for Manchester United again."

Rangnick mostly used the 4-2-3-1 or, on occasion, 4-3-3 towards the end of the season, often selecting players whose contracts were due to expire in a matter of weeks. When results and performances dipped, and questions were asked about commitment levels, Rangnick often criticised the players and even said he'd asked about signing players in January only to be refused. These comments were music to the ears of disgruntled supporters at first, as they wanted to see poor performing players held accountable, but it soon seemed apparent that it was indicative of a rift between the coach and the squad.

United won just three of their last 14 games, a poor run including 4-0 defeats at Liverpool and Brighton. In the end, supporters just wanted to see the back of another dismal season, as it was clear another manager would soon be leaving. And he did, to be replaced by Erik ten Hag, the Dutch coach who was manager of Ajax; there were hopes that his more modern take on the national philosophy would allow for more freedom and expression than the interpretation of his compatriot Louis van Gaal.

Rangnick, who had been pencilled in to remain as a consultant, left the club altogether to coach the Austria national team, making it one of the more bewildering appointments in United's history. Performances were below standard, formation changes yielded little improvement, and what started off as a fresh transparency, as though Rangnick was exposing a number of serial underachievers at the club, began to evolve into a sense of understanding why the German hadn't previously been given one of the truly big jobs. Just as with Van Gaal, the club dipped their toes into a vision of football not traditionally associated with Manchester United; a vision of the football of tomorrow – but the spell ended with a concern that the manager had been yesterday's man.

30

ERIK TEN HAG

ERIK TEN HAG COACHED AJAX FROM 2017 UNTIL HE was appointed by Manchester United in May 2022. So far so good, as to how you might presume his education in football was concerned, but he wasn't raised in the club of Michels and Cruyff – so what exactly was his philosophy? "When it comes to Ten Hag's favoured style of play, the Cruyffian influence is unavoidable," Will Magee wrote in the *Independent* in 2019. "There is a reason that his approach has been dubbed 'Total Football 2.0'. If the original premise of Total Football was that outfield players should be flexible, adaptable and to some degree interchangeable in their positioning as they sought to create and exploit space, Ten Hag's side live up to their billing." With Ajax, he won three Eredivisie titles, two KNVB Cups, and also qualified for the Champions League semi-final in 2019.

Prior to his time at Ajax, Ten Hag had spent time coaching Bayern Munich's reserve side from 2013 to 2015, where he worked closely with Pep Guardiola. In April 2019, Ten Hag explained 'since Pep, football in Germany is different', and went on to give an insight into his own personal beliefs. "I want to hurt the opponent. It's about possession, about movement, about vertical attacking patterns, about pressing, wingers moving into the middle to make room for the full-backs. Everyone is attacking, everyone is defending."

There's no guarantee of what will be successful in football. You might argue, though, given all the evidence proposed, the chances were weighted in favour of Ten Hag succeeding so long as his interpretation of Total Football included that element of accommodating instinct in the expression of his players. It did, initially; but it is equally true to hail the transformative impact of the players he brought in – in particular, Lisandro Martinez and Casemiro. Martinez, a proactive centre-back, did what Harry Gregg did over 60 years earlier, pushing United's starting position in defence 20 yards further up the pitch and defending with a snarl. Casemiro, meanwhile, brought all the class one would expect from a player who had won five European Cups, as well as a level of tackling ability not seen since Robson or Keane.

After a bumpy start to his reign with two disappointing defeats, Ten Hag ordered his players into training on their day off and instructed them to run 8.5 miles – the differing distance in running statistics between the Brentford players and the United players the day before. The manager joined his players on the run, showing that he was part of it too.

There was an immediate on-pitch response. United defeated Liverpool 2-1, and then beat Arsenal 3-1, with new signing Antony scoring a goal that showcased the new style of the team – 18 passes in the build-up, featuring almost every player in the side.

There was active discipline after early attempts to assert control over the dressing room. He disciplined Cristiano Ronaldo for leaving a pre-season game early. The relationship never truly recovered, and when Ronaldo agreed to an interview with broadcaster Piers Morgan where he criticised the club, it was mutually agreed between club and player that his contract should be terminated, just before the winter break for the 2022 World Cup in Qatar.

Ronaldo's exit seemed to lighten the mood around the club after domestic football resumed, following the World Cup and Ten Hag's side enjoyed a fine run of form. When Marcus Rashford scored the winning goal against Crystal Palace on February 4th, the game closest to the 65th anniversary of the Munich disaster, the manager felt it was a fitting tribute to the traditions of the club.

"It was a great team goal," said Ten Hag. "I think it really gives a reference to the attacking football from the Busby Babes. So many players were involved by switching the play and in between the lines. Great actions, short combinations and a great finish by a player out of the youth academy and that is brilliant on a day like today."

The club's tradition for fantastic football and winning silverware was also reflected later in the month, thanks to a thrilling win over Barcelona in the Europa League and then a 2-0 win in the League Cup final against Newcastle United. The 4-2-3-1 deployed was Ten Hag's most-used, with Martinez aggressively pushing the play high, the full-backs either overlapping or inverting into deep midfield roles, almost like the vintage half-back position, and Fred pushing higher instead of sitting deep.

Wout Weghorst, a Dutch striker signed on loan in January, was required to exhaust defenders, but was not much of a goal threat. Casemiro and Rashford scored in the first half to secure a win that was as routine as one might hope for in a final.

FOOTBALL, TAUGHT BY MATT BUSBY

DE GEA
DALOT VARANE MARTINEZ SHAW
CASEMIRO FRED
ANTONY FERNANDES RASHFORD
WEGHORST

A third-placed finish in the league concluded a promising start for Ten Hag (despite defeat in the FA Cup final against Manchester City, who went on to complete the treble that United had won 24 years earlier) but late-season concerns about injuries and form seemed to dog the pre-season and most of his second season. In truth, those concerns had been aired the very week after the League Cup final, when United suffered a horrendous 7-0 defeat at Anfield, where everything that could go wrong, did.

Early in Ten Hag's second campaign, chastening defeats at Arsenal and at home to City were accompanied by defensive capitulations in the Champions League which meant elimination from Europe at the group stage. Bournemouth defeated United 3-0 at Old Trafford before Christmas, and it seemed as though Ten Hag was already on borrowed time. The injuries had been catastrophic, with all of the club's recognised left-sided defenders out with long-term problems, but few were sympathetic when the results and performances were so concerning. Empathy for the manager's circumstances, and a sure conviction of his tactical suitability for the job at hand, was lacking in most. However, speculation over the club at the time was going right to the very top, with a change in ownership structure imminent – Sir Jim Ratcliffe, a British billionaire and boyhood United fan born in Failsworth, had agreed to become a significant investor in exchange for control over the football operations. Those changes happened in the winter, earning Ten Hag a stay of execution until at least the end of the season.

Using the law of averages, everyone was hoping for some relief probably has never been defined, or labelled," he smiles. "I've never really thought about it but, maybe, does not being able to label something give it a higher existence? Possibly…. can you label art? Probably not. There's a mystique… yeah, maybe, I've just undone the premise of the book because there's a label for it right here!"

in the second half of the campaign, but injuries continued to take their toll – the club suffered over 60 individual injuries throughout the season. That might have explained the defensively torrid defeats to Fulham, Manchester City, Chelsea and Crystal Palace, yet it might have also contributed to an increased defiance that appeared in the FA Cup run, which bore similarities to the Alex Ferguson triumph in 1990 and Louis van Gaal's success in 2016.

Casemiro's last-minute winner in the fifth round at Nottingham Forest, of all places, had its own romantic links after Mark Robins scored a third round winner at the City Ground in January 1990 to set United on the road to Wembley when the pressure was piling up on Alex Ferguson.

But even that was nothing compared to a breathless 4-3 win over Liverpool after extra-time in the quarter-final at Old Trafford, sealed by a 121st-minute winner by Amad Diallo. That was a match which ended with chief playmaker Bruno Fernandes playing at centre-half and Antony – normally a right-winger – filling in at left-back. No tactical deconstruction here folks, just utter chaos and faith in youth, with the likes of Alejandro Garnacho and Kobbie Mainoo now fearlessly leaving impressions on big games. Both started the semi-final, and were substituted with United comfortably in front of Championship side Coventry City – but the Midlands side came back from 3-0 down after 70 minutes to draw the match 3-3, only to lose on penalties. Ten Hag's side had scraped through – it seemed as though their name was on the trophy. In the final, they faced Manchester City again; it was the only time in FA Cup history where the same teams competed in successive finals.

ONANA

WAN-BISSAKA   VARANE   MARTINEZ   DALOT

GARNACHO   MAINOO   AMRABAT   RASHFORD

FERNANDES   MCTOMINAY

Though not a system the manager would have preferred, he did at least have his first choice central defence back, and it made a significant difference. This was almost a 4-6-0, with a concession that United would not be on the ball much, and that they would seek to make hay on the counter.

The gameplan was executed magnificently, with Garnacho taking advantage of defensive confusion to tap into an empty net just after the half-hour mark. With City rocking, United had the ball in the net again – only for Rashford's tap-in to be disallowed for offside. That second goal did arrive moments later, when Mainoo started a breakaway that included Fernandes, a fine cross-field pass from Rashford, a measured ball from Garnacho and a beautiful rolled assist from Fernandes to Mainoo, both of whom had raced the length of the pitch, with the latter stroking the ball into the goal. City scored a late consolation, but Mainoo's had been the decisive strike. The young midfielder was named man of the match, his composure and dominance on such an important occasion defying his teenage years.

Two years earlier, Mainoo and Garnacho had been the stars of United's Youth Cup-winning side. That it was those two who scored the goals in the FA Cup final win could scarcely have been more fitting.

City, the Premier League champions, had been favourites to win the double. This was not vintage United, but it was nonetheless a performance which called upon all of the hallmarks of what made the club great – youth, determination, an assertiveness, and just as significantly, players being asked to do something out of their favoured position for the greater good. It was conviction for those who believed the manager still had the tactical nous to succeed when his squad was not decimated by injuries. There were still criticisms, and plenty of them valid, but any finger pointed at the manager's tactical ideas for most of his second season could be rebutted with a finger pointed at the injury list.

Mainoo was not the only local player winning the FA Cup for United in 2024. That privilege was shared by Ella Toone, for Manchester United Women – Toone scored a wonderful individual effort to start the scoring in United's 4-0 win over Tottenham at Wembley. Toone, born in Tyldesley, wore the number seven – a lifelong United fan, she had trained at the club as a young girl. Only one problem – the club did not have a professional side. In the 1970s, there was a Manchester United Supporters Club Ladies side that was more formally aligned with the club in 1989, but this was disbanded in 2005 after the Glazer family takeover. Years of campaigns followed and Manchester United Women Football Club was officially founded in 2018. The FA Cup win in 2024 was their first major honour. One day, it could well be that someone writes a book on their own cultural and tactical history; it is romantic to think that in a youth product wearing the number seven and scoring a sensational goal to win a trophy.

The summer brought the first big changes of the Ratcliffe era. Omar Berrada was lured from Manchester City to become the Chief Executive Officer. Dan Ashworth, the highly-rated sporting director, was snared acrimoniously from Newcastle United, and Jason Wilcox – a member of Blackburn Rovers' 1995 Premier League-winning team – joined as Technical Director. Ten Hag's backroom staff received a shake-up, with club legend Ruud van Nistelrooy becoming assistant manager, despite having coached PSV Eindhoven's senior team in recent years. René Hake, the Go Ahead Eagles head coach, also joined as an assistant. Andreas Georgson came from Lillestrom where he too had been head coach. It marked a dramatic sign of the times from when Ernest Mangnall had grand ideas backed singularly by the owner, or when Matt Busby handpicked Jimmy Murphy as his assistant to oversee the change he wanted to make. Manchester United as a business had grown into an enterprise with over a thousand employees and it was no surprise that this eventuality was reached; after all, Alex Ferguson had been famed for the skill of his delegation.

All of these measures were put in place to assist Ten Hag with ensuring United came as close to looking like themselves as he could achieve. The jury was out on assessing whether his interpretation of Total Football from Ajax had seemed more free than that of Louis van Gaal's, or of Dave Sexton's earlier dreams, due to the injury crisis which had prohibited a fair assessment. That arrived swiftly in the 2024/25 campaign.

With most players back and fit, United appeared to be static in their positions, and a goal conceded in the opening moments of a 3-0 home defeat to Spurs – where away defender Micky van de Ven was able to stride 70 yards unchallenged – seemed to align the tactical system closely to that of Van Gaal and Sexton. Like those two, the chaotic moments and introduction of younger players seemed more accident than design, and, again, like those two, that the chaos seemed to introduce moments of what supporters recognised as the old United was a matter of concern.

When the team suffered a 2-1 defeat at West Ham in late October, albeit to a hugely controversial late penalty, Ten Hag was dismissed less than a day later. With some justification he had pointed to the fact he'd won trophies in both of his full seasons; but the progress wasn't enough, and the football was rarely entertaining to watch. Ruud van Nistelrooy was given the managerial job on an interim basis, but there would be no repeat of a legendary former striker being given the responsibility permanently. The Dutchman would depart to an emotional Old Trafford farewell, a 3-0 victory over

Leicester City concluding an almost flawless caretaker stint (three wins, one draw) and with morale seemingly restored.

Ruben Amorim, the 39-year-old Sporting Lisbon manager, had quickly been identified as the man to follow Ten Hag. He was the youngest man to be appointed manager since Sir Matt Busby. A favouring of a three-man defensive system appeared to conflict with United's traditional way; talk of an emphasis on pleasing supporters with entertaining football prior to starting in the job, however, was just what they wanted to hear. Still, as the Ten Hag era showed (just as it did with Sexton and Van Gaal), true conclusions could only be formed with evidence.

Ten Hag's sacking left a curious juxtaposition when it came to analysing how close his reign had come to encapsulating the club's traditional identity. The winning goal in the FA Cup final of 2024 was a masterpiece of football aesthetics, a moment to treasure, and a moment of potential encapsulated perfectly by a teenager from Stockport. It was the Manchester United way. It was football taught by Matt Busby.

We could, however, say the same for FA Cup final goals scored by Sammy McIlroy in 1979, and Jesse Lingard in 2016. Perhaps the most salient point to make here is to refer to the academy.

When the senior side has endured struggle in recent years, as always, the greatest connection between the crowd and the team has been with the younger players breaking through. Mainoo and Garnacho, the FA Cup winners in 2024 and Youth Cup final stars of 2022, represented more than themselves – they were the ideology of the club. There was a multi-faceted response to that Youth Cup final in May 2022, which drew a record attendance of 67,492 at Old Trafford. The first was that it came at the end of a long difficult season for the first team, and a secondary reason could be that people voted with their feet to reconnect with something which represented the core values of the club, particularly after a period of time where they had not been allowed to attend matches due to the coronavirus pandemic.

"The youth system is just like a metronome here that ticks, constantly, it doesn't waver," says academy director Nick Cox. "It just keeps ticking along, and then sometimes we'll have some incredible highs and the academy ticks along, and there'll be some incredible lows and the academy ticks along and it just felt like that Youth Cup final in 2022 was people recognising that it was their opportunity to recognise that. There is historical significance about the youth programme. On these greatest days, young people have stood up to the test, and in the darkest moments, young people have been there as a constant to rescue us. Some of our greatest players are some of the greatest players ever to play the game, Ballon d'Or winners who were young people that came through the programme. There is historical pressure, historical expectation, and it means our fans are as obsessed about a young talent breaking into the team, as they are about the team winning a trophy."

It brings sharper focus on the responsibility of Cox, whose role is effectively that held and introduced by Jimmy Murphy. Cox was brought into the club for his own abilities and innovative approaches but quickly understood his role as a custodian. "The success of our programme is that it's been an iterative process, if that's the right word, over 92 years," explains Cox. "It's been layers of advancement, with a knowledge of what's come before and a desire to protect some of the non-negotiables. Money can't buy what United have created, we will never ever recreate it, so you couldn't let it die. It's our competitive advantage.

"The lineage is more powerful than somewhere that doesn't have a feel for its soul… look, *notionally* you *could* rip it up, start again and do it differently but you would be inviting your competitors to knock you off the throne. One of the greatest principles is innovation and doing things differently. Sir Matt was an innovator, that's why we have our European tradition. We will always innovate, we will make sure that we stay ahead of the crowd, and my job is about holding that tension between wherever we've come from, and where we're trying to get to, and to just get the balance right, that we don't crush something valuable that has been gifted to us. That we don't just become complacent, we don't stagnate where we're so wedded to a way of working that we don't know how to produce players for the future game."

And what does that look like? "You're trying to think about what the future game might look like," admits Cox, "but it's also got to be a developmental model, so it's not necessarily a model that's designed to win – it's designed to be competitive, but it's got to develop the individuals so our teams in an academy are really just a vehicle for individual development. You're looking at 'how do I set the team up?' or 'what principles of play do we have to teach in order to give the individuals the best chance of individual success?' and you're trying to think about, also, we want to be playing in such a way that is aligned to our first team and aligned to our spirit. There's a way that Man United plays and there are certain non-negotiables, so it's quite a challenge to think about how you weave all of those things into a group of players on matchday over a period of time."

We are back where we started. There's a way that United plays. A way that has a clearly defined origin in the Busby era, adopting a system that even he inherited. Academy directors at other clubs are fortunate enough to call upon something that is well-established in the football lexicon. Cox, meanwhile, has had to work with something almost ethereal. He has enjoyed that challenge. "It

31

PERFECTION

SIRS MATT BUSBY AND ALEX FERGUSON BOTH SPOKE of perfection in their teams. Busby was more sparing with his use, reserving it for just two performances – the 1948 FA Cup final and the 10-0 win over Anderlecht in 1956. Ferguson was a little more liberal in his application of the term – after the 1994 FA Cup win against Wimbledon he spoke of such levels being reached 'only' five or six times a season – but then again, he was in charge of a team who spoiled supporters with their frequency of brilliance.

It brings to mind the question – how many games have Manchester United played that resemble perfection, if perfection is a complete representation of what the club's identity is supposed to be? And, on the same theme, how many goals have they scored that represent these qualities?

Anyone can appreciate such a list will still be fairly comprehensive so in order to make it more succinct, I'll start from the Busby era (so, excluding the 1909 FA Cup final and the famous match where United escaped relegation to the third division by defeating Millwall) and only concentrate on games where United did not lose – though there are certain defeats that do tie into the tapestry. As painful as it was, and as literal as it wasn't, who can deny the symbolism of Denis Law scoring a back-heel flick to send United down? And, as poignant as it was, the same criteria means that Manchester City's visit to Old Trafford in February 2008, commemorating the 60th anniversary of Munich, isn't included. You have to draw the line somewhere, so forgive the author for drawing it there.

24/4/48 Blackpool N W4-2

31/8/55 Tottenham A W2-1

26/9/56 Anderlecht Maine Road W10-0

25/4/57 Real Madrid H D2-2

1/2/58 Arsenal A W5-4

5/2/58 Red Star Belgrade A D3-3

19/2/58 Sheff Wed H W3-0

9/3/66 Benfica A W5-1

6/5/67 West Ham A W6-1

15/5/68 Real Madrid A D3-3

29/5/68 Benfica N W4-1

30/11/74 Sunderland H W3-2

3/4/76 Derby County N W2-1

21/5/77 Liverpool N W2-1

2/11/77 Porto H W5-2

21/3/84 Barcelona H W3-0

17/4/85 Liverpool N W2-1

18/5/85 Everton N W1-0

15/5/91 Barcelona N W2-1

5/4/93 Norwich A W3-1

10/4/93 Sheff Wed H W2-1

3/5/93 Blackburn H W3-1

PERFECTION

22/1/94 Everton H W1-0

20/2/94 Wimbledon A W3-0

16/3/94 Sheff Wed H W5-0

10/4/94 Oldham N D1-1

25/1/95 Crystal Palace A D1-1

1/10/95 Liverpool H D2-2

11/5/96 Liverpool N W1-0

1/10/97 Juventus H W3-2

25/11/98 Barcelona A D3-3

24/1/99 Liverpool H W2-1

14/4/99 Arsenal N W2-1

21/4/99 Juventus A W3-2

26/5/99 Bayern Munich N W2-1

30/11/99 Palmeiras N W1-0

25/02/01 Arsenal H W6-1

29/09/01 Tottenham A W5-3

6/1/02 Aston Villa A W3-2

1/2/05 Arsenal A W4-2

3/3/07 Liverpool A W1-0

4/4/07 Roma H W7-1

29/4/08 Barcelona H W1-0

21/5/08 Chelsea N D1-1 (win on penalties)

21/12/08 LDU Quito N W1-0

5/4/09 Aston Villa H W3-2

5/5/09 Arsenal A W3-1

14/5/11 Blackburn A D1-1

12/5/13 Swansea H W2-1

17/3/24 Liverpool H W4-3

25/4/24 Manchester City N W2-1

That is a subjective list and takes in all of what Manchester

United is supposed to be and represent; only some of those matches focus solely on the quality of performance. Blackpool 1948, Anderlecht 1956, Arsenal 1958, Benfica 1966, West Ham 1967, Wimbledon 1994, Arsenal and Juventus 1999, Arsenal 2001, Roma 2007, Arsenal 2009. The others have elements of the club's identity and sense of occasion tied to them, whether following it or creating something new, making them memorable for different reasons. For everything that Manchester United are, then it feels difficult to look past the first match post-Munich and the end of the 10-year journey which followed – so the 3-0 win over Sheffield Wednesday in February 1958, and the 4-1 win over Benfica in May 1968 – as two apt bookends.

How many goals truly summarise the Manchester United way? This is a much more difficult question because first of all, you could make an argument that every single goal is a product of an effective implementation of a tactic or philosophy. And you could also make the case that every team has, at one point or another, scored goals after long passing movements – is that Total Football? There might be only a handful of goals where the United 'pattern' of football was on show, yes in terms of movement and execution but also as a consequence of patience and team-building. Duncan Edwards' goal at Tottenham Hotspur in 1955, where he cleared a shot off the line, played a one-two and then hit a 50-yard pass only to be in a position to receive the ball after an upfield sprint, thrashing the ball in from 30 yards, was possibly the first. A 15-pass move in that game at Wimbledon in the FA Cup in 1994 that featured every outfield player except Steve Bruce before it was finished by Denis Irwin. Another move with the same number of passes earlier in that Cup run at Sheffield United, scored by Mark Hughes. 16 passes at Stamford Bridge to create a goal for Paul Scholes in October 1995. Almost twice that number against Panathinaikos in November 2000, when Scholes again was the scorer.

It's not just about the number of passes. Ashley Young netted after 37 passes in a game at Blackburn in 2012 and Juan Mata scored after 45 passes at Southampton under Louis van Gaal in September 2015 but what puts the above goals in a different category is the craft, movement, intent and incision. There is no definite number where possession of the ball becomes passing for the sake of passing, and even a manager who champions that approach would say there is always a point to possession, that being to wear down an opponent's concentration. That wasn't the case with the goals scored by Edwards, Hughes, Irwin and Scholes; these were combinations to create the quickest way to the scoresheet and unlock a defence.

Sometimes that takes 15 passes. Sometimes it takes five, like in the one-touch break at Carrow Road in 1993 that resulted in Andrei Kanchelskis scoring a thrilling goal. Sometimes it can take just four – Vidic to Ronaldo, to Park, to Rooney, back to Ronaldo at Arsenal in May 2009 for a counter-attack goal which took 13 seconds. Rooney scored a similar goal at the same ground in January 2010. Rooney and Ronaldo combined to score a breakaway goal against Bolton in 2007 that deserves to be mentioned in the same breath. Then there was the five-man, one-touch move against Bolton in 1995, featuring Scholes, Beckham and Terry Cooke before it was finished by Giggs – a Premier League goal crafted from the training pitch of The Cliff. More recently we have the evidence of the seven-pass lacerating counter that concluded with Kobbie Mainoo's match-winning strike in the 2024 FA Cup final. Those are the goals that are products of the pattern of play, products of investment of time and patience. The right amount of creative expression.

Edwards' goal also fits a different criteria – the one scored by the talisman, the extraordinary individual, in his own unique fashion. Denis Law's goal in the 1963 FA Cup final. George Best against Benfica in 1966. Bobby Charlton in the 1967 Charity Shield. Gordon Hill against Derby County in 1976. Bryan Robson in the FA Cup semi-final in 1985. Eric Cantona's chip against Southampton in 1993. David Beckham from the halfway line at Wimbledon in 1996. Ryan Giggs' run against Arsenal in 1999. Cristiano Ronaldo's free-kick at Arsenal or long-range screamer against Porto. Wayne Rooney's overhead kick against Manchester City that Alex Ferguson described as the best ever seen at Old Trafford.

Then there are the cinematic goals. The ones that seem part of a script. Those goals may or may not be aesthetically pleasing but the context associated with them is deeper than another goal. It feels like they were meant to be. Shay Brennan scoring the first goal after Munich. Bobby Charlton scoring first in the European Cup final. Mark Robins against Nottingham Forest. Steve Bruce's late double against Sheffield Wednesday. Mark Hughes against Oldham. Eric Cantona in the 1996 FA Cup final. Andy Cole against Barcelona. Ole Gunnar Solskjaer against Liverpool in January 1999 and then again against Bayern Munich in May of the same year. Roy Keane against Juventus. John O'Shea against Liverpool at Anfield. Amad Diallo against Liverpool in the FA Cup. There is an emotional resonance, and not just because some of them were last-minute winners, which of course carries a drama in and of itself. They're attached to United in a way that runs deeper than their status as a last-minute goal.

There are too many to mention so plenty have not been included on this non-exhaustive list, but I ought to put forward my own theory for the most *Manchester United* goal Manchester United have ever scored – George Best's in the 1968 European Cup final. This writer had the fortune of discussing the goal with members of United's squad on that day. Jimmy Rimmer and Pat Crerand both describe it as the most important goal in the club's history. So does Alex Stepney. "Whatever a club achieves, someone has to go first," he says. "There were three men from Munich who were still there – Bobby as captain, Bill Foulkes, and obviously Matt. As a group of players we never spoke of the emotional significance. But I knew, and I know for sure the others did, that we were playing for those three men, all of those who passed away, and all of the people who suffered as a result of the disaster. This was the journey the club started under Matt, to be the first to win the European Cup. So to score the goal which brought the club to that achievement couldn't ever be anything other than the most important in United's history. And it was scored in a way that was so unique to George, it was a product of his imagination, and that was a benefit of the freedom given to him by Matt."

Unless you have a 15-pass combination executed in injury time to deliver a trophy, preferably with a sensational finish from your star man with a mazy dribble included, then you have to decide which side of the fence you're on; the aesthetic, or the emotion. You have to then select the goal that appears to contain as many of the elements of what make the club so unique as possible. Best's was as close to perfect as could be and still did possess some of Busby's philosophy in that courage and determination to entertain. Best had been desperate to play at Wembley in a cup final. In the months before he had been writing a book, *Best of Both Worlds*, where he spoke about his vision of a perfect goal at the famous stadium. He spoke about trapping the ball with his backside after a long kick from Stepney; of juggling the ball on his thigh; of 'denying all the known laws of balance' to 'fly into a handstand

and volley the ball' into the goal. In the weeks before the game he was driving his team-mates mad with the idea that he was going to dribble around the goalkeeper and either backheel it in on the line, or stop the ball dead on the line and then stoop to the ground and nod it over.

Best showed no little courage and conviction; Benfica's man-marking plan repeatedly testing the line of what was legal. He would not be shaken and when the moment arrived, he showed fresh ingenuity, bending the match to his will at a time where every other player on the pitch was striving to merely compete. Stepney described Best as embodying the spirit of the Busby Babes to deliver the trophy that was forever connected to them. To do so in his own style, and with the liberation encouraged by Busby – and for that to be the crucial difference – makes the goal, in only this writer's humble opinion, the one which defines the United way more than any other.

32

THE UNITED WAY

AS WE REACH A CONCLUSION FOLLOWING OVER A century of analysis, we now have to ask how easily Manchester United's identity can be broken down and presented in a form that's straightforward to understand. It is clear that *Football Taught By Matt Busby* is a philosophy as vivid and real as total football, tiki-taka, catenaccio and gegenpress. On first impression, five words feels too long to serve as a catchy phrase that can be used as a reference and introduced into the general footballing dictionary.

Busbyball? Hollywood? *Hollywoodball*? Some might say the time has been and gone; others might feel it is still worthy of a name. This book took a decade to write, the idea for it formulating at the same time as I was writing a biography of Jimmy Murphy. I was so fascinated by the vague descriptions of this brand of football – and how it was simultaneously elevated to almost mythical status and almost disregarded as not being in the same lane as that for the true football connoisseur.

The juxtaposition for anyone who moonlights as a historian is that life goes on, we're constantly in the present and the present moment is constantly resigned to history. In the post-Ferguson years, as United underwent another transition after a successful period, the idea of the club's identity has almost become a stick to beat it with. Nonetheless, knowing that any such endeavour might still prove fruitless, I embarked upon this task with the intention of first and foremost being a supporter and wanting to know for myself.

You begin trying to explain a philosophy of football but, at Manchester United in particular, the 'United way' is more than just an attitude on the pitch. It also applies to behaviours off it, even though it is difficult to translate conduct on a sports field to conduct in an office or another environment. There are some qualities that easily lend themselves. A blend of humility in talent but arrogance in performance; a pride in representing the best and trying to be the best. An attitude of working harder to help a team-mate, or a colleague, achieve. Creativity and the element of surprise on the pitch can read as innovation off the pitch.

Tactics and philosophies in football can be influenced by practically anything. The lightness of the balls, the greater athletic nature of players in the 21st century and implementation of video technology have all had a major impact on the game since the mid 1970s, and even a consciousness of the identity itself, as this book took a natural course away from how these things impacted the Manchester United philosophy and focused more on that philosophy in and of itself.

After consuming and scouring the evidence, what have we learned? Success, the youth system and style of play are the three key elements of United's first team DNA – so how much of this is philosophical, how much can be traced to Matt Busby, how much of it was introduced by different managers, and how much of it can be traced via tactical systems?

Success

Busby himself said a Manchester United manager must be successful. It is likely the media would have created a pressurised environment for his successors. So, does success influence tactics and philosophy? Yes – it encourages consistency of selection and formation. Success over a longer period allows a manager to take a gamble which might not be too costly in consequence. In times where there is little success, a new shape might be used. Curiously, this was not generally the case in the pre-Ferguson era. In United's history it can only be said that Van Gaal, Mourinho, Solskjaer and Rangnick made pronounced tactical changes, particularly towards the end of their reigns, adding to the feeling of instability and subsequently the lack of conviction a squad could have in their manager. Ruben Amorim's appointment in November 2024 was the only time other than the appointment of Van Gaal where the club was braced for tactical reinvention from the outset.

A Manchester United manager must be successful. So, what determines success? Atkinson, for example, was not deemed a failure by Martin Edwards, nor were the players who Ferguson signed who were already out of the team by the time of the Cup Winners' Cup final in 1991. In the post-Ferguson era, managers were sacked for failure to qualify for the Champions League.

Success as determined by Busby was trophies, so all trophy winners were successful; how beloved they become in United folklore is another matter, and becomes a subjective argument.

Success via trophies is, however, the most straightforward principle and the easiest to measure.

"I never wanted Manchester United to be second to anybody," Matt Busby once said. "Only the best would be good enough." This is not a point made expecting United to win the league every season, it was a point of reference to the standards held internally. This was substantiated by another Busby line, from Tony Pullein's *The History of Manchester United Football Club*: "I had never believed Manchester United to be an ordinary club."

Success wasn't just winning trophies. It was a matter of internal standards not concerned with the standard of the opposition. These were the standards demanded of a United team by every opponent they faced but few managers seemed to truly understand it. That did not mean that a manager had to be fully tuned in to the Old Trafford psyche; but they would have to hold those internal standards themselves, like, for example, Alex Ferguson showed after the 1983 Scottish Cup final.

Perhaps we can excuse the managers, to an extent, if their vision of football was incompatible with that of United, and if that played a part in their eventual exit. Van Gaal admitted the identity of the club wasn't even discussed prior to his arrival, so it stands to reason that he believed he was hired to implement his own way.

You have to consider the size of the institution and its resistance to change. Arsenal are the third biggest English club after Manchester United and Liverpool. Those three were the biggest in the 70s, and 80s, and 90s. When George Graham won two league titles, an FA Cup, a League Cup and a European Cup Winners' Cup at Highbury, there was a disparaging chant – 'boring boring Arsenal' such was their reputation for defensive football. Arsene Wenger became manager in 1996 and their entire identity changed. It helped that they were successful, but they were not more successful to such an extent that you would say the change in philosophy was justified in trophy count (Wenger won three league titles and seven FA Cups). It was justified aesthetically and today, Arsenal have a reputation as an attractive football club. They were not resistant to change.

Manchester United, on the other hand, has tried to embrace change in the same way, but its traditions are ultimately much too strong to be abandoned. Mourinho was embraced with his traditionally pragmatic way, and even Rangnick's first few days were shrouded in talk about his way of playing football. Solskjaer understood the club's philosophy, but just like McGuinness, understanding and conveying can be two very different things.

Youth

The fact that Ryan Giggs was the only youth product in the team that would jump into most people's heads from the 1993/94 side (Lee Sharpe and Clayton Blackmore might have cause to state their own case), coupled with the fact that this team was beloved, suggests that the importance of youth could be overstated – certainly when it comes to how accepted a team will be by supporters. In fact it's this truism which presents the theory that supporters will accept any team so long as they're successful.

The Jose Mourinho era is a great example as his two trophies made him, objectively, the most successful manager in the 10 years after Ferguson retired. This writer took a quick poll on social media in 2022 to ask United supporters what they did not enjoy about the Mourinho era, if indeed they didn't. Almost 1,300 votes rated poor quality of football at 57 per cent, Mourinho himself at

13 per cent, and both at 30 per cent. Only two players (and you have to include Pogba in this) started in the Europa League final who came through the youth system but it wasn't this factor which made Mourinho's reign so divisive; however, just as we saw with Van Gaal, introducing more kids into the team may have had a positive impact.

There is definitely truth in the premise that the number of youth players in the team has a correlation with the backing of the support, especially at the start as they encourage them to do well. The power of this cannot be understated – the evidence can be seen in the 1958 FA Cup run as it literally willed a team to ride a wave of grief to the final.

It is clear that youth, and to be more precise, interpersonal relationships, have some bearing on how successful a philosophy of football will be. A player is more inclined to work harder to compensate for a team-mate's error if they have a close personal relationship. That part is human nature. It is no coincidence that Gary Neville and David Beckham, best mates, had such a strong partnership on the right. It is no coincidence that Eddie Colman was so often selected as Duncan Edwards' midfield partner. It is no coincidence that Beckham, Scholes, Butt and Giggs (and throw in Keane) formed the most successful midfield in English football history. Those players were all incredibly gifted but the value of the principle of their work-rate – which was partly inherent, partly inspired by driven coaches, partly inspired by their close relationships – cannot be understated and although it takes a while to cultivate, the long-term value of this sort of philosophy is so strong that it makes you wonder why every team doesn't try and build the same structure.

The benefit of strong player relationships is hardly groundbreaking but the value of that investment of time, when up against an opponent with a team full of star names, can not be underestimated. The consistency, familiarity and patience provided to and by those players is profoundly important; it has been a cornerstone upon which the club's greatest successes are built. The work-rate of those unsung players was crucial. Oftentimes, when those players eventually moved on from Old Trafford, they would adopt similar roles in their following team, to the surprise of most who probably expected a star name doing star name things. But you can name just a few – Phil Neville, Nicky Butt, John O'Shea and Wes Brown, all players who went on to do the dirty work at the clubs they went to after United. Perhaps they weren't flashy enough to be adored by supporters but their work-rate and principles were valuable; coveted by managers and deeply appreciated by team-mates, their Manchester United education a stamp of quality, almost a guarantee of a sound investment when it came to character and hard work.

This too was a Busby mandate. "Players are human beings, not pieces of furniture to be dumped when new equipment is installed," Busby once said. "They had given the club wonderful service and I felt it my duty to see them all fixed up with reasonable jobs within the game."

It is no coincidence that managers who took young United players either on loan or on a permanent transfer would usually be repeat customers. When Tony Pulis was manager of Stoke City, he signed Danny Higginbotham, Ryan Shawcross and Danny Pugh. Stoke were one of the success stories of the Premier League in terms of character, with a reputation for punching above their weight, and that was thanks in no small part to the hard work of the former United academy products. You could even use the example of David Beckham, arguably the world's most famous footballer, becoming renowned as a workhorse when he went to Real Madrid. The Spanish were expecting a superstar and he delivered on that front; they were not, however, expecting someone who worked as hard as Beckham did.

The likes of Joe Armstrong and Jimmy Murphy and later, Brian Kidd and others, were not only looking for talent, but character. Would that boy be prepared to work hard? Would that personality fit into what was already at the club? It was a value system established by the club and filtered through to the scouts – so much so that those scouts would take a sense of pride in their own reputation. Northern Irish boys would go with Bob Bishop to the farm he used in Helen's Bay, so desperate were they to follow George Best – and Bishop reported back to the club about the obedience of the boys and how likely they were to be able to adapt away from home.

The players you inherit influence the tactics you use and the success of any philosophy you attempt to instil. Managers are forced to adapt when they go into a new club because rarely do they inherit a squad perfectly suited for their philosophy. The individual personalities of players influences tactics – Harry Gregg, for one example, and Eric Cantona, another – especially Cantona, as Ferguson tried to sign Alan Shearer and David Hirst, two traditional number nines who would not have had the same impact.

Youth players influence tactics thanks in large part to their familiarity with each other. The ability to call upon a number of players to play in an area close to each other helps with flowing combinations, movement and protection of space. If proper attention is spent on the development of a player then time is dedicated to trying the player in different positions. This is one of the staples of Total Football and it is one of the fundamental principles of Manchester United's ideal style of football. It doesn't appear to be coincidental that the three periods of greatest success of the club (let's say 1957, 1999 and 2009 are our yardsticks) have this as a strong part of their composition.

This is the internal mechanism, the inner-working of a football club. But the external factor – the connection this has with a crowd – has become a thing of perpetual motion at Manchester United. One minute you're creating history and the next you're attempting to live up to it. The capability for this unique set of circumstances to ignite an atmosphere is second to none and becomes a palpable tool of its own. Imagine if you will, the moment that Federico Macheda came on in the 61st minute against Aston Villa in April 2009 and Danny Welbeck followed him in the 87th minute. This wasn't just a case of two rookies coming on to have an impact. Ferguson's gamble was a loaded gun. Villa were playing a hundred years of history – Munich, Edwards, Murphy, Busby, relegation, promotion, Steve Bruce, Fergie Time. This was what the gamble represented. It's a battle of concentration and momentum. You can disregard quality. It's about controlling the elements. It's a psychological contest.

The greatest factor without doubt was that Ferguson was ramping up the atmosphere in Old Trafford, knowing the supporters would get behind the kids instead of showing anxiety about a possible poor result. It is a trait quite impossible to articulate but if a series of events could provide the explanation, that match did so. Ferguson used – quite deliberately – the reputation of the club, created by himself and his predecessors.

The success of this approach can only be achieved by the introduction of the elements that are so ingrained within Manchester United. To reach that level of control as a manager, it's not only true to say patience is a virtue – it is, in fact, a crucial part of the journey. 2009 is a good example. So is the period between January and May of 1999. What you have is evidence of just how important Manchester United's youth policy has become to the club; true and tangible results and threads to understand the significance and its uniqueness. The story itself has a value to be harnessed, to connect to something significant.

Style of Play

The simplest way to describe United's traditional style of play is that its roots are in Total Football and largely adherent to the most common tactical shape of the day. What makes it unique and therefore apparently so undefinable comes down to four factors. The youth element, as articulated above. The accommodation of a wildcard, such as Ferguson's use of Cantona or Ronaldo. Thirdly, the quirks within the system. For example, having Colman at right-half and Edwards at left-half. Playing two creative inside-forwards. Overlapping full-backs and having half-backs cover those spaces. Busby's specific use of Stiles, or his constant work in repositioning. Docherty's use of two sweeper defenders and two attacking midfielders. Ferguson having Ronaldo start in a false position on the right. And, finally, perhaps the edict from Ferguson himself, where he listed qualities (speed, power, penetration and unpredictability) in preference over strategy.

And, really, that's it. Progressive Total Football. The most common formation. A healthy balance of youth players brought up playing this way. A difference-maker in terms of an individual catalyst encouraged to do their own thing. The embrace of every player as an individual and the accommodation of that player's qualities into the pattern – for example, the inclusion of Paul Parker at right-back even though he didn't usually overlap, as opposed to Gary Neville, who did overlap, whereas a specific system might require that a player should do one or the other. A fundamental adherence to playing with speed and penetration. And finally, though not always crucial, some form of tactical surprise within the otherwise fairly common shape, aiding that desire for unpredictability.

At its strongest, at its healthiest, these elements are cultivated by coaches who believe strongly in the ethos of man-management. Busby wanted to create a club where players were treated as people. He wanted them to be proud of where they were and that attitude came from the top – he made it his purpose to know the name of every person who worked for the club. He made it his business to know their business. To know them as people. Ferguson was this way too, influenced heavily by Jock Stein.

These things are specific to Manchester United in the way they combine to create an over-arching philosophy and how that manifests into a pattern of play. The other things – tricks, speed and movement, strong wing play, wanting to play entertaining football… well, you could argue that any football fan wants to see these things. And plenty of football clubs do have some of these qualities.

It would be ludicrous to suggest that United's is an objectively superior brand of football; it is just the subjective favourite of this writer. It would also not be wise to assert that some of the elements mentioned – such as United embracing Total Football at club level in Britain or Ron Atkinson using the diamond – were cast-iron inventions created or embraced first at Old Trafford. This record exists just to make it known that these things did *happen* at Old Trafford; making sure the truth is noted. Because Atkinson *did* use a version of the diamond. And United's style, as introduced by Busby and Murphy, *was* heavily influenced by the Hungarian, or Hogan philosophy – of that there is incontrovertible eye-witness proof. The closest United have played to the Hungarian style came between 1952 and 1958; for spells between 1965 and 1968; under

Docherty between 1975 and 1977; for a spell under Atkinson; for a period between 1993 and 1994; and for the time between 2007 and 2009 where Rene Meulensteen's influence as coach was most keenly felt. That can be observed by the records, reports, tapes of games and eyewitness accounts in addition to all we know about the philosophies held by those managers.

Football taught by Matt Busby was, at its purest, the perseverance with his pattern to entertain the crowd. He was right to have a tremendous conviction that this style would be successful – and when handling challenges, he ensured his team were still playing to win. This was the spirit of his way and could be found even in the moving of, for example, Duncan Edwards to play at inside-forward to control the play in Dortmund. He wanted to make progressive amendments to win the game.

As evolution of the game introduced pragmatism, Busby embraced its necessity. Harry Gregg, Pat Crerand and Alex Stepney to name just three would take an oath insisting Busby never sent his team out to do anything other than win a game. A feature of the Busby team-talk which was present throughout his reign was to keep it tight for the first 15 minutes. On reflection, this was probably as much an attempt to eradicate the infamous way his side could make it difficult for themselves. Ferguson would often refer to this characteristic in his own side. Maybe that too is just the Manchester United way. After all, wasn't this remarked upon in the first trophy-winning season under Busby? The way his team almost needed to fall behind to start playing.

O'Farrell and Sexton concentrated on the opposition, as did Mourinho. Atkinson was, his players found, often surprisingly good on the detail when it came to rival players. Docherty's complete reckless abandon – Cavanagh screwing up the team sheet and all that – was almost *too* ignorant of opponents and that possibly prohibited them from making the leap from entertainers to clinical winners.

It should be noted that in Docherty, Atkinson and Ferguson, United hired men who were strong enough to implement their own style on the club. It was coincidental that Docherty and Atkinson were taught by Jimmy Hogan but it was not coincidental that Old Trafford responded to that brand of football. It was not coincidental that Ferguson was influenced so profoundly by Stein's style of management, that he had a track record of bringing through young players, and that he had high personal standards. He would recall on numerous occasions how Stein had blooded young players at Dunfermline and, within months at Celtic, had created a 'will to win'.

The plot thickens, however. Jimmy Hogan's time at Celtic preceded that of Stein but only by a year (Stein joining as a player in 1951), so the impression made on the club was still quite prominent. Stein had been impressed by the Hungarian victory over England (who hadn't been?), but the website theCelticwiki.com theorises 'Possibly, Jock Stein learned one set of valuable lessons more than others from Jimmy Hogan. Players were at times children and had to be bullied at times (a method in madness) for their own sake.' It may be too contrived to link Hogan directly to Ferguson in methodology, but it does not seem too great a leap to draw a logical line via Stein's personality.

Ferguson always wanted his team to impose themselves on the game. The two times he willingly encouraged pragmatic play, against Juventus in 1996 and against Barcelona in 2008, his natural reaction was almost to rebel against that and ensure his team would forevermore be proactive; in the Busby mould without question. He had an innovative approach to man-marking – McClair on Koeman, Park on Pirlo, and against Arsenal, strategies were employed not to man-mark their creative players like Nasri and Fabregas, but to stop the ball getting into them in the first place. Pragmatic concessions did not have to mean a pragmatic overview. They were sensible adaptations.

How much of the above was dictated or led by the ownership of the club? Davies and Gibson were influential in the identity of Manchester United. Busby was so dominant that Louis Edwards was almost led by him when it came to the major decisions with managers. Martin Edwards seemed to be more proactive – hiring Atkinson for his flamboyance and dismissing Sexton for his lack of it. Hiring Ferguson for his winning attitude and commitment to youth. Building a museum at the club, overseeing the implementation of a Former Players' Association in the mid-80s and then making a commitment to the development of Old Trafford to make it the grandest arena in the domestic game. Edwards was a controversial figure with supporters, but the above contributions cannot be disputed. Edwards was the first man with leadership of the club to speak about the importance of being a custodian of its legacy. The Glazer family took over the club in 2005 and had to deal with a number of manager dismissals. Even though Van Gaal and Mourinho were criticised for their brand of football, the decision to sack them was taken because of results and not because of any perceived abandonment of the club's identity.

Success, youth and style of play – these are the three key internal elements to United's identity. There are other factors to consider.

History

Even Matt Busby had to follow someone. Even Matt Busby benefitted from the work of others. Before him, United had an identity that focused on entertaining football with its heavy Scottish influence. There are seeds of the elements that were to become important to the cultural legacy of Manchester United before they even took the name. From being founded, Newton Heath were taking on foreign opponents in a trendsetting fashion. Alfred Albut was credited with resourcefulness to find players and bringing in a number of Scottish players to play the passing game. When Newton Heath ended and Manchester United began, the era was signalled by a trophy win earned by a goal scored by the longest-serving player on his final appearance. Ernest Mangnall arrived with grandiose ideas and decorated his side with star individuals before taking them overseas. Mangnall oversaw the period where United moved to Old Trafford, and saw some of those players create a professional union. Jack Robson was the first to really focus on his team having a younger average age. It was under John Chapman that players were rewarded in a fashion that connected them to their locality.

Crickmer and Rocca had observed these qualities and it's reasonably safe to assume it had a significant influence on the vision they shared for the club and presented to Gibson before hiring Scott Duncan, who was well-loved. Duncan was well-loved and was enjoying some success before deciding to move elsewhere. Crickmer, Rocca and Gibson clearly believed in the direction the club was headed and stayed true to that when choosing who came next after the war.

When Busby became a part of Manchester United history, it could be said that he unwittingly added to the problem for his successor by speaking honestly about his own expectations for who should follow. They became standards instead of opinions. In some sense, you might say that is helpful. It is not just the history of Busby and Ferguson that is important when it comes to whoever the incumbent manager is. Dave Sexton suffered because he wasn't Docherty. Solskjaer suffered because he didn't win trophies even if the football was usually more entertaining than under Mourinho. Any successful manager embraces the history of the club without being burdened by it. As history itself has told us – that's not as straightforward as it reads.

Munich

The sight of two survivors in the first line-up after the disaster set a tone. Bill Foulkes recalled that Albert Quixall, then of Sheffield Wednesday, wore an expression that suggested he didn't want to have to play the game. Jimmy Murphy had taken the young players to Blackpool and when they returned to play football, they were a squad bonded by what they had been through. The knockout nature of cup football must have helped because it became *their* competition – the increased attention and United's winning streak created a momentum of its own.

Faced with a choice to bring in players or to stay as true as he could to what had been built before the disaster, Murphy went with the latter, cementing its importance. He used grief to fuel and motivate – he had no other way – and, then, as soon as the time came to rebuild, Munich became an unspoken element of the club's identity. It remained that way until May 1968, when the fulfilment of the dreams all at Manchester United had, were met.

It wasn't until Alex Ferguson's arrival – shortly after which, the club marked 30 years since Munich – that the club became more proactive in commemorating it. So the work of Busby and Murphy became more prominent factors in actual education for the players. Introductions to survivors of the disaster. Pointing out the presence of Jimmy Murphy Jnr on the sidelines of youth games at The Cliff and Carrington.

"Telling them what Jimmy did," Ferguson said, "is the most important thing you can tell a young player who is representing Manchester United... if you don't know your history, you don't know your future, and your future is to be what was happening in those early days of Matt Busby and Jimmy Murphy."

This embrace of the past and the fact it came when the club were beginning to introduce the largest number of young players into the first team since Busby – one can call it coincidental that United's propensity to battle for late results seemed to increase. If Ferguson himself says that it was a deliberate tactic, then we can take it as read. His ability to almost sense the timing of a game that wasn't in his favour and make the changes that would create a shift in the atmosphere almost made him a conductor of sorts. Rather than being coincidental, you can't help but feel it's *necessary* for there to be a core of homegrown players in order to yield the best sort of results in this atmosphere.

Again – great timing by a manager and his use of substitutes or ability to inspire a team to a late win or a comeback isn't the sole ownership of Manchester United. Nor could it be said that the emotional power of Munich is partly responsible for every comeback; that is too sentimental. Clearly the balance has to be right. What is motivation to some can be a burden to another. That is where a good man-manager comes in. It all forms a major part of the tapestry and Ferguson's openness in using the past to motivate his players cannot be dismissed as merely coincidental.

Personality

As the club moved back and forth between O'Farrell, Docherty, Sexton and Atkinson, it was clear it wasn't just a style of play that the club were struggling with. In fact you might say Docherty's sacking was key in this timeline as Sexton was brought in, in part, thanks to his uncontroversial nature. As he faced the same sort of criticism as O'Farrell, it seemed set in stone that the man who was given the job of manager of Manchester United was a footballing politician. He led an institution. He was required to be the public face of the club – to be the father protecting his family. That feeling went back beyond Busby all the way to Rocca and J H Davies. That burden, that pressure, was a feeling carried by Martin Edwards, who said amidst the Cantona controversy in 1995, "Manchester United is bigger than Eric Cantona, and football is bigger than Manchester United."

A manager of Manchester United must be confident enough to lead the club and feel that they belong to be there. They should have charisma, in order to present a public front of calm. They have a responsibility to follow that Busby line – never portray United as second best to anyone. He must always be prepared to face the press even in times of difficulty. As that paternal figure, he was required to be the man who took the start and end of the criticism – no throwing players under the bus. No peeling back the curtain to expose fractured relationships; those happen at every football club, but not every football club gets an automatic back page on a newspaper at the hint of trouble. Another book could be written on the psychological demands on a Manchester United manager and the unique qualities the job requires, but it is included here to note its relative importance, and how even the merest contravention of one of the above qualities could invite pressure.

Education and Patience

There is, simply, no substitute for time. Singular examples of the benefit of patience can include the development of Bobby Charlton, from learning to kick with both feet at the back of the Stretford End, to playing outside-left for a number of years, and moving inside to central midfield where he became one of the most feared strikers of a ball to ever play the game. You could also think of Darren Fletcher, who spent three or four years receiving criticism even from some United fans before he became one of the most important players in the squad.

Any team can only benefit from time spent together but the rewards are potentially far greater if that time together begins at an earlier age. This is crucial in the development of any pattern or philosophy and can be seen at Ajax and Barcelona to name just two famous examples, just as it has been at Manchester United. The successful graduation of that pattern becoming dominant can only come with experience. You have to allow for hiccups. There will be setbacks. What is learned in defeat can be valuable too. So any introduction of those players into the first team has to be gradual, just as it was from 1953 to 1955 and 1993 to 1995. Fate robbed the world of seeing the Busby Babes grow against Real Madrid but they did see another group of young players grow a decade later, and then again against Juventus in the 1990s, where their traceable improvement through the experience of those games finally concluded with the ultimate victory. To a lesser extent, overcoming a pragmatic Chelsea side a few years later helped instil a level of consistency arguably no United team had ever exhibited.

The value of patience is therefore clear – it yields the greatest results. This is not just the case for the players – there is evidence to show that both Busby and Ferguson evolved with time, Busby in his embracing of growing pragmatism to strategise counters, and Ferguson with his concession that he wanted his team to play 4-4-2 and not try unfamiliar shapes against strong opponents. Compare this to the many modern examples that will instantly jump to mind regarding managers who are sometimes criticised and praised in equal measure in their refusal to adapt.

Evolution of style does not necessarily mean abandonment of the original vision. Football careers are short for managers and shorter for players. A cycle of a great team can be expected to last for five years. It stands to reason that there is a much greater chance of success if time has been spent before that peak with the same group of players; it is why it is easy to predict that the Busby Babes would have been dominant in the Ferguson or Paisley mould if not for Munich, because we have evidence of the same philosophy under Ferguson resulting in a multi-generationally dominant side thanks to the ethos of the likes of Giggs, Scholes and Neville. This same standard of success can be reached by spending an exorbitant amount of money but is very unlikely to be replicated through mere coaching and philosophy – putting into perspective just how unique Busby and Ferguson were, but also laying bare the incalculable value of time and patience.

If Hungarian football is the tree, then Football Taught By Matt Busby is a branch closely connected to another which is Total Football. What it is today is the creation of the elements of the time and events of the journey along the way. It is, fundamentally, movement of the player and movement of the ball. It is a rhythm established in brotherhood. It is a machine of perpetual motion. There is innovation inside the most popular contemporary tactical shape to make it adaptable to the set-up of an opponent. There is encouragement of individual expression. There is a commitment to entertain and an ambition to win. It is bigger than football; it is poetic. It is romantic. Tragic. Shakespearean. It is alchemical.

It is fitting that a reference to Manchester United's philosophy should bear the name of Matt Busby. To deviate from that reference now would probably feel contrived, even if there is a temptation to give it a quicker, catchier reference, like Harry Gregg's reference to Hollywood. *Football Taught By Matt Busby* isn't as vague, unexplainable and incomprehensible as many would have you think; and it's much more tactically complex and innovative than many would have you believe. The reward, for anyone choosing to undertake that journey of research, is surely a deeper connection to Manchester United Football Club.

It has taken this many words and this many pages to try and explain, in all its inexplicable detail and nuance, the identity of Manchester United. It took over 100 years of history and over 20 years as manager for Alex Ferguson to be able to manifest everything as masterfully as he did against Tottenham and Aston Villa at Old Trafford in early 2009. At its heart the explanation for it all, the key to unlocking it all, feels infuriatingly and inexplicably simple. What did Alex Ferguson tell Federico Macheda and Danny Welbeck as they took to the pitch against Aston Villa? The same as he did to the countless young hopefuls before.

"Go out there son," he said, "and enjoy yourself."

Bibliography

Manchester United (Percy M. Young – The Sportsmans Book Club)
My Story (Matt Busby – Souvenir Press)
Manchester United (Alf Clarke – Convoy)
Soccer At The Top (Matt Busby – Weidenfeld & Nicolson)
Best Of Both Worlds (George Best – Corgi)
Matt, United and Me (Jimmy Murphy – Souvenir Press)
The Manchester United Football Book series
(David Meek – Stanley Paul)
Tackle Soccer (Dave Sexton – Hutchinson)
There's Only One United (Geoffrey Green – Coronet Book)s
Winners And Champions
(Alex Shorrocks – Weidenfield & Nicholson)
Champions Again (Ralph L. Finn – Robert Hale)
Sir Matt Busby's Manchester United Scrapbook (Souvenir Press)
The History Of Manchester United Football Club
(Tony Pullein – Direct Printing Ltd)
Six Years At United
(Alex Ferguson and David Meek – Mainstream Publishing)
Year In the Life – The Manager's Diary
(Alex Ferguson w/ Peter Ball – Virgin Books)
A Will To Win – The Manager's Diary
(Alex Ferguson w/ David *Meek* – Andres Deutsch)
Managing My Life (Alex Ferguson – Coronet)
The Birth Of The Babes (Tony Whelan – Empire Publications)
My Autobiography (Alex Ferguson – Hodder and Stoughton(
Red News (Barney Chilton)

ACKNOWLEDGEMENTS

THIS BOOK HAS BEEN A WORK IN PROGRESS FOR OVER a decade and as such it feels like an almost futile exercise to even begin to list everybody who deserves to be thanked for their help. I will start, though, with some of the significant names when it comes to the very existence of the project, and that list commences with the late Harry Gregg, who planted the seed which started my research.

Tony Whelan is perhaps the man who has the most credibility when it comes to studying the cultural identity of Manchester United; thank you Tony, for reading this and giving me such generous feedback. I remember the first conversation when you read it, and you were so enthusiastic. I was so emotional; I value your opinion so highly. It would be remiss of me not to reference Tony's book, The Birth Of The Babes, which is the definitive account of Manchester United's youth policy in the 1950s, and by extension, one of the most important books ever written on the club.

Just before this book went to print, I learned of the passing of Patrick Barclay. I worked with Paddy for the last few years of his life. The last communication I had with him was an email he sent which included his review of this book, which you can read on the back cover.

Paddy was my writing hero. The greatest football writer ever. I am extremely fortunate to have benefitted from his generosity of spirit and so many kind words. There is nothing I could write to justify the profound sense of loss and gratitude I feel. That I was able to work with my hero was an indulgence. That he treated me like a peer was a privilege. He will be, and already is, sorely missed.

The late Tom Clare and Barry Shmeizer read all of my work before it was published. The last drafts they read before they passed away were of this book, and my gratitude for their kindness is something that will live on as long as the memory of both of them. The family of the late Tom Tyrrell, whose books gave me my early education on the club, must also be mentioned, as must the kindness of Roy Cavanagh, who conducted an interview with Sir Matt Busby in 1983 and permitted me to use it exclusively for this book.

The title of this book is of course a nod to the United Calypso, my favourite United chant, written by Eric Watterson, composed by Ken Jones and performed notably by Edric Connor before the choir of the Stretford End.

There is an extensive list of people I interviewed over a decade, who have contributed to the historical identity of the club. Sir Alex Ferguson, Martin Edwards, Tommy Docherty, Wilf McGuinness, Ron Atkinson, Paul McGuinness, Rene Meulensteen, Tony Whelan, Nick Cox, Frank Blunstone, Jimmy Murphy Junior, Nick Murphy, Mark Armstrong, Alan Embling, Harry Turnbull, Sammy McIlroy, Harry Gregg, Brian Greenhoff, David Ryan, Alan Wardle, Jimmy Elms – just a few of the people I owe a debt of gratitude to. I particularly wish to thank Martin Edwards for giving his time.

There are a number of interviews in this book that have never been heard before, and those were included from the archive of Tom Tyrrell, featuring Sir Alex, Denis Law, George Best, Mick Brown, Jack Rowley, Sir Bobby Charlton and Tommy Cavanagh.

Thank you to Pete Johnson, and Chris Lepkowski, for additional

ACKNOWLEDGEMENTS

insight about Frank O'Farrell and Ron Atkinson before they became United manager.

Thank you to Rob Smyth, Charlotte Duncker and Neil Harman for the investment of time in reading this and taking the time to provide feedback.

Thank you to Barney Chilton, Nicolas Berg, Ben McManus, Ben Greenwood, Luke Smalley, Matthew Smallwood, Brian McFadden, Eifion Evans, Satyajit Dutt, Robbie Norman, Ben Thornley, Bjarte Valen, Deiniol Graham, Alan Monger, Jimmy Williams, Dips, Kevin Pilkington, Matthew Galea, David Blatt, Stel Stylianou, Steve Hobin, Stan Chow, Andy Birkett, Ben Allen, Phil Marsh, Steve Whittle, Matthew Battle, Jon Wilson, Mark Foster, Alan Keegan, Keith Norris, Andy Gillespie, Paul Anthony, Mike Carney, JD Deitch, Pete Summers, Blaine Humbles, Nathan Thomas, Magda Walker, Aggie Johnson, Calum Best, Angie Best, Stylianos Ioannou, Eivind Nybakk, Bob Mehr, Krishan Puvvada, Ryan Michael, Damian Ginty, Mark Henshall, Jason Leach, Des McKibbin, Nipun Chopra, Mark Welsh, Ilkay Glatter, Chris Culkin, David O'Callaghan, Li Yan, Mark Froggatt. To Mark Graham, Kyle Diller, Preben Walle, James Murphy, Maurice Murphy, Emma Priestley, Les Richardson, Phil Martin, Danny Woodvine, Linda Gregg, John Gregg, Jordan Eyre, Tom Boswell, Paul Murphy, Stephen Murphy, Roy Taylor, Tony Russell, Meurig Wyn Jones, Alan Gordon, Liam McGibbon, Lee Lawrence. Thanks to Andrew Yates, David Craigen, Matt Webster, Mona Shehata, Micky Dillon, Paul Reid, Darren Hall. Thank you to Les and Dion Brown.

Thank you to Ben Redpath. To Laurence Brownhill, Rose Cook Monk and Andy Monk. To Ed Barker, thanks for everything, mate. Tony Walsh, your generosity is always gratefully appreciated. A special thanks to Sacha Jakovljevich. Thank you to Leslie Millman for your generosity and kindness. Thanks to Craig Park and Kerry Rutkin for your friendship.

Thank you to Scott Martin, who helped me to do something that was quite beyond my wildest dreams, and that was to finish writing this book inside Old Trafford.

In my introduction to these acknowledgements I spoke about the people who were crucial when it came to this book even existing but I missed one person from that part, to include him here. Tony Park, who this book is dedicated to. I had written notes and articles and large parts of a manuscript because I was so interested in the subject but it was Tony who convinced me to put it all together. Of course, Tony, you know that isn't the only thing you've done for me. You are a mentor, a sounding board, a man of advice and guidance. Your friendship is so valuable to me, and it was inevitable that I would dedicate a book to you… considering you are the person who I have discussed this subject with more than any other, it is fitting that it is this one. Thank you for being all that you are.

Thanks to Reach Sport for always proving such a beautiful home for my work. Claire Brown, I am so fortunate that you have worked with me for a decade or so, you really are the best. As are you, Chris Brereton, although for different reasons! Your enthusiasm for this has meant so much to me. Huge thanks also to Simon Monk for honing the manuscript with a meticulous edit, and to Chris Collins and Christine Costello who designed the cover and inside.

Thank you to my agent Nick Walters for his support of this book and his patience with me. Nick, I know I must have driven you mad. I really cannot say how much I value you, you are always honest and straightforward and are always considering what is the best for me.

ACKNOWLEDGEMENTS

If the above list wasn't quite long enough, there are still some more friends and family who have been so supportive, still now as always. Rory Tompkins. Mozza. Steve and Gem. Oyvind Enger. Thank you to Charlie and family. Thanks PY. Thank you Gruff, Hayley and Elfyn. To Steven Marrable, whose support means so much to me. To Phil, Mikiel and Charlotte Gatt, I am so proud to know you.

Thank you to Paul Parker. You usually hate the hero worship, but here I can put it in print and you can't answer back. You have given your time over six years to talk about the club we both love, and you know because I tell you often enough that you played for my favourite team in history. Some of the conversations we have had in that time have been some of the most important in my life; you have taken the time to consider what is best for me, and given me so much confidence at crucial times, that really, a paragraph of embarrassment to tell you that you're as much a hero as a man as you were as a player is the least I could do.

Thanks to Dan Kersh, Nicki and the boys, for your generosity, friendship and time. My deep gratitude to Mike Pieri for everything.

Thank you to Dan, Kim and Alex Burdett, for always being so incredibly supportive. Thank you to my best friend Dave Murphy for everything, especially permitting me to waffle on about Jimmy Hogan for five years. I'll never stop. A great big thank you to my mum. Thanks to my in-laws, especially my mother-in-law Lisa and my three little sisters-in-law, Teide, Macy and Maddy.

Thank you to my wonderful wife Stacey, whose support is always the most crucial thing for me; your faith and belief in getting everything right with this book, right down to the timing of everything, has been possibly even stronger than my own.

As a gentleman approaching middle age, it is sometimes a natural step for us to become disillusioned with the changes of the modern game and bore on with our assertion that it was better in our day. Well, I confess I do that, but my enthusiasm for the game remains burning bright mostly thanks to my nephews. It could be Logan learning to kick a ball, or Noah's obsession with cards and United, or Freddy's interest in learning so much about the history of the club and now collecting autographs; all of it always brings me so much joy. You boys mean everything to me.